Mgr

[(

Organizational Culture
and Leadership

Edgar H. Schein

Organizational Culture and Leadership

Third Edition

JOSSEY-BASS
A Wiley Imprint
www.josseybass.com

Published by Jossey-Bass
A Wiley Imprint
989 Market Street, San Francisco, CA 94103-1741   www.josseybass.com

Jossey-Bass books and products are available through most bookstores. To contact Jossey-Bass
directly call our Customer Care Department within the U.S. at 800-956-7739, outside the
U.S. at 317-572-3986 or fax 317-572-4002.

Jossey-Bass also publishes its books in a variety of electronic formats. Some content that
appears in print may not be available in electronic books.

Library of Congress Cataloging-in-Publication Data
Schein, Edgar H.
  Organizational culture and leadership / Edgar H. Schein.—3rd ed.
     p. cm.—(The Jossey-Bass business & management series)
  Includes bibliographical references and index.
  ISBN 0-7879-6845-5 (alk. paper)
  1. Corporate culture. 2. Culture. 3. Leadership. I. Title. II. Series.
  HD58.7.S33 2004
  302.3'5—dc22

                                                              2004002764

Printed in the United States of America
THIRD EDITION
HB Printing   10 9 8 7 6 5 4 3 2 1

The Jossey-Bass

Business & Management Series

Contents

Preface

Organizational culture has come of age. Not only did the concept have staying power but it is even being broadened to occupational cultures and community cultures. Culture at the national level is more important than ever in helping us to understand intergroup conflict. As it turns out, culture is essential to understanding intergroup conflict at the organizational level as well. My years of consulting experience with Digital Equipment Corporation (DEC) provided useful case material (as the Action Company) in my previous editions, but it was only through my attempt to fully understand why DEC initially succeeded—and, in the end, failed as a business—that I came to realize the true importance of organizational culture as an explanatory concept. *What* happens in organizations is fairly easy to observe; for example, leadership failures, marketing myopia, arrogance based on past success, and so on; but in the effort to understand *why* such things happen, culture as a concept comes into its own (Schein, 2003).

In an age in which leadership is touted over and over again as a critical variable in defining the success or failure of organizations, it becomes all the more important to look at the other side of the leadership coin—how leaders create culture and how culture defines and creates leaders. The first and second editions of this book attempted to show this connection, and I hope that I have been able to strengthen the connection even more in this third edition.

The conceptual models of how to think about the structure and functioning of organizational culture, and the role that leadership plays in the creation and management of culture have remained more or less the same in this third edition. However, I have been able to add material based on more recent clinical research and to make the concepts more vivid by identifying more of the organizations with whom I have worked over the years.

All of the chapters have been redone and edited. Some have been shortened; more have been lengthened with additional case material that I was able to incorporate. In addition, I have selectively incorporated relevant material from a great many other books and papers that have been written about organizational culture since the last edition. It is clear that there are still different models available to scholars and practitioners on how to think about culture. I have not reviewed all of them in detail but have tried to show, wherever possible, variations in point of view. I apologize to those colleagues whose work I may have overlooked or chosen not to include, but my purpose is not to write the definitive textbook on culture; rather, it is to explore a way of thinking about culture that I believe best suits our efforts to understand groups, organizations, and occupations.

This edition is organized into three parts. Part One focuses on organizational and occupational cultures—how to think about them, how to define them, and how to analyze them. Leadership is referred to throughout and leadership issues are highlighted, but the focus is clearly on getting a better feel for what culture is and does.

Part Two focuses on the content of culture. In a sense, culture covers all of a given group's life; hence the content is, in principle, endless and vast. Yet we need categories for analysis, and here we can draw on anthropology and group dynamics to develop a set of dimensions that are most likely to be useful in making some conceptual sense of the cultural landscape as applied to organizations.

In Part Three the focus shifts to the leader as founder, manager, and, ultimately, a victim of culture if the leader does not understand how to manage culture. A crucial element in this analysis is to understand how culture coevolves with the organization as success brings growth and aging. The issues that leaders face at each of these different organizational growth stages are completely different, partly because the role that culture plays at each stage is completely different. This aspect of leadership is almost completely ignored in most leadership books.

Acknowledgments

My most profound gratitude is to the readers of the first and second edition. Were it not for their positive and critical feedback, and their use of this book in their courses and their consulting work, I would not have had the energy to write a third edition. Support and stimulation from colleagues again played a key role, especially the feedback from John Van Maanen, Otto Scharmer, Joanne Martin, Mary Jo Hatch, Majken Schultz, and Peter Frost.

The publisher, Jossey-Bass, has always been totally encouraging and their editorial staff, especially Byron Schneider, urged me on relentlessly but in a positive and supportive way. The reviews they provided were essential to gaining perspective on a book that was first published in 1985. I got many good ideas about what was working and should be preserved, what needed to be cut out, and what needed to be added or enhanced. I thank each of them.

I think it is also important to acknowledge the tremendous positive impact of word processing technology. Work on this edition was launched with a set of chapters scanned in from the second edition, permitting immediate on-line editing. Material from the first edition that I decided to bring back in the third edition could be scanned and immediately incorporated where it belonged. Feedback from readers could be incorporated into the text directly and used or not used, without additional retyping. Final copy could be sent to the publisher directly on discs or electronically. Once errors were corrected they stayed corrected. All of this is a most unusual and pleasant experience for an author who can remember what writing was like with carbons, ditto paper, and endless retyping.

Last but not least I thank my wife, Mary, for sitting by patiently while I disappeared to work at the computer from time to time. But she too has gotten hooked on the power of e-mail and other electronic marvels, so she is now more understanding of how screens capture our attention.

May 2004   EDGAR H. SCHEIN
Cambridge, Massachusetts

The Author

EDGAR H. SCHEIN was educated at the University of Chicago; at Stanford University, where he received a master's degree in psychology in 1949; and at Harvard University, where he received his Ph.D. in social psychology in 1952. He was chief of the Social Psychology Section of the Walter Reed Army Institute of Research while serving in the U.S. Army as a captain from 1952 to 1956. He joined the Sloan School of Management at the Massachusetts Institute of Technology (MIT) in 1956 and was made a professor of organizational psychology and management in 1964.

From 1968 to 1971 Schein was the undergraduate planning professor for MIT, and in 1972 he became the chairman of the Organization Studies Group at the Sloan School, a position he held until 1982. He was honored in 1978 when he was named the Sloan Fellows Professor of Management, a chair he held until 1990.

At present he is Sloan Fellows Professor of Management Emeritus and continues at the Sloan School part time as a senior lecturer. He is also the founding editor of *Reflections*, the journal of the Society for Organizational Learning, which is devoted to connecting academics, consultants, and practitioners around the issues of knowledge creation, dissemination, and utilization.

Schein has been a prolific researcher, writer, teacher, and consultant. Besides his numerous articles in professional journals, he has authored fourteen books, including *Organizational Psychology* (third edition, 1980), *Career Dynamics* (1978), *Organizational Culture and Leadership* (1985, 1992), *Process Consultation Vol. 1 and Vol. 2*

(1969, 1987, 1988), *Process Consultation Revisited* (1999), and *The Corporate Culture Survival Guide* (1999).

Schein wrote a cultural analysis of the Singapore Economic Development Board, entitled *Strategic Pragmatism* (MIT Press, 1997), and he has published an extended case analysis of the rise and fall of Digital Equipment Corporation, entitled *DEC Is Dead; Long Live DEC: The Lasting Legacy of Digital Equipment Corporation* (Berrett-Koehler, 2003). He was coeditor with the late Richard Beckhard of the Addison Wesley Series on Organization Development, which has published over thirty titles since its inception in 1969.

His consultation focuses on organizational culture, organization development, process consultation, and career dynamics; among his past and current clients are major corporations both in the U.S. and overseas, such as Digital Equipment Corporation (DEC), Ciba-Geigy, Apple, Citibank, General Foods, Procter & Gamble, Imperial Chemical Industries (ICI), Saab Combitech, Steinbergs, Alcoa, Motorola, Hewlett-Packard, Exxon, Shell, Amoco, Con Edison, the Economic Development Board of Singapore, and the International Atomic Energy Agency (on the subject of "safety culture").

Schein has received many honors and awards for his writing, most recently the Lifetime Achievement Award in Workplace Learning and Performance of the American Society of Training Directors, February 3, 2000; the Everett Cherrington Hughes Award for Career Scholarship from the Careers Division of the Academy of Management, August 8, 2000; and the Marion Gislason Award for Leadership in Executive Development from the Boston University School of Management Executive Development Roundtable, December 11, 2002.

He is a Fellow of the American Psychological Association and the Academy of Management. Schein is married and has three children and seven grandchildren. He and his wife, Mary, live in Cambridge, Massachusetts.

Organizational Culture
and Leadership

Part One

ORGANIZATIONAL CULTURE AND LEADERSHIP DEFINED

In this section of the book I will define the concept of culture and show its relationship to leadership. Culture is both a dynamic phenomenon that surrounds us at all times, being constantly enacted and created by our interactions with others and shaped by leadership behavior, and a set of structures, routines, rules, and norms that guide and constrain behavior. When one brings culture to the level of the organization and even down to groups within the organization, one can see clearly how culture is created, embedded, evolved, and ultimately manipulated, and, at the same time, how culture constrains, stabilizes, and provides structure and meaning to the group members. These dynamic processes of culture creation and management are the essence of leadership and make one realize that leadership and culture are two sides of the same coin.

Leadership has been studied in far greater detail than organizational culture, leading to a frustrating diffusion of concepts and ideas of what leadership is really all about, whether one is born or made as a leader, whether one can train people to be leaders, and what characteristics successful leaders possess. I will not review this literature, focusing instead on what I consider to be *uniquely* associated with leadership—the creation and management of culture.

As we will see, this requires an evolutionary perspective. I believe that cultures begin with leaders who impose their own values and assumptions on a group. If that group is successful and the assumptions come to be taken for granted, we then have a culture that will define for later generations of members what kinds of leadership are acceptable. The culture now defines leadership. But as the group runs into adaptive difficulties, as its environment changes to the point where some of its assumptions are no longer valid, leadership comes into play once more. Leadership is now the ability to step outside the culture that created the leader and to start evolutionary change processes that are more adaptive. This ability to perceive the limitations of one's own culture and to evolve the culture adaptively is the essence and ultimate challenge of leadership.

If leaders are to fulfill this challenge, they must first understand the dynamics of culture, so our journey begins with a focus on definitions, case illustrations, and a suggested way of thinking about organizational culture. In this part, I begin in Chapter One with some brief illustrations and a definition. Chapter Two expands the concept and argues for a multilevel conception of culture. In Chapter Three, I examine in some detail two cases that illustrate well the complexity of culture and will be used throughout the rest of the book. And in Chapter Four, I show how culture arises in the process of human interaction.

At this point, the most important message for leaders is this: "try to understand culture, give it its due, and ask yourself how well you can begin to understand the culture in which you are embedded.

In Part Two of this book we turn to the content of culture, and in Part Three, to the dynamic processes involved in the interaction of leadership and culture.

1

THE CONCEPT OF ORGANIZATIONAL CULTURE: WHY BOTHER?

Culture is an abstraction, yet the forces that are created in social and organizational situations that derive from culture are powerful. If we don't understand the operation of these forces, we become victim to them. To illustrate how the concept of culture helps to illuminate organizational situations, I will begin by describing several situations I have encountered in my experience as a consultant.

Four Brief Examples

In the first case, that of Digital Equipment Corporation (DEC), I was called in to help a management group improve its communication, interpersonal relationships, and decision making. After sitting in on a number of meetings, I observed, among other things, (1) high levels of interrupting, confrontation, and debate; (2) excessive emotionality about proposed courses of action; (3) great frustration over the difficulty of getting a point of view across; and (4) a sense that every member of the group wanted to win all the time.

Over a period of several months, I made many suggestions about better listening, less interrupting, more orderly processing of the agenda, the potential negative effects of high emotionality and conflict, and the need to reduce the frustration level. The group members said that the suggestions were helpful, and they modified certain aspects of their procedure; for example, they scheduled more time for some of their meetings. However, the basic pattern did not change. No matter what kind of intervention I attempted, the basic style of the group remained the same.

In the second case, that of the Ciba-Geigy Company—a large multinational chemical and pharmaceutical company located in Basel, Switzerland—I was asked, as part of a broader consultation project, to help create a climate for innovation in an organization that felt a need to become more flexible in order to respond to its increasingly dynamic business environment. The organization consisted of many different business units, geographical units, and functional groups. As I got to know more about these units and their problems, I observed that some very innovative things were going on in many places in the company. I wrote several memos that described these innovations and presented other ideas from my own experience. I gave the memos to my contact person in the company with the request that he distribute them to the various geographic and business unit managers who needed to be made aware of these ideas.

After some months, I discovered that those managers to whom I had personally given the memo thought it was helpful and on target, but rarely, if ever, did they pass it on, and none were ever distributed by my contact person. I also suggested meetings of managers from different units to stimulate lateral communication, but found no support at all for such meetings. No matter what I did, I could not seem to get information flowing, especially laterally across divisional, functional, or geographical boundaries. Yet everyone agreed in principle that innovation would be stimulated by more lateral communication and encouraged me to keep on "helping."

In the third example, Amoco, a large oil company that was eventually merged with British Petroleum (BP), decided to centralize all of its engineering functions in a single service unit. Whereas engineers had previously been regular parts of projects, they were now supposed to sell their services to clients who would be charged for these services. The engineers resisted violently and many of them threatened to leave the organization. We were unable to reorganize this engineering organization to fit the new company requirements.

In the fourth example, Alpha Power, an electric and gas utility that services a large urban area, was faced with having to become more environmentally responsible after the company was brought up on criminal charges for allegedly failing to report the presence of asbestos in a local unit that had suffered an accident. Electrical workers, who took pride in their "heroic" self-image of keeping the lights on no matter what, also held the strong norm that one did not report spills and other environmental and safety problems if such reports would embarrass the group. I was involved in a multi-year project to change this self-image to one in which the "heroic" model would be to report all safety and environmental hazards, even if that meant reporting on peers—or bosses. All employees were supposed to adopt a new concept of personal responsibility, teamwork, and openness of communication. Yet no matter how clear the new mandate was made, safety problems continued wherever peer group relations were involved.

I did not really understand the forces operating in any of these cases until I began to examine my own assumptions about how things should work in these organizations and began to test whether my assumptions fitted those operating in my clients' systems. This step—examining the shared assumptions in the organization or group one is dealing with and comparing them to one's own—takes one into cultural analysis and will be the focus from here on.

It turned out that at DEC, an assumption was shared by senior managers and most of the other members of the organization: that one cannot determine whether or not something is "true" or "valid" unless one subjects the idea or proposal to intensive debate; and further, that only ideas that survive such debate are worth acting on, and only ideas that survive such scrutiny will be implemented. The group assumed that what they were doing was discovering truth, and in this context being polite to each other was relatively unimportant. I became more helpful to the group when I realized this and went to the flip chart and just started to write down the various ideas they were processing. If someone was interrupted, I could ask them to restate their point instead of punishing the interrupter. The group began to focus on the items on the chart and found that this really did help their communication and decision process. I had finally understood and entered into an essential element of *their* culture instead of imposing my own.

At Ciba-Geigy I eventually discovered that there was a strong shared assumption that each manager's job was his or her private "turf," not to be infringed on. The strong impression was communicated that one's job is like one's home, and if someone gives one unsolicited information, it is like walking into one's home uninvited. Sending memos to people implies that they do not already know what is in the memo, and that is potentially insulting. In this organization managers prided themselves on knowing whatever they needed to know to do their job. Had I understood this, I would have asked for a list of the names of the managers and sent the memo directly to them. They would have accepted it from me because I was the paid consultant and expert.

At Amoco I began to understand the resistance of the engineers when I learned that in their occupational culture there are strong assumptions that "good work should speak for itself" and "engineers should not have to go out and sell themselves." They were used to having people come to them for services and did not have a good role model for how to sell themselves.

At Alpha Power I learned that all work units had strong norms and values of self-protection that often overrode the new requirements imposed on the company by the courts. The groups had their own experience base for what was safe and what was not, which they were willing to trust, whereas the tasks of reporting environmental spills and cleaning them up involved *new* skills that workers were eventually willing to learn and collaborate on.

In each of these cases I initially did not understand what was going on because my own basic assumptions about truth and turf and group relations differed from the shared assumptions of the members of the organization. And my assumptions reflected my occupation as a social psychologist and organization consultant, while the group's assumptions reflected in part their occupations as electrical engineers, chemists, and electrical workers.

To make sense of such situations requires taking a cultural perspective; learning to see the world through *cultural lenses*; becoming competent in cultural analysis—by which I mean being able to perceive and decipher the cultural forces that operate in groups, organizations, and occupations. Once we learn to see the world through cultural lenses, all kinds of things begin to make sense that initially were mysterious, frustrating, or seemingly stupid.

Culture: An Empirically Based Abstraction

Culture as a concept has had a long and checkered history. It has been used by the layman as a word to indicate sophistication, as when we say that someone is very "cultured." It has been used by anthropologists to refer to the customs and rituals that societies develop over the course of their history. In the last several decades it has been used by some organizational researchers and managers to refer to the climate and practices that organizations develop around their handling of people, or to the espoused values and credo of an organization.

In this context, managers speak of developing the "right kind of culture," a "culture of quality" or a "culture of customer service," suggesting that culture has to do with certain values that managers are trying to inculcate in their organizations. Also implied in this usage is the assumption that there are better or worse cultures and stronger or weaker cultures, and that the "right" kind of culture will influence how effective the organization is. In the managerial literature there is often the implication that having a culture is necessary for effective performance, and that the stronger the culture, the more effective the organization.

Researchers have supported some of these views by reporting findings that cultural "strength" or certain kinds of cultures correlate with economic performance (Denison, 1990; Kotter and Heskett, 1992; Sorensen, 2002). Consultants have touted "culture surveys" and have claimed that they can improve organizational performance by helping organizations create certain kinds of cultures, but these claims are based on very different definitions of culture than what I will be arguing for here. As we will see, many of these usages of the word *culture* display not only a superficial and incorrect view of culture, but also a dangerous tendency to evaluate particular cultures in an absolute way and to suggest that there actually are "right" cultures for organizations. As we will also see, whether or not a culture is "good" or "bad," "functionally effective" or not, depends not on the culture alone, but on the relationship of the culture to the environment in which it exists.

Perhaps the most intriguing aspect of culture as a concept is that it points us to phenomena that are below the surface, that are powerful in their impact but invisible and to a considerable degree unconscious. In that sense, culture is to a group what personality or character is to an individual. We can see the behavior that results, but often we cannot see the forces underneath that cause certain kinds of behavior. Yet, just as our personality and character guide and constrain our behavior, so does culture guide and constrain the behavior of members of a group through the shared norms that are held in that group.

To complicate matters further, one can view personality and character as the accumulation of cultural learning that an individual has experienced in the family, the peer group, the school, the community, and the occupation. In this sense, culture is within us as individuals and yet constantly evolving as we join and create new groups that eventually create new cultures. Culture as a concept is thus an abstraction but its behavioral and attitudinal consequences are very concrete indeed.

If an abstract concept is to be useful to our thinking, it should be observable and also increase our understanding of a set of events that are otherwise mysterious or not well understood. From this point of view, I will argue that we must avoid the superficial models of culture and build on the deeper, more complex anthropological models. Culture as a concept will be most useful if it helps us to better understand the hidden and complex aspects of life in groups, organizations, and occupations, and we cannot obtain this understanding if we use superficial definitions.

What Needs to Be Explained?

Most of us, in our roles as students, employees, managers, researchers, or consultants, work in and have to deal with groups and organizations of all kinds. Yet we continue to find it amazingly difficult to understand and justify much of what we observe and experience in our organizational life. Too much seems to be bureaucratic or political or just plain irrational—as in the four cases that I described at the beginning of this chapter.

People in positions of authority, especially our immediate bosses, often frustrate us or act incomprehensibly; those we consider the leaders of our organizations often disappoint us. When we get into arguments or negotiations with others, we often cannot understand how our opponents could take such ridiculous positions. When we observe other organizations, we often find it incomprehensible that smart people could do such dumb things. We recognize cultural differences at the ethnic or national level, but find them puzzling at the group, organizational, or occupational level.

As managers, when we try to change the behavior of subordinates, we often encounter resistance to change to an extent that seems beyond reason. We observe departments in our organization that seem to be more interested in fighting with each other than getting the job done. We see communication problems and misunderstandings between group members that should not be occurring between reasonable people. We explain in detail why something different must be done, yet people continue to act as if they had not heard us.

As leaders who are trying to get our organizations to become more effective in the face of severe environmental pressures, we are sometimes amazed at the degree to which individuals and groups in the organization will continue to behave in obviously ineffective ways, often threatening the very survival of the organization. As we try to get things done that involve other groups, we often discover that they do not communicate with each other and that the level of conflict between groups in organizations and in the community is often astonishingly high.

As teachers, we encounter the sometimes mysterious phenomenon that different classes behave completely differently from each other, even though our material and teaching style remains the same. As employees considering a new job, we realize that companies differ greatly in their approach, even in the same industry and geographic locale. We feel these differences even as we walk through the doors of different organizations, such as restaurants, banks, stores, or airlines.

As members of different occupations, we are aware that being a doctor, lawyer, engineer, accountant, or other professional involves not only the learning of technical skills but also the adoption of certain values and norms that define our occupation. If we violate some of these norms we can be thrown out of the occupation. But where do these come from and how do we reconcile the fact that each occupation considers its norms and values to be the correct ones?

The concept of culture helps to explain all of these phenomena and to normalize them. If we understand the dynamics of culture, we will be less likely to be puzzled, irritated, and anxious when we encounter the unfamiliar and seemingly irrational behavior of people in organizations, and we will have a deeper understanding not only of why various groups of people or organizations can be so different, but also why it is so hard to change them. Even more important, if we understand culture better we will better understand ourselves—better understand the forces acting within us that define who we are, that reflect the groups with which we identify and to which we want to belong.

Culture and Leadership

When we examine culture and leadership closely, we see that they are two sides of the same coin; neither can really be understood by itself. On the one hand, cultural norms define how a given nation or organizations will define leadership—who will get promoted, who will get the attention of followers. On the other hand, it can be argued that the only thing of real importance that leaders do is to create and manage culture; that the unique talent of leaders is their ability to understand and work with culture; and that it is an ultimate act of leadership to destroy culture when it is viewed as dysfunctional.

If one wishes to distinguish leadership from management or administration, one can argue that leadership creates and changes cultures, while management and administration act within a culture. By defining leadership in this manner, I am not implying that culture is easy to create or change, or that formal leaders are the only determiners of culture. On the contrary, as we will see, culture refers to those elements of a group or organization that are most stable and least malleable.

Culture is the result of a complex group learning process that is only partially influenced by leader behavior. But if the group's survival is threatened because elements of its culture have become maladapted, it is ultimately the function of leadership at all levels of the organization to recognize and do something about this situation. It is in this sense that leadership and culture are conceptually intertwined.

Toward a Formal Definition of Culture

When we apply the concept of culture to groups, organizations, and occupations, we are almost certain to have conceptual and semantic confusion, because such social units are themselves difficult to define unambiguously. I will use as the critical defining characteristic of a *group* the fact that its members have a shared history. Any social unit that has some kind of shared history will have evolved a culture, with the strength of that culture dependent on the length of its existence, the stability of the group's membership, and the emotional intensity of the actual historical experiences they have shared. We all have a commonsense notion of this phenomenon, yet it is difficult to define it abstractly. In talking about organizational culture with colleagues and members of organizations, I often find that we agree that "it" exists and that it is important in its effects, but when we try to define it, we have completely different ideas of what "it" is.

To make matters worse, the concept of culture has been the subject of considerable academic debate in the last twenty-five years and there are various approaches to defining and studying culture (for example, those of Hofstede, 1991; Trice and Beyer, 1993; Schultz, 1995; Deal and Kennedy, 1999; Cameron and Quinn, 1999; Ashkanasy, Wilderom, and Peterson, 2000; and Martin, 2002). This debate is a healthy sign in that it testifies to the importance of culture as a concept, but at the same time it creates difficulties for both the scholar and the practitioner if definitions are fuzzy and usages are inconsistent. For the purpose of this introductory chapter, I will give only a quick overview of this range of usage and then offer a precise and formal definition that makes the most sense from my point of view. Other usages and points of view will be further reviewed in later chapters.

Commonly used words relating to culture emphasize one of its critical aspects—the idea that certain things in groups are shared or held in common. The major categories of observables that are associated with culture in this sense are shown in Exhibit 1.1.

All of these concepts relate to culture or reflect culture in that they deal with things that group members *share* or hold in common, but none of them can usefully be thought of as "the culture" of an organization or group. If one asks why we need the word *culture* at

Exhibit 1.1. Various Categories Used to Describe Culture.

Observed behavioral regularities when people interact: the language they use, the customs and traditions that evolve, and the rituals they employ in a wide variety of situations (Goffman, 1959, 1967; Jones, Moore, and Snyder, 1988; Trice and Beyer, 1993, 1985; Van Maanen, 1979b).

Group norms: the implicit standards and values that evolve in working groups, such as the particular norm of "a fair day's work for a fair day's pay" that

---

Exhibit 1.1. Various Categories Used to Describe Culture, Cont'd.

---

evolved among workers in the Bank Wiring Room in the Hawthorne studies (Homans, 1950; Kilmann and Saxton, 1983).

Espoused values: the articulated, publicly announced principles and values that the group claims to be trying to achieve, such as "product quality" or "price leadership" (Deal and Kennedy, 1982, 1999).

Formal philosophy: the broad policies and ideological principles that guide a group's actions toward stockholders, employees, customers, and other stake-holders, such as the highly publicized "HP Way" of Hewlett-Packard (Ouchi, 1981; Pascale and Athos,1981; Packard, 1995).

Rules of the game: the implicit, unwritten rules for getting along in the organization; "the ropes" that a newcomer must learn in order to become an accepted member; "the way we do things around here" (Schein, 1968, 1978; Van Maanen, 1979a, 1979b; Ritti and Funkhouser, 1987).

Climate: the feeling that is conveyed in a group by the physical layout and the way in which members of the organization interact with each other, with customers, or other outsiders (Ashkanasy, Wilderom, and Peterson, 2000; Schneider, 1990; Tagiuri and Litwin, 1968).

Embedded skills: the special competencies displayed by group members in accomplishing certain tasks, the ability to make certain things that gets passed on from generation to generation without necessarily being articulated in writing (Argyris and Schön, 1978; Cook and Yanow, 1993; Henderson and Clark, 1990; Peters and Waterman, 1982).

Habits of thinking, mental models, and linguistic paradigms: the shared cognitive frames that guide the perceptions, thought, and language used by the members of a group and taught to new members in the early socialization process (Douglas, 1986; Hofstede, 2001; Van Maanen, 1979b; Senge and others, 1994).

Shared meanings: the emergent understandings created by group members as they interact with each other (as in Geertz, 1973; Smircich, 1983; Van Maanen and Barley, 1984; Weick, 1995).

"Root metaphors" or integrating symbols: the ways in which groups evolve to characterize themselves, which may or may not be appreciated consciously but become embodied in buildings, office layout, and other material artifacts of the group. This level of the culture reflects the emotional and aesthetic response of members as contrasted with the cognitive or evaluative response (as in Gagliardi, 1990; Hatch, 1990; Pondy, Frost, Morgan, and Dandridge, 1983; Schultz, 1995).

Formal rituals and celebrations: the ways in which a group celebrates key events that reflect important values or important "passages" by members, such as promotion, completion of important projects, and milestones (as in Deal and Kennedy, 1982, 1999; Trice and Beyer, 1993).

---

all when we have so many other concepts—such as norms, values, behavior patterns, rituals, traditions, and so on—one recognizes that the word *culture* adds several other critical elements to the concept of sharing: structural stability, depth, breadth, and patterning or integration.

Structural Stability

Culture implies some level of structural stability in the group. When we say that something is "cultural," we imply that it is not only shared, but also stable, because it defines the group. Once we achieve a sense of group identity, it is our major stabilizing force and will not be given up easily. Culture survives even when some members of the organization depart. Culture is hard to change because group members value stability in that it provides meaning and predictability.

Depth

Culture is the deepest, often unconscious part of a group and is, therefore, less tangible and less visible than other parts. From this point of view, most of the concepts reviewed above can be thought of as manifestations of culture, but they are not the essence of what we mean by culture. Note that when something is more deeply embedded it also gains stability.

Breadth

A third characteristic of culture is that once it has developed, it covers *all* of a group's functioning. Culture is pervasive; it influences all aspects of how an organization deals with its primary task, its various environments, and its internal operations. Not all groups have cultures in this sense, but the concept connotes that when we refer to the culture of a group we are referring to all of its operations.

Patterning or Integration

The fourth characteristic that is implied by the concept of culture and that further lends stability is patterning or integration of the elements into a larger paradigm or "gestalt" that ties together the various elements and that lies at a deeper level. Culture somehow implies that rituals, climate, values, and behaviors tie together into a coherent whole; this patterning or integration is the essence of what we mean by "culture." Such patterning or integration ultimately derives from the human need to make our environment as sensible and orderly as we can (Weick, 1995). Disorder or senselessness makes us anxious, so we will work hard to reduce that anxiety by developing a more consistent and predictable view of how things are and how they should be. Thus "organizational cultures, like other cultures, develop as groups of people struggle to make sense of and cope with their worlds" (Trice and Beyer, 1993, p. 4).

How then should we think about the "essence" of culture and how should we formally define it? The most useful way to arrive at a definition of something as abstract as culture is to think in dynamic evolutionary terms. If we can understand where culture comes from and how it evolves, then we can grasp something that is abstract; that exists in a group's unconscious, yet that has powerful influences on a group's behavior.

How Does Culture Form?

Culture forms in two ways. In Chapter Four I will show how spontaneous interaction in an unstructured group gradually lead to patterns and norms of behavior that become the culture of that group—often within just hours of the group's formation. In more formal groups an individual creates the group or becomes its leader. This could be an entrepreneur starting a new company, a religious person creating a following, a political leader creating a new party, a teacher starting a new class, or a manager taking over a new department of an organization. The individual founder—whether an entrepreneur or just the convener of a new group—will have certain personal visions, goals, beliefs, values, and assumptions about how things should be. He or she will initially impose these on the group and/or select members on the basis of their similarity of thoughts and values.

We can think of this imposition as a primary act of leadership, but it does not automatically produce culture. All it produces is compliance in the followers to do what the leader asks of them. Only if the resulting behavior leads to "success"—in the sense that the group accomplishes its task and the members feel good about their relationships to each other—will the founder's beliefs and values be confirmed and reinforced, and, most important, come to be recognized as *shared*. What was originally the founder's *individual* view of the world leads to shared action, which, if successful, leads to a *shared* recognition that the founder "had it right." The group will then act again on these beliefs and values and, if it continues to be successful, will eventually conclude that it now has the "correct" way to think, feel, and act.

If, on the other hand, the founder's beliefs and values do not lead to success, the group will fail and disappear or will seek other leadership until someone is found whose beliefs and values will lead to success. The culture formation process will then revolve around that new leader. With continued reinforcement, the group will become less and less conscious of these beliefs and values, and it will begin to treat them more and more as nonnegotiable assumptions. As this process continues, these assumptions will gradually drop out of awareness and come to be taken for granted. As assumptions come to be taken for granted they become part of the identity of the group; are taught to newcomers as the way to think, feel, and act; and, if violated, produce discomfort, anxiety, ostracism, and eventually excommunication. This concept of assumptions, as opposed to beliefs and values, implies nonnegotiability. If we are willing to argue about something, then it has not become taken for granted. Therefore, definitions of culture that deal with *values* must specify that culture consists of *nonnegotiable values*—which I am calling *assumptions*.

In summary, we can think of culture as the accumulated shared learning of a given group, covering behavioral, emotional, and cognitive elements of the group members' total psychological functioning. For such shared learning to occur, there must be a history of shared experience that, in turn, implies some stability of membership in the group. Given such stability and a shared history, the human need for stability, consistency, and meaning will cause the various shared elements to form into patterns that eventually can be called a culture.

Culture Formally Defined

The culture of a group can now be defined as *a pattern of shared basic assumptions that was learned by a group as it solved its problems of external adaptation and internal integration, that has worked well enough to be considered valid and, therefore, to be taught to new members as the correct way to perceive, think, and feel in relation to those problems*.

I am not arguing that all groups evolve integrated cultures in this sense. We all know of groups, organizations, and societies in which certain beliefs and values work at cross purposes with other beliefs and values, leading to situations full of conflict and ambiguity (Martin, 2002). This may result from insufficient stability of membership, insufficient shared history of experience, or the presence of many subgroups with different kinds of shared experiences. Ambiguity and conflict also result from the fact that each of us belongs to many groups, so that what we bring to any given group is influenced by the assumptions that are appropriate to our other groups.

But if the concept of culture is to have any utility, it should draw our attention to those things that are the product of our human need for stability, consistency, and meaning. Culture formation is always, by definition, a striving toward patterning and integration, even though in many groups their actual history of experiences prevents them from ever achieving a clear-cut, unambiguous paradigm.

If a group's culture is the result of that group's accumulated learning, how do we describe and catalogue the content of that learning? All group and organizational theories distinguish two major sets of problems that all groups, no matter what their size, must deal with: (1) survival, growth, and adaptation in their environment; and (2) internal integration that permits daily functioning and the ability to adapt and learn. Both of these areas of group functioning will reflect the larger cultural context in which the group exists and from which are derived broader and deeper basic assumptions about the nature of reality, time, space, human nature, and human relationships. Each of these areas will be explained in detail in later chapters.

At this point, it is important to discuss several other elements that are important to our formal definition of culture.

The Process of Socialization

Once a group has a culture, it will pass elements of this culture on to new generations of group members (Louis, 1980; Schein, 1968; Van Maanen, 1976; Van Maanen and Schein, 1979). Studying what new members of groups are taught is, in fact, a good way to discover some of the elements of a culture; however, by this means one only learns about surface aspects of the culture—especially because much of what is at the heart of a culture will not be revealed in the rules of behavior taught to newcomers. It will only be revealed to members as they gain permanent status and are allowed into the inner circles of the group in which group secrets are shared.

On the other hand, how one learns and the socialization processes to which one is subjected may indeed reveal deeper assumptions. To get at those deeper levels one must try to understand the perceptions and feelings that arise in critical situations, and one must observe and interview regular members or "old-timers" to get an accurate sense of the deeper-level assumptions that are shared.

Can culture be learned through anticipatory socialization or self-socialization? Can new members discover for themselves what the basic assumptions are? Yes and no. We certainly know that one of the major activities of any new member when she enters a new group is to decipher the operating norms and assumptions. But this deciphering can be successful only through the feedback that is meted out by old members to new members as they experiment with different kinds of behavior. In this sense, there is always a teaching process going on, even though it may be quite implicit and unsystematic.

If the group does not have shared assumptions, as will sometimes be the case, the new member's interaction with old members will be a more creative process of building a culture. But once shared assumptions exist, the culture survives through teaching them to newcomers. In this regard culture is a mechanism of social control and can be the basis for explicitly manipulating members into perceiving, thinking, and feeling in certain ways (Van Maanen and Kunda, 1989; Kunda, 1992; Schein, 1968). Whether or not we approve of this as a mechanism of social control is a separate question that will be addressed later.

Behavior Is Derivative, Not Central

This formal definition of culture does not include overt behavior patterns (although some such behavior—particularly formal rituals—does reflect cultural assumptions). Instead, it emphasizes that the critical assumptions deal with how we perceive, think about, and feel about things. Overt behavior is always determined both by the cultural predisposition (the perceptions, thoughts, and feelings that are patterned) and by the situational contingencies that arise from the immediate external environment.

Behavioral regularities can occur for reasons other than shared culture. For example, if we observe that all members of a group cower in the presence of a large, loud leader, this could be based on biological, reflex reactions to sound and size, or on individual or shared learning. Such a behavioral regularity should not, therefore, be the basis for defining culture—though we might later discover that, in a given group's experience, cowering is indeed a result of shared learning and, therefore, a manifestation of deeper shared assumptions. To put it another way, when we observe behavior regularities, we do not know whether or not we are dealing with a cultural manifestation. Only after we have discovered the deeper layers that I define as the essence of culture can we specify what is and what is not an artifact that reflects the culture.

Can a Large Organization or Occupation Have One Culture?

My formal definition does not specify the size of social unit to which it can legitimately be applied. Our experience with large organizations tells us that at a certain size the variations among the subgroups is substantial, suggesting that it might not be appropriate to talk of the culture of an IBM or a General Motors or Shell. In the evolution of DEC over its thirty-five-year history one can see both a strong overall corporate culture and the growth of powerful subcultures that reflected the larger culture but also differed in important ways (Schein, 2003). In fact, the growing tensions among the subcultures were partly the reason why DEC as an economic entity ultimately failed to survive.

Do Occupations Have Cultures?

If an occupation involves an intense period of education and apprenticeship, there will certainly be a shared learning of attitudes, norms, and values that eventually will become taken-for-granted assumptions for the members of those occupations. It is assumed that the beliefs and values learned during this time will remain stable as assumptions even though the person may not always be in a group of occupational peers. But reinforcement of those assumptions occurs at professional meetings and continuing education sessions, and by virtue of the fact that the practice of the occupation often calls for teamwork among several members of the occupation, who reinforce each other. One reason why so many occupations rely heavily on peer-group evaluation is that this process preserves and protects the culture of the occupation.

Determining which sets of assumptions apply to a whole society, or a whole organization, or a whole subgroup within an organization or occupation, should be done empirically. I have found all kinds of combinations; their existence is one reason why some theorists emphasize that organizational cultures can be integrated, differentiated, or fragmented (Martin, 2002). But for the purpose of defining culture, it is important to recognize that a fragmented or differentiated organizational culture usually reflects a multiplicity of subcultures, and within those subcultures there are shared assumptions.

Are Some Assumptions More Important than Others?

As we will see when we examine some of our cases more closely, organizations do seem to function primarily in terms of some core of assumptions, some smaller set that can be thought of as the cultural paradigm or the governing assumptions, or as critical "genes" in the "cultural DNA." For the researcher, the problem is that different organizations will have different paradigms with different core assumptions. As a result, cultural typologies can be very misleading. One could measure many organizations on the same core dimensions, but in some of those organizations a particular dimension could be central to the paradigm, whereas in others its influence on the organization's behavior could be quite peripheral.

If the total set of shared basic assumptions of a given organizational culture can be thought of as its DNA, then we can examine some of the individual genes in terms of their centrality or potency in forcing certain kinds of growth and behavior, and other genes in terms of their power to inhibit or prevent certain kinds of behavior. We can then see that certain kinds of cultural evolution are determined by the "genetic structure," the kind of "autoimmune system" that the organization generates, and the impact of "mutations and hybridization."

Summary and Conclusions

In this chapter I introduced the concept of culture and have argued that it helps to explain some of the more seemingly incomprehensible and irrational aspects of what goes on in groups and organizations. The variety of elements that people perceive to be "culture" was reviewed, leading to a formal definition that puts the emphasis on shared learning experiences that lead, in turn, to shared, taken-for-granted basic assumptions held by the members of the group or organization.

It follows that any group with a stable membership and a history of shared learning will have developed some level of culture, but a group that has had either considerable turnover of members and leaders or a history lacking in any kind of challenging events may well lack any shared assumptions. Not every collection of people develops a culture; in fact, we tend to use the term *group* rather than, say, *crowd* or *collection* of people only when there has been enough of a shared history for some degree of culture formation to have taken place.

Once a set of shared assumptions has come to be taken for granted, it determines much of the group's behavior, and the rules and norms are taught to newcomers in a socialization process that is itself a reflection of culture. To define culture one must go below the behavioral level, because behavioral regularities can be caused by forces other than culture. Even large organizations and entire occupations can have a common culture if there has been enough of a history of shared experience. Finally, I noted that the shared assumptions will form a paradigm, with more or less central or governing assumptions driving the system, much as certain genes drive the genetic structure of human DNA.

Culture and leadership are two sides of the same coin, in that leaders first create cultures when they create groups and organizations. Once cultures exist they determine the criteria for leadership and thus determine who will or will not be a leader. But if elements of a culture become dysfunctional, it is the unique function of leadership to be able to perceive the functional and dysfunctional elements of the existing culture and to manage cultural evolution and change in such a way that the group can survive in a changing environment.

The bottom line for leaders is that if they do not become conscious of the cultures in which they are embedded, those cultures will manage them. Cultural understanding is desirable for all of us, but it is essential to leaders if they are to lead.

A final note: from this point on I will use the term *group* to refer to social units of all sizes—including organizations and subunits of organizations—except when it is necessary to distinguish the type of social unit because of subgroups that exist within larger groups.

2

THE LEVELS OF CULTURE

The purpose of this chapter is to show that culture can be analyzed at several different levels, with the term *level* meaning the degree to which the cultural phenomenon is visible to the observer. Some of the confusion surrounding the definition of what culture really is results from not differentiating the levels at which it manifests itself. These levels range from the very tangible overt manifestations that one can see and feel to the deeply embedded, unconscious, basic assumptions that I am defining as the essence of culture. In between these layers are various espoused beliefs, values, norms, and rules of behavior that members of the culture use as a way of depicting the culture to themselves and others.

Many other culture researchers prefer the term *basic values* to describe the concept of the deepest levels. I prefer *basic assumptions* because these tend to be taken for granted by group members and are treated as nonnegotiable. Values are open to discussion and people can agree to disagree about them. Basic assumptions are so taken for granted that someone who does not hold them is viewed as a "foreigner" or as "crazy" and is automatically dismissed.

The major levels of cultural analysis are shown in Figure 2.1.

Artifacts

At the surface is the level of artifacts, which includes all the phenomena that one sees, hears, and feels when one encounters a new group with an unfamiliar culture. Artifacts include the visible products of the group, such as the architecture of its physical

Figure 2.1. Levels of Culture.

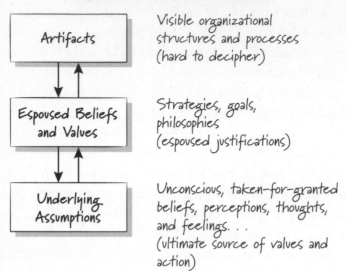

Artifacts	Visible organizational structures and processes (hard to decipher)
Espoused Beliefs and Values	Strategies, goals, philosophies (espoused justifications)
Underlying Assumptions	Unconscious, taken-for-granted beliefs, perceptions, thoughts, and feelings . . . (ultimate source of values and action)

environment; its language; its technology and products; its artistic creations; its style, as embodied in clothing, manners of address, emotional displays, and myths and stories told about the organization; its published lists of values; its observable rituals and ceremonies; and so on.

The "climate" of the group is an artifact of the deeper cultural levels, as is the visible behavior of its members. Artifacts also include, for purposes of cultural analysis, the organizational processes by which such behavior is made routine, and structural elements such as charters, formal descriptions of how the organization works, and organization charts.

The most important point to be made about this level of the culture is that it is both easy to observe and very difficult to decipher. The Egyptians and the Mayans both built highly visible pyramids, but the meaning of pyramids in each culture was very different—tombs in one, temples as well as tombs in the other. In other words, observers can describe what they see and feel, but cannot reconstruct from that alone what those things mean in the given group, or whether they even reflect important underlying assumptions.

On the other hand, one school of thought argues that one's own response to physical artifacts such as buildings and office layouts can lead to the identification of major images and root metaphors that reflect the deepest level of the culture (Gagliardi, 1990). This kind of immediate insight would be especially relevant if the organization one is experiencing is in the same larger culture as the researcher. The problem is that symbols are ambiguous, and one can only test one's insight into what something may mean if one has also experienced the culture at the deeper levels of values and assumptions.

It is especially dangerous to try to infer the deeper assumptions from artifacts alone, because one's interpretations will inevitably be projections of one's own feelings and reactions. For example, when one sees a very informal, loose organization, one may interpret that as inefficient if one's own background is based on the assumption that informality means playing around and not working. Or, alternatively, if one sees a very formal organization, one may interpret that to be a sign of lack of innovative capacity, if one's own experience is based on the assumption that formality means bureaucracy and formalization.

Every facet of a group's life produces artifacts, creating the problem of classification. In reading cultural descriptions, one often notes that different observers choose to report on different sorts of artifacts, leading to noncomparable descriptions. Anthropologists have developed classification systems, but these tend to be so vast and detailed that cultural essence becomes difficult to discern.

If the observer lives in the group long enough, the meanings of artifacts gradually become clear. If, however, one wants to achieve this level of understanding more quickly, one can attempt to analyze the espoused values, norms, and rules that provide the day-to-day operating principles by which the members of the group guide their behavior. This kind of inquiry takes us to the next level of cultural analysis.

Espoused Beliefs and Values

All group learning ultimately reflects someone's original beliefs and values, their sense of what ought to be, as distinct from what is. When a group is first created or when it faces a new task, issue, or problem, the first solution proposed to deal with it reflects some individual's own assumptions about what is right or wrong, what will work or not work. Those individuals who prevail, who can influence the group to adopt a certain approach to the problem, will later be identified as leaders or founders, but the group does not yet have any *shared* knowledge as a group because it has not yet taken a common action in reference to whatever it is supposed to do. Whatever is proposed will only be perceived as what the leader wants. Until the group has taken some joint action and together observed the outcome of that action, there is not as yet a shared basis for determining whether what the leader wants will turn out to be valid.

For example, in a young business, if sales begin to decline a manager may say "We must increase advertising" because of her belief that advertising always increases sales. The group, never having experienced this situation before, will hear that assertion as a statement of that manager's beliefs and values: "She believes that when one is in trouble it is a good thing to increase advertising." What the leader initially proposes, therefore, cannot have any status other than a value to be questioned, debated, challenged, and tested.

If the manager convinces the group to act on her belief, and if the solution works, and if the group has a shared perception of that success, then the perceived value that advertising is good gradually becomes transformed: first into a shared value or belief, and ultimately into a shared assumption (if actions based on it continue to be successful). If this transformation process occurs, group members will tend to forget that originally they were not sure and that the proposed course of action was at an earlier time just a proposal to be debated and confronted.

Not all beliefs and values undergo such transformation. First of all, the solution based on a given value may not work reliably. Only those beliefs and values that can be empirically tested and that continue to work reliably in solving the group's problems will become transformed into assumptions. Second, certain value domains—those dealing with the less controllable elements of the environment or with aesthetic or moral matters—may not be testable at all. In such cases, consensus through social validation is still possible, but it is not automatic.

By *social validation* I mean that certain values are confirmed only by the shared social experience of a group. For example, any given culture cannot prove that its religion and moral system are superior to another culture's religion and moral system, but if the members reinforce each others' beliefs and values, they come to be taken for granted. Those who fail to accept such beliefs and values run the risk of "excommunication"—of being thrown out of the group. Such beliefs and values typically involve the group's internal relations; the test of whether they work or not is how comfortable and anxiety-free members are when they abide by them. Social validation also applies to those broader values that are not testable, such as ethics and aesthetics.

In these realms the group learns that certain beliefs and values, as initially promulgated by prophets, founders, and leaders, "work" in the sense of reducing uncertainty in critical areas of the group's functioning. And, as they continue to work, they gradually become transformed into nondiscussible assumptions supported by articulated sets of beliefs, norms, and operational rules of behavior. The derived beliefs and moral and ethical rules remain conscious and are explicitly articulated because they serve the normative or moral function of guiding members of the group in how to deal with certain key situations, and in training new members how to behave. A set of beliefs and values that become embodied in an ideology or organizational philosophy thus can serve as a guide and as a way of dealing with the uncertainty of intrinsically uncontrollable or difficult events. An example of such an ideology is Hewlett-Packard's *The HP Way* (Packard, 1995).

Beliefs and values at this conscious level will predict much of the behavior that can be observed at the artifacts level. But if those beliefs and values are not based on prior learning, they may also reflect only what Argyris and Schön (1978) have called "espoused theories," which predict well enough what people will *say* in a variety of situations but which may be out of line with what they will actually *do* in situations in which those beliefs and values should, in fact, be operating. Thus, a company may say that it values people and that it has high quality standards for its products, but its record in that regard may contradict what it says.

If the espoused beliefs and values are reasonably congruent with the underlying assumptions, then the articulation of those values into a philosophy of operating can be helpful in bringing the group together, serving as a source of identity and core mission. But in analyzing beliefs and values one must discriminate carefully between those that are congruent with underlying assumptions and those that are, in effect, either rationalizations or only aspirations for the future. Often such lists of beliefs and values are so abstract that they can be mutually contradictory, as when a company claims to be *equally* concerned about stockholders, employees, and customers, or when it claims both highest quality and lowest cost. Espoused beliefs and values often leave large areas of behavior unexplained, leaving us with a feeling that we understand a piece of the culture but still do not have the culture as such in hand. To get at that deeper level of understanding, to decipher the pattern, and to predict future behavior correctly, we have to understand more fully the category of basic underlying assumptions.

Basic Underlying Assumptions

When a solution to a problem works repeatedly, it comes to be taken for granted. What was once a hypothesis, supported only by a hunch or a value, gradually comes to be treated as a reality. We come to believe that nature really works this way. Basic assumptions, in this sense, are different from what some anthropologists called "dominant value orientations" in that such dominant orientations reflect the *preferred* solution among several basic alternatives, but all the alternatives are still visible in the culture, and any given member of the culture could, from time to time, behave according to variant as well as dominant orientations (Kluckhohn and Strodtbeck, 1961).

Basic assumptions, in the sense in which I want to define that concept, have become so taken for granted that one finds little variation within a social unit. This degree of consensus results from repeated success in implementing certain beliefs and values, as previously described. In fact, if a basic assumption comes to be strongly held in a group, members will find behavior based on any other premise inconceivable. For example, a group whose basic assumption is that the individual's rights supersede those of the group members would find it inconceivable that members would commit suicide or in some other way sacrifice themselves to the group even if they had dishonored the group. In a capitalist country, it is inconceivable that one might design a company to operate consistently at a financial loss, or that it does not matter whether or not a product works. In an occupation such as engineering, it would be inconceivable to *deliberately* design something that is unsafe; it is a taken-for-granted assumption that things should be safe. Basic assumptions, in this sense, are similar to what Argyris has identified as "theories-in-use"—the implicit assumptions that actually guide behavior, that tell group members how to perceive, think about, and feel about things (Argyris, 1976; Argyris and Schön, 1974).

Basic assumptions, like theories-in-use, tend to be nonconfrontable and nondebatable, and hence are extremely difficult to change. To learn something new in this realm requires us to resurrect, reexamine, and possibly change some of the more stable portions of our cognitive structure—a process that Argyris and others have called "double-loop learning," or "frame breaking" (Argyris et al., 1985; Bartunek, 1984). Such learning is intrinsically difficult because the reexamination of basic assumptions temporarily destabilizes our cognitive and interpersonal world, releasing large quantities of basic anxiety.

Rather than tolerating such anxiety levels, we tend to want to perceive the events around us as congruent with our assumptions, even if that means distorting, denying, projecting, or in other ways falsifying to ourselves what may be going on around us. It is in this psychological process that culture has its ultimate power. Culture as a set of basic assumptions defines for us what to pay attention to, what things mean, how to react emotionally to what is going on, and what actions to take in various kinds of situations. Once we have developed an integrated set of such assumptions—a "thought world" or "mental map"—we will be maximally comfortable with others who share the same set of assumptions and very uncomfortable and vulnerable in situations where different assumptions operate, because either we will not understand what is going on, or, worse, we will misperceive and misinterpret the actions of others (Douglas, 1986).

The human mind needs cognitive stability; therefore, any challenge or questioning of a basic assumption will release anxiety and defensiveness. In this sense, the shared basic assumptions that make up the culture of a group can be thought of at both the individual and the group level as psychological cognitive defense mechanisms that permit the group to continue to function. Recognizing this connection is important when one thinks about changing aspects of a group's culture, for it is no easier to do that than to change an individual's pattern of defense mechanisms. As was pointed out in Chapter One, we can also think of culture at this level as the group's DNA, so if new learning or growth is required, the genes have to be there to make such growth possible and the autoimmune system has to be neutralized to sustain new growth. In any case, the two keys to successful culture change are (1) the management of the large amounts of anxiety that accompany any relearning at this level and (2) the assessment of whether the genetic potential for the new learning is even present.

To illustrate how unconscious assumptions can distort data, consider the following example. If we assume, on the basis of past experience or education, that other people will take advantage of us whenever they have an opportunity, we expect to be taken advantage of and we then interpret the behavior of others in a way that coincides with those expectations. We observe people sitting in a seemingly idle posture at their desk and interpret their behavior as "loafing" rather than "thinking out an important problem." We perceive absence from work as "shirking" rather than "doing work at home."

If this is not only a personal assumption but also one that is shared and thus part of the culture of an organization, we will discuss with others what to do about our "lazy" workforce and institute tight controls to ensure that people are at their desks and busy. If employees suggest that they do some of their work at home, we will be uncomfortable and probably deny the request because we will figure that at home they would loaf (Bailyn, 1992; Perin, 1991).

In contrast, if we assume that everyone is highly motivated and competent, we will act in accordance with that assumption by encouraging people to work at their own pace and in their own way. If someone is discovered to be unproductive in such an organization, we will make the assumption that there is a mismatch between the person and the job assignment, not that the person is lazy or incompetent. If the employee wants to work at home, we will perceive that as evidence of his wanting to be productive even if circumstances required him to be at home.

In both cases there is the potential for distortion, in that the cynical manager will not perceive how highly motivated some of the subordinates really are, and the idealistic manager will not perceive that there are subordinates who are lazy and who are taking advantage of the situation. As McGregor noted many decades ago, such assumptions about "human nature" become the basis of management and control systems that perpetuate themselves because if people are treated consistently in terms of certain basic assumptions, they come eventually to behave according to those assumptions in order to make their world stable and predictable (McGregor, 1960).

Unconscious assumptions sometimes lead to ridiculously tragic situations, as illustrated by a common problem experienced by American supervisors in some Asian countries. A manager who comes from an American pragmatic tradition assumes and takes it for granted that *solving* a problem always has the highest priority. When that manager encounters a subordinate who comes from a different cultural tradition, in which good relationships and protecting the superior's "face" are assumed to have top priority, the following scenario has often resulted.

The manager proposes a solution to a given problem. The subordinate knows that the solution will not work, but his unconscious assumption requires that he remain silent because to tell the boss that the proposed solution is wrong is a threat to the boss's face. It would not even occur to the subordinate to do anything other than remain silent or, if the boss were to inquire what the subordinate thought, to even reassure the boss that they should go ahead and take the action.

The action is taken, the results are negative, and the boss, somewhat surprised and puzzled, asks the subordinate what he would have done. When the subordinate reports that he would have done something different, the boss quite legitimately asks why the subordinate did not speak up sooner. This question puts the subordinate into an impossible double bind because the answer itself is a threat to the boss's face. He cannot possibly explain his behavior without committing the very sin he was trying to avoid in the first place—namely, embarrassing the boss. He may even lie at this point and argue that what the boss did was right and only "bad luck" or uncontrollable circumstances prevented it from succeeding.

From the point of view of the subordinate, the boss's behavior is incomprehensible because it shows lack of self-pride, possibly causing the subordinate to lose respect for that boss. To the boss, the subordinate's behavior is equally incomprehensible. He cannot develop any sensible explanation of his subordinate's behavior that is not cynically colored by the assumption that the subordinate at some level just does not care about effective performance and therefore must be gotten rid of. It never occurs to the boss that another assumption—such as "one never embarrasses a superior"—is operating, and that, to the subordinate, that assumption is even more powerful than "one gets the job done."

If assumptions such as these operate only in an individual and represent her idiosyncratic experience, they can be corrected more easily because the person will detect that she is alone in holding a given assumption. The power of culture comes about through the fact that the assumptions are shared and, therefore, mutually reinforced. In these instances probably only a third party or some cross-cultural education could help to find common ground whereby both parties could bring their implicit assumptions to the surface. And even after they have surfaced, such assumptions would still operate, forcing the boss and the subordinate to invent a whole new communication mechanism that would permit each to remain congruent with his or her culture—for example, agreeing that, *before* any decision is made and before the boss has stuck his neck out, the subordinate will be asked for suggestions and for factual data that would not be face threatening. Note that the solution has to keep each cultural assumption intact. One cannot in these instances simply declare one or the other cultural assumption "wrong." One has to find a third assumption to allow them both to retain their integrity.

I have dwelled on this long example to illustrate the potency of implicit, unconscious assumptions and to show that such assumptions often deal with fundamental aspects of life—the nature of time and space, human nature and human activities, the nature of truth and how one discovers it, the correct way for the individual and the group to relate to each other, the relative importance of work, family, and self-development, the proper role of men and women, and the nature of the family. These assumptions form the core cultural content as will be discussed in Chapters Seven, Eight, and Nine.

We do not develop new assumptions about each of these areas in every group or organization we join. Members of any new group will bring their own cultural learning from prior groups, from their education, and from their socialization into occupational communities, but as the new group develops its own shared history, it will develop modified or brand-new assumptions in critical areas of its experience. It is those new assumptions that make up the culture of that particular group.

Any group's culture can be studied at these three levels—the level of its artifacts, the level of its espoused beliefs and values, and the level of its basic underlying assumptions. If one does not decipher the pattern of basic assumptions that may be operating, one will not know how to interpret the artifacts correctly or how much credence to give to the articulated values. In other words, the essence of a culture lies in the pattern of basic underlying assumptions, and once one understands those, one can easily understand the other more surface levels and deal appropriately with them.

Summary and Conclusions

Though the essence of a group's culture is its pattern of shared, basic taken-for-granted assumptions, the culture will manifest itself at the level of observable artifacts and shared espoused beliefs and values. In analyzing cultures, it is important to recognize that artifacts are easy to observe but difficult to decipher and that espoused beliefs and values may only reflect rationalizations or aspirations. To understand a group's culture, one must attempt to get at its shared basic assumptions and one must understand the learning process by which such basic assumptions come to be.

Leadership is originally the source of the beliefs and values that get a group moving in dealing with its internal and external problems. If what leaders propose works, and continues to work, what once were only the leader's assumptions gradually come to be shared assumptions. Once a set of shared basic assumptions is formed by this process, it can function as a cognitive defense mechanism both for the individual members and for the group as a whole. In other words, individuals and groups seek stability and meaning. Once achieved, it is easier to distort new data by denial, projection, rationalization, or various other defense mechanisms than to change the basic assumption. As we will see, culture change, in the sense of changing basic assumptions is, therefore, difficult, time-consuming, and highly anxiety-provoking—a point that is especially relevant for the leader who sets out to change the culture of the organization.

The most central issue for leaders, therefore, is how to get at the deeper levels of a culture, how to assess the functionality of the assumptions made at that level, and how to deal with the anxiety that is unleashed when those levels are challenged.

3

CULTURES IN ORGANIZATIONS: TWO CASE EXAMPLES

In the last chapter I indicated in a rather abstract manner how one should think about the complex concept of culture as it applies to groups, occupations, and organizations. I emphasized the need to go beyond the surface levels of artifacts and espoused beliefs and values to the deeper, taken-for-granted shared assumptions that create the pattern of cognitions, perceptions, and feelings displayed by the members of the group. Unless one understands what is going on at this deeper level, one cannot really decipher the meaning of the more surface phenomena, and, worse, one might misinterpret them because of the likelihood that one will be projecting one's own cultural biases onto the observed phenomena.

In this chapter I would like to illustrate this multilevel analysis by describing two companies with whom I worked for some period of time, permitting me to begin to identify some key elements of their cultures. I say elements because it is not really possible to describe an entire culture. But one can get at enough elements to make some of the key phenomena in these companies comprehensible.

The Digital Equipment Corp.

Digital Equipment Corp. (DEC) will be a major case running throughout this book because it not only illustrates aspects of how one describes and analyzes organizational culture, but also reveals some important cultural dynamics that explain both DEC's rise to the position of number two computer company in the world and its rapid decline in the 1990s (Schein, 2003). I was a consultant to the founder, Ken Olsen, and to the various executive committees and engineering groups that ran the company from 1966 to 1992; therefore I had a unique opportunity to see cultural dynamics in action over a long period of time.

Artifacts: Encountering the Company

DEC was the first major company to introduce interactive computing, and it became a very successful manufacturer, initially of what came to be called "mini computers" and eventually of a whole line of computer products. It was located primarily in the northeastern part of the United States, with headquarters in an old mill in Maynard, Massachusetts, but it had branches throughout the world. At its peak it employed over 100,000 people, with sales of $14 billion; in the mid-1980s it became the second largest computer manufacturer in the world after IBM. The company ran into major financial difficulties in the 1990s and was eventually sold to the Compaq Corp. in 1998. Compaq was in turn merged into Hewlett-Packard in 2001.

To gain entry into any of DEC's many buildings, one had to sign in with a guard who sat behind a counter where there were usually several people chatting, moving in and out, checking the badges of employees who were coming into the building, accepting mail, and answering phone calls. Once one had signed in, one waited in a small, casually furnished lobby until the person one was visiting came personally or sent a secretary to escort one to one's destination.

What I recall most vividly from my first encounters with this organization some thirty-eight years ago is the ubiquitous open office architecture, the extreme informality of dress and manners, a very dynamic environment in the sense of rapid pace, and a high rate of interaction among employees, seemingly reflecting enthusiasm, intensity, energy, and impatience. As I would pass cubicles or conference rooms, I would get the impression of openness. There were very few doors. The company cafeteria spread out into a big open area where people sat at large tables, hopped from one table to another, and obviously were intensely involved in their work even at lunch. I also observed that there were many cubicles with coffee machines and refrigerators in them and that food seemed to be part of most meetings.

The physical layout and patterns of interaction made it very difficult to decipher who had what rank, and I was told that there were no status perquisites such as private dining rooms, special parking places, or offices with special views and the like. The furniture in the lobbies and offices was very inexpensive and functional, and the company was mostly headquartered in an old industrial building that had been converted for their use. The informal clothing worn by most managers and employees reinforced this sense of economy and egalitarianism.

I had been brought into DEC to help the top management team improve communication and group effectiveness. As I began to attend the regular staff meetings of the senior management group, I was quite struck by the high level of interpersonal confrontation, argumentativeness, and conflict. Group members became highly emotional at the drop of a hat and seemed to get angry at each other, though it was also noticeable that such anger did not carry over outside the meeting.

With the exception of the president and founder, Ken Olsen, there were very few people who had visible status in terms of how people deferred to them. Olsen himself, through his informal behavior, implied that he did not take his position of power all that seriously. Group members argued as much with him as with each other and even interrupted him from time to time. His status did show up, however, in the occasional lectures he delivered to the group when he felt that members were not understanding something or were "wrong" about something. At such times Olsen could become very emotionally excited in a way that other members of the group never did.

My own reactions to the company and these meetings also have to be considered as artifacts to be documented. It was exciting to be attending top management meetings—and surprising to observe so much behavior that seemed to me dysfunctional. I was made quite nervous by the level of confrontation I observed and I had a sense of not knowing what this was all about, as I indicated in the example in Chapter One. I learned from further observation that this style of running meetings was typical and that meetings were very common, to the point where people would complain about all the time spent in committees. At the same time, they would argue that without these committees they could not get their work done properly.

The company was organized in terms of functional units and product lines, but there was a sense of perpetual reorganization and a search for a structure that would "work better." Structure was viewed as something to tinker with until one got it right. There were many levels in the technical and managerial hierarchy, but I got the sense that the hierarchy was just a convenience, not something to be taken very seriously. On the other hand, the communication structure was taken very seriously. There were many committees already in existence and new ones were constantly being formed; the company had an extensive electronic mail network that functioned worldwide, engineers and managers traveled frequently and were in constant telephone communication with each other, and Olsen would get upset if he observed any evidence of under- or miscommunication.

Many other artifacts from this organization will be described later but, for the present, this will suffice to give a flavor of what I encountered at DEC. The question now is, what does any of it mean? I knew what my emotional reactions were, but I did not really understand why these things were happening and what significance they had for members of the company. To gain some understanding one has to get to the next level: the level of espoused beliefs and values.

Espoused Beliefs and Values

As I talked to people at DEC about my observations, especially those things that puzzled and scared me, I began to elicit some of the espoused beliefs and values by which the company ran. Many of these were embodied in slogans or in parables that Olsen wrote from time to time and circulated throughout the company. For example, a high value was placed on personal responsibility. If one made a proposal to do something and it was approved, one had a clear obligation to do it or, if it was not possible to do, to come back and renegotiate. The phrase "He who proposes, does" was frequently heard around the organization.

Employees at all levels were responsible for thinking about what they were doing and were enjoined at all times to "do the right thing," which, in many instances, meant being insubordinate. If the boss asked you to do something that you considered wrong or stupid, you were supposed to "push back" and attempt to change the boss's mind. If the boss insisted, and you still felt that it was not right, then you were supposed to not do it and take your chances on your own judgment. If you were wrong, you would get your wrist slapped but would gain respect for having stood up for your own convictions. Because bosses knew these rules they were, of course, less likely to issue arbitrary orders, more likely to listen to you if you pushed back, and more likely to renegotiate the decision. So actual insubordination was rarely necessary, but the principle of thinking for yourself and doing the right thing was very strongly reinforced.

It was also a rule that you should not do things without getting "buy-in" from others who had to implement the decision, who had to provide needed services, or who would be influenced by it. One had to be very individualistic and, at the same time, very willing to be a team player; hence the simultaneous feeling that committees were a big drain on time but one could not do without them. To reach a decision and to get buy-in, one had to convince others of the validity of one's idea and be able to defend it against every conceivable argument. This caused the high levels of confrontation and fighting that I observed in groups, but once an idea had stood up to this level of debate and survived, it could then be moved forward and implemented because everyone was now convinced that it was the right thing to do. This took longer to achieve, but once achieved, led to more consistent and rapid action. If somewhere down the hierarchy the decision "failed to stick" because someone was not convinced that it was "the right thing to do," that person had to push back, her arguments had to be heard, and either she had to be convinced or the decision had to be renegotiated up the hierarchy.

In asking people about their jobs, I discovered another strong value: one should figure out for oneself what the essence of one's job was and get very clear about it. Asking the boss what was expected was considered a sign of weakness. If one's own job definition was out of line with what the group or department required, one would hear about it soon enough. The role of the boss was to set broad targets, but subordinates were expected to take initiative in figuring out how best to achieve them. This value required a lot of discussion and negotiation, which often led to complaints about time wasting, but, at the same time, everyone defended the value of doing things in this way, and continued to defend it even though it created difficulties later at DEC's life.

I also found out that people could fight bitterly in group meetings, yet be very good friends. There was a feeling of being a tight-knit group, a kind of extended family under a strong father figure, Ken Olsen, which led to the norm that fighting does not mean that people dislike or disrespect each other. This norm seemed to extend even to "bad-mouthing" each other: people would call each other "stupid" behind each others' backs or say that someone was a real "turkey" or "jerk," yet they would respect each other in work situations. Olsen often criticized people in public, which made them feel embarrassed, but it was explained to me that this only meant that the person should work on improving his area of operations, not that he was really in disfavor. Even if someone fell into disfavor, he or she was viewed merely as being in the "penalty box"; stories were told of managers or engineers who had been in this kind of disfavor for long periods of time and then rebounded to become heroes in some other context.

When managers talked about their products they emphasized quality and elegance. The company was founded by engineers and was dominated by an engineering mentality in that the value of a proposed new product was generally judged by whether the engineers themselves liked it and used it, not by external market surveys or test markets. In fact, customers were talked about in a rather disparaging way, especially those who might not be technically sophisticated enough to appreciate the elegance of the product that had been designed.

Olsen emphasized absolute integrity in designing, manufacturing, and selling. He viewed the company as highly ethical and he strongly emphasized the work values associated with the Protestant work ethic—honesty, hard work, high standards of personal morality, professionalism, personal responsibility, integrity, and honesty. Especially important was being honest and truthful in their relations with each other and with customers. As this company grew and matured it put many of these values into formal statements and taught them to new employees. They viewed their culture as a great asset and felt that the culture itself had to be taught to all new employees (Kunda, 1992).

Basic Assumptions: The DEC Paradigm

To understand the implications of these values and to show how they relate to overt behavior, one must seek the underlying assumptions and premises on which this organization was based (see Figures 3.1 and 3.2).

The founding group, by virtue of their engineering background, was intensely individualistic and pragmatic in its orientation. They developed a problem solving and decision making system that rested on five interlocking assumptions:

1. The individual is ultimately the source of ideas and entrepreneurial spirit.
2. Individuals are capable of taking responsibility and doing the right thing.

Figure 3.1. DEC's Cultural Paradigm: Part One.

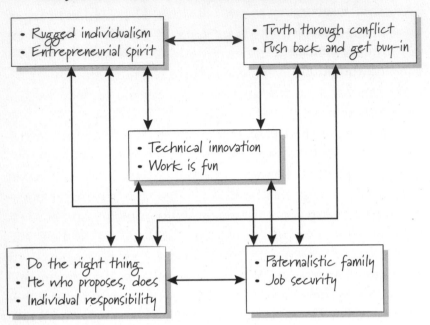

Copyright © E. H. Schein. *DEC Is Dead; Long Live DEC*. Berrett-Koehler, 2003.

3. No one individual is smart enough to evaluate his or her own ideas, hence one should push back and get buy-in. (In effect, the group was saying that "truth" cannot be found without debate; that there is no arbitrary way of figuring out what is true unless one subjects every idea to the crucible of debate among strong and intelligent individuals; therefore, one must get others to agree before taking action.)

4. The central assumption: the basic work of the company is technological innovation and such work is and always should be "fun."

Without understanding these first four assumptions, one cannot decipher most of the behavior observed, particularly the seeming incongruity between intense individualism and intense commitment to group work and consensus. Similarly, one cannot understand why there was simultaneously intense conflict—with authority figures, insubordination, and bad-mouthing of bosses—and intense loyalty to the organization and personal affection across hierarchical boundaries, without also understanding the fifth interlocking assumption:

5. We are one family whose members will take care of each other (implying that no matter how much of a troublemaker one was in the decision process, one was valued in the family and could not be kicked out of it).

It is only when one grasps these first five assumptions that one can understand, for example, why my initial interventions of trying to get the group to be "nicer" to each other in the communication process were politely ignored. I was seeing the group's "effectiveness" in terms of my values and assumptions of how a "good" group should act. The DEC senior management committee was trying to reach "truth" and make valid decisions in the only way they knew how and by a process that they believed in. The group was merely a means to an end; the real process going on in the group was a basic, deep search for solutions in which they could have confidence because they stood up even after intense debate.

Once I shifted my focus to helping them in this search for valid solutions, I figured out what kinds of interventions would be more relevant and I found that the group accepted them more readily. For example, I began to emphasize agenda setting, time management, clarifying some of the debate, summarizing, consensus testing once debate was running dry, and in other ways focused more on the task process rather than the interpersonal process. The interrupting, the emotional conflicts, and the other behavior I observed initially continued, but the group became more effective in its handling of information and in reaching consensus. It was in this context that I gradually developed the philosophy of being a "process consultant" instead of trying to be an expert on how groups should work (Schein, 1969, 1988, 1999a, 2003).

As I learned more about DEC, I also learned that the cultural DNA contained another five key assumptions, shown in Figure 3.2. These five additional assumptions reflected some of the group's beliefs and values pertaining to customers and marketing:

6. The only valid way to sell a product is to find out what the customer's problem is and to solve that problem, even if that means selling less or recommending another company's products.

7. People can and will take responsibility and continue to act responsibly no matter what.

8. The market is the best decision maker if there are several product contenders (internal competition was viewed as desirable throughout DEC's history).

Figure 3.2. DEC's Cultural Paradigm: Part Two.

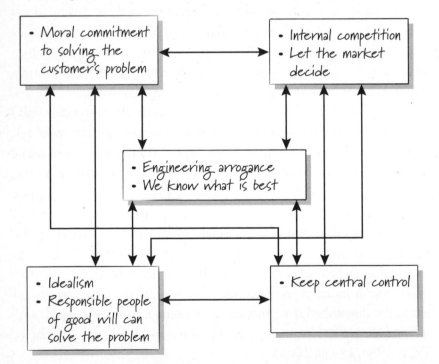

9. Even as the company gets very large and differentiated, it is desirable to keep some central control rather than divisionalizing.

10. DEC engineers "know best" what a good product is, based on whether or not they personally like working with that product.

These ten assumptions can be thought of as the DEC cultural paradigm—its cultural DNA. What is important in showing these interconnections is the fact that single elements of the paradigm could not explain how this organization was able to function. It was only by seeing the *combination* of assumptions—around individual creativity, group conflict as the source of truth, individual responsibility, commitment to each other as a family, commitment to innovation and to solving customer problems, and belief in internal competition and central control—that one could explain the day-to-day behavior one observed. It is this level of basic assumptions and their interconnections that defines some of the essence of the culture—the key genes of the cultural DNA.

How general was this paradigm in Digital? That is, if one were to study workers in the plants, salesmen in geographically remote units, engineers in technical enclaves, and so on, would one find the same assumptions operating? One of the interesting aspects of the DEC story is that at least for its first twenty or so years this paradigm would have been observed in operation across all of its rank levels, functions, and geographies. But, as we will also see later, some elements of the DEC culture began to change and the paradigm no longer fitted in some parts of the company.

Ciba-Geigy

The Ciba-Geigy Company in the late 1970s and early 1980s was a Swiss multidivisional, geographically decentralized chemical company with several divisions dealing with pharmaceuticals, agricultural chemicals, industrial chemicals, dyestuffs, and some technically based consumer products. It eventually merged with a former competitor,

Sandoz, to become what is today Novartis. I was originally asked to give some talks at their 1979 annual meeting of top executives on the topic of innovation and creativity, and this encounter evolved into a variety of consulting activities that lasted into the mid-1980s. Some of these are described in greater detail in Chapter Eighteen.

Artifacts—Encountering Ciba-Geigy

I learned during my initial briefings that the company was run by a board of directors and an internal executive committee of nine people who were legally accountable as a group for company decisions. The chairman of this executive committee, Sam Koechlin, functioned as the chief executive officer, but the committee made most decisions by consensus.

Each member of the committee had oversight responsibility for a division, a function, and a geographic area, and these responsibilities rotated from time to time. The company had a long history of growth and had merged with another similar company a decade or more ago. The merger of Ciba and Geigy was considered to be a success, but there were still strong identifications with the original companies, according to many managers.

My original clients were the director of management development, Dr. Jurg Leupold, and his immediate boss, Sam Koechlin, who was clearly the originator of the project I became involved in. Ciba-Geigy ran annual meetings of their top forty to fifty executives worldwide and had a tradition of inviting one or two outsiders to the three-day meetings held at a Swiss resort. The purpose was to stimulate the group by having outside lecturers present on topics of interest to the company.

I was originally contacted by Dr. Leupold by phone; he asked me to give lectures and do some structured exercises to improve the group's understanding of creativity and to increase "innovation" and "leadership" in the company. Prior to the annual meeting I was to visit the company headquarters to be briefed, to meet some other key executives—especially Koechlin—and to review the material that was to be presented at the annual meeting. I got the impression that things were highly organized and carefully planned.

My first visit to Ciba-Geigy offered a sharp contrast to what I had encountered at DEC. I was immediately struck by the formality as symbolized by large gray stone buildings and stiff uniformed guards in the main lobby. This spacious, opulent lobby was the main passageway for employees to enter the inner compound of office buildings and plants. It had high ceilings, large heavy doors, and a few pieces of expensive modern furniture in one corner to serve as a waiting area.

(I should point out that I reacted differently to the Ciba-Geigy and DEC environments. I liked the DEC environment more. In doing a cultural analysis, one's reactions are themselves artifacts of the culture that must be acknowledged and taken into account. It would be impossible and undesirable to present any cultural analysis with total objectivity because one's emotional reactions and biases are also primary data to be analyzed and understood.)

Upon entering the Ciba-Geigy lobby, I was asked by the uniformed guard to check in with another guard who sat in a glassed-in office. I had to give my name and state where I was from and whom I was visiting. The guard then asked me to take a seat while he did some telephoning, and to wait until an escort could take me to my appointed place. As I sat and waited, I noticed that the guard seemed to know most of the employees who streamed through the lobby or went to elevators and stairs leading from it. I had the distinct feeling that any stranger would have been spotted immediately and would have been asked to report as I had been.

Dr. Leupold's secretary arrived in due course and took me up the elevator and down a long corridor of closed offices. Each office had a tiny nameplate that could be covered over by a hinged metal plate if the occupant wanted to remain anonymous. Above each office was a light bulb, some of which showed red and some green. I asked on a subsequent visit what this meant and was told that if the light was green it was OK to knock, whereas red meant that the person did not want to be disturbed under any circumstances.

We went around a corner and down another such corridor, and did not see another soul during the entire time. When we reached Dr. Leupold's office the secretary knocked discreetly; when he opened the door, she ushered me in, then went to her own office and closed the door behind herself. I was offered some tea or coffee, which was brought by the secretary on a large tray with a small plate of cookies.

Following our meeting, my client took me to the executive dining room in another building, where we again passed guards. This was the equivalent of a first-class restaurant, with a hostess who clearly knew everyone, reserved tables, and provided discreet guidance on the day's specials. Aperitifs and wine were offered with lunch, and the whole meal took almost two hours. I was told that there was a less fancy dining room in still another building and an employee cafeteria as well, but that this dining room clearly had the best food and was the right place for senior management to conduct business and to bring visitors. I got the impression that whereas at DEC kitchens and food were used as vehicles to get people to interact with each other, at Ciba-Geigy, food, drink, and graciousness had some additional symbolic meaning, possibly having to do with status and rank.

Various senior officers of the company were pointed out to me, and I noticed that whenever anyone greeted another it was always with their formal titles, usually Dr. This or Dr. That. Observable differences in deference and demeanor made it fairly easy to determine who was superior to whom in the organization. It was also obvious that the tables in the room were assigned to executives on the basis of status and that the hostess knew exactly the relative status of all her guests.

Throughout the time of my consultation, in moving around the company I always felt a hushed atmosphere in the corridors, a slower, more deliberate pace, and much more emphasis on planning, schedules, and punctuality. Whereas at DEC I got the impression of frantic activity in order to make the most of what time there was, at Ciba-Geigy time was carefully managed to maintain order. If I had an appointment with a manager at 2 P.M., the person I was with just prior to that meeting would start walking down the hall with me at 1:58 so that we would arrive almost exactly on the dot. Only rarely was I kept waiting if I arrived on time, and if I was even a few minutes late I had the strong sense that I had to apologize and explain.

Ciba-Geigy managers came across as very serious, thoughtful, deliberate, well prepared, formal, and concerned about protocol. I learned later that whereas DEC allocated rank and salary fairly strictly to the actual job being performed by the individual, Ciba-Geigy had a system of managerial ranks based on length of service, overall performance, and the personal background of the individual rather than on the actual job being performed at a given time. Rank and status therefore had a much more permanent quality at Ciba-Geigy, whereas at DEC one's fortunes could rise and fall precipitously and frequently.

In Ciba-Geigy meetings I observed much less direct confrontation and much more respect for individual opinion. Recommendations made by managers in their specific area of accountability were generally respected and implemented. Insubordination was never observed and I got the impression that it would not be tolerated. Rank and status thus clearly had a higher value at Ciba-Geigy than at DEC, whereas personal negotiating skill and the ability to get things done in an ambiguous social environment had a higher value at DEC.

Espoused Beliefs and Values

Beliefs and values tend to be elicited when one asks about observed behavior or other artifacts that strike one as puzzling, anomalous, or inconsistent. If I asked managers at Ciba-Geigy why they always kept their doors closed, they would patiently and somewhat condescendingly explain to me that this was the only way they could get any work done, and they valued work very highly. Meetings were a necessary evil and were useful only for announcing decisions or gathering information. "Real work" was done by thinking things out and that required quiet and concentration. In contrast, at DEC real work was done by debating things out in meetings!

It was also pointed out to me that discussion among peers was not of great value, and that important information would come from the boss. Authority was highly respected, especially authority based on level of education, experience, and rank. The use of titles such as doctor or professor symbolized their respect for the knowledge that education bestowed on people. Much of this had to do with a great respect for the science of chemistry and the contributions of laboratory research to product development.

At Ciba-Geigy, as at DEC, a high value was placed on individual effort and contribution, but at Ciba-Geigy one never went outside the chain of command and never did things that would be out of line with what one's boss had suggested. At Ciba-Geigy a high value was placed on product elegance and quality, and, as I discovered later, what might be called product significance. Ciba-Geigy managers felt very proud of the fact that their chemicals and drugs were useful in crop protection, in curing diseases, and in other ways helping to improve the world.

Basic Assumptions— The Ciba-Geigy Company Paradigm

Many of the values that were articulated gave a flavor of this company, but without digging deeper to basic assumptions one could not fully understand how things worked. For example, the artifact that struck me most as I worked with this organization on the mandate to help them to become more innovative was the anomalous behavior around my memos, previously mentioned in Chapter One. I realized that there was very little lateral communication occurring between units of the organization, so that new ideas developed in one unit never seemed to get outside that unit. If I inquired about cross-divisional meetings, for example, I would get blank stares and questions such as "Why would we do that?" Since the divisions were facing similar problems, it would obviously have been helpful to circulate some of the better ideas that came up in my interviews, supplemented with my own ideas based on my knowledge of what went on in other organizations.

Elaborating on the example provided in Chapter One, I wrote a number of memos along these lines and asked my contact client, Dr. Leupold, the director of management development, to distribute them to those managers who he thought could most benefit from the information. Since he reported directly to Sam Koechlin, he seemed like a natural conduit for communicating with those divisional, functional, and geographic managers who needed the information I was gathering. When I would return on a subsequent visit to the company and be meeting with one of the unit managers, without fail I would discover that he did not have the memo, but if he requested it from Dr. Leupold it would be sent over almost immediately.

This phenomenon was puzzling and irritating, but its consistency clearly indicated that some strong underlying assumptions were at work here. When I later asked one of my colleagues in the corporate staff unit that delivered training and other development programs to the organization why the information did not circulate freely, he revealed that he had similar problems in that he would develop a helpful intervention in one unit of the organization, but that other units would seek help outside the organization before they would "discover" that he had a solution that was better. The common denominator seemed to be that unsolicited ideas were generally not well received.

We had a long exploratory conversation about this observed behavior and jointly figured out what the explanation was. As previously mentioned, at Ciba-Geigy, when a manager was given a job, that job became the private domain of the individual. Managers felt a strong sense of turf or ownership and made the assumption that each owner of a piece of the organization would be completely in charge and on top of his piece. He would be fully informed and make himself an expert in that area. Therefore, if someone provided some unsolicited information pertaining to the job, this was potentially an invasion of privacy and possibly an insult, as it implied that the manager did not already have this information or ideas.

The powerful metaphor that "giving someone unsolicited information was like walking into their home uninvited" came from a number of managers in subsequent interviews. It became clear that only if information was asked for was it acceptable to offer ideas. One's superior could provide information, though even that was done only cautiously, but a peer would rarely do so, lest he unwittingly insult the recipient. To provide unsolicited information or ideas could be seen as a challenge to the information base the manager was using, and that might be regarded as an insult, implying that the person challenged had not thought deeply enough about his own problem or was not really on top of his own job.

By not understanding this assumption I had unwittingly put Dr. Leupold into the impossible position of risking insulting all his colleagues and peers if he circulated my memos as I had asked him to do. Interestingly enough, this kind of assumption is so tacit that even he could not articulate just why he had not followed my instructions. He was clearly uncomfortable and embarrassed about it, but had no explanation until we uncovered the assumption about organizational turf and its symbolic meaning.

To further understand this and related behavior, it was necessary to consider some of the other underlying assumptions that this company had evolved (see Figure 3.3). It had grown and achieved much of its success through fundamental discoveries made by a number of basic researchers in the company's central research laboratories. Whereas at DEC truth was discovered through conflict and debate, at Ciba-Geigy truth had come more from the wisdom of the scientist/researcher.

Both companies believed in the individual, but the differing assumptions about the nature of truth led to completely different attitudes toward authority and the role of conflict. At Ciba-Geigy, authority was much more respected, and conflict tended to be avoided. The individual was given areas of freedom by the boss and

Figure 3.3. Ciba-Geigy's Cultural Paradigm.

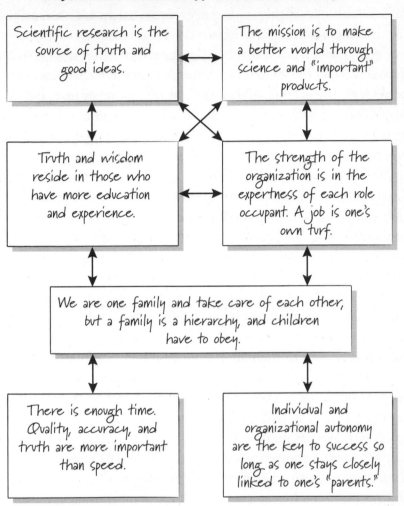

then was totally respected in those areas. If role occupants were not well enough educated or skilled enough to make decisions, they were expected to train themselves. If they performed poorly in the meantime, that would be tolerated for quite a while before a decision might be made to replace them. In both companies there was a "tenure" assumption that once one had been accepted one was likely to remain unless one failed in a major way.

At DEC, conflict was valued and the individual was expected to take initiative and fight for ideas in every arena. At Ciba-Geigy, conflict was suppressed once a decision had been made. At DEC, it was assumed that if a job was not challenging or was not a good match between what the organization needed and what the individual could give, the individual should be moved to a new assignment or would quit anyway. At Ciba-Geigy, the person would be expected to be a good soldier and do the job as best he could, and as long as he was perceived as doing his best he would be kept in the job.

Both companies talked of being families but the meaning of the word *family* was quite different in each culture. At DEC, the essential assumption was that family members could fight but they loved each other and could not lose membership. At Ciba-Geigy, the assumption was that the family works well when parental authority is respected, when the children behave according to the rules and obey their parents. If they do so, they will be well treated, taken care of, and supported by the parents. In each case the family model also seemed to reflect the wider cultural assumptions of the countries in which these companies were based.

The Ciba-Geigy paradigm has many implications that will be brought out later, but one immediate consequence of understanding their culture at this level was that I was able to figure out how to operate more effectively as a consultant. As I interviewed more managers and gathered information that would be relevant to what they were trying to do, instead of attempting to circulate memos to the various branches of the Ciba-Geigy organization through my contact client, I found that if I gave information directly, even if it was unsolicited, it was accepted because I was an "expert." If I wanted information to circulate, I sent it out to the relevant parties on my own initiative, or, if I thought it needed to circulate down into the organization, I gave it to the boss and attempted to convince him that the information would be relevant lower down. If I really wanted to intervene by having managers do something different, I could accomplish this best by being an expert and formally recommending it to CEO Sam Koechlin. If he liked the idea, he would then order "the troops" to do it.

Other facets of Ciba-Geigy will be discussed in other sections of this book. For example, their patience and their attitude toward time, and their formality along with their ability to be playful and informal during organizational "time outs" are important in understanding how they were able to get their work done.

Summary and Conclusions

In the above case analyses I have tried to illustrate how organizational culture can be analyzed at several levels: (1) visible artifacts, (2) espoused beliefs, values, rules, and behavioral norms, and (3) tacit, taken-for-granted, basic underlying assumptions. My argument is that unless one digs down to the level of the basic assumptions one cannot really decipher the artifacts, values, and norms. On the other hand, if one finds some of those basic assumptions and explores their interrelationship, one is really getting at the essence of the culture and can then explain a great deal of what goes on. This essence can sometimes be analyzed as a paradigm in that some organizations function by virtue of an interlocking, coordinated set of assumptions. Whereas each one alone might not make sense, the pattern explains the behavior and the success of the organization in overcoming its external and internal challenges.

Because I have only described certain elements of the culture as these pertained to key goals that the organizations were trying to achieve, we should not assume that these paradigms describe the whole culture, nor should we assume that we would find the same paradigm operating in every part of the organization. The generality of the assumptions is itself something to be investigated and determined empirically.

I discovered these assumptions primarily through exploring with inside informants some of the anomalies that I experienced and observed between the visible artifacts and the espoused beliefs and values. It is when we do not understand something that we need to pursue vigorously why we do not, and the best way to search is to use one's own ignorance and naïveté.

This method of research, labeled "clinical research," will be described in greater detail in Chapter Eleven and will be contrasted to various other research models that imply a lower level of involvement of the research subject (Schein, 1987a). In dealing with culture it is necessary to "triangulate," using all of the methods available, but the clinical method is central because only by involving the members of the group can one get at their deeper assumptions. The "subjects" have to be motivated to reveal themselves, and this only occurs when they perceive themselves to be benefiting from the inquiry process itself.

What are some the lessons to be learned from these cases, and what implications do they have for leadership? The most important lesson for me is the realization that culture is deep, pervasive, complex, patterned, and morally neutral. In both cases I had to overcome my own cultural prejudices about the right and wrong way to do things, and to learn that culture simply exists. Both companies were successful in their respective technological, political, economic, and broader cultural environments for a long time, but both companies also experienced environmental changes that led to their disappearance as independent economic entities. The role that their cultures played in causing economic problems will be explored in a later chapter.

In both cases the powerful influence of early leaders and historical circumstance was evident. Cultural assumptions have their roots in early group experience and in the pattern of success and failure experienced by these companies. Their current leaders strongly valued their cultures, were proud of them, and felt it important for members of their organizations to accept the basic assumptions. In both organizations stories were told of misfits who left because they did not like the way the company operated, or who were not hired in the first place because they either would be disruptive or would not like it there anyway.

As will be analyzed in more detail later, in both companies leaders were struggling with changing environmental demands and faced the issue of whether and how to evolve or change their ways of operating, but in both companies this was initially defined as reaffirmation of portions of the existing culture, not as changes in the culture. Though the companies were at different stages in their evolution, they both valued their cultures as important assets and were anxious to preserve and enhance them.

4

HOW CULTURE EMERGES IN NEW GROUPS

In Chapter Three, I illustrated how to think about and describe culture in organizations; in Chapters Twelve and Thirteen, I will describe how leaders create and embed culture as organizations form and grow. However, culture is also created in the interactions we have with others in our normal day-to-day life, and the best way to demystify the concept of culture is first of all to become aware of culture in our own experience, to perceive how something comes to be *shared* and *taken for granted*, and to observe this particularly in new groups that we enter and belong to. We bring culture with us from our past experience but we are constantly reinforcing that culture or building new elements as we encounter new people and new experiences.

The strength and stability of culture derives from the fact that it is group based—that the individual will hold on to certain basic assumptions in order to ratify his or her membership in the group. If someone asks us to change our way of thinking or perceiving, and that way is based on what we have learned in a group that we belong to, we will resist the change because we will not want to deviate from our group even if privately we think that the group is wrong. This process of trying to be accepted by our membership and reference groups is unconscious and, by virtue of that fact, very powerful. But how does a group develop a common way of thinking in the first place?

To examine how culture actually begins—how a group learns to deal with its external and internal environment and develops assumptions that then get passed on to new members—we need to analyze group situations in which such events are actually observable. The bulk of this chapter will therefore deal with data from my own experience in running training groups for the National Training Laboratories and various companies, supplemented by observations made in small groups within organizations during my consulting activities (Bradford, Gibb, and Benne, 1964; Schein and Bennis, 1965; Schein, 1999a, 1999b). If we become sensitive to the issues that will be presented here, we can more readily see cultural phenomena in organizations and occupations.

In making a detailed analysis of small groups, I am not implying that group phenomena can be automatically treated as models for organizational phenomena. Organizations bring in additional levels of complexity and new phenomena that are not visible in the small group. Still, if we look at organizations in an evolutionary sense, we must realize that all organizations started as small groups and continue to function in part through various small groups within them. So the understanding of culture formation in small groups also is necessary to understanding how culture may evolve in the large organization through small-group subcultures and through the interplay of small groups within the organization.

Group Formation Through Originating and Marker Events

All groups start with some kind of originating event: (1) an environmental accident (for instance, a sudden threat that occurs in a random crowd and requires a common response), (2) a decision by an "originator" to bring a group of people together for some purpose, or (3) an advertised event or common experience that attracts a number of individuals. Human relations training groups start in the third mode: a number of people come together to participate in a one- or two-week workshop for the advertised purpose of learning more about themselves, groups, and leadership (Bradford, Gibb, and Benne, 1964; Schein and Bennis, 1965; Schein, 1993a). The workshops are typically held in a geographically remote, isolated location and require full, round-the-clock participation.

The staff of the workshop, usually one trainer per ten to fifteen participants, have typically met for several days to plan the basic structure of lectures, group meetings, focused exercises designed to bring out certain points about leadership and group behavior, and free time. The staff members start out with their own assumptions, values, and behavior patterns in initiating the groups and therefore will bias the culture that is eventually formed. But culture formation really occurs in the T (training) group, the key component of every workshop. The T group consists of ten to fifteen people who will meet for four to eight hours every day with one or two staff members. Because such groups typically develop distinct cultures within a matter of days, what goes on in these groups will be the focus of this chapter.

When the group first comes together, the most fundamental issue facing it as a whole is "What are we really here for? What is our task?" At the same time, each individual is facing basic social survival issues such as: "Will I be included in this group?" "Will I have a role to play?" "Will my need to influence others be met?" "Will we reach a level of intimacy that meets my needs?" As the group gathers in its appointed space, various participants, coming to terms with the new situation, will display their own coping style. Some will silently await events; some will form immediate alliances with others; and some will begin to assert themselves by telling anyone who cares to listen that they know how to deal with this kind of situation (Schein, 1999a).

Once the group has settled down to begin its first meeting, it faces the issue of its basic mission. Statements about the goal of "learning about itself" will have been spelled out in the training literature, the workshop brochure, and the initial introductory lecture to the entire workshop, and again by the staff member who launches the group. Some people may even have had prior experiences with similar groups. But initially everyone is acutely aware of how ambiguous the words of the staff member are when he or she says: "This is the first meeting of our T group. Our goal is to provide for ourselves a climate in which we can all learn. There is no one correct way to do this. We will have to get to know each other, find out what our individual needs and goals are, and build our group to enable us to fulfill those goals and needs. My role as staff member will be to help this process along in any way that I can, but I will not be the formal leader of the group, and I have no answers as to the right way to proceed."

The ensuing silence, as each person experiences feelings of anxiety in the face of this ambiguous agenda and power vacuum, is usually a key *marker event* that almost everyone remembers vividly at a later time. Even though all the members usually come from the same host culture and share the same formal language, everyone is aware that this group is a unique combination of personalities and that those personalities are initially unknown. What makes the initial silence a marker event, even if it is only a few seconds long, is that every person is aware of his own emotional intensity level in response to the sudden silence. Whether or not the emotional tone is recognized as one of anxiety will vary from individual to individual; but once the silence is identified as something to be understood, all group members can easily recognize how much of their own response to the silence can best be characterized in terms of tension or anxiety.

To facilitate learning about group dynamics, the formal agenda, leadership structure, and procedural rules or even suggestions are deliberately removed as part of the training design. This novel situation heightens members' awareness of how much they typically depend on those external "crutches" to define the rules of the game. The group is deliberately thrown onto its own resources to allow members to observe their own feelings and reactions as they cope with this initially normless and ruleless situation. Everyone suddenly realizes how dependent we are on culture and how uncomfortable it is to be deprived of procedures and rules. Physically locating the workshop in a remote area further deprives participants of cues; hence the term that's come to be used for such places: *cultural islands*.

Each member brings to this new situation a wealth of prior learning in the form of assumptions, expectations, and patterns of coping, but, as the group gets started by someone's making a suggestion or revealing a feeling, it immediately becomes apparent that there is little consensus within the group on how to proceed, and that the group cannot become a copy of any other group. Thus, even though individual members bring prior cultural learning to the new situation, by definition this particular group starts out with no culture of its own. Goals, means, working procedures, measurements, and rules of interaction all must be forged out of common experience, and a sense of mission—what the group is ultimately all about—develops only as members begin genuinely to understand each other's needs, goals, talents, and values, and as they begin to integrate these into a shared mission.

How does group formation now proceed? Often, the very first thing said by any person in the group will become the next marker event if it succeeds in reducing some of the tension. The silence is broken, there is a huge sigh of relief, and the group becomes aware through this *joint sensing of relief* that it is sharing something unique to it. No other group in the world will have this particular pattern of initial tension and manner of resolving the initial silence. Members also become aware of something that is easy to forget—that one cannot, in an interpersonal situation, *not* communicate. Everything that happens has potential meaning and consequences for the group.

If whatever suggestion or comment is made gets the group started, not only will it have provided emotional relief and anxiety reduction, but the forward movement produced will also be positively reinforcing. This piece of behavior may then become more probable as a future means of starting meetings. For example, one of the more active members often will initiate with a suggestion of how to get started: "Why don't we go around the group and each introduce ourselves?" Or "Let's each of us say what we are here for" or "I feel pretty tense right now. Does anyone else feel the same way?" or "Ed, can you give us some suggestion on how best to get started?" And so on.

If that suggestion fits the mood of the group or at least of some other members who are ready to speak up, it will be picked up and may become the beginning of a pattern. If it does not fit the mood, it will elicit disagreement, countersuggestions, or some other response that will make members aware that they cannot easily agree. Whatever the response, however, the crucial event of group formation has taken place when the group, including the staff member, has participated in a *shared emotional reaction*. What makes the event *shared* is the fact that all members have been witnesses to the same behavior on the part of one of their members and have observed the responses together. After the meeting they can refer to the event and people will remember it. This initial sharing is what defines, at an emotional level, that "we are a group; we have been launched."

The most fundamental act of culture formation, the defining of crude group boundaries, has occurred with the shared emotional response. Everyone who has shared the response is now, by definition, *in the group* at some level, and anyone who has not shared the experience is initially *not in the group*. And this fact of being in or out of the group is quite concrete, in that the person who did not attend and witness the events cannot know what happened or how people reacted. A new member who arrives one hour late will already feel the presence of a group and will want to know "what has gone on so far." And the group will already feel that the newcomer is a "stranger" who "has to be brought on board."

The nature of that initial shared response in various other kinds of groups will, of course, differ. Some theorists have speculated that early tribal formation may have resulted from a joint emotionally involving act, such as defeating an enemy or making a sacrifice. For our purposes the important thing to recognize is that the original intention to do something may have been *individually* motivated, but the result, if it leads to a shared emotional experience, may have important *group* consequences.

Thus, in any new group situation—whether we are talking about a new company, a task force, a committee, or a team—much of the initial behavior of founders, leaders, and other initiators is individually motivated and reflects their own particular assumptions and intentions. But, as the individuals in the group begin to do things together and share experiences around such individually motivated acts, *groupness* arises.

Initially, this groupness is only an emotional substrate that permits the defining of who is in and who is not. For the group to begin to understand its sense of groupness, someone must articulate what the experience has been and what it means. Such articulation is again an individual act, motivated by individual intentions to lead, or be a prophet, or whatever, but the consequences are group consequences if the articulation "works," if things are stated in a way that makes sense and helps group members to understand what has happened and why they are feeling the way they are. Examples of such articulation might be "We all seem to be pretty tense right now," or "I guess we won't get much help from the staff member," or "I don't know how the rest of you feel, but I feel the need to get going, so here's a suggestion. . . ." Such statements help to make some sense of the situation and are, therefore, crucial components of what we call leadership and can be understood as acts of *culture creation* if the process imparts meaning to an important shared emotional experience. Some of the deepest and most potent shared experiences occur within the first few hours of group life, so the deepest levels of consensus on who we are, what our mission is, and how we will work are formed very early in the group's history.

The subsequent progress of group formation can best be understood as the confrontation of a sequence of shared underlying assumptions that are likely to arise in each of the major group stages, as outlined in Table 4.1. Culture formation takes place around the efforts to deal with the anxieties characteristic of each of the basic assumptions.

Table 4.1. Stages of Group Evolution.

Stage	Dominant Assumption	Socioemotional Focus
1. Group formation	*Dependence:* "The leader knows what we should do."	*Self-Orientation:* Emotional focus on issues of (a) inclusion, (b) power and influence, (c) acceptance and intimacy, and (d) identity and role.
2. Group Building	*Fusion:* "We are a great group; we all like each other."	*Group as Idealized Object:* Emotional focus on harmony, conformity, and search for intimacy. Member differences are not valued.
3. Group Work	*Work:* "We can perform effectively because we know and accept each other."	*Group Mission and Tasks:* Emotional focus on accomplishment, teamwork, and maintaining the group in good working order. Member differences are valued.
4. Group Maturity	*Maturity:* "We know who we are, what we want, and how to get it. We have been successful, so we must be right."	*Group Survival and Comfort:* Emotional focus on preserving the group and its culture. Creativity and member differences are seen as threat.

Stages of Group Evolution

Every group goes through some version of evolution that can best be described in terms of the following stages.

Stage One: Group Formation

Initially, the group is not really a group but a collection of individual members, each focused on how to make the situation safe and personally rewarding while struggling with personal issues of inclusion, identity, authority, and intimacy. In other words, even with the early marker events that create some shared emotional responses, at this stage the new members are much more preoccupied with their own feelings than with the problem of the group as a group and, most likely, they are operating on the unconscious assumption of *dependency*—namely, that "the leader [staff member] knows what we are supposed to do." Therefore, the best way to achieve safety is to find out what the group is supposed to do and do it. This group stage, with its associated feelings and moods, is, in my experience, similar to what Bion (1959) described in his work as the *dependence assumption* and what other theories note as the first issue the group has to deal with; that is, authority (Bennis and Shepard, 1956).

The evidence for the operation of this assumption is the behavior one sees in the early minutes and hours of the group's life. First of all, much of the initial behavior of group members is, in fact, directed to the staff member in the form of questions, requests for explanations and for suggestions about how to proceed, and constant checking for approval. Even if the behavior is not directed to the staff member, one notices that members constantly look at him or her, pay extra attention if the staff member does speak, and in other nonverbal ways indicate their preoccupation with the staff member's reaction.

Members may share the common assumption of being dependent on the leader (staff member), yet react very differently. These differences can best be understood in terms of what they have learned in their prior group experience, probably starting in the family. One way to deal with authority is to suppress one's aggression, accept dependence, and seek guidance. If the staff member makes a suggestion, members who cope in this way will automatically accept it and attempt to do what is asked of them. Others have learned that the way to deal with authority is to resist it. They also will seek to find out what the leader wants, but their motive is to find out in order to resist rather than to comply; to be counterdependent. Still others will attempt to find people to share their feelings of dependence and, in effect, set up a subgroup within the larger group.

The mixture of tendencies in the personalities of group members is, of course, not initially predictable, nor is any given person inflexible. The range of possible variations in response to the initial leadership/authority vacuum is thus immense in a ten- to fifteen-person group. What one observes in watching the early interaction can best be described as a mutual testing out—testing of the staff member to see how much guidance will be offered, and testing by members of other members to see who can influence whom and who will control whom—a process not unlike the barnyard process of establishing a pecking order.

Several members will emerge as competitors for leadership and influence. If any one of these members suggests something or makes a point, one of the others will contradict it or try to go off in a different direction. This aggressive competition among the "sturdy battlers" keeps the group from achieving any real consensus early in its life, and one paradox of group formation is that there is no way to short-circuit this early power struggle. If it is swept under the rug by formal procedures, it will surface around the task issues that the group is trying to address.

From the point of view of the staff member, confirmation that this process is indeed going on comes from the frequent experience of trying to give the group guidance and finding that some members leap at the help, while others almost blindly resist it. If frustration is high, one or the other extreme mode may build up in the group as a whole, what Bion labeled "fight or flight." The group may collectively attack the staff member, aggressively deny his suggestions, and punish him for his silence, or the group may suddenly go off on its own, led by a group member, with the implicit or explicit statement "We need to get away from the disappointing leader and do it on our own."

Building Behavioral Norms.   The group in its early life cannot easily find consensus on what to do, so it bounces from one suggestion to another and becomes increasingly more frustrated and discouraged at its inability to act. And this frustration keeps the shared emotional assumption of dependency alive. The group continues to act as if the leader knows what to do. In the meantime members are, of course, beginning to be able to calibrate each other, the staff member, and the total situation. A common language slowly gets established; and, as shared experience accumulates, more of a sense of groupness arises at the emotional level, providing some reassurance to all that they are being included. Primary cognitive and social anxieties are slowly reduced.

This sense of groupness arises through successive dealings with marker events—those that arouse strong feelings and then are dealt with definitively. The group is not consciously aware of this process of norm building, however, unless attention is drawn to it. For example, within the first few minutes, a member may speak up strongly for a given course of action. Joe suggests that the way to proceed is to take turns introducing ourselves and stating why we are in the group. This suggestion requires some behavioral response from other members; therefore, no matter what the group does, it will be setting some kind of precedent for how to deal with future suggestions that are "controlling"—that require behavior from others (Blake and Mouton, 1969).

What are the options at this point? One common response in groups is to act as if the suggestion had not even been made. There is a moment of silence, followed by another member's comment irrelevant to the suggestion. In the jargon of group training, this is called a *plop*—a group decision by nonaction. The member who made the suggestion may feel ignored. At the same time, a group norm has been established. The group has, in effect, said that members need not respond to every suggestion, that it is permissible to ignore someone. A second common response is for another person to agree or disagree overtly with the suggestion. This response begins to build a different norm—that one should respond to suggestions in some way. If there has been agreement, the response may also begin to build an alliance; if there has been disagreement, it may begin a fight that will force others to take sides. A third possibility is for another member to make a *process* comment, such as "I wonder if we should collect some other suggestions before we decide what to do?" or "How do the rest of you feel about Joe's suggestion?" Again, a norm is being established—that one does not have to plunge into action but can consider alternatives. A fourth possibility is to plunge ahead into action. The suggestion is made to introduce ourselves, and the next person to speak launches into an introduction. This response not only gets the group moving but may set two precedents: (1) that suggestions should be responded to and (2) that Joe is the one who can get us moving. Finally, the group may ignore the suggestion yet come back to it later, demonstrating that what may have felt like a plop at the time was not forgotten.

Norms are thus formed when an individual takes a position and the rest of the group deals with that position by either letting it stand (by remaining silent), actively approving it, processing it, or rejecting it. Three sets of consequences are always observed: (1) the personal consequences for the member who made the suggestion (he may gain or lose influence, disclose himself to others, develop a friend or enemy, and so on); (2) the interpersonal consequences for those members immediately involved in the interplay; and (3) the normative consequences for the group as a whole. So here again we have a situation in which an *individual* has to act, but the subsequent shared reaction turns the event into a *group* product. It is the joint witnessing of the event and the reaction that makes it a group product.

The early life of the group is filled with thousands of such events and the responses to them. At the *cognitive* level, they deal with the effort to define working procedures to fulfill the primary task—to learn. Prior assumptions about how to learn will operate initially to bias the group's effort, and limits will be set by the staff member in the form of calling attention to the consequences of behavior considered clearly detrimental to learning—behavior such as failure to attend meetings, frequent interruptions, personally hostile attacks, and the like. At the *emotional* level, such events deal with the problem of authority and influence. The most critical of such events will be ones that overtly test or challenge the staff member's authority.

Thus, one will note that the group pays special attention to the responses that occur immediately after someone has directed a comment, question, or challenge to the staff member.

One will also note anomalous behavior that can be explained only if one assumes that an authority issue is being worked out. For example, the group will actively seek leadership by stating that some member should help the group to get moving, but then systematically ignore or punish anyone who attempts to lead. One can understand this behavior if one remembers that feelings toward authority are always ambivalent and that the anger felt toward the staff member for not leading the group cannot be expressed directly if one feels dependent on the staff member. The negative feelings are split off and projected onto a "bad leader," thus preserving the illusion that the staff member is the "good leader." Acts of insubordination or outbursts of anger at the staff member may be severely punished by other group members, even though those members have themselves been critical of the staff member.

How, then, does a group learn what "reality" is? How does it develop workable and accurate assumptions about how to learn and how to deal with influence and authority?

Reality Test and Catharsis. Though members begin to feel they know each other better, the group continues to be frustrated by its inability to act in a consensual manner, because the unconscious dependence assumption is still operating and members are still working out their influence relationships with each other. The event that moves the group forward at such times, often many hours into the group's life, is an insightful comment by a member who is less conflicted about the authority issue and, therefore, able to perceive and articulate what is really going on. In other words, while those members who are most conflicted about authority are struggling in the dependent and counterdependent mode, some members find that they care less about this issue, are able psychologically to detach themselves from it, and come to recognize the reality that *the leader does not, in fact, know what to do.*

The less conflicted members may intervene in any of a number of ways that expose this reality: (1) by offering a direct *interpretation*—"Maybe we are hung up in this group because we expect the staff member to be able to tell us what to do"; (2) by offering a direct *challenge*—"I think the staff member doesn't know what to do; we better figure it out ourselves"; (3) by offering a direct *suggestion* for an alternative agenda—"I think we should focus on how we feel about this group right now, instead of trying to figure out what to do"; or (4) by making a *process* suggestion or observation—"I notice that we ask the leader for suggestions but then don't do what he suggests" or "I wonder why we are fighting so much among ourselves in this group" or "I think it is interesting that every time Joe makes suggestion, Mary challenges him or makes a countersuggestion."

If the timing is right, in the sense that many members are ready to hear what may be going on because they have all observed the process for a period of time, there will be a strong cathartic reaction when the assumption-lifting intervention is made. The group members will suddenly realize that they have been focusing heavily on the staff member and that, indeed, that person is not all-knowing and all-seeing and therefore probably does not, in fact, know what the group should do. With this insight comes the feeling of responsibility: "We are all in this together, and we each have to contribute to the group's agenda." The magical leader has been killed, and the group begins to seek realistic leadership from whoever can provide it.

Leadership comes to be seen as a shared set of activities rather than a single person's trait, and a sense of ownership of group outcomes arises. Some work groups never achieve this state, remaining dependent on whatever formal authority is available and projecting magically onto it; but in the training situation, the emphasis on process analysis makes it very likely that the issue will be brought to the surface and dealt with.

A comparable process occurs in formally constituted groups, but it is less visible. The group founder or chairperson does have real intentions and plans, but the group initially tends to attribute far more complete and detailed knowledge to the leader than is warranted by reality. Thus, early in the life of a company the entrepreneur is viewed much more magically as the source of all wisdom, and only gradually is it discovered that he or she is only human and that the organization can function only if other members begin to feel responsible for group outcomes as well. But all this may occur implicitly and without very visible marker events. If such events occur, they will most likely be in the form of challenges of the leader or outright insubordination. How the group and the leader then handle the emotionally threatening event will determine, to a large extent, the norms around authority that will become operative in the future.

The insight that the leader is not omniscient or omnipotent gives members a sense of relief not to be struggling any longer with the staff member. They are likely to develop a feeling of euphoria that they have been able to deal with the tough issue of authority and leadership. There is a sense of joy in recognizing that everyone in the group has a role and can make a leadership contribution; this, in turn, strengthens the group's sense of itself.

At this point the group often takes some joint action, as if to prove to itself that it can do something, and gets a further sense of euphoria from being successful at it. Such action is often externally directed—winning a competition with another group or tackling a difficult task under time pressure and completing it. Whatever the task, the end result is a feeling of "We are a great group" and possibly, at a deeper level, even the feeling of "We are a better group than any of the others." It is this state of affairs that leads to the unconscious assumption of *fusion*.

Stage Two: Group Building

At stage 2, the primary operating assumption is the fusion assumption. The essence of this assumption is "We all like each other"; this, in turn, is buttressed by the assumption "We are a great group," based on the euphoria of having solved the problem of dependence and put the formal authority in its proper place. Turquet (1973) used the same label (*fusion*) to reflect a strong emotional need to feel merged with the group and to deny internal differences.

How do we know when this assumption is operating? What one observes at the overt behavior level is a marked absence of interpersonal conflict, a tendency to bend over backward to be nice to each other, emotional expressions of affection, a mood of euphoria, and group solidarity in the face of any challenge. Symptoms of conflict or lack of harmony are ignored or actively denied. Hostility is suppressed or, if it occurs, punished severely. An image of solidarity must be presented at all costs.

Different members of the group will vary in their need to attain and maintain a high level of intimacy, and those who care most, the "overpersonals," will become the most active guardians of the group harmony image and will suppress the "counterpersonals," who are made anxious by the level of intimacy. In particular, some members will resolve conflicts about intimacy by seeking it and by attempting to maintain harmony at all costs. But other group members, those who resolve their conflict about intimacy by avoiding it, will rock the boat and challenge the harmony image because the harmony makes them anxious. They will complain that the group is wasting time, is being too "cozy," and is ignoring conflicts that are visible. But their complaints will be ignored or actively put down if the need to prove group harmony is strong.

The staff member suddenly is now "one of the regulars" and is labeled as "no different from the rest of us," which is, of course, just as unrealistic as the assumption that the staff member is omniscient and omnipotent. At this stage, interventions that may be disturbing to the group are simply ignored or laughed off.

The strength of the fusion assumption will be a function of the individual needs of group members and the actual experience of the group. The more the group feels itself to be in a hostile environment or vulnerable to destruction, the more it may cling to the assumption as a way of claiming strength. Or, to put it the other way, only when the group feels reasonably secure can it give up the false solidarity that the fusion assumption claims. Such security comes gradually from increasing experience, success with tasks, and tests of strength against other groups.

The group moods of fight or flight are likely to arise around the fusion assumption, because both fight and flight involve solidarity and joint action. Thus, if the authority issue arises again, the group may at this point turn collectively against the staff member or may deliberately run away from its real task of learning about itself by rationalizing that it has overcome all of its problems already, that there is nothing more to learn. Or the group may project its negative feelings onto someone outside the group—the administration of the workshop or some other group—and fight or flee from that outside enemy.

What Bion (1959) called "pairing" will also be common at this stage, since the need for love and intimacy that is operating can easily be projected onto those members who display such feelings overtly. By projecting the fate of the group into the pair, by hoping for a magic solution through what the pair will produce, the group can maintain its sense of solidarity. All these responses preserve the assumption that the group is great and can do things together.

Many organizations get stuck at this level of group evolution, developing an adequate authority system and a capacity to defend themselves against external threat but never growing internally to a point of differentiation of roles and clarification of personal relationships.

Reality Test and Catharsis. The fusion assumption will not be given up until some marker event brings its falsity into consciousness. There are four group events that have the potential for revealing the assumption: (1) the subtle disagreements and conflicts that occur in the attempts to take joint action, (2) the noticeable avoidance of confrontation, (3) the overt denial of the fact that some members may not like each other, and (4) the occasional eruptions of negative feelings toward other members. The actual marker event that tests the reality of the fusion assumption is most likely to come from those group members who are least conflicted about intimacy issues and who, therefore, are most likely to have insight into what is happening. For example, on one of the many occasions when a "counterpersonal" member challenges the solidarity of the group, one of the less conflicted members may support the challenge by providing incontrovertible examples indicating that group members actually do not seem to get along all that well. This introduction of data that cannot be denied will pierce the illusion and thus force the recognition of the assumption.

I have frequently observed similar events in more formally constituted groups. A work group in a growing company erupts into a hostile confrontation between two members. The manner in which the group handles the ensuing tense silence builds a norm for future expressions of feeling. If the group or the leader punishes either or both combatants, norms get built that feelings should be kept in check; if the group or leader encourages resolution, norms get built that hostility is OK and that feelings can be expressed, as was consistently the case at DEC. The moments when these norm-building activities occur are often very brief and easy to miss if one is not alert to them. But it is at those moments that culture begins to form, and the eventual assumptions about what is appropriate and right will reflect a long series of such incidents and the reactions to them.

The Role of Learning: Which Norms Survive? How are norms reinforced and built up into the assumptions that eventually come to be taken for granted? The two basic mechanisms of learning involved are (1) *positive problem solving*, to cope with *external integration* issues, and (2) *anxiety avoidance*, to cope with *internal integration* issues. For example, if a group challenges its formal leader and begins to build norms that support more widely shared leadership and higher levels of member involvement, it is an empirical matter whether or not this way of working is effective in solving real-word problems. In the T group, it is an empirical matter whether or not the group feels that such norms are enabling it to fulfill its primary task of *learning*. In formal work groups, it is a matter of actual experience whether or not the work gets done better with a given set of norms that have evolved.

If the group fails repeatedly, sooner or later someone will propose that a new leadership process be found or that the original leader be reinstated in a more powerful role, and the group will find itself experimenting with new norms of how to work with authority. It then again must test against reality how successful it is. The norms that produce the greatest success will be the ones that survive. As they continue to work, they gradually turn into assumptions about how things really are. At the same time, as new norms form, there is always an immediate test of whether the members of the group are more or less comfortable as a result of the new way of working; that is, do the new norms enable them to avoid the anxiety inherent in the initially unstable or uncertain situation? If the leader is challenged, gives up some authority, and shares power with the group, some group members, depending on their own pattern of needs and prior experiences, may feel less comfortable than before. In some groups a greater comfort level may be achieved by norms that, in effect, reassert the authority of the leader and make members more dependent on the leader. The needs of the leader will also play a role in this process, so the ultimate resolution—what makes everyone most comfortable—will be a set of norms that meet the many internal needs as well as the external experiences. Because so many variables are involved, the resultant group culture will usually be a unique and distinctive one.

Learning by Seeking Rewards Versus Learning to Avoid Pain. The kinds of norms—and, eventually, assumptions—that evolve out of a group's experience will reflect whether the learning has been primarily the result of success, or has resulted from trying to avoid in the future some painful trauma that has happened in the past. The way in which cultural assumptions were learned will strongly influence how changes in that culture can be made at some later time, if necessary. If a group has learned primarily through positive successes, the mentality will be "Why change something that has been successful?" If a group has learned something in order to avoid pain, the mentality will be "We cannot try something that has hurt us in the past." The implications of these differences will be explored later in this chapter.

Stage Three: Group Work and Functional Familiarity

If the group deals successfully with the fusion assumption, it usually achieves an emotional state that can best be characterized as *mutual acceptance*. The group will have had enough experience so that members not only know what to expect of each other—what we can think of as *functional familiarity*—but also will have had the chance to learn that they can coexist and work together even if they do not all like each other. The emotional shift from maintaining the illusion of mutual liking to a state of mutual acceptance and functional familiarity is important in that it frees up emotional energy for work. Being dominated by either the dependence or the fusion assumption ties up emotional energy because of the denial and defensiveness required to avoid confronting the disconfirming realities. Therefore, if a group is to work effectively, it must reach a level of emotional maturity at which reality-testing norms prevail.

At this stage a new implicit assumption arises, the *work assumption*: "We know each other well enough, both in a positive and negative light, that we can work well together and accomplish our external goals."

Now the group exerts less pressure to conform and builds norms that encourage some measure of individuality and personal growth, on the assumption that the group ultimately will benefit if all members grow and become stronger. However, because many groups never get to this stage, some observers judge groups as inherently demanding of conformity. In my own experience, high conformity pressures are symptomatic of unresolved issues in the group, and the best way to get past them is to help the group to a more mature stage.

As Bion (1959) pointed out, groups always have some kind of task, even if that task is to provide learning or therapy to its members; so the need to work, to fulfill the task, is always psychologically present. But the ability to focus on the task is a function of the degree to which group members can reduce and avoid their own anxieties. Such anxieties are intrinsically highest when the group is very young and has not yet had a chance to build up cultural assumptions to control the anxiety. Therefore, the energy available for work is lowest in the early stages of group formation, though a focus on work is often a convenient way to work out underlying group issues. The important point to note is that a focus on work does not necessarily produce good results if members' energy and attention are bound up in personal issues.

One way of thinking about group evolution, then, is to recognize that the work of the group gradually attracts more and more of the members' attention, with the periods of regression into dependence, fusion, fight or flight, or pairing becoming less frequent as the group evolves a culture, stabilizes its way of working, and thus releases energy for the task at hand. On the other hand, the quickest way for the group to lose its ability to work productively is to question some of its cultural assumptions, because such a threat rearouses the primary anxieties that the cultural solutions dealt with in the first place.

As the group works on its tasks, a new issue arises. Do members seek solutions that "satisfy," then institutionalize them because they reduce anxiety? Or do they seek optimal solutions and create a climate for perpetual creativity in order to remain externally adaptive even though internally more anxious? It is a paradox of evolution or development that the more we learn how to do things and to stabilize what we have learned, the more unwilling or unable we become to adapt, change, and grow into new patterns, even when our changing environment demands such new patterns.

Stage Four: Group Maturity

Only a few remarks will be made about this final group stage because it will receive much more focus in later chapters. If a group works successfully, it will inevitable reinforce its assumptions about itself and its environment, thus strengthening whatever culture it has developed. Because culture is a learned set of responses, culture will be as strong as the group's learning history has made it. The more the group has shared emotionally intense experiences, the stronger the culture of that group will be.

Given these forces, a group or organization inevitably will begin to develop the assumption that it knows who it is, what its role in the world is, how to accomplish its mission, and how to conduct its affairs. If the culture that develops *works*, it will ultimately be taken for granted as the only correct way for group members to see the world. The inevitable dilemma for the group, then, is how to avoid becoming so stable in its approach to its environment that it loses its ability to adapt, innovate, and grow. How this works out in various kinds of organizations will be examined in subsequent chapters.

Summary and Conclusions

To understand organizational or occupational cultures, it is necessary to understand cultural origins. In this chapter I have reviewed how this happens in a group by examining the stages of group growth and development based on social psychological concepts and what we know about group dynamics. By examining in detail the interactions of members, it is possible to reconstruct how norms of behavior arise through what members do or do not do when critical incidents occur.

The basic sociopsychological forces that operate in all of us are the raw material around which a group organizes itself both to accomplish its task and to create for itself a viable and comfortable organization. Thus every group must solve the problems of member identity, common goals, mechanisms of influence, and how to manage both aggression and intimacy. Culture arises around the learned solutions to these problems.

We have now presented in this part of the book the structure of culture and the sociodynamics of culture formation in our daily relationships. In Part Two we turn to a more detailed analysis of the *content* of culture—of the dimensions one looks at in trying to describe and decipher a given culture in a group, organization, or occupation.

Part Two

THE DIMENSIONS
OF CULTURE

Thus far I have defined and described culture as a structural concept. In this part of the book I want to describe what culture consists of— what an observer would view as the *content* of culture. If culture consists of shared basic assumptions, we still need to specify: assumptions about what? The content of organizational or occupational cultures reflects the ultimate problems that every group faces: dealing with its external environment (Chapter Five) and managing its internal integration (Chapter Six). Culture is pervasive and ultimately embraces everything that a group is concerned about and must deal with. Beyond these external and internal problems, cultural assumptions reflect deeper issues about the nature of truth, time, space, human nature, and human relationships. A way of thinking about and describing these deeper issues is spelled out in Chapters Seven, Eight, and Nine.

In trying to understand the bewildering variety of different cultures that one encounters, it is tempting to develop typologies that allow us to categorize different organizations into types. Such typologies have the advantage of simplifying and building higher-order theoretical categories, but they have the disadvantage of being so abstract that they often fail to describe accurately a particular organization. A number of such typologies have been proposed. They are reviewed in Chapter Ten.

Having defined ways of describing culture content, there remains the issue of how one can measure or decipher such content from a researcher or consultant point of view. In Chapter Eleven I describe a number of available alternatives and argue for what I call a *clinical* view that takes into account and uses what members of the organization are trying to do.

These chapters focus more on the concept of culture and less on the concept of leadership. Nevertheless, the reader should remember that it is leadership in the history of the group that has created the particular culture content that the group ends up with. The categories of culture content that will be reviewed are therefore also categories of content that exist within the leader's head. *Every leader should be highly conscious of his or her own assumptions in each of those content areas.*

5

ASSUMPTIONS ABOUT
EXTERNAL ADAPTATION ISSUES

A formal definition of organizational culture can tell us what culture is from a structural point of view, but it does not tell us what the content of culture is—what cultural assumptions are about. What kinds of issues does any group face that lead ultimately to cultural assumptions? To put it another way, what critical functions does culture perform for the group? Why do certain cultural assumptions survive? We examined these issues in some detail in the last chapter as they arise in the initial formation of a group. As groups grow and develop into organizations, those issues are supplemented by other issues that become the groundwork for culture formation.

The most relevant model is that evolved by sociology and group dynamics, based on the fundamental distinction between any group's problems of (1) survival in and adaptation to its external environment and (2) integration of its internal processes to ensure the capacity to continue to survive and adapt. In other words, from an evolutionary perspective, we need to identify the issues that any group faces from the moment of its origin through to its state of maturity and decline. Although it may be difficult—sometimes even impossible—to study cultural origins and functions in ethnic units whose history is lost in antiquity, it is not at all impossible to study these matters in groups, organizations, or occupations whose history and evolution are available.

The process of culture formation is, in a sense, identical to the process of group formation in that the very essence of groupness or group identity—the shared patterns of thought, belief, feelings, and values that result from shared experience and common learning—results in the pattern of shared assumptions that I am calling the *culture* of that group. Without a group there can be no culture, and without some shared assumptions, some minimal degree of culture, we are really talking about just an aggregate of people, not a group. So group growth and culture formation can be seen as two sides of the same coin, and both are the result of leadership activities and shared experiences.

We need, then, to understand the dimensions along which leaders think in creating and managing groups and the issues they face as they attempt to cope with the external context in which they are trying to create an organization. The issues or problems of external adaptation basically specify the coping cycle that any system must be able to maintain in relation to its changing environment. The essential elements of that cycle are shown in Exhibit 5.1. Though the steps in the cycle are presented in sequential order, any given organization probably works on most of the steps simultaneously, once it is a going concern (Schein, 1980, 1983).

Exhibit 5.1. The Steps of External Adaptation and Survival.

1. *Mission and Strategy*. Obtaining a shared understanding of core mission, primary task, and manifest and latent functions.

2. *Goals*. Developing consensus on goals, as derived from the core mission.

3. *Means*. Developing consensus on the means to be used to attain the goals, such as the organization structure, division of labor, reward system, and authority system.

4. *Measurement*. Developing consensus on the criteria to be used in measuring how well the group is doing in fulfilling its goals, such as the information and control system. This step also involves the cycle of obtaining information, getting that information to the right place within the organization, and digesting it so that appropriate corrective action can be taken.

5. *Correction*. Developing consensus on the appropriate remedial or repair strategies to be used if goals are not being met.

Shared Assumptions
About Mission and Strategy

Every new group or organization must develop a shared concept of its ultimate survival problem, from which usually is derived its most basic sense of core mission, primary task, or "reason to be." In most business organizations, this shared definition revolves around the issue of economic survival and growth, which, in turn, involves the maintenance of good relationships with the major stakeholders of the organization: (1) the investors and stockholders; (2) the suppliers of the materials needed to produce; (3) the managers and employees; (4) the community and government; and, last but not least, (5) the customers willing to pay for the product or service.

Several recent studies of organizations have shown that the key to long-range growth and survival is to keep the needs of these constituencies in some kind of balance, and that the mission of the organization, as a set of beliefs about its core competencies and basic functions in society, is usually a reflection of this balance (Donaldson and Lorsch, 1983; Kotter and Heskett, 1992; Porras and Collins, 1994). It has been a mistake to think in terms of a total focus on any one of these constituencies, because all of them together make up the environment in which the organization must succeed.

In religious, educational, social, and governmental organizations, the core mission or primary task is clearly different, but the logic that it ultimately derives from a balancing of the needs of different stakeholders is the same. Thus, for example, the mission of a university must balance the learning needs of the students (which includes housing, feeding, and often acting in loco parentis), the needs of the faculty to do research and further knowledge, the needs of the community to have a repository for knowledge and skill, the needs of the financial investors to have a viable institution, and, ultimately, even the needs of society to have an institution to facilitate the transition of late adolescents into the labor market and to sort them into skill groups.

Though core missions or primary tasks are usually stated in terms of a single constituency, such as customers, a more useful way to think about ultimate or core mission is to change the question to "What is our function in the larger scheme of things?" or "What justifies our continued existence?" Posing the question this way reveals that most organizations have multiple functions reflecting the multiple stakeholders and that some of these functions are public justifications, whereas others are "latent" and, in a sense, not spoken of (Merton, 1957). For example, the manifest function of a school system is to educate. But a close examination of what goes on in school systems suggests several latent functions as well: (1) to keep children (young adults) off the streets and out of the labor market until there is room for them and they have some relevant skills, (2) to sort and group the next generation into talent and skill categories according to the needs of the society, and (3) to enable the various occupations associated with the school system to survive and maintain their professional autonomy. In examining the manifest and latent functions, the organization's leaders and members will recognize that to survive, the organization must to some degree fulfill all of these functions.

Core mission thus becomes a complex multifunctional issue, whereby some of the functions must remain latent to protect the manifest identity of the organization. To announce publicly the babysitting, sorting, and professional autonomy functions would be embarrassing, but these functions often play an important role in determining the activities of school organizations. In business organizations the latent functions include, for instance, the provision of jobs in the community where the business is located; the provision of economic resources to that community, in the form of goods and raw materials purchased; and the provision of managerial talent to be used in activities other than running the business. The importance of these latent functions does not surface until an organization is forced to contemplate closing or moving; then a number of interest groups that were in one way or another counting on that organization, even though implicitly, suddenly come forward to protest the decision to move or to close.

Internal debates start among members for whom the priorities among the different functions are different, forcing the organization to confront what collectively it has assumed to be at the top of this hierarchy. If no such overarching priority is found, the group may splinter and even dissolve. On the other hand, if the debate leads to an affirmation of what the ultimate mission and identity of the group is, a strong cultural element has been formed that will carry forward through the beliefs and assumptions of senior management.

Mission relates directly to what organizations call *strategy*. From the point of view of an *outside* analyst of an organization, one can define what the strategy should be for that organization to survive and prosper. However, from the point of view of *insiders*, the strategic options are limited by the culture of the organization. Strategy consultants are often frustrated by the fact that their recommendations are not acted upon. They forget that unless those recommendations are feasible, given the organization's assumptions about itself, they will not make sense and hence will not be implemented.

For example, at one stage in the evolution of Ciba-Geigy, I heard lengthy debates among top managers on the question of whether Ciba-Geigy should design and produce any product, provided it could be sold at a profit, or whether designs and products should be limited to what some senior managers believed to be sound or valuable products, based on their conception of what their company had originally been built on and what their unique talents were. The debate focused on whether or not to keep Airwick, which had been acquired in the American subsidiary, to help Ciba-Geigy become more competent in consumer-oriented marketing. Airwick made air fresheners to remove pet or other odors, and at one of the annual meetings of top management the president of the U.S subsidiary was very proudly displaying some TV ads for their new product Carpet Fresh. I was sitting next to a senior member of the internal board, a Swiss researcher who had developed several of the company's key chemical products. He was visibly agitated by the TV ads and finally leaned over to me and loudly whispered, "You know, Schein, those things are not even *products*.

In the later debates about whether to sell Airwick (even though it was financially sound and profitable), I only understood this comment when it was revealed that Ciba-Geigy could not stomach the image of being a company that produced something as seemingly trivial as an air freshener. Thus a major strategic decision was made on the basis of the company's culture, not on marketing or financial grounds. Ciba-Geigy sold this company and affirmed the assumption that they should only be in businesses that had a clear scientific base and that dealt with major problems such as disease and starvation.

This issue came up in a different way at General Foods when it had to face the accusation from consumer groups and nutrition experts that some of its products, although they tasted good because of high sugar and artificial flavoring content, had no nutritional value. The accusation raised for the top management not merely an economic question but an identity question: Is this company a food company or a consumer-oriented edibles company (that is, producing anything that tastes good), or both, or neither?

At first the company responded by attempting to develop and sell more nutritious products, but it found that customers genuinely preferred the cheaper, less nutritious but better-tasting ones. An advertising campaign to sell nutrition did not overcome this customer resistance, nor did lowering the price. A debate ensued in the company about its basic mission beyond economic survival, and in this debate the pragmatic market-oriented philosophy could be argued much more successfully by managers. The company discovered that its commitment to nutrition was not fundamental and that its identity rested much more on the assumption that they were in the consumer-oriented edibles business. They would make and sell any kind of food that people were willing to pay money for.

In summary, one of the most central elements of any culture will be the assumptions the members of the organization share about their identity and ultimate mission or functions. These are not necessarily very conscious but can be brought to the surface if one probes the strategic decisions that the organization makes.

Shared Assumptions About Goals Derived from the Mission

Consensus on the core mission does not automatically guarantee that the members of the group will have common goals. The mission is often understood but not well articulated. In order to achieve consensus on goals, the group needs a common language and shared assumptions about the basic logistical operations by which one moves from something as abstract or general as a sense of mission to the concrete goals of designing, manufacturing, and selling an actual product or service within specified and agreed-upon cost and time constraints.

For example, at DEC there was a clear consensus on the mission of bringing out a line of products that would "win in the marketplace," but this consensus did not solve for senior management the problem of how to allocate resources among different product development groups, nor did it specify how best to market such products. Mission and strategy can be rather timeless, whereas goals have to be formulated for what to do next year, next month, and tomorrow. Goals concretize the mission and facilitate the decisions on means. In that process, goal formulation also often reveals unresolved issues or lack of consensus around deeper issues.

At DEC, the debate around which products to support and how to support them revealed a deep lack of semantic agreement on how to think about marketing. For example, one group thought that marketing meant better image advertising in national magazines so that more people would recognize the name of the company; one group was convinced that marketing meant better advertising in technical journals; one group thought it meant developing the next generation of products; and another group emphasized merchandizing and sales support as the key elements of marketing.

Senior management could not define clear goals because of lack of consensus on the meaning of key functions and how those functions reflected the core mission of the organization. Senior management had to come to agreement on whether it was better to develop the company through being well known in the technical community or through being recognized nationally as a brand name in their industry. The deeper shared assumption that came to dominate this debate was derived from the identity that most senior DEC people had as electrical engineers and innovators. As engineers they believed that good products would sell themselves, that their own judgment of goodness was sufficient, and that one should not waste money on image building.

At Ciba-Geigy there was a clear consensus on the mission to remain in the pharmaceuticals business because it fitted the broad self-concept of senior management and was profitable, but there was considerable disagreement on goals, such as the rate of return that should be expected from that division and the length of time over which its growth and performance should be measured.

Because operational goals have to be more precise, organizations typically work out their issues of mission and identity in the context of deciding annual or longer-range goals. If one really wants to understand cultural assumptions, one must be careful not to confuse assumptions about goals with assumptions about mission. Ciba-Geigy's concern with being only in businesses that make science-based, useful products did not become evident in their discussions about business goals until they hit a strategic issue like whether or not to buy another company. In fact, one way of looking at what we mean by *strategy* is to realize that strategy concerns the evolution of the basic mission, whereas operational goals reflect the short-run tactical survival issues that the organization identifies. Thus, when a company gets into basic strategy discussions, it is usually trying to assess in a more fundamental way the relationship between its sense of its mission and its operational goals.

In summary, goals can be defined at several levels of abstraction and in different time horizons. Is our goal to be profitable at the end of next quarter, or to make ten sales next month, or to call twelve potential customers tomorrow? Only as consensus is reached on such matters, leading to solutions that work repeatedly, can we begin to think of the goals of an organization as potential cultural elements. Once such consensus is reached, however, the assumptions about goals become a very strong element of that group's culture.

Shared Assumptions About Means to Achieve Goals

The group cannot achieve its goals and fulfill its mission unless there is clear consensus on the means by which goals will be met. The means that are to be used have to do with day-to-day behavior, and therefore require a higher level of consensus. One can have ambiguous goals, but if anything is to happen at all one must agree on how to structure the organization, how to design, finance, build, and sell the products or services. From the particular pattern of these agreements will emerge not only the style of the organization, but also the basic design of tasks, division of labor, reporting and accountability structure, reward and incentive systems, control systems, and information systems.

The skills, technology, and knowledge that a group acquires in its effort to cope with its environment then also become part of its culture if there is consensus on what they are and how to use them. For example, in his study of several companies that make the world's best flutes, Cook (personal communication, 1992) shows that for generations the craftsmen were able to produce flutes that artists would recognize immediately as having been made by a particular company, but neither management nor the craftsmen could describe exactly what they had done to make it so. It was embedded in the processes of manufacturing and reflected a set of skills that could be passed on for generations through an apprentice system, but was not formally identifiable.

In evolving the means by which the group will accomplish its goals, many of the internal issues that the group must deal with get partially settled. The external problem of division of labor will structure who will get to know whom and who will be in authority. The work system of the group will define its boundaries and its rules for membership. The particular beliefs and talents of the founders and leaders of the group will determine which functions become dominant as the group evolves. For example, engineers founding companies based on their inventions will create very different kinds of internal structures than venture capitalists creating organizations by putting technical and marketing talent under the direction of financially or marketing oriented leaders.

The founders of Ciba-Geigy believed that solutions to problems result from hard thought, scientific research, and careful checking of that research in the marketplace. From the beginning this company had clearly defined research roles and distinguished them sharply from managerial roles. The norm had developed that one must become an expert in one's own area, to the point where one knows more about that area than anyone else—a norm clearly derived from some of the assumptions of the scientific model on which the company operated. Historically, this link to the culture of science may have accounted, in part, for the assumption that one's area of expertise was one's own property or turf and the feeling that it might be considered insulting to be given advice in that area. The defined turf included one's subordinates, budget, physical space, and all other resources that one was allocated. This level of felt autonomy and the formal relationships that developed among group members then became their means of getting work done. The high degree of reliance on hierarchical authority also derived from the core technology in which Ciba-Geigy was working. Chemistry and chemical engineering are fairly precise hierarchical fields in which being an experienced expert helps to prevent serious accidents or explosions.

At DEC, on the other hand, a norm developed that the only turf one really owns is one's accountability for certain tasks and accomplishments. Budget, physical space, subordinates, and other resources were really seen as common organizational property over which one had only influence. Others in the organization could try to influence the accountable manager or her subordinates, but there were no formal boundaries or walls, physical space was viewed as common territory, and sharing of knowledge was highly valued. Whereas at Ciba-Geigy to give ideas to another was considered threatening, at DEC it was considered mandatory to survival. The core technology of electrical engineering and circuit design lent itself much more to experimentation and individual innovation in that mistakes were mostly a waste of time and resources but not physically threatening.

At DEC, lack of consensus on who "owned" what could be a major source of conflict. For example, at one time in DEC's history there was a lack of consensus on the rules for obtaining key engineering services, such as drafting and the use of the model-building shop. Some engineers believed that work would be done in the order in which it was submitted; others believed that it would be done according to the importance of the work, and they often persuaded the service manager to break into the queue to give their work priority. This aroused great anger on the part of those who were waiting their turn patiently and, as might be expected, it made the service managers very anxious.

The whole engineering group eventually had to get together to establish a common set of policies, which, interestingly enough, reinforced the existing pattern and legitimized it. Both engineering and service managers were to do the "sensible" thing, and if they could not figure out what that was they were to refer the matter to the next higher level of management for resolution. The policy discussion ended up reinforcing the assumption that, since no one is smart enough to have a formula for how to do things, people should use their intelligence and common sense at all times. Ambiguity was considered to be a reality that must be lived with and managed sensibly.

Feelings around territory, property, and turf also have a biological basis. Few things arouse as much aggression in animals as having their defined territory invaded. Few circumstances cause as much breakdown of normal behavior patterns as excessive crowding, rendering any private space a physical impossibility (Hall, 1966). In cultures where crowding is inevitable because of shortage of space, defensive cultural assumptions form to deal with the stress this creates. Butterfield (1982) notes in his description of China that when one bumps into someone in a crowded bus, one need not even say "sorry," as Westerners would do routinely, because one has only bumped into a stranger, an impersonal object. The same kind of depersonalization operates in the Japanese subway, and, for that matter, in any kind of intense crowding situation.

Division of labor—the allocation of various kinds of roles—can be seen as an extension of the allocation of physical and other kinds of property, since various amounts of status, access to rewards, and certain privileges inevitably accompany the assigned roles. Therefore, the way in which those roles are allocated and the consensus on criteria for allocation not only become the means by which tasks are accomplished but also resolve major internal group issues. Because the means by which things get done in the external environment become "property" in the internal environment, we often see the means controlling the ends. An efficient assembly line may mechanize behavior to such a degree that the organization begins to be perceived as caring more about efficiency and profit than the welfare of its employees. The production manager's "turf" can become sacred even though it may lead to organizational activities that violate other elements of its identity and mission.

Changing an organization's structures and processes is therefore difficult because it involves not only considerations of efficiency and effectiveness vis-à-vis the external task but also the reallocation of internal "property." Similarly, changing reward systems and status allocation systems in the internal working of the organization may be difficult because such changes will affect how work is done and how well goals are achieved. It is for this reason that organizational analysis is increasingly moving toward what has been labeled *sociotechnical* system analysis, acknowledging the degree to which the formal technical means for task accomplishment are intrinsically intertwined with the internal status, turf, and role systems

(Hanna, 1988; Pasmore and Sherwood, 1978; Rice, 1963; Trist and others, 1963).

In summary, as cultural assumptions form around the means by which goals are to be accomplished, they will inevitably involve the internal issues of status and identity, thus highlighting the complexity of both the analysis of means and the issues surrounding efforts to change how an organization accomplishes its goals. Consensus on the means to be used creates the behavioral regularities and many of the artifacts that eventually come to be identified as the visible manifestations of the culture. Once these regularities and patterns are in place, they become a source of stability for members and are, therefore, strongly adhered to.

Shared Assumptions About Measuring Results

Measurement of performance has two elements around which consensus must be achieved: what to measure and how to measure it. Strong cultural elements will form around each of these issues, and often they become the primary issue that newcomers to the organization are concerned about.

Measurement Criteria: Consensus on What to Measure

Once the group is performing, it must have consensus on how to judge its own performance in order to know what kind of remedial action to take when things do not go as expected. For example, we have noted that early in DEC's history the evaluation of engineering projects hinged on whether certain key engineers in the company liked the product. The company assumed that internal acceptance was an acceptable surrogate for external acceptance. At the same time, if several engineering groups each liked what they were designing the criterion shifted to letting the market decide. These criteria could work in tandem as long as there were enough resources to support all the projects, because DEC was growing at a rapid rate. In another high-technology company, the criterion was completely different. Products had to be built and thoroughly market tested before it was considered legitimate to mass-produce them.

At the Wellmade flute company, evaluation was done at each node in the production process, so that by the time an instrument reached the end of the line it was likely to pass inspection and to be acceptable to the artist. If a craftsman at a given position did not like what he felt or saw, he simply passed it back to the preceding craftsman and it was the norm that it would be reworked without resentment. Each person trusted the person in the next position (S.D.N. Cook, personal communication, 1992).

Cook also found a similar process at a French brandy company: not only was each step evaluated by an expert, but the ultimate role of taster—the person who makes the final determination of when a batch is ready—could only be assumed by a son of the previous taster. In this company the last taster had no sons. Rather than pass the role on to the eldest daughter, it was passed on to a nephew, on the assumption that female taste preferences were in some fundamental way different from male taste preferences!

I was involved at one point in the 1980s with the exploration and production division management of the U.S. Shell Oil Company. My consulting assignment was to help them do a cultural analysis to develop better measurements of the division's performance. As we collectively began to examine the artifacts and espoused beliefs and values of this group, it immediately became apparent that the exploration group and the production group had completely different concepts of how they wanted to be measured, yet within each group there was complete consensus. We were dealing with two subcultures.

The exploration group wanted to be measured on finding evidence of oil, which they felt should be determined on a statistical basis over a long period of time, because most wells proved to be dry. In contrast, the production group, which was charged with safely removing oil from an active well, wanted to be measured on a short-term basis in terms of safe and efficient production. For the exploration group the risk was in not finding anything over a long period of time; for the production group the risk was of an accident or fire, which could occur at any moment. In the end, both groups wanted to contribute to the financial performance of the company, so the cost of exploration and the cost of safe production had to be factored in, but these were not the primary criteria on which either group wanted to be measured.

Some companies teach their executives to trust their own judgment as a basis for decisions; others teach them to check with their bosses; still others teach them not to trust results unless they are based on hard data, such as test markets or at least market research; and still others teach them to rely on staff experts. If members of the group hold widely divergent concepts of what to look for and how to evaluate results, they cannot decide when and how to take remedial action.

For example, senior managers within companies often hold different views of how to assess financial performance—debt/equity ratio, return on sales, return on investment, stock price, credit rating, and other indicators could all be used. If senior management cannot agree on which indicator to pay primary attention to, they cannot decide how well they are doing and what corrective action, if any, they need to take.

Debates can occur over whether financial criteria should override criteria such as customer satisfaction, market share, or employee morale. These debates are complicated by potential disagreements on the correct time horizons to use in making evaluations—daily, monthly, quarterly, annually, or what? Even though the information systems may be very precise, such precision does not guarantee consensus on how to evaluate information.

The potential complexity of achieving consensus on measurement criteria was illustrated at an international refugee organization. Field workers measured themselves by the number of refugees processed, but senior management paid more attention to how favorable the attitudes of host governments were, because those governments financed the organization through their contributions.

Senior management therefore checked every decision that was to be made about refugees with virtually every other department and several layers of management, to ensure that the decision would not offend one of the supporting governments. However, this process markedly slowed decision making and often led to "lowest common denominator" conservative decisions. This, in turn, led to great irritation on the part of field workers, who felt that they were usually dealing with crisis situations in which a slowdown might mean death for significant numbers of refugees. They perceived top management to be hopelessly mired in what they considered to be simply bureaucratic tangles, and they did not understand the caution that top management felt it had to exercise toward sponsoring governments.

Lack of agreement across the hierarchy on how to judge success—the amount of money contributed or the number of refugees processed—was the major source of difficulty in improving the overall performance and level of employee satisfaction in this organization. In addition, there may have been a basic lack of consensus even on the core mission. Whereas the field workers tended to think of the core mission as helping the survival of refugees, senior management was clearly more concerned with the survival of the total organization, which, in its view, depended on how it related to the United Nations and to the host governments. Senior management had to decide whether to indoctrinate field workers more effectively on what the core organizational survival problem really was, or to live with the internal conflict that the lack of consensus seemed to generate. On the other hand, the younger, idealistic field workers could well argue (and did) that to survive as an organization made no sense if the needs of refugees were not met. In this organization, then, one would have to speak of conflicting cultural assumptions or conflicting subcultures in that the headquarters and field each had consensus but there was an absence of a total organizational consensus on mission, goals, and means.

At Ciba-Geigy a comparable issue arose in evaluating the performance of different divisions. The high-performing divisions chose to compare themselves internally to the low-performing divisions and were therefore complacent about pushing for even higher performance levels. Senior management chose to compare these same divisions to their *external* competitors in the same product/market space and found that they were underperforming by this criterion. For example, the pharmaceutical division outperformed the other chemical divisions but did poorly relative to other pharmaceutical companies. But the tradition of being one family made it hard to convince the pharma division managers to accept the tougher external standards.

Many so-called culture change programs actually deal only with this one element of the culture—the measurements to be applied to future performance. Thus, new chief executives come in and announce that they will emphasize product quality, or bring costs under control, or get the organization to be more customer oriented. This sometimes sounds like a real change in mission but on closer examination turns out to be merely a new focus on how to measure success. From this perspective it is clear that such new signals will change only one element of the culture. If only the results signals are changed, without concern for mission, goals, and means, very little actual change may come about.

Consensus on Means of Measurement

Consensus must be achieved both on the criteria and on the means by which information is to be gathered. For example, at DEC during its early years there developed a very open communication system, built around high levels of acquaintance and trust among the members of the organization. This system was supported by a computerized electronic mail network, constant telephone communications, frequent visits, formal and informal surveys and sensing meetings, and two- to three-day committee meetings in settings away from the office. Individual managers developed their own systems of measurement and were trusted to report progress accurately. DEC operated on the powerful shared assumption that information and truth were the lifeblood of the organization, and the company built many formal and informal mechanisms to ensure a high rate of internal communication, such as the rule in the early years that engineers' offices were not to have doors. They were to be easily accessible to each other physically and through the worldwide electronic network.

Ken Olsen measured things by walking around, talking to people at all levels of the organization, sensing morale from the climate he encountered as he walked around. The informal measures were much more important initially than formal financial controls, and consensus developed around the assumption that "we will always be open and truthful with each other."

In contrast, at Ciba-Geigy there was a tightly structured reporting system, which involved weekly telephone calls, monthly reports to the financial control organization in headquarters, semiannual visits to every department by headquarters teams, and formal meetings and seminars at which policy was communicated downward in the organization. At Ciba-Geigy the main assumption appeared to be that information flowed primarily in designated channels, and informal systems were to be avoided because they could be unreliable.

In summary, the methods an organization decides to use to measure its own activities and accomplishments—the criteria it chooses and the information system it develops to measure itself—become central elements of its culture as consensus develops around these issues. If consensus fails to develop and strong subcultures form around different assumptions, the organization will find itself in serious conflict that can potentially undermine its ability to cope with its external environment.

Shared Assumptions About Remedial and Repair Strategies

The final area of consensus crucial for external adaptation concerns what to do if a change in course is required and how to make that change. If information surfaces that the group is not on target—sales are off, market share is down, profits are down, product introductions are late, key customers complain about product quality, or the like—by what process is the problem diagnosed and remedied?

Consensus is needed about how to gather external information, how to get that information to the right parts of the organization that can act on it, and how to alter the internal production processes to take the new information into account. Organizations can become ineffective if there is lack of consensus on any part of this information gathering and utilization cycle (Schein, 1980). For example, at General Foods the product managers used market research to determine whether or not the product they were managing was meeting sales and quality goals. At the same time, sales managers who were out in the supermarkets were getting information on how store managers were reacting to different products by giving them better or worse positions on the shelves. It was well established that shelf position was strongly correlated with sales. Sales managers consistently attempted to get this information to the product managers, who refused to consider it relative to their more "scientifically conducted" market research, thus unwittingly undermining their own performance. In the same vein, in the early days at DEC the person who knew the most about what competitors were doing was the purchasing manager, because he had to buy parts from competitor companies. Yet his knowledge was often ignored because engineers trusted their own judgment more than his information.

If information gets to the right place, where it is understood and acted upon, there is still the matter of reaching consensus on what kind of action to take. For example, if a product fails in the marketplace, does the organization fire the product manager, reexamine the marketing strategy, reassess the quality of the research and development process, convene a diagnostic team from many functions to see what can be learned from the failure, or brush the failure under the rug and quietly move the good people into different jobs?

At DEC, both the diagnosis and the proposed remedy were likely to result from widespread open discussion and debate among members at all levels of the organization, but more weight was consistently given to the technical people over the financial, marketing, or purchasing people. After the discussion and debate, self-corrective action was often taken locally because people now recognized problems about which they could do something. Thus, by the time top management ratified a course of action and announced it, most of the problem had already been dealt with. However, if the discussion led to proposals that violated some of Ken Olsen's assumptions or intuitions, he would step into the debate and attempt to influence thinking. If that did not work, he sometimes empowered different groups to proceed along different paths in order to "play it safe," to stimulate internal competition and to "let the market decide." Though this process was at times haphazard, it was well understood and consensually agreed to as the way to get things done in the kind of dynamic marketplace that DEC found itself in.

At Ciba-Geigy, remedial action was taken locally, if possible, to minimize the upward delegation of bad news. However, if problems surfaced that were company wide, top management went through a formal period of diagnosis, often with the help of task forces and other specific processes. Once a diagnosis had been made and remedial action decided on, the decision was formally disseminated through systematic meetings, memoranda, phone calls, and other formal means, as will be illustrated in Chapter Eighteen.

At General Foods it was found that one of the most difficult remedial actions was for the product development function to stop working on a product that was not successful. If market test data showed that customers would not buy a particular product, it was assumed that they had tested the wrong population or that a minor change in the product would cure the problem. No matter what the data showed, the development team would rationalize them away and assume that sooner or later the product would sell. Management had to develop tough rules and time limits that, in effect, forced the abandonment of projects over the objections of the development team.

Corrective processes are not limited to problem areas. If a company is getting signals of success, it may decide to grow faster, or develop a careful strategy of controlled growth, or take a quick profit and risk staying small. Consensus on these matters becomes crucial to effectiveness, and the kind of consensus achieved is one of the determinants of the style of the company. Organizations that have not had periodic survival problems may not have a style of responding to such problems. However, those organizations that have had survival crises have often discovered in their responses to such crises what some of their deeper assumptions really were. In this sense an important piece of an organization's culture can be genuinely latent. No one really knows what response it will make to a severe crisis, yet the nature of that response will reflect deep elements of the culture.

For example, many organizations about to go out of business have discovered, to their surprise, high levels of motivation and commitment among their employees. One also hears the opposite kinds of stories, often from wartime, of military units that were counting on high levels of commitment only to find individuals losing their will to fight, seeking excuses to get out of combat, and even shooting their own officers in the back. Crisis situations reveal whether worker subcultures have developed around restriction of output and hiding ideas for improvement from management, or whether these subcultures support productivity goals.

In a first-generation company, crises will reveal some of the deeper assumptions of the founder, and as these become manifested the culture of the group may be elaborated around them. At one company the founder reacted to poor economic circumstances by massive layoffs of even his closest colleagues. In contrast, at another company the founder in a similar situation put everyone on part-time work and suggested that everyone take a percentage pay cut. He made it clear that he valued his people and wanted to retain as many of them as possible. "Neurotic" organizations, whose culture becomes chronically dysfunctional, often arise from a series of such crisis resolutions, which produce a systematic bias in how problems are responded to (Kets de Vries and Miller, 1984; Miller, 1990). Responses to crises thus provide opportunities for culture building and reveal aspects of the culture that have already been built. From that point of view, this area of organizational adaptation is one of the most important to analyze, understand, and, if possible, manage.

The remedial or corrective strategies that an organization employs in response to the information it gathers about its performance is an important area around which cultural assumptions form. These assumptions are likely to reveal other assumptions about mission and identity, and are likely to be closely connected to the assumptions that the organization makes about its internal functioning.

Once remedial or corrective action has been taken, new information must be gathered to determine whether results have improved or not. Sensing changes in the environment, getting the information to the right place, digesting it, and developing appropriate responses is thus a perpetual learning cycle that will ultimately characterize how a given organization maintains its effectiveness.

Summary and Conclusions

In this chapter I have reviewed how cultural assumptions evolve around all aspects of a group's relationship to its external environment. The group's ultimate mission, goals, means used to achieve goals, measurement of its performance, and remedial strategies all require consensus if the group is to perform effectively. If there is conflict between subgroups that form subcultures, such conflict can undermine group performance; however, if the environmental context is changing, such conflict can also be a potential source of adaptation and new learning. As we will see, degree of consensus is more functional in the early growth of the group and can become dysfunctional in later stages.

How these external survival issues are worked out strongly influences the internal integration of the group. Ultimately all organizations are sociotechnical systems in which the manner of external adaptation and the solution of internal integration problems are interdependent and intertwined. Although we are discussing them in serial order for purposes of exposition, in reality, of course, the external and internal processes are occurring at the same time.

The most important conclusion to be derived from this analysis is that culture is a multidimensional, multifaceted phenomenon, not easily reduced to a few major dimensions. Culture ultimately reflects the group's effort to cope and learn; it is the residue of that learning process. Culture thus not only fulfills the function of providing stability, meaning, and predictability in the present but is the result of functionally effective decisions in the group's past.

The implications for leadership are several. First, the external issues described are usually the leader's primary concern in that it is the leader who creates the group and wants it to succeed. Even if the group precedes the leader historically, it will generally put one of its members into the leadership role to worry about external boundary management, survival, and growth. Second, it is the successful management of these several functions that is usually the basis on which leaders are assessed. If they cannot create a group that succeeds, they are considered to have failed as leaders. Internal dissent can be forgiven, but if a leader fails in the external functions, he or she is usually abandoned, voted out, or gotten rid of in a more dramatic way. The steps of the coping cycle and the issues groups face thus make a useful checklist for leaders against which to assess their own performance.

6

ASSUMPTIONS ABOUT MANAGING INTERNAL INTEGRATION

If a group is to accomplish tasks that enable it to adapt to its external environment, it must be able to develop and maintain a set of internal relationships among its members. The processes that build and develop the group occur at the same time as the processes of problem solving and task accomplishment. What we ultimately find to be the culture of the group will reflect both externally and internally oriented processes. The processes that allow a group to internally integrate itself reflect the major internal issues that any group must deal with, as shown in Exhibit 6.1 and as was reviewed in Chapter Four.

Creating a Common Language and Conceptual Categories

To function as a group, the individuals who come together must establish a system of communication and a language that permits interpretation of what is going on. The human organism cannot tolerate too much uncertainty or stimulus overload. Categories of meaning that organize perceptions and thought filter out what is unimportant while focusing on what is important. Such categories not only reduce overload and anxiety but also are a necessary precondition for any coordinated action.

Two children on a see-saw not only need to be able to signal each other that they want to operate the see-saw together; they also need some verbal or nonverbal means of signaling when to push and

Exhibit 6.1. Internal Integration Issues.

- *Creating a common language and conceptual categories.* If members cannot communicate with and understand each other, a group is impossible by definition.
- *Defining group boundaries and criteria for inclusion and exclusion.* The group must be able to define itself. Who is in and who is out, and by what criteria does one determine membership?
- *Distributing power and status.* Every group must work out its pecking order, its criteria and rules for how members get, maintain, and lose power. Consensus in this area is crucial to helping members manage feelings of anxiety and aggression.
- *Developing norms of intimacy, friendship, and love.* Every group must work out its rules of the game for peer relationships, for relationships between the sexes, and for the manner in which openness and intimacy are to be handled in the context of managing the organization's tasks. Consensus in this area is crucial to help members manage feelings of affection and love.
- *Defining and allocating rewards and punishments.* Every group must know what its heroic and sinful behaviors are and must achieve consensus on what is a reward and what is a punishment.
- *Explaining the unexplainable—ideology and religion.* Every group, like every society, faces unexplainable events that must be given meaning so that members can respond to them and avoid the anxiety of dealing with the unexplainable and uncontrollable.

when to relax, or how far back to sit if their weight is different, or how fast to move. Members of a founding group coming together to create a new organization need to learn about each other's semantic space (even if they start with a common basic language, such as English) in order to determine what they mean by such abstractions as "a good product," of "high quality," produced at "low cost," to get into the "market" "as rapidly as possible."

If several members of a group are using different category systems, not only will they not agree on what to do, they will not even agree on their definition of what is real, what is a fact, when something is true or false, what is important, what needs attention, and so on. Most communication breakdowns between people result from their lack of awareness that at the outset they are making basi-

"Little Jack Horner sat in a corner, eating . . . What's a corner?"

Reprinted by permission of J. Whiting

cally different assumptions about meaning categories, as the cartoon above shows.

For example, in my role as a consultant to a small family-owned food company, I asked some managers whether they experienced any conflicts with subordinates, peers, or superiors in their daily work. Unless I happened to be talking to a particularly disgruntled person, I usually elicited an immediate and flat denial of any conflict whatsoever. This response puzzled me because I had been called in by the president to help figure out what to do about "severe conflicts" that members of the organization were perceiving and/or experiencing. I finally realized that I was assuming that the word *conflict* was a generally understood term referring to any degree of disagreement between two or more people, and that conflict was a normal human condition that is always present to some degree.

My interviewees, on the other hand, held two quite different assumptions. In their view, (1) the word *conflict* referred to a severe disagreement that is difficult if not impossible to reconcile (a different semantic interpretation of the word itself), and (2) conflict was bad in the sense that a person who has conflicts is not managing well. Once I realized that different semantic assumptions were at the root of the communication problem, I could change my request to "Tell me about the things that make it easy or hard for you to get your job done." If any evidence of interpersonal disagreements began to surface, I made explicit my own assumption that such disagreements were, in my view, completely normal in organizations. I then often got vivid and detailed stories of severe conflicts and, in subsequent discussions, found that I could use the word *conflict* itself without further misunderstanding or defensiveness. In this example, my clients and I were building a common language for our own work.

In this same organization, I observed in group meetings that the president often got angry with a member who was not contributing actively and he began to draw conclusions about the competence of that member. The president assumed (as I learned later by asking about the situation) that the silence meant ignorance, incompetence, or lack of motivation. The silent member, it turned out, was usually ready to make a presentation and was very frustrated because he was never called on to give it. He assumed that he was not supposed to volunteer, and he began to believe that his boss did not value him because he was not called on. If their different assumptions about the meaning of silence were not brought into the open, the danger was that both would validate their own incorrect assumption, thus setting up a classic case of a self-fulfilling prophecy. In this group the absence of a consensually validated communication system undermined effective action. A total group culture had not yet formed, though various subgroups might already have been operating on shared assumptions, such as "Our boss does not value our contributions."

It is often the creators of groups who build the common category system. For example, the founder of a small high-technology company whose own sense of his mission was to give the world a cheaper yet technically better product had to teach his engineers how to design an optimal level of elegance and quality into the product. He had to point out in detail what they should look for and pay special attention to among the myriad details involved in design; how to analyze customer responses; how to think about costs; and how to react to feedback from manufacturing and marketing. One might label such teaching as getting across certain values, but in fact the process went much deeper than that. The values were embedded in the conceptual categories themselves, and what was being taught was really a category system, along with the values embedded in the rules of how to respond.

Critical conceptual categories are usually built into the basic language a group uses. Thus, English speakers learn through English words the major cultural categories of the Anglo-Saxon cultural tradition. For example, the word *management* reflects the proactive, optimistic, pragmatic approach that characterizes the U.S. culture. It is a surprise to many people who speak only English that a comparable word does not exist in other languages, such as German. Even more important, if the word does not exist, the concept also may not exist in the same sense. For example, in German there are words for leadership, leading, and directing; but *managing,* as English speakers mean it, does not readily translate either as a word or as a concept.

Because new groups always emerge from a host culture, it is often difficult to distinguish what is culturally new in a new group. Does the new company simply reflect its members' culture of origin? The founders will, of course, bring their own prior cultural assumptions to the new situation. But as the new group begins to experience its own issues of survival and growth and begins to develop its own history, it will develop, in addition, its own language and conceptual categories that refine and elaborate on the basic language.

In summary, a common language and common conceptual categories are clearly necessary for any other kind of consensus to be established and for any communication to occur at all. This common understanding begins with the categories of action, gesture, and speech that are often provided by the person who brought the group together or by the more active members of the group once it is together. Because the members are usually all from the same host culture, a common language is initially available. However, as the group matures, it invests common words with special meanings, and the assumptions of what certain words really mean ultimately become one of the deepest layers of that group's culture.

Defining Group Boundaries and Identity

If a group is to function and develop, one of the most important areas for clear consensus is the perception of who is in the new group and who is out (or not in), and the criteria by which inclusionary decisions are made. New members cannot really function and concentrate on their primary task if they are insecure about their membership, and the group cannot really maintain a good sense of itself if it does not have a way of defining itself and its boundaries.

Initially, the criteria for inclusion are usually set by the leader, founder, or convener, but as the group members interact, those criteria are tested and a group consensus arises around the criteria that survive the test. In a young company, there is often intense debate over who should be an owner or a partner, who should have stock options, who should be hired for key functions or be an officer, and who should be ejected because he or she does not fit in. In this debate, real personnel decisions are being made, and at the same time the criteria of inclusion are themselves being forged, tested, and articulated so that they become clear to everyone. Such debate also provides opportunities for testing mission statements, goal clarity, and means clarity, illustrating how several cultural elements are simultaneously being created, tested, articulated, and reinforced.

One way of determining a group's core assumptions is to ask present members what they really look for in new members and to examine carefully the career histories of present members in order to detect what accounts for their inclusion in the group. For example, when one inquired about DEC's hiring process, the answer was that every potential new member of the technical or managerial staff had to be interviewed by at least five to ten people, and only if that individual was acceptable to the entire set was he or she offered a job. If one asked what the interviewers looked for, one found that intelligence, self-reliance, the ability to articulate clearly, tolerance for ambiguity, and high motivation were all central criteria used in selection, though most of them operated implicitly. What interviewers tended to say when they were questioned was more vague: "We want someone who will fit in."

Once DEC hired people, they were provisionally accepted as permanent members. If they failed in an initial job assignment, the assumption was that they were competent but had been put in the wrong job. In other words, once a person was "in," it was difficult to lose that status. In an economic crisis, the company tended to slow down its rate of hiring but was typically reluctant to lay off anybody. And when pressures for staff reduction mounted, the organization redefined layoffs as "transitions" in which employees were given a great deal of latitude and choice.

It was important to preserve the assumption that no one is so bad that he or she deserves to be laid off, but that economic and technological changes can create conditions in which it is in the person's own best interest to make a transition to a new job inside the company, if it is available, or to another company. As pressures to improve efficiency by cutting many more people arose in the late 1980s and early 1990s, conflicts arose between subgroups that believed that growth would be sufficient to absorb the excess people and subgroups that had come to believe that a more fundamental reorganization around fewer people was essential. Ken Olsen felt strongly that DEC was still a family that should not eject its own children and that layoffs were the wrong way to deal with excess costs and inefficiencies. In the end the board forced the issue, first by insisting that more layoffs be made and finally by forcing Ken Olsen to resign.

At Ciba-Geigy prior education was a key criterion for membership. Most of the young technical and managerial staff members came from a scientific background, highlighting the assumption that if one is to succeed in the company, one must understand the scientific base on which it was built. Having an advanced degree, such as a doctorate, was a distinct advantage even if one was being hired into a marketing or managerial job.

Both DEC and Ciba-Geigy had difficulty hiring and absorbing what they called MBAs, by which they meant all-purpose generalists who do not have a solid technical or scientific background and who might be more concerned with personal ambition than contributing to the technical work of the organization. Behind these perceptions lay the further assumption (at both of these companies) that general management, though necessary, was not the key to success. Scientific and technical know-how was essential. These assumptions had a powerful impact on DEC's ability to develop in different directions and to divisionalize, because there was always a shortage of experienced general managers.

Who is in and who is out not only applies to the initial hiring decision but continues to have important symbolic meaning as one progresses in the group. One of the immediate consequences of defining who is in and who is out is that differential treatment rules begin to be applied. Insiders get special benefits, are trusted more, get higher basic rewards, and most important, get a sense of identity from belonging to a defined organization. Outsiders not only get fewer of the various benefits and rewards but, more important, lose specific identity. They become part of a mass that is simply labeled "outsiders" and they are more likely to be stereotyped and treated with indifference or hostility.

Organizations can be thought of, then, as involving three dimensions of career movement: (1) lateral movement from one task or function to another, (2) vertical movement from one rank to another, and (3) inclusionary movement from outsider to insider (Schein, 1978, 1987b). Consensus forms around criteria not only for promotion but also for inclusionary movement. As one moves farther "in," one becomes privy to some of the more secret assumptions of the group. One learns the special meanings attached to certain words and the special rituals that define membership—such as the secret fraternity handshake—and one discovers that one of the most important bases for status in the group is to be entrusted with group secrets. Such secrets involve historical accounts of how and why some of the things in the past really happened, who is really part of the dominant coalition or insider group, and what some of the latent functions of the organization are. At Ciba-Geigy there was in senior management a "Basel aristocracy"—board members or senior executives who were in their jobs by virtue of their social position as well as their technical excellence—but you had to be a real insider to know who they were.

As organizations age and become more complex, the problem of defining clear external and inclusionary internal boundaries becomes more complex. More people—such as salespeople, purchasing agents, distributors, franchisees, board members, and consultants—come to occupy boundary-spanning roles. In some industries economic circumstances have made it necessary for companies to reduce the size of their work force, causing an increase in the hiring of temporaries or contract workers, who can be laid off more easily if necessary. Cultural assumptions then come into bold relief when certain questions are raised from a policy perspective: what is a temporary, for how long can one keep people in that status, to what benefits if any are they entitled, how does one train them quickly in the essentials of the culture, and how does one deal with the threat that temporaries pose to more permanent members of the organization (Kunda, 1992)?

In a complex society, individuals belong to many organizations, so their identity is not tied up exclusively with any one organization. Locating and defining what a given cultural unit is then becomes more difficult because a given organization may really be a complex set of overlapping subcultures (Louis, 1983). But consensus on criteria for membership is always one means of determining whether a cultural unit exists in any given group, and seeking such consensus will always be a preoccupation of any given group in order to differentiate itself from other groups. A set of communication rules—the meaning of acronyms and special jargon developed within the culture—is one of the clearest ways that a group speci-fies who is *us* and who is *them*. Wearing special badges or uniforms is, of course, another obvious means of showing identity.

From the point of view of the individual moving through the organization during her or his career, frequent rotational movement from one functional or geographic group to another can result in a failure to absorb any of the deeper assumptions operating in any of the groups. The person may continue to feel marginal and experi-ence intrapsychic conflict if the assumptions of different groups are different. This suggests that if an individual is to be socialized into a complex multi-unit organization, each assignment must be long enough for that individual to absorb some key assumptions, but not so long as to cause oversocialization into any one subculture.

In summary, defining the criteria for deciding who is in and who is out of an organization or any of its subunits is one of the best ways to begin to analyze a culture. Moreover, the very process by which a group makes those judgments and acts on them is a process of culture formation that forces some integration of the external survival issues and the internal integration issues being discussed in this chapter.

Distributing Power and Status

A critical issue in any new group is how influence, power, and au-thority will be allocated. The process of stratification in human sys-tems is typically not as blatant as the dominance-establishing rituals of animal societies, but it is functionally equivalent in that it con-cerns the evolution of workable rules for managing aggression and mastery needs. Human societies develop pecking orders just as chickens do, but both the process and the outcome are, of course, far more complex and varied.

DEC and Ciba-Geigy differed dramatically in their methods of allocating power and channeling aggression. At DEC, power was derived from personal success and the building of a network of sup-port. Formal rank, seniority, and job description had relatively less influence than personal characteristics and track record. Personal characteristics such as the ability to negotiate, to convince, and to be proved right by circumstance were emphasized. The formal system of status was deliberately de-emphasized in favor of an assumption that everyone has a right to participate, to voice an opinion, and to be heard, because it was assumed that good ideas can come from anyone. As previously mentioned, however, because no one was considered smart enough to evaluate the quality of his or her own idea, one always had to get buy-in if others were involved in the implementation of that idea, and anyone had a right and obligation to challenge it. Aggression was thus channeled into the daily working routines but directed at ideas, not people. The further assumption—that once one was in the organization, one was a member of "the family" and could not really lose membership—protected people from feeling personally threatened if their ideas were challenged.

Ciba-Geigy, in contrast, had a very formal system of allocating power: a system based on personal background, educational credentials, seniority, loyalty, and successful performance of whatever jobs were allocated to the person by higher authority. After a certain number of years, an employee acquired a rank similar to the kind of rank one acquires with promotion in military service or the civil service, and this rank was independent of particular job assignments. Status and privileges went with this rank and could not be lost even if the employee was given reduced job responsibilities. The working climate emphasized politeness, formality, and reason. Displays of aggression were taboo, but behind-the-scenes complaining, badmouthing, and politicking were the inevitable consequences of suppressing overt aggression.

Both organizations could be labeled paternalistic from some points of view in that they generated strong family feelings and a degree of emotional dependence on leaders or formal authorities. However, the drastic difference in how the rules of power allocation actually worked in these two organizations serves to remind us how vague and potentially unhelpful broad labels such as *autocratic* or *paternalistic* are in characterizing particular organizational cultures.

One should also note once again the tight interrelationship between the external issues of mission and task, on the one hand, and the internal issues of power distribution, on the other hand. The kind of technology and task involved in each organization had a direct effect on the kind of power distribution that eventually arose. The more autocratic assumptions of the science of chemistry and the more egalitarian assumptions of the engineering community of an emerging technology could be seen as powerful influences through the assumptions brought into the organizations by the founders and new members.

To understand how an authority system works requires one to be sensitive to the nuances of language, as illustrated by my experience in a meeting at a British oil company in the 1980s. I was asked by the incumbent chairman to attend the three-day meeting of all of the senior managers from around the world, observe the culture in action, and facilitate a discussion of the culture during the third day. It developed that at this meeting a major structural change was to be discussed. Whereas previously countries had been fairly autonomous in managing all product lines, in the new organization worldwide business units would be created for each major product line and these would be managed from London. This change meant that the country managers would lose a great deal of autonomy and power, while the headquarters and business units would gain power.

Most of the meeting was devoted to the present chairman's efforts to help the country managers to accept their new role as more of a "diplomat" locally and less of a business unit manager. My observation was that the chairman handled their disappointment and obvious resentment in a most gentle and kindly manner, while reaffirming repeatedly the new reality of their positions. It came across as gently giving the disempowered country managers some advice on how their roles might be restructured in the future. When I reported these observations to my client, the incumbent chairman, he burst out laughing and said: "Ed, what you have just witnessed in that meeting was the worst bloodbath we have ever had; I have never seen our chairman more aggressive in putting down people and asserting the new power structure." So much for my understanding of the British culture and the culture of this company!

Sociologists have shown very convincingly how manners and morals, politeness and tact are not niceties of social life, but essential rules for how to keep from destroying each other socially (Goffman, 1959, 1967). Our functioning as human beings requires us to develop not only a self-image of who we are, but also a degree of self-esteem—a sense that we have enough value to continue to function. That self-esteem is based on others' accepting the claims we make for ourselves. When we tell a joke, others laugh no matter how unfunny the joke; when someone breaks wind in public we pretend not to have noticed no matter how loud the sound. In other words, human society of any sort hinges on the cultural agreements to try to uphold each others' identities and illusions, even if that means lying. We compliment people to make them feel good even if we don't believe it; we teach little children not to say "Look at that fat lady over there," even though an obese person is clearly visible.

One reason why performance appraisal in organizations is emotionally resisted so strongly is that managers know full well they are violating the larger cultural rules and norms when they sit a subordinate down to give him or her "feedback." To put it bluntly, when we tell a person what we really think of them in an aggressive way, this is functionally equivalent to social murder. Someone who goes around doing this is viewed as unsafe to have around, and if the behavior persists we often declare such a person mentally ill and lock them up. In his analysis of mental hospitals, Goffman showed brilliantly how "therapy" was in many cases teaching the patients the rules of polite society so that they could be let free to function in that society without making *others* too anxious (Goffman, 1961).

To conclude, every group, organization, and occupation develops norms around the distribution of influence, authority, and power. If those norms work in the sense of providing a system that gets external tasks done and leaves members in the group reasonably free of anxiety, the norms gradually become shared tacit assumptions and critical genetic elements in the cultural DNA.

Developing Rules for
Intimacy, Friendship, and Love

Every new group must decide simultaneously how to deal with authority problems and how to establish workable peer relationships. Authority issues derive ultimately from the necessity of dealing with feelings of aggression; peer relationship and intimacy problems derive ultimately from the necessity of dealing with feelings of affection, love, and sexuality. Thus, societies develop clear sex roles, kinship systems, and rules for friendship and sexual conduct that serve to stabilize current relationships while ensuring procreation mechanisms and thereby the survival of the society.

For the new group or organization, the deeper issues of sex and procreation are typically irrelevant unless we are talking about a family firm that is specifically concerned with keeping succession in the family. Then who marries whom and which children come into the firm are indeed major problems, and the emerging norms of the organization will reflect the assumptions of the founding family about succession (Beckhard and Dyer, 1983a, 1983b; Dyer, 1986). Recall Cook's (1992) finding that the role of chief taster in the French brandy company could only pass to another male, so the succession went to a nephew instead of a daughter.

One of the most salient features of family firms is that certain levels of intimacy and trust appear to be reserved for family members, creating a kind of dual intimacy system in the organization. At Steinbergs, a large Canadian supermarket chain (to be described in greater detail in Chapter Twelve), the founder hired another person who became virtually a partner in all business affairs, but the owner would never allow this person to own any voting stock. The two were very intimate in all business relations and were close friends, but ownership had a special meaning to the founder and could only be shared with blood relatives.

As Freud pointed out long ago, one of the models we bring to any new group situation is our own model of family, the group in which we spent most of our early life. Thus, the rules that we learned from our own parents for dealing with them and with our siblings are often our initial model for dealing with authority and peer relationships in a new group. Because the different members of a new group are likely to have had widely varying experiences in their families of origin, they may start with very different models of what those relationships should be, leading to potential disagreement and conflict over the right way to relate to others in the new group.

If the group's founder is a very dominant person with a very clear model of how these relationships should function, he or she may, over time, be able to impose that model on the other new members (Kets de Vries and Miller, 1984, 1987). Yet even with a strong founder, the outcome is, in the end, a negotiated one, and the norms that gradually evolve in the group will reflect the initial underlying assumptions of a number of the influential members as well as the group's actual experiences.

Relationships within DEC were paradoxical. On the one hand, "pushing back, doing the right thing, and getting buy-in" made the environment extremely individualistic and competitive. On the other hand, the repeated shared experience of building consensus before leaping into action created a high degree of personal intimacy. The many off-site meetings that involved roughing it together in the woods for several days at a time brought DEC groups into much more intimate contact, reflecting the family feeling previously referred to.

Teamwork at DEC was strongly espoused, but the meaning of the concept was unique to Digital in that being a good team player meant pushing back even if that disrupted meetings and slowed projects down. This assumption was the opposite of the Hewlett-Packard assumption that being a good team player meant going along with where the group seemed to want to go, not objecting too much. An insightful internal organization consultant told me recently that he had finally achieved some insight into what kind of a team DEC was. He said it was "a track team or a gymnastics team in which you want the total score to be high, but you get the score by a lot of superior individual efforts."

At Ciba-Geigy, relationships were much more aloof and formal, reflecting the larger culture in which Ciba-Geigy was embedded and the personalities of most of the current leaders of the group. However, Ciba-Geigy formalized informality and closeness by a particular ritual that occurred at each annual management meeting of the top forty or fifty people. One afternoon and evening of the three-day meeting were always devoted to an event that was planned by the meeting organizer but kept secret until the group actually boarded buses. The event always involved some sport at which everyone would be relatively incompetent and would therefore look foolish in everyone else's eyes, for example shooting an old-style cross-bow. Rank and status were thus deliberately equilibrated and a level of kidding and teasing replaced the workaday formality. Following the sports event, everyone went to an informal dinner at which humorous speeches were given, laced with more teasing and jibes at each other. With the consumption of much alcohol, people really let their hair down and interacted in a way that would never have been possible at work. The secrecy surrounding what would be done each year heightened the emotionality associated with the event and made the ritual comparable to a group of children anticipating what their Christmas gifts would be. One could almost say that in this organization intimacy was achieved through periodic regression rituals.

A similar point is made about the role of the after-hours meetings, including much drinking, common at Japanese companies. Formal relations in Japan, especially across authority lines, have to preserve face, but this prevents certain kinds of necessary feedback to the boss. By getting drunk together (faking inebriation is not allowed) they create a climate in which subordinates can say things to the boss that would ordinarily be much too face-threatening.

Allocating Rewards and Punishment

Every group must develop a system of sanctions for obeying or disobeying its norms and rules. There must evolve some consensus on what symbolically and actually is defined as a reward or punishment and on the manner in which it is to be administered. The shared assumptions concerning this issue constitute some of the most important elements of an emerging culture in a new organization. Change in the reward and punishment system is also one of the quickest and easiest ways to begin to change some elements of the culture.

At General Foods the norm developed that a product manager who did his job competently could expect to be moved to a bigger and better product within approximately eighteen months. Managers who did not move every eighteen months began to feel that they were failing. By way of contrast, in the early years of DEC the assumption developed that the designer of a product should see it through from cradle to grave, so a reward was defined as being allowed to stay with one's product through manufacturing and marketing all the way to sales. Being pulled off a project would have been perceived as a punishment.

At General Foods, promotion to a higher rank also correlated with all kinds of perquisites, notably a more spacious office in a better location with better furniture, higher-quality carpeting and higher-quality art on the walls. All this was drawn from a central supply of these "status resources" very carefully allocated to each rank level. The headquarters building was designed to have movable walls so that office size could be quickly adjusted as promotions and job reassignments required. By contrast, at DEC if a manager used promotion as an excuse for getting a bigger house or better car, senior management began to distrust him as being more concerned about personal welfare than company performance.

At Ciba-Geigy the key short-run rewards were the personal approval of senior management and public recognition in the company newspaper. Longer-range rewards were promotion to a higher rank or movement to a clearly more important job assignment. Length of assignment to a given job could mean that the person was either dead-ended or doing such a good job that he or she was irreplaceable. DEC used bonuses, stock options, and raises as signals of good performance, whereas Ciba-Geigy relied much more heavily on symbolic nonmonetary rewards such as special privileges like attendance at a scientific meeting. Salary was tied more to rank and length of service.

Punishments, like rewards, will have local meanings in different organizations. At several high-tech companies that have clear espoused values about not laying people off, people can lose the particular task they are working on and become "boat people" or "wander the halls" while looking for another job within the organization. They will be carried on the payroll indefinitely, but it is clear that they have been punished. Often the signals are subtle, but colleagues know when someone is in the "doghouse" or in the "penalty box." Actual loss of bonuses or the failure to get a raise may follow, but the initial punishment is clear enough already.

In fact, for newcomers in organizations, deciphering when one has been rewarded and when one has been punished is one of the most difficult tasks because the signals are so often ambiguous from an outsider's point of view. Being yelled at by the boss may be a reward, being ignored may be a punishment, and only someone farther along in the understanding of the culture can reassure the yelled-at newcomer that she or he is, in fact, doing well. At many companies, teamwork is espoused as a major characteristic of how work gets done, but only after some time does a newcomer learn what teamwork means at a given company. Being open and confrontational in meetings can be rewarded or punished, depending on such meanings.

One dramatic example was revealed in a cultural analysis of Amoco some years before it was acquired by British Petroleum. Amoco's managers and engineers called it a "blaming culture" in which the norm was that if something went wrong on a project, one had to identify who was responsible as quickly as possible. *Who* was more important than *why*, but the really destructive aspect was that the person who was blamed was not necessarily punished in any overt way, and often was not even told that others considered him or her responsible. Instead, it was noted in the memory of senior managers as a reason to be less trustful of this person, leading to career limitation. People who were not given good assignments or promotions might never find out just why they were not. Consequently, it was viewed as essential to distance oneself as quickly as possible from any project that might fail, lest one be blamed for the failure. This belief prevented Amoco from engaging in a joint venture with another company, because if a project failed, any of their employees on the project felt vulnerable, even if it was clear that the failure was due to people in the other company.

The system of rewards and punishments usually reflects and is correlated with other important cultural themes. For example, acquired rewards can be treated as acquired social "property" and serve as a basis for increased status and power. Thus, just as a bonus or a stock option can be translated into acquired material property, approval on the part of the boss or a formal promotion can be translated into social property or status. Rewards and punishments from more senior or higher-status members of the organization are the key signals by which the person measures his or her progress along the inclusionary dimension. Being told company secrets is a major reward; being frozen out by *not* being told can be a major punishment that signals ultimate excommunication. Being no longer in the loop is a clear signal that one has done something wrong.

The reward system, viewed as a dynamic process, usually has both short- and long-range implications. Many of the short-range aspects concern the organization's performance in its defined external environment—getting a product out, reducing inventory, cutting costs, and so on. When studying the culture of an organization, one must investigate the reward and punishment system because it reveals fairly quickly some of the important rules and underlying assumptions in that culture. Once one has identified what kinds of behavior are considered "heroic" and what kinds of behavior are "sinful," one can begin to infer the assumptions that lie behind those evaluations.

Managing the Unmanageable
and Explaining the Unexplainable

Every group inevitably faces some issues not under its control, events that are intrinsically mysterious and unpredictable and hence frightening. At the physical level, such events as natural disasters and the weather require explanation. At the biological level, such events as birth, growth, puberty, illness, and death require one to have a theory of what is happening and why.

In a culture heavily committed to reason and science, there is a tendency to treat everything as explainable; the mysterious is only as yet unexplained. But until science has demystified an event that we cannot control or understand, we need an alternative basis for putting what has happened into a meaningful context. Religious beliefs can provide such a context and can also offer justification for events that might otherwise seem unfair and meaningless. Superstitions explain the unexplainable and provide guidelines for what to do in ambiguous, uncertain, and threatening situations. Those guidelines usually specify and reinforce what is considered heroic and what is considered sinful, thus creating an "ideology" that ties together into a coherent whole the various deeper assumptions of the culture (see Chapter Seven).

Ideology often contains various myths of origin and stories of heroic behavior, thus articulating and illustrating some of the overarching values that can serve as a prescription for action in ambiguous situations. In a society that is dominated by religion, ideology merges with religion. The more the society is based on reason, logic, and science, the more ideology has a secular base and comes to be clearly distinguishable from religion.

The organizational equivalent of this general cultural process tends to occur around critical events in the organization's history, especially ones that are difficult to explain or justify because they were not under organizational control. Organizations are capable of developing the equivalent of religion and/or ideology on the basis of the manner in which such critical events were managed. Myths and stories develop around the founding of the company, times when the company had particular difficulty surviving or an unusual growth spurt, times when a challenge to core assumptions brought about a fresh articulation of those assumptions, and times of transformation and change.

For example, certain individual contributors and managers at DEC were associated with getting the company out of trouble whenever a severe crisis occurred. Certain processes were viewed almost superstitiously as "the way" to get out of trouble. One such process was to bring together a task force under the leadership of one of these heroic managers and give that task force complete freedom for a period of time to work on the problem. Sometimes consultants are brought into organizations with the same kind of faith that something constructive will happen as a result of the presence of the outsider.

In a study of the introduction of computerized tomography into hospital radiology departments, Barley (1984a, 1984b) observed that if the computer went down at an awkward time, such as when a patient was in the middle of a scan, the technicians tried all kinds of remedial measures, including the proverbial kicking of the machine. If the computer resumed operating, as it did occasionally, the technician carefully documented what he or she had just done and passed on this "knowledge" to colleagues, even though there was no technical or logical basis for it. In a real sense, this was superstitious behavior, even in a realm in which logical explanation was possible.

Stories and myths about how the organization dealt with key competitors in the past, how it survived a downturn in the economy, how it developed a new and exciting product, how it dealt with a valued employee, and so on not only spell out the basic mission and specific goals (and thereby reaffirm them) but also reaffirm the organization's picture of itself, its own theory of how to get things done and how to handle internal relationships (Dandridge, Mitroff, and Joyce, 1980; Koprowski, 1983; Martin, 1982; Mitroff and Kilmann, 1975, 1976; Ouchi, 1981; Pettigrew, 1979; Wilkins, 1983).

For example, a story widely circulated about Hewlett-Packard is that during a severe recession no one was laid off because management and hourly people alike were willing to work shorter hours for less pay, thus enabling the company to cut its costs without cutting people. The lesson to be derived is the affirmation of strong values around people (Ouchi, 1981). A similar story is told at DEC about the "rehabilitation" of a key engineer who was associated with several important projects, all of which failed. Instead of firing him, the company—reaffirming its core assumption that if someone fails, it is because he or she is mismatched with the job—found an assignment for him in which he could succeed and once again become a hero. Buried in this story is also the assumption that individuals count and any person whom the company has hired is by definition competent.

A story from DEC's early history concerns an engineer who was sent to the West Coast to repair some equipment. He caught the midnight plane but did not have time to pack any clothing. The work took a week, requiring the engineer to buy clothing, which he duly charged to the company. When the accounting department refused to approve the charge, the engineer threatened to quit. Ken Olsen heard about this and severely punished the accounting department, thereby reaffirming the company's dedication to technical values and to its highly motivated technical employees.

An organization's ideology in this context can be any of several things. Sometimes it is the conscious component of the total set of assumptions that make up the culture. Sometimes it is a set of rationalizations for essentially unexplained or superstitious behavior. Sometimes ideology reflects ideals and future aspirations as well as current realities and thereby functions as a guide and incentive system for members. Ideologies often involve statements about the core mission, the goals, the preferred means for accomplishing them, and the preferred set of relationships among organizational members.

Ideologies often are partially stated in formal company documents as the organization's key values. They are likely to be embodied in company charters, annual reports, and orientation and training materials, but in this form they are often merely a list of espoused values and may not even make up a coherent ideology. Only when there are stories supporting the values and when the underlying assumptions behind the values are articulated can one determine what the substance of the ideology really is.

Through stories, parables, and other forms of oral or written history, an organization can communicate its ideology and basic assumptions—especially to newcomers, who need to know what is important not only in abstract terms but by means of concrete examples that can be emulated. Even in this domain, however, the point of a story or parable may not be clear until insiders in the culture explain the meaning to the newcomer. Published ideologies and philosophies are, therefore, little more than cultural artifacts that are easy to see but hard to decipher.

Summary and Conclusions

Every group must learn how to become a group. The process is not automatic; in fact, it is complex and multifaceted. Humans, being what they are, must deal with a finite and describable set of issues in any new group situation. At the most basic level they must develop a common language and category system that clearly define what things mean. Formal languages do not specify with enough precision what *work, teamwork, respect, quality,* and so on mean. Groups must reach consensus on the boundaries of the group, who is in and who is not in. They must develop consensus on how to distribute influence and power so that aggression can be constructively channeled and formal status accurately determined. They must develop rules that define peer relationships and intimacy so that love and affection can be appropriately channeled.

Groups must develop clear assumptions about what is a reward and what is a punishment so that group members can decipher how they are doing. And finally, groups must develop explanations that help members deal with unpredictable and unexplainable events— the functional equivalents of religion, mythology, and ideology.

The assumptions that develop around these issues constitute— along with the assumptions about mission, goals, means, results detection, and correction mechanisms—a set of dimensions along which one can study and describe a culture. These are not necessarily the only dimensions one could use, but they have the advantage of being tied to a large body of research on groups and they permit one to begin to get a sense of the dynamics of culture—how cultural assumptions begin and evolve. They also represent a conceptual grid into which one can sort the cultural data that one observes.

Ultimately, what makes it possible for people to function comfortably with each other and to concentrate on their primary task is a high degree of consensus on the management of the issues discussed in this chapter. If internal issues are not settled, if people are preoccupied with their position and identity, if they are insecure, if they do not know the rules of the game and therefore cannot predict or understand what is going on, they cannot concentrate on the important survival issues the group may face. On the other hand, the confrontation of survival issues most often is the critical stimulus that creates rapid consensus around the internal integration issues.

The internal integration and external adaptation issues are thus interdependent. The environment sets limits on what the organization can do, but within those limits not all solutions will work equally well. Feasible solutions are also limited by the characteristics of the members of the group. The culture that eventually evolves in a particular organization is thus a complex outcome of external pressures, internal potentials, responses to critical events, and, probably to some unknown degree, chance factors that could not be predicted from a knowledge of either the environment or the members. I have tried to identify the common issues that every new group faces, recognizing that the manner in which those issues are dealt with will result in a unique outcome.

Leadership comes into play once again as the original source of ideas or the original behavioral models that are then tested against the internal and external environments. Norms, rules, languages, reward systems, and so on do not come out of thin air; nor is it sufficient to say, as some sociologists argue, that such things are enacted by and result from the interaction of members. This is true but insufficient by itself. In any group situation, some members will be more active than others and will propose verbally or by example how things should be. These acts of leadership can come from different members at different times, but they are always there in some form. As we will see in later chapters, leader behavior by group founders plays a major role in how the group evolves. In the meantime, the culture categories identified so far can again serve as a kind of checklist to enable leaders to assess their own behavior.

7

DEEPER CULTURAL ASSUMPTIONS
ABOUT REALITY AND TRUTH

As groups and organizations evolve, the assumptions they develop about external adaptation and internal integration reflect deeper assumptions about more abstract general issues around which humans need consensus in order to have any kind of society at all. If we cannot agree on what is real, how to determine the truth or falsity of something, how to measure time, how space is allocated, what human nature is, and how people should get along with each other, society is not possible in the first place.

But different societies have evolved different answers to these questions; hence we have many different cultures in the world, and these broader cultures influence how groups and organizations within them will evolve. Thus individualistic competitive behavior would be taken for granted in a U.S. company, just as teamwork would be taken for granted in a Japanese company. It is when one examines the formation of groups that are initially multinational, such as cross-national mergers like that of Daimler-Benz and Chrysler or joint ventures between companies from different countries, that one sees how disagreement on this higher level of abstraction can make group formation and performance extremely difficult.

The dimensions to be reviewed in this and the chapters that follow are based on concepts originally developed by the sociologist Talcott Parsons (1951) and were evolved into a set of value dimensions by Kluckhohn and Strodtbeck (1961) in order to do their classic comparative study of four cultures in the U.S. Southwest— Anglo, Hispanic, Mormon, and Navajo. To varying degrees these dimensions overlap others, such as those promoted by Hofstede

(2001, first published 1980), Hampden-Turner and Trompenaars (1993, 2000) and others, but I have also added to and elaborated on them, based on my own experience in different countries. The dimensions I will review are shown in Exhibit 7.1.

These deeper dimensions clearly will influence how external adaptation and internal integration issues are handled; thus, they relate directly to those previously discussed dimensions. For exam-

Exhibit 7.1. Deeper Dimensions Around Which Shared Basic Underlying Assumptions Form.

- *The Nature of Reality and Truth.* The shared assumptions that define what is real and what is not, what is a fact in the physical realm and the social realm, how truth is ultimately to be determined, and whether truth is revealed or discovered.

- *The Nature of Time.* The shared assumptions that define the basic concept of time in the group, how time is defined and measured, how many kinds of time there are, and the importance of time in the culture.

- *The Nature of Space.* The shared assumptions about space and its distribution, how space is allocated, the symbolic meaning of space around the person, and the role of space in defining aspects of relationships such as degree of intimacy or definitions of privacy.

- *The Nature of Human Nature.* The shared assumptions that define what it means to be human and what human attributes are considered intrinsic or ultimate. Is human nature good, evil, or neutral? Are human beings perfectible or not?

- *The Nature of Human Activity.* The shared assumptions that define what is the right thing for human beings to do in relating to their environment on the basis of the above assumptions about reality and the nature of human nature. In one's basic orientation to life, what is the appropriate level of activity or passivity? At the organizational level, what is the relationship of the organization to its environment?

- *The Nature of Human Relationships.* The shared assumptions that define what is ultimately the right way for people to relate to each other, to distribute power and love. Is life cooperative or competitive; individualistic, group-collaborative, or communal? What is the appropriate psychological contract between employers and employees? Is authority ultimately based on traditional lineal authority, moral consensus, law, or charisma? What are the basic assumptions about how conflict should be resolved and how decisions should be made?

ple, organizational missions, primary tasks, and goals reflect basic assumptions about the nature of human activity and the ultimate relationship between the organization and its environment. The means chosen to achieve the goals will reflect assumptions about truth, time, space, and human relationships in the sense that the kind of organization that is designed will automatically reflect those deeper assumptions. Similarly, the measurement system and assumptions about how to take corrective action will reflect assumptions about the nature of truth and the appropriate psychological contract for employees.

The internal integration issues also tie in closely with these more abstract categories. Language and conceptual systems certainly reflect directly some of the fundamental assumptions about time, space, and truth. Status systems, reward systems, and rules for intimacy and for the channeling of aggression all reflect deeper assumptions about the nature of human nature, human activity, and human relationships. The kinds of ideologies that organizations evolve can certainly be seen as directly connected to deeper assumptions about truth, time, and space and, especially, about human nature.

When any new group forms, its members will bring with them cultural assumptions at this deeper level. If the members of the group come from different ethnic or occupational cultures, they are likely to have different assumptions on this level. These differences will cause initial difficulty in the group's efforts to work and to make life safe for itself. As members get to know each other, they will gradually develop some common assumptions at this fundamental level, and such new assumptions may, in the end, differ somewhat from any given member's original assumptions. As we will see, however, some data on joint ventures between parent companies from different countries show that sometimes the new group forms because one culture comes to dominate the other, or a new group fails to form because neither set of cultural assumptions gives way (Salk, 1997).

An example from DEC will make some aspects of this dynamic clear. DEC's French subsidiary was managed by an American who knew the DEC culture very well and implemented it. He hired a young Parisian to be the manager of human resources and told him,

"Define your own job; figure out how you can best help," which was the typical DEC way. When I talked to this personnel manager about a year after he had been hired, he said that the first six months were absolutely traumatic because he had been brought up in the best French tradition of expecting a strong boss who would tell a subordinate what to do. The manager kept searching for guidance and for someone to lean on, but he found neither.

As he tells the story, one day he finally decided to take some initiative and try out some of his own ideas. He found immediate support and positive reinforcement for this behavior. So he took some further initiatives and again found that he was encouraged by his boss and peers. He was learning how to work at DEC, but in describing this socialization process, he said, "I had to give up my 'Frenchness' to work in this company. I like it, but I don't think I could ever work in a traditional French company after this experience." Other DEC alumni confirm that the DEC culture was so unusual that once one had learned to work in it, one probably could not work in any other company again! The DEC culture ended up modifying some of the assumptions this man had brought with him from his culture of origin.

Because of the ultimate importance of these assumptions, we must understand them at some level of detail so that we can compare organizations and subunits within them and also begin to compare national and ethnic cultures on a broader scale. In the remainder of this chapter we will take up the first three dimensions, those dealing with reality and truth, time, and space; in Chapters Eight and Nine we will examine the other three dimensions—those dealing with human nature, human activity, and human relationships.

Shared Assumptions About the Nature of Reality and Truth

A fundamental part of every culture is a set of assumptions about what is real and how one determines or discovers what is real. Such assumptions tell members of a group how to determine what is relevant information, how to interpret information, and how to determine when they have enough of it to decide whether or not to act, and what action to take?

For example, as I have already pointed out several times, at DEC reality and truth were defined by debate and by pragmatic criteria of whether things work. If an objective test was impossible or too difficult to construct, the idea was debated to see whether it stood the test of being subjected to severe critical analysis. At Ciba-Geigy much more emphasis was given to research results from the laboratory and to the opinions of those considered wise and experienced. Both companies existed in broader Western cultures dominated by concepts of science and rationally based knowledge. But the fact that these companies differed greatly from each other shows that even within this broader cultural context different levels of reality can be distinguished.

Levels of Reality

External physical reality refers to those things that can be determined empirically by objective or, in our Western tradition, "scientific" tests. For example, if two people are arguing about whether or not a piece of glass will break, they can hit it with a hammer and find out (Festinger, 1957). If two managers are arguing over which product to introduce, they can agree to define a test market and establish criteria by which to resolve the issue. On the other hand, if two managers are arguing over which of two political campaigns to support, both would have to agree that there are no physical criteria by which to resolve their conflict.

Different cultures have different assumptions about what constitutes external physical reality. For example, many of us would not regard the spirit world or extrasensory perception as having a physical reality basis, but in other cultures such phenomena might be regarded as very real. Vivid examples of how ambiguous the borderline can be are provided in Castaneda's (1968, 1972) descriptions of his experiences with the Indian shaman Don Juan and in

the controversies that surround research on extrasensory perception. At its core physical reality is obvious; at its boundaries it becomes very much a matter of cultural consensus, raising the issue of
"social reality."

Social reality refers to those things that members of a group regard
as matters of consensus, that are not externally, empirically testable.
The nature of human nature, the correct way for humans to relate to
nature and to each other, the distribution of power and the entire
political process, and assumptions about the meaning of life, ideology, religion, group boundaries, and culture itself are obviously matters of consensus, not empirically determinable. How a group defines
itself, the values it chooses to live by, obviously cannot be tested in
terms of our traditional notions of empirical scientific testing but certainly can be strongly held and shared unanimously. If people believe
in something and define it as real, it becomes real for that group, as
sociologists pointed out long ago.

In the international context, there is no way to test who is right
about a territorial conflict or a belief system, as the continuing war
in the Middle East has amply demonstrated. Negotiation becomes
very difficult if people hold different assumptions about reality, leading nations to resort to the use of economic and military power. The
bad joke about the naïve diplomat who tells the Arabs and the
Israelis to settle their differences in a good Christian manner makes
the point well.

One of the reasons why business decisions are often difficult to
make and why management is an intrinsically complex activity is
the lack of consensus on whether a given decision area belongs in
the realm of physical or social reality. If an organization is to have
coherent action, there must be shared assumptions about which
decisions can be empirically resolved and which ones are based on
consensual criteria such as "Let the most experienced person decide"
or "Let's decide by majority vote." Notice that the consensus must
be on the *criteria* and on the *process* to be used, not necessarily on the
ultimate substance of the decision. For example, in the western
democratic tradition we *assume* that "majority rules," yet there is no
empirical basis for that criterion at all. In fact, for many kinds of

decisions majority rule can be the worst kind of decision rule because it polarizes the debate into the two camps of "winners" and "losers."

Individual reality refers to what a given person has learned from her or his own experience, which therefore has a quality of absolute truth to that person. However, that truth may not be shared by anyone else. When we disagree at this level, it becomes very hard to move forward until we can clearly articulate what our actual experience base is. We must also have some kind of consensus on whose experience we are willing to trust. In a traditional, lineal society, based on hierarchical authority, if so-called elder statesmen speak, we take their experience as valid and act as if what they say is objectively true. In a pragmatic, individualistic society, on the other hand, the attitude may well be "Prove it to me," and beyond that, what is accepted as proof may be all over the map.

What is defined as physical, social, or individual reality is itself the product of social learning and hence, by definition, a part of a given culture (Van Maanen, 1979b; Michael, 1985). But cultural assumptions are assumed to have relatively less importance in the area of physical reality, which in Western society is assumed to operate according to natural laws as discovered by the scientific method. Cultural assumptions become relatively more important in the area of social reality, or what Louis (1981) calls intersubjective reality, as distinct from universal objective reality or individual subjective reality. In fact, the bulk of the content of a given culture will concern itself primarily with those areas of life in which objective verification is assumed not to be possible and in which, therefore, a social definition becomes the only sound basis for judgment. It is in this area that we are most susceptible to discomfort and anxiety if we do not have a common way of deciphering what is happening and how to feel about it.

High Context and Low Context

A useful distinction can be found in Hall's (1977) differentiation between what he calls high-context and low-context cultures and Maruyama's (1974) contrast between unidirectional and mutual causal cultural paradigms. In the low-context, unidirectional culture, events have clear universal meanings; in the high-context, mutual causality culture, events can be understood only in context, meanings can vary, categories can change, and causality cannot be unambiguously established.

Though this distinction has more meaning when one compares countries or large ethnic units, it has utility for organizations as well. For example, DEC was a high-context culture in which the meaning of words and actions depended on who was speaking and under what conditions. Managers knew each other well and always took into account who the actors were. When a senior manager was observed publicly punishing a subordinate for doing something "dumb," this sometimes simply meant that the subordinate should have gotten buy-in from a few more people before going off on his own. Ciba-Geigy, by contrast, was a low-context culture in which messages tended to have the same meaning no matter whom they were coming from. To be labeled "dumb" at Ciba-Geigy would have been a severe negative judgment.

When we refer to "language," we often overlook the role of context. We assume that when one has learned the language of another country, one will be able to understand what is going on and take action. But as we know all too well from our own cross-cultural travel experiences, language is embedded in a wider context in which nonverbal cues, tone of voice, body language, and other signals determine the true meaning of what is said. A vivid example from my own experience was the previously cited senior management meeting of the British oil company at which I thought I observed polite explanations from the chairman, only to be told later that he had never been more brutal than he was at that meeting.

Moralism-Pragmatism

A useful dimension for comparing groups on their approach to reality testing is an adaptation of England's (1975) moralism-pragmatism scale. In his study of managerial values, England found that managers in different countries tended to be either pragmatic, seeking validation in their own experience, or moralistic, seeking validation in a general philosophy, moral system, or tradition. For example, he found that Europeans tended to be more moralistic, whereas Americans tended to be more pragmatic. If we apply this dimension to the basic underlying assumptions that a group makes, we can specify different bases for defining what is true, as shown in Table 7.1.

This dimension not only highlights the basis on which truth is determined but also can be related to uncertainty avoidance, a major dimension derived in Hofstede's survey-based cross-national study, and tolerance for ambiguity, an important dimension that has come out of post-World War II research (Hofstede, 2001; Adorno and others, 1950). Managers and employees in different countries and in different companies vary in the degree to which they share a certain level of comfort with varying degrees of uncertainty and ambiguity. Some researchers argue that higher tolerance levels in certain managerial areas are associated with more effectiveness (Davis and Davidson, 1991; Pascale and Athos, 1981; Peters, 1987), but those results may themselves apply only in broader cultural contexts that are more tolerant of and even value ambiguity. Analysts concerned about planning for and adapting to an uncertain and uncontrollable future would argue that as environments become more turbulent, the ability to tolerate uncertainty becomes more necessary for survival and learning, suggesting that organizational and national cultures that can embrace uncertainty more easily will be inherently more adaptive (Michael, 1985).

For the purpose of this analysis, one needs to determine whether or not there is consensus on the underlying assumptions held by the members of a group. If such consensus does not exist, the collection of people will not evolve as a group in the first place.

This discussion can be summarized best by showing how it applies to our two organizations. DEC had both high consensus that reality was defined by pragmatic criteria and debate, and a very high tolerance of ambiguity. In my consultation work with DEC, for instance, I was never asked for a recommendation. If I gave one, it

Table 7.1. Criteria for Determining Truth.

Pure dogma, based on tradition and/or religion	It has always been done this way. It is God's will. It is written in the Scriptures.
Revealed dogma; that is, wisdom based on trust in the authority of wise men, formal leaders, prophets, or kings	Our president wants to do it this way. Our consultants have recommended that we do it this way. She has had the most experience, so we should do what she says.
Truth derived by a "rational-legal" process (as when we establish the guilt or innocence of an individual by means of a legal process that acknowledges from the outset that there is no absolute truth, only socially determined truth)	We have to take this decision to the marketing committee and do what they decide. The boss will have to decide this one because it is his area of responsibility. We will have to vote on it and go by majority rule. We agreed that this decision belongs to the production department head.
Truth as that which survives conflict and debate	We thrashed it out in three different committees, tested it on the sales force, and the idea is still sound, so we will do it. Does anyone see any problems with doing it this way . . . ? If not, that's what we'll do.
Truth as that which works, the purely pragmatic criterion	Let's try it out this way and evaluate how we are doing.
Truth as established by the scientific method, which becomes, once again, a kind of dogma, especially in the social sciences, where even the scientific method is a matter of consensus among social scientists.	Our research shows that this is the right way to do it. We've done three surveys and analyzed the statistics very carefully; they all show the same thing, so let's act on them. Our survey results may not be completely valid, but our focus group follow-up data support the findings so we should go ahead and do it."

was usually overridden immediately by various ideas from the client, which were then debated among the members. At Ciba-Geigy I was always treated as an authority and asked what I knew from my research and other consulting experience and what I would recommend. I was treated as a scientist who was bringing some knowledge to the organization, and I often found that my recommendations were implemented exactly. However, if what I recommended conflicted with processes based on other cultural elements—for example, when I suggested more lateral communication—the recommendation was dismissed outright. Ciba-Geigy did not tolerate ambiguity well and operated much closer to the moralistic end of the dimension.

What Is "Information"?

How a group tests for reality and makes decisions also involves consensus on what constitutes *data*, what is *information*, and what is *knowledge*. As information technology has grown, the issue has become sharpened because of debates about the role of computers in providing information. Information technology "professionals" often hold shared assumptions that differ in substantial ways from the assumptions of senior managers. For example, many company presidents will point out that all you get on a computer screen is data and what they really need is information, which implies a level of analysis of the data that is typically not available unless a sophisticated decision support system or expert system has been programmed in (Rockart and DeLong, 1988). For a group to be able to make realistic decisions, there must be a degree of consensus on which information is relevant to the task at hand.

Dougherty's research on new product development teams showed that when such groups do not develop a common definition of relevant information, they are more likely to come up with products that do not make it in the marketplace (Dougherty, 1990). She identified five separate "thought worlds" that operate in the functional specialists who are usually brought together in product development teams. Each member of the team believes that he or she "knows a lot" about the team's customers, but what these members know turns out to be very different.

- The engineers know just how big the product should be, what its technical specifications should be, where the power plug should go, and so on.
- The manufacturing people know what the potential volumes are and how many models might be needed.
- Marketers/business planners know in general whether or not a market exists, the size of the potential market, what price and volume would produce appropriate profit levels, what the market trends are, and so on.
- The field salespeople know what the potential customers will use the product for, what the users' specific needs are, and how important the product is to customers relative to competitors' products.
- The distribution people know how the product will be sold, what the merchandising plans are, and how many sales channels there will be.

Each of these groups, by virtue of its members' occupational background and functional experience, has built up concepts and language that are common to the group members but not necessarily understood clearly or valued by others.

When members of these subcultures are brought together into a product development team, their ability to discover the others' realities is, according to Dougherty, a major determinant of whether or not the product that is developed will succeed in the marketplace. All organizations advocate teamwork at this level and have formal processes that are supposed to be followed. However, Dougherty's data indicate that only if the team goes outside the formally defined process is there a chance that enough mutual understanding will arise to permit real coordination of relevant information. Apparently, when the process is formalized, groups get only the illusion that they are communicating relevant information to each other and never discover that what they define as information is itself different from subgroup to subgroup. If they go outside the formal channel, they are more likely to feel the need to become a real group, to get to know each other at a more personal level, thus providing opportunities to discover where they agree and disagree and how their information sets differ in content.

In summary, one of the most important dimensions of culture is the nature of how reality, truth, and information are defined. Reality can exist at physical, group, and individual levels, and the test for what is real will differ according to the level—overt tests, social consensus, or individual experience. Groups develop assumptions about information that determine when they feel they have enough information to make a decision, and those assumptions reflect deeper assumptions about the ultimate source of truth. What is a fact, what is information, and what is truth—each depends not only on shared knowledge of formal language but also on context.

8

ASSUMPTIONS ABOUT THE NATURE OF TIME AND SPACE

The deep structure of culture consists not only of how we perceive reality and truth, but also of how we orient ourselves toward our physical and human environment, and that orientation involves unconscious and taken-for-granted experiences and concepts of time and space.

Assumptions About Time

The perception and experience of time are among the most central aspects of how any group functions. When people differ in their experience of time, tremendous communication and relationship problems typically emerge. Consider how anxious and/or irritated we get when someone is "late," or when we feel our time has been "wasted," or when we feel that we did not get "enough air time" to make our point, or when we feel "out of phase" with someone, or someone is taking on "too much at one time," or when we can never get our subordinate to do things "on time" or to show up "at the right time."

In an analysis of time, Dubinskas (1988, p. 14) points out its central role in human affairs: "Time is a fundamental symbolic category that we use for talking about the orderliness of social life. In a modern organization, just as in an agrarian society, time appears to impose a structure of work days, calendars, careers, and life-cycles that we learn and live in as part of our cultures. This temporal order has an 'already made' character of naturalness to it, a model of the way things are."

But time itself is not a unidimensional, clear construct. It has been analyzed from many perspectives, and a number of these are particularly relevant to cultural analysis.

Basic Time Orientation

Anthropologists have noted that every culture makes assumptions about the nature of time and has a basic orientation toward the past, present, or future (Kluckhohn and Strodtbeck, 1961; Redding and Martyn-Johns, 1979; Hampden-Turner and Trompenaars, 1993). For example, in their study of the various cultures in the U.S. Southwest, Kluckhohn and Strodtbeck noted that some of the Indian tribes lived mostly in the past, the Spanish-Americans were oriented primarily toward the present, and the Anglo-Americans were oriented primarily toward the near future.

Time orientation is a useful way to distinguish national cultures. In their cross-cultural study, Hofstede and Bond identified a dimension that contrasted a past/present orientation with a future orientation and found that economic development was correlated with a future orientation (Hofstede and Bond, 1988; Hofstede, 2001, first published 1980). Hampden-Turner and Trompenaars, based on their own survey, show that among Asian countries Japan is at the extreme of long-range planning while Hong Kong is at the extreme of short-run planning.

At the level of the organization, one can distinguish companies that are primarily oriented to (1) the past, thinking mostly about how things used to be; (2) the present, worrying only how to get the immediate task done; (3) the near future, worrying mostly about quarterly results; and (4) the distant future, investing heavily in research and development or in building market share at the expense of immediate profits.

Cultural assumptions about time influence the role that planning will play in the management process. For example, one high-tech company I have worked with operated by the assumption that "only the present counts." Employees worked extremely hard on the immediate tasks that challenged them, but they had little sense of past history and did not care much about the future. People in the planning department complained that plans were made in a ritualistic way, planning books were filled with things to do, but nothing ever got implemented.

One can find many organizations that live in the past, reflecting on their past glories and successes while ignoring present and future challenges. They make the basic assumption that if things worked in the past, they must be good enough to work in the present and future and therefore do not need to be reexamined. That assumption can indeed be valid if the technology and the environment have remained stable, but it can lead an organization to destruction if new environmental demands and technological changes require changes in how the organization defines its mission, its goals, and the means by which to accomplish them.

How future oriented an organization should be is the subject of much debate, with many arguing that one of the problems of U.S. companies is that the financial context in which they operate (the stock market) forces a near-future orientation at the expense of longer-range planning. From an anthropological point of view, it is of course not clear what is cause and what is effect. Is the United States, culturally speaking, a near-future-oriented pragmatic society that has therefore created certain economic institutions to reflect our need for quick and constant feedback, or have our economic institutions created the short-run pragmatism? In either case, the important point is that these cultural assumptions about time dominate daily thinking and activity to the point where a U.S. manager may have a hard time imagining the alternative of a long-range planning process such as would be typical in some Japanese industries.

Monochronic and Polychronic Time

Edward Hall, in several very insightful books about culture (1959, 1966, 1977), points out that in the United States most managers view time as monochronic, an infinitely divisible linear ribbon that can be divided into appointments and other compartments but within which only one thing can be done at a time. If more than one thing must be done within, say, an hour, we divide the hour into as many units as we need and then do "one thing at a time." When we get disorganized or have a feeling of being overloaded, we are advised to "do one thing at a time." Time is viewed as a valuable commodity that can be spent, wasted, killed, or made good use of; but once a unit of time is over, it is gone forever.

In contrast, some cultures in southern Europe, Africa, and the Middle East regard time as polychronic, a kind of medium defined more by what is accomplished than by a clock and within which several things can be done simultaneously. Even more extreme is the Asian cyclical concept of time "as phases, rather circular in form. One season follows the next, one life leads into another" (Sithi-Amnuai, 1968, p. 82). The manager who operates according to this kind of time "holds court" in the sense that she or he deals simultaneously with a number of subordinates, colleagues, and even bosses, keeping each matter in suspension until it is finished.

This distinction is usefully applied by Hampden-Turner and Trompenaars (1993, 2000) to nations and organizations in terms of whether they are more focused on sequential thinking (mono-chromic clock time) or synchronization of activities (polychronic). They point out, for example, that the Japanese approach to manu-facturing is based on making as many of the sequential activities of a product line as possible into synchronous activities so that at the point where a given part such as an engine is inserted, a number of different engines can be ready to fit into the different models that may be coming down the line. Supplies have to arrive "just in time" so that the costs of keeping things in inventory are minimized.

How a culture views time is, of course, related to other cultural themes, such as the importance of relationships in getting a job done. If relationships are thought of as being more important than short-run efficiency, there is likely to be more emphasis on poly-chronicity. Punctuality or the rapid completion of a task may not be valued as highly as dealing with all the relationship issues that are brought up in relation to the task. But a monochronically oriented manager can become very impatient and frustrated in a polychronic culture when his boss gives attention to several subordinates at the same time, or in a more relationship-oriented culture when he must give time to social events before business can be discussed.

Though there is an emphasis on monochronicity in the United States, polychronic time concepts do exist in U.S. organizations. A doctor or dentist, for example, may simultaneously see several patients in adjacent offices, and a supervisor is usually totally available at all times to all of his or her machine operators. Parents and homemakers may simultaneously cook, clean house, and deal with each of several children. In an airport check-in line an agent will ask whether any of the people in the line are scheduled for an immediate flight and pull them out of the line so as not to hold up the flight departure. When Alpha Power was required by a court order to become environmentally responsible, electrical workers were told that cleaning up an oil spill from the emergency truck was just as important as fixing the hospital generator—that, in effect, they had to view these tasks synchronously, not sequentially.

Time concepts such as these also define in a subtle way how status is displayed, as illustrated by the frustrating experiences that Americans and northern Europeans have in Latin cultures, where "lining up" and "doing things one at a time" are less common. I have stood in line at a small post office in Southern France only to discover that some people barge to the head of the line and actually get service from the clerk. My friends have pointed out to me that in this situation not only does the clerk have a more polychronic view of the world, leading her to respond to whoever seems to shout loudest, but a higher-status person considers it legitimate to break into the line and get service first as a legitimate display of his status. If others live in the same status system, they do not get offended by being kept waiting. In fact, it was pointed out to me that by staying in line and fulminating, I was displaying a low sense of my own status; otherwise, I would be up at the head of the line demanding service as well.

Monochronic time controls human behavior and is therefore well suited to situations that require highly coordinated actions ("Synchronize your watches!"). Because this form of time facilitates coordination, it is well suited to the management of large systems and is the form of time taken for granted in most organizations as the only way to get things done efficiently. Polychronic time assumptions are more effective for building relationships and for solving complex problems where information is widely scattered and highly interactive so that all channels must be kept open at all times. Polychronic time is therefore more suitable for the early stages of an organization, for smaller systems, and for organizations where one person is the central point of coordination.

Bluedorn (2000) decided that polychronicity, in the sense of preference for doing more than one thing at a time, was a dimension that could be measured, and he developed a scale for this purpose. Onken (1999) applied this measure to a number of organizations and found that even within a seemingly more monochromic cultural context—that is, U.S. society—polychronicity correlated positively with the degree to which an organization valued speed and with some measures of organizational performance. Paradoxically, it is sometimes faster and more efficient to work in a polychronic manner!

Planning Time and Development Time

In a study of biotechnology companies, Dubinskas (1988) found that when biologists who had become entrepreneurs worked with managers who came from an economics or business background, subtle misunderstandings would occur over how long things took, how one viewed milestones, and how one perceived the future in general during the planning process. The managers viewed time in a linear, monochronic way, with targets and milestones that were tied to external objective realities like market opportunities and the stock market. Dubinskas labeled this form of time "planning time."

In contrast, the biologists seemed to operate from something they called "development time," best characterized as "things will take as long as they will take," referring to natural biological processes that have their own internal time cycles. To caricature the distinction, a manager might say we need the baby in six months to meet a business target, while the biologist would say, sorry, but it takes at least nine months to make one. The person operating from planning time sees herself more in a world of objects that can be manipulated and as a "finished adult" operating in an external world. The person operating from development time sees herself more in a process world, where her own development and that of other things in her world are more oriented to natural processes that cannot be easily speeded up or slowed down, and development is a never-ending, open-ended process. Planning time seeks closure; development time is open ended and can extend far into the future. Managers and scientists operating in terms of these two types of time can work together and even influence each other's concepts, but they must first understand the differences in each other's assumptions.

Discretionary Time Horizons and Degree of "Accuracy"

Another dimension of time on which group members need consensus has to do with the size of relevant time units in relation to given tasks (Jaques, 1982, 1989). Do we measure and plan for things annually, quarterly, monthly, daily, hourly, or by the minute? What is considered accurate in the realm of time? Does a given task have to be measured in terms of seconds, minutes, or longer units? How long after an appointed time can one show up and still be considered "on time" and how long after expected time of arrival can a plane land and still be listed as "on time"? What are the expected timetables for certain events, such as promotions? How much time is it appropriate to spend on a given task, and what is the length of a feedback loop? How long should a task take?

As Lawrence and Lorsch (1967) noted years ago, one of the reasons why sales and R&D people have trouble communicating with each other is that they work with totally different time horizons. For salespeople, they pointed out, the time horizon involved the completion of a sale, which could take minutes, hours, days, or weeks. In general, however, even their longer time horizons were much shorter than those of the research people, for whom a one- or two-year horizon was normal. In other words, research people would not get closure, in the sense of knowing that they had a good product, until a much longer period of time had elapsed, partly because they operated more in terms of "development time," as described above, and partly because in many industries it is not known whether the new product or process will work when it is scaled up to greater volume production. Particularly in the chemical industry, a researcher does not know whether he has been successful until his product has passed the pilot plant and full production facility hurdles. At each step the larger scale can change the process and reveal things that will require new research and development.

If we now consider the communication process between the researcher and the salesperson/marketer, when the latter says that she wants a product "soon" and the researcher agrees that the product will be ready "soon," they may be talking about completely different things and not realize it. For example, at DEC I constantly heard complaints from the sales department that engineering was not getting the products out on time. If I talked to engineering, I was told that the product was on schedule and doing just fine, which often meant "we are only six months late, which is nothing in a several-year development cycle." Each function got angry at the other. Neither recognized that the judgments being made about what it meant to be on time differed because different assumptions about time units were being used.

DEC and Ciba-Geigy differed in their overall time horizons, probably because of their underlying technologies and markets. The slow deliberateness of the research process at Ciba-Geigy spilled over into the management process. Things were done slowly, deliberately, and thoroughly. If a project was going to take several years, so be it. Time was expressed in spatial terms in a phrase commonly heard around the company: "The first thousand miles don't count."

In other words, be patient and persistent; things will eventually work out.

Time horizons differ not only by function and occupation but by rank. The higher the rank, the longer the time horizon over which a manager has discretion (Jaques, 1982, 1989) or what Bailyn (1985) has called "operational autonomy." This period of time is usually defined as the time between formal reviews of whether or not one is doing one's basic job. Production workers may get reviewed every few minutes or hours, supervisors may get reviewed monthly or annually, and top executives may get reviewed only once every several years, depending upon the nature of their industry. Different norms about time arise, therefore, at different rank levels. Senior managers assume that one must plan in cycles of several years, whereas such an assumption may not make sense to the middle manager or the worker, whose time cycle is daily, weekly, or monthly.

Different assumptions about discretionary periods can cause difficulty in managing. Bailyn (1985) found that senior managers in one large R&D organization believed that their scientists wanted to set their own research goals (they were given goal autonomy), but because those scientists were perceived to be undisciplined in their management of budgets and time, they were reviewed frequently (they were not given operational autonomy). When Bailyn talked to the scientists, she discovered two of the main reasons why they felt demoralized: management was "not telling them what range of problems to work on" (because they were in industry, they wanted to work on relevant problems as specified by management) and "they were constantly being reviewed and never allowed to get any work done." In other words, the scientists wanted just the opposite of what management was providing—they wanted less goal autonomy and more operational autonomy.

Jaques (1982, 1989) takes the argument about discretionary time horizons even further by noting that managerial competence can be judged by whether or not a given manager is functioning in terms of the time horizons appropriate to the level of his or her job.

A production worker thinking in terms of years and a senior manager thinking in terms of hours and days are equally likely to be
ineffective in terms of what their jobs demand of them. As one
moves up the hierarchy of jobs that require longer-range planning,
one can assess the manager's potential for promotion partly in terms
of his or her ability to take longer-range points of view. When
senior managers operate with too short a time horizon, they are
likely to overmanage and to fail to plan appropriately.

Temporal Symmetry, Pacing, and Entrainment

A subtle but critical aspect of time is the way in which activities are
paced. In a study of the introduction of computerized equipment
into radiology departments, Barley (1988) discovered that one of
the major impacts of the technology was the degree to which the
pacing of the activities of the technicians and the radiologists
became more or less symmetrical. In the traditional X-ray department, the technicians worked monochronically as far as scheduling
patients and making films. But if they needed to consult a radiologist, the technicians became frustrated by the polychronic world of
the radiologists. For example, if a technician needed the services of
a radiologist to give an injection to a patient, to conduct a fluo-
roscopy, or to review preliminary films, the technician would often
have to wait. The following quotation captures the asymmetry well.

> To locate a radiologist, a technologist often had to search several
> offices and ask other technologists about the radiologist's last known
> whereabouts. Even after the tech found a radiologist, there was no
> guarantee that he would be immediately available. At the time of the
> tech's arrival, the radiologist could be talking on the telephone, dis-
> cussing a film with a physician, consulting a colleague, or about to
> assist with another examination. In each instance the technologist
> would have to wait. But even if the technologist successfully engaged
> the radiologist's attention, he or she still had no firm claim on the
> radiologist's time. The radiologist could always be diverted by a num-

ber of events, including a telephone call, a consultation, or even another technologist with a request that the radiologist deemed more important. [Barley, 1988, p. 145]

When computerized tomography, magnetic resonance, and ultrasound came into the departments, the temporal orders of the two sets of people became more symmetrical because of 1) the greater duration of each test, 2) the technician's greater level of expertise in reading the results, and 3) the degree to which the special procedures involved in the new technologies often required the radiologists and technicians to work side by side throughout. Furthermore, the diagnostic procedures in ultrasound could not be done in the first place unless the technicians knew how to read results as they were forthcoming. The technicians acquired, de facto, more operational autonomy, which gave them more status, as did the reality that because of their greater amount of experience they often knew better than the radiologist how to read the results. The new technologies created a world in which both technician and radiologist worked in a monochronic manner, making it easier to coordinate their efforts and achieve efficiency for the patient and in the use of the equipment.

Polychronically driven work always has the potential for frustrating the person who is working monochronically, as exemplified in the interaction between an air traffic controller (polychronic) and the pilot of a single aircraft waiting for landing clearance (monochronic). Similar issues arise when a patient gets frustrated waiting in the emergency room because she is not aware of the fact that the physician is treating many at once. Because the monochronically driven person typically does not understand the multiple demands being placed on the polychronically driven person, there is a very high potential for misunderstanding and drawing inaccurate conclusions, such as perceiving the polychronically driven one as lazy or inefficient.

The temporal context within which groups work, involving the pacing of activities, rhythms, and cycles of work activities, are obviously relevant to how groups will perform and will be the source of frustration if there is insufficient consensus within and between groups (Ancona, 1988; Bluedorn, 1997, 2000). To prevent dysfunctional conflicts in pacing, some researchers have noted that organizations tend to try to "entrain" interdependent activities. Entrainment, a concept taken from the natural sciences, can be defined as "the adjustment of the pace or cycle of one activity to match or synchronize with that of another" (Ancona and Chong, 1996, p. 251). A growing body of research on time, reported in the October 2001 issue of the *Academy of Management Review*, reflects the degree to which the sense of time and the management of time is becoming more and more acknowledged as crucial to understanding cultural phenomena.

Summary

There is probably no more important category for cultural analysis than the study of how time is conceived and used in a group or organization. Time imposes a social order, and the manner in which things are handled in time conveys status and intention. The pacing of events, the rhythms of life, the sequence in which things are done, and the duration of events all become subject to symbolic interpretation. Misinterpretations of what things mean in a temporal context are therefore extremely likely unless group members are operating from the same sets of assumptions.

Some of the main aspects of time reviewed, such as (1) past, present, near-, or far-future orientation; (2) monochronicity or polychronicity; (3) planning or developmental time; (4) time horizons; and (5) symmetry of temporal activities, can form an initial diagnostic grid to help one begin to understand how time is viewed in a given organization.

Ultimately, time is so critical because it is, in a sense, so invisible, so taken for granted, and so difficult to speak about. When we are late or early, for example, we mumble apologies and possibly provide explanations, but rarely do we ask, "When did you expect me?" or "What does it mean to you when I am late?" One of the most important contributions of Forrester's systems dynamics models is that they deal explicitly with the dynamics of time and invite managers who are learning to develop these models to think through their own assumptions about time and to study the effects on a total system of time delays at various stages in a production process (Forrester, 1969; Senge, 1990; Sterman, 2000).

Shared Assumptions About the Nature of Space

The meaning and use of space are among the most subtle aspects of organizational culture because assumptions about space, like those about time, operate outside of awareness and are taken for granted. At the same time, when those assumptions are violated, very strong emotional reactions occur because space comes to have very powerful symbolic meanings, as expressed in the current phrase, "Don't get into my 'space.'" One of the most obvious ways that rank and status is symbolized in organizations is by the location and size of offices.

Hall (1966) points out that in some cultures, if one is walking in a certain direction, the space ahead of one is perceived to be one's own, so that if someone crosses in front of one, that person is "violating" one's space. In other cultures, notably some Asian ones, space is initially defined as communal and shared, allowing for the complex flow of people, bicycles, cars, and animals one may see in a Chinese city street with everyone somehow moving forward and no one getting killed or trampled. Space, like time, can be analyzed from a number of different points of view.

Distance and Relative Placement

Space has both a physical and a social meaning (Van Maanen, 1979b). For coordinated social action to occur, one must share assumptions about the meaning of the placement of physical objects in an environment and also know how to orient oneself spatially in relation to other members of one's group. Placement of oneself in relation to others symbolizes status, social distance, and membership. For example, Hall (1966) points out that in the United States there is high consensus on four kinds of "normal distance" and that within each of these there is consensus on what it means to be "very near" or "very far."

1. *Intimacy distance.* Among those who consider themselves to be intimate with each other, contact and touching are defined as being very near; six to eighteen inches is the range for being far. This is what sociologists call the "ideal sphere" around each of us that defines the space we only allow to be entered by people with whom we feel we have an intimate relationship.

2. *Personal distance.* Eighteen to thirty inches is being near, two to four feet is being far. This is the range within which we have personal conversations with another individual even if we are in a crowd or at a party. This distance permits a normal or soft tone of voice to be used and is usually accompanied by intense eye contact. The easiest way to appreciate the power of this distance norm is to recall what happens at parties when someone from another culture—in which personal distance is defined as closer than it is in the United States—moves in "too close." We find ourselves backing up, only to discover that the other person is pursuing us, trying to make the distance seem right to him or her. Eventually we feel cornered, and all kinds of irrelevant motives or personality attributes get called into play, when in fact the only thing operating is the fact that in two different cultures, the norm of what is appropriate personal distance varies. When personal distance is violated one often hears the phrase "You're in my face," or "Get out of my face."

3. *Social distance.* Four to seven feet is near; seven to twelve feet is far. Social distance defines how we talk to several people at once, as at a dinner party or a seminar; it usually involves some raising of the voice and less personal focus on any given individual. Our eyes will scan the group or be focused on the floor or ceiling. Designers of seminar rooms or tables for committee meetings have to work around these kinds of norms if they are concerned about making

the room feel appropriate for the kinds of meeting that are supposed to go on there. The more we want to meet informally and really get to know each other, the more the room has to be scaled down to allow that to happen.

4. *Public distance*. Twelve to twenty-five feet is near; more than twenty-five feet is far. At this distance the audience is defined as undifferentiated, and we raise our voice even more or use a microphone. Our eyes rove systematically or do not focus on anyone, as when we read a speech to an audience.

Feelings about distance have biological roots. Animals have a clearly defined *flight distance* (the distance that will elicit fleeing if the animal is intruded upon) and *critical distance* (the distance that will elicit attacking behavior if the animal is intruded upon or "cornered"). Conditions of *crowding* not only elicit pathological behavior in nonhuman species but elicit aggression in humans. Hence, most cultures have fairly clear rules about how to define personal and intimate space through the use of a variety of cues to permit what Hall calls *sensory screening*. We use partitions, walls, sound barriers, and other physical devices, and we use eye contact, body position, and other personal devices to signal respect for the privacy of others (Goffman, 1959; Hatch, 1990; Steele, 1973, 1981).

We also learn how to manage what Hall calls *intrusion distance*; that is, how far away to remain from others who are in personal conversation without interrupting the conversation yet making it known that one wants attention when appropriate. In some cultures, including ours, intrusion occurs only when one interrupts with speech (one can stand close by without "interrupting"), whereas in other cultures even entering the visual field of another person constitutes a bid for attention and hence is seen as an interruption. In these cultural settings, the use of physical barriers such as closed offices has an important symbolic meaning—it is the only way to get a feeling of privacy (Hall, 1966).

At the organizational level, one can clearly see that DEC and Ciba-Geigy had contrasting assumptions about space. DEC opted for a completely open office layout, with partitions low enough to permit everyone to see over the tops. At Ciba-Geigy the offices were arranged along corridors and had heavy doors that were kept shut.

The Symbolics of Space

Organizations develop different norms of who should have how much and what kind of space. They also hold different implicit assumptions about the role of space utilization in getting work accomplished. In most organizations the best views and locations are reserved for the highest-status people. Senior executives are typically on the higher floors of buildings and often are allocated special spaces such as private conference rooms and private bathrooms. Sociologists point out that one important function of private bathrooms is to preserve the image of leaders as "super-human" beings who do not have the ordinary needs of those at lower levels. In some organizations, it would not be comfortable for the employee to find himself urinating next to the president of the corporation.

Some organizations use very precise space allocation as a direct status symbol. As was mentioned before, the headquarters building of General Foods was designed with movable walls so that, as product managers were promoted, their office size could be adjusted to reflect their new rank. At the same time the company had a department that allocated the kind of carpeting, furniture, and wall decorations that went with particular rank levels. In contrast, DEC aggressively tried to reduce status and privileges by not allocating private parking spaces; by reserving the good locations, such as corners, for conference rooms; and by putting higher-status managers in inside offices so that clerical and secretarial employees could work on the outside, next to windows. Whereas in many organizations the way in which the employees can decorate their own work space is prescribed, in DEC employees were left entirely on their own with regard to decoration.

Where buildings are located, how they are built, and the kind of architecture involved will vary from one organization to the next and may well reflect deeper values and assumptions held in the larger culture and by the key leaders. Because buildings and the environment around them are highly visible and relatively permanent, organizations attempt to symbolize important values and assumptions through the design. The physical layout not only has this symbolic function but is often used to guide and channel the behavior of members of the organization, thereby becoming a powerful builder and reinforcer of norms (Berg and Kreiner, 1990; Gagliardi, 1990; Steele, 1973, 1981).

For example, DEC reinforced its values of autonomy and empowerment by being highly decentralized geographically but, at the same time, reinforced its value of communication by employing a fleet of helicopters and shuttle buses to transport people around easily among the decentralized units. The value of frugality was reinforced by opting for inexpensive, unobtrusive, low-rise buildings. The interior open-office layout was designed to stimulate high levels of communication and to symbolize efficiency and cost consciousness. In contrast, Ciba-Geigy, with its greater emphasis on work as a private activity, enclosed areas as much as possible, was comfortable with private dining rooms for different levels of executives, and enclosed its buildings in an almost fortress-like manner.

Body Language

One of the more subtle uses of space is our use of gestures, body position, and other physical cues to communicate our sense of what is going on in a given situation and how we relate to the other people in it. On the gross level, whom we sit next to, whom we physically avoid, whom we touch, whom we bow to, and so on convey our perceptions of relative status and intimacy. As sociologists have observed, however, there are many more subtle cues that convey our deeper sense of what is going on and our assumptions about the right and proper way to behave in any given situation (Goffman, 1967; Van Maanen, 1979b).

Rituals of deference and demeanor that reinforce hierarchical relationship are played out in the physical and temporal positioning of behavior, as when a subordinate knows just where to stand at a meeting relative to the boss and how to time his questions or comments when he is disagreeing with the boss. The boss, for her part, knows that she must sit at the head of the table in the boardroom and time her remarks to the group appropriately. But only insiders know the full meaning of all these time/space cues, reminding us forcefully that what we observe around spatial arrangements and the behavioral use of time are only cultural artifacts, difficult to decipher if we do not have additional data obtained from insiders through interview, observation, and joint inquiry. It would be highly dangerous to use our own cultural lenses to interpret what we observe, as when I misjudged the feeling tone of the meeting at the British company mentioned earlier.

Time, Space, and Activity Interaction

Orienting oneself in both time and space is fundamental in any new situation. Thus far we have analyzed time and space as separate dimensions, but in reality they always interact in complex ways around the activity that is basically supposed to occur. It is easiest to see this in relation to the basic forms of time. Monochronic time assumptions have specific implications for how space is organized. If one has to have individual appointments and privacy, one needs areas in which they can be held, thus requiring either desks that are far enough apart, cubicles, or offices with doors. Because monochronic time is linked with efficiency, one also requires a space layout that allows a minimum of wasted time. Thus it must be easy for people to contact each other, distances between important departments must be minimal, and amenities such as toilets and eating areas must be placed in such a way as to save time. In fact, at DEC the liberal distribution of water coolers, coffee machines, and small kitchens around the organization clearly signaled the importance of continuing to work even as one satisfied bodily needs.

Polychronic time, in contrast, requires spatial arrangements that make it easy for simultaneous events to occur, where privacy is achieved by being near someone and whispering rather than by retreating behind closed doors. Thus one finds large rooms built more like amphitheaters that permit a senior person to hold court, or sets of offices or cubicles built around a central core that permits easy access to everyone. One might also expect more visually open environments such as the office bullpens that permit supervisors to survey the entire department so that they can easily see who might need help or who is not working.

When buildings and offices are designed in terms of certain intended work patterns, both distance and time are usually considered in the physical layout. These design issues get very complex, however, because information and communication technology is increasingly able to shrink time and space in ways that may not have been considered. For example, a group of people in private offices can communicate by telephone, electronic mail, fax, and videophone and even be a virtual team by using conference calls enhanced by various kinds of computer software, now called Group-Ware (Grenier and Metes, 1992; Johansen and others, 1991).

The difficulty of introducing some of these technologies points up the interaction of assumptions, in that some managers become conscious of the fact that they need face-to-face interaction to gauge whether or not their message is getting through and how the other person is reacting. At DEC, for example, electronic mail was widely used by certain sets of engineers who felt comfortable solving problems with each other by this means even if they did not know each other personally; senior executives, on the other hand, usually insisted on meetings and face-to-face communication.

The introduction of new information technologies such as e-mail or groupware sometimes forces to the surface assumptions that had been taken for granted, thereby revealing cultural elements that may be incongruent with behavior that would be optimal from the point of view of the technology. Conference calls, for example, might be resisted because participants can not read each other's body language and facial expressions. E-mail, on the other hand, can facilitate communication because it does not require the sender to "interrupt" the receiver in the way that a phone call would. New cultural norms about time then arise in terms of the expectations that e-mails will be answered within a certain length of time and that everyone will have e-mail service.

Summary and Conclusions

It is important to recognize that (1) how we conceptualize reality, what concepts and dimensions guide our perception of time, and how we construct and utilize our physical spatial environment are very much a matter of prior cultural learning, and (2) in any given new organization, shared assumptions arise only over the course of time and common experience. The analyst of culture must be careful not to project his or her own conceptions of time and space onto groups and must remember that the visible artifacts surrounding these conceptions are easy to misinterpret.

What are the implications of all this for leaders and managers? The most obvious implication has already been stated—they must learn to decipher cultural cues so that the normal flow of work is not interrupted by cultural misunderstandings. More important than this point, however, is the implication that the way in which leaders act out their own assumptions about time and space comes to train their subordinates and ultimately their entire organization to accept those assumptions. Most leaders are not aware of how much the assumptions they take for granted are passed on in day-to-day behavior by the way they manage the decision-making process, time, and space. If the external context then changes, requiring new kinds of responses, not only will it be difficult for the leader to learn new things, but it will be even more difficult to retrain members of the organization who have become used to the way the leader structured things in the past. How we define reality, time, and space represents the deepest level of assumptions and, hence, is the level we will most cling to in order to avoid uncertainty and anxiety.

9

ASSUMPTIONS ABOUT HUMAN NATURE, ACTIVITY, AND RELATIONSHIPS

This chapter will explore what it means to be human, what a culture's basic assumptions are about the appropriate kinds of action for humans to take with respect to their environment, and most important, what a culture's basic assumptions are about the right and proper forms of human relationships. It is this last category that frequently receives all the attention and defines for many people what the word *culture* is all about. However, it is important to recognize that assumptions about human relationships are deeply connected not only to assumptions about human nature and activity but also to assumptions about time, space, and the nature of truth, as discussed in Chapters Seven and Eight.

Assumptions About the Nature of Human Nature

In every culture there are shared assumptions about what it means to be human, what our basic instincts are, and what kinds of behavior are considered inhuman and therefore grounds for ejection from the group. Being human is not just a physical property but also a cultural construction, as we have seen throughout history. Slavery was often justified by a particular society by defining slaves as not human. In ethnic and religious conflicts the "other" is often defined as not human. Within the category of those defined as human we have further variation. Kluckhohn and Strodtbeck (1961) in their classic comparative study noted that in some societies humans are seen as basically evil, in others as basically good, and in still others as mixed or neutral, capable of being either good or bad. Closely related are assumptions about how perfectible human nature is. Is our goodness or badness intrinsic and do we simply accept what we are, or can we, through hard work, generosity, or faith, overcome our badness and earn our salvation?

At the organizational level, the basic assumptions about the nature of human nature are often expressed most clearly in how workers and managers are viewed. Within the Western tradition we have seen an evolution of assumptions about human nature, as follows:

1. Humans as rational-economic actors

2. Humans as social animals with primarily social needs

3. Humans as problem solvers and self-actualizers, with primary needs to be challenged and to use their talents

4. Humans as complex and malleable (Schein, 1980, first published 1965)

Early theories of employee motivation were almost completely dominated by the assumption that the only incentives available to managers are monetary ones because it was assumed that the only essential motivation of employees was economic self-interest. The Hawthorne studies (Roethlisberger and Dickson, 1939; Homans, 1950) launched a new series of "social" assumptions, postulating that employees are motivated by the need to relate well to their peer and membership groups and that such motivation often overrides economic self-interest. The main evidence for these assumptions came from studies of restriction of output, which showed clearly that workers will reduce their take-home pay rather than break the norm of a fair day's work for a fair day's pay. Furthermore, workers will put pressure on high producers ("rate busters") to work less hard and make less money in order to preserve the basic norm of a fair day's work.

Subsequent studies of work, particularly on the effects of the assembly line, introduced another set of assumptions: employees are self-actualizers who need challenge and interesting work to provide self-confirmation and valid outlets for the full use of their talents (Argyris, 1964). Motivation theorists, such as Maslow (1954), organized these vying assumptions into a hierarchy: if the individual is in a survival mode, economic motives will dominate; if survival needs are met, social needs come to the fore; if social needs are met, self-actualization needs are released.

McGregor (1960) observed that within this broad framework an important second layer of assumptions was held by managers vis-à-vis employees. Ineffective managers tended to hold an interlocked set of assumptions that McGregor labeled Theory X. Theory X managers assumed that people are lazy and must therefore be motivated with economic incentives and controlled by constant surveillance. In contrast, effective managers held a different set of assumptions that he labeled Theory Y. These managers assumed that people are basically self-motivated and therefore need to be challenged and channeled, not controlled. McGregor and other researchers saw insufficient financial incentives as "demotivators" but observed that adding financial incentives would not increase motivation. Only challenge and use of one's talents could increase motivation (Herzberg, 1968). Whereas Theory X assumes that employees are intrinsically in conflict with their employing organization, Theory Y assumes that it is possible to design organizations that make it possible for employee needs to be congruent with organizational needs.

Most current theories are built on still another set of assumptions, namely, that human nature is complex and malleable and that one cannot make a universal statement about human nature; instead, one must be prepared for human variability. Such variability will reflect (1) changes in the life cycle in that motives may change and grow as we mature and (2) changes in social conditions in that we are capable of learning new motives as may be required by new situations (Schein, 1978, 1990). Such variability makes it essential for organizations to develop some consensus on what their own assumptions are, because management strategies and practices reflect those assumptions. Both the incentive and control systems in most organizations are built on assumptions about human nature, and if those assumptions are not shared by the managers of the organization, inconsistent practices and confusion will result.

McGregor (1960) also noted that because humans are malleable, they will often respond adaptively to the assumptions that are held about them. This is particularly a problem in organizations that are run by managers who share a Theory X set of assumptions, because the more that employees are controlled and treated as untrustworthy, the more likely they are to behave in terms of those expectations. The cynical Theory X manager then feels vindicated but fails to note that the employee behavior was learned and does not reflect *intrinsic* human nature.

The initial assumptions that members of a new group adopt may well reflect the personal biases of the founders or owners of an organization because founders tend to select associates who share assumptions similar to their own. These assumptions then become embedded in the incentive, reward, and control systems of the organization so that new members are motivated to share those assumptions or, if they cannot share them, to leave the organization (Schein, 1983).

As noted previously, the core assumption about human nature at DEC was that individuals are self-motivated and capable of responsible and creative decision making. At some level, DEC was one of the most Theory Y–driven organizations I have ever encountered. The core assumption at Ciba-Geigy was more difficult to decipher, but there were strong indications that individuals were viewed ultimately as good soldiers, who would perform responsibly and loyally and whose loyalty the organization would reward. Individuals were expected to do their best in whatever was asked of them, but loyalty was ultimately assumed to be more important than individual creativity. One gets the sense that at DEC the individual was ultimately more important than the organization and that at Ciba-Geigy the organization was ultimately more important than the individual. In such an organization neither Theory X nor

Theory Y applies. Ouchi (1981) referred to this type of organization as being dominated by "Theory Z": a more clanlike, paternalistic, holistic view of the organization and its members.

Assumptions About Appropriate Human Activity

Closely connected to assumptions about human nature are shared assumptions about the appropriate way for humans to act in relation to their environment. Several basically different orientations have been identified in cross-cultural studies and these have direct implications for variations one can see in organizations.

The Doing Orientation

Kluckhohn and Strodtbeck (1961) noted in their comparative study that at one extreme one can identify a "doing" orientation, which correlates closely with (1) the assumption that nature can be controlled and manipulated, (2) a pragmatic orientation toward the nature of reality, and (3) a belief in human perfectibility. In other words, it is taken for granted that the proper thing for people to do is to take charge and actively control their environment and their fate.

"Doing" is the predominant orientation of the United States and is certainly a key assumption of U.S. managers, reflected in the World War II slogan "We can do it" as immortalized in the Rosie the Riveter posters, and in the stock American phrases "getting things *done*" and "let's *do* something about it." The notion that "the impossible just takes a little longer" is central to United States business ideology. DEC was a prime example of commitment to "doing the right thing": when there is a difficulty, do something about it, solve the problem, involve other people, get help, but do something; don't let it fester. The doing orientation focuses on the task, on efficiency, and on discovery. Organizations driven by this assumption seek to grow and to dominate the markets they are in.

The Being Orientation

At the other extreme from the doing orientation is a "being" orientation, which correlates closely with the assumption that nature is powerful and humanity is subservient to it. This orientation implies a kind of fatalism: since one cannot influence nature, one must become accepting and enjoy what one has. One must focus more on the here and now, on individual enjoyment, and on acceptance of whatever comes. Organizations operating according to this orientation look for a niche in their environment that allows them to survive and they always think in terms of adapting to external realities rather than trying to create markets or dominate some portion of the environment.

The Being-in-Becoming Orientation

A third orientation, which lies between the two extremes of doing and being, is "being-in-becoming," referring to the idea that the individual must achieve harmony with nature by fully developing his or her own capacities and, thereby, achieving a perfect union with the environment. Through detachment, meditation, and control of those things that can be controlled (for instance, feelings and bodily functions), one achieves full self-development and self-actualization. The focus is on what the person *is* rather than what the person can *accomplish*, on achieving a certain state of development rather than doing and accomplishing. In short, "the being-in-becoming orientation emphasizes that kind of activity which has as its goal the development of all aspects of the self as an integrated whole" (Kluckhohn and Strodtbeck, 1961, p. 17).

The relevance of this dimension can be seen most clearly in organizational attitudes and norms about the expression of emotions. At Essochem, the European subsidiary of the chemical branch of Exxon, senior managers complained that they could not find any competent managers to put on their internal board of directors. In observing their meetings devoted to succession planning and management development, I observed that French and Italian managers were frequently labeled as "too emotional" and that this disqualified them from further consideration for higher-level jobs. Apparently, the assumption in this organization was that good management involves being unemotional, an assumption that I later found out was very dominant in the U.S. headquarters organization. This organization's assumptions limited human growth and development and, through limiting its diversity at senior levels, limited the strategic options available to it.

In contrast, DEC was extreme in the degree to which it allowed and encouraged all forms of self-development, which was later reflected in the degree to which "alumni" of DEC, now working on their own or in other organizations, used the phrase "I grew up at DEC." At Ciba-Geigy, it was clear that one had to fit in and become part of the organizational fabric and that socialization into the existing mode was therefore more common than self-development.

Organization/Environment Relations

Activity orientation translates fairly quickly into concepts of how organizations—especially business organizations—should relate to their external economic and market environment. In every organization there will evolve a deeply held view of whether (1) nature, the perceived total environment, can be subjugated and controlled (the Western tradition), or (2) nature must be harmonized with (the assumption of many Asian religions and societies), or (3) one must subjugate oneself to nature (the assumption of some Southeast Asian religions and societies). Does the organization view itself as capable of dominating and changing its environment? Or does it assume that it must coexist with other organizations and harmonize with its environment by developing its proper niche? Or does it assume that it must subjugate itself to its environment and accept whatever niche is available?

At this level we are talking about the deep assumptions underlying an organization's primary task, core mission, or basic functions, whether manifest or latent. If the organization's assumptions about itself at this level are out of line with environmental realities, sooner or later it may face a survival problem. Therefore, when organizations examine their strategy, they should focus heavily on initial assumptions about the environment and attempt, as much as possible, to validate those assumptions before deciding on goals and means.

When DEC was founded in the mid-1950s, computing technology was just beginning to evolve, which permitted DEC to develop and validate the assumption that it could dominate the mini-computer market and that it could innovate fast enough to stay ahead by this means. This set of assumptions even led DEC in the mid-1980s to decide to compete directly with IBM; some DEC strategists saw DEC overtaking IBM by the mid 2000s. However, the technology, the economic environment in terms of numbers of competitors, and the market in terms of commodification all changed to create a very different total environment in which DEC's assumptions no longer fit, creating the conditions for DEC's ultimate economic failure (Schein, 2003).

Ciba-Geigy, in its major turnaround (which is described in Chapter Eighteen) realized that it existed in multiple environments. Its chemical business existed in an environment that had huge "overcapacity," leading to decisions to scale that business way down. On the other hand, pharmaceuticals was a business with high potential for growth and one in which size and the ability to dominate markets mattered. It was this latter assumption that ultimately led to Ciba-Geigy's merging with one of its former competitors, Sandoz, to become Novartis, a more powerful and more focused pharmaceutical giant.

Assumptions About the Nature of Human Relationships

At the core of every culture are assumptions about the proper way for individuals to relate to each other in order to make the group safe, comfortable, and productive. When such assumptions are not widely shared, we speak of anarchy and anomie. Whereas the previous assumption areas deal with the group's relationship to the external environment, this set of assumptions deals more with the nature of the group itself and the kind of internal environment it creates for its members. Here we proceed with a more general analysis of what was covered in Chapter Four as the issues groups face when a culture first emerges and the internal integration problems that were reviewed in Chapter Six.

What Problems Must be Resolved?

Assumptions about relationships must solve four basic problems for each member:

1. Identity and Role—Who am I supposed to be in this group and what will be my role?
2. Power and Influence—Will my needs for influence and control be met?
3. Needs and Goals—Will the group's goals allow me to meet my own needs?
4. Acceptance and Intimacy—Will I be accepted, respected, and loved in this group? How close will our relationships be?

Every group, organization, and society will develop different solutions to each of these problem areas, but some kind of solution must be found for people to get past self-oriented defensive behavior and be able to function in the group. How this process works out in a new group was illustrated in Chapter Four. In organizations we have to assume that sometime early in their history the group learned certain ways of relating that worked and hence became the norm. For example, at DEC you were supposed to develop and push your own identity and formulate your own role. Power and influence were to be perpetually negotiated rather than being fixed in any positions. The open climate encouraged employees to define their jobs in such a way that they could meet their own needs, and the required openness and commitment to truth made for a very informal and intimate environment.

At Ciba-Geigy, roles were very structured and if your identity did not match role requirements you found identity outlets elsewhere. Power and influence were clearly derivative from education, research experience, and position in the organization. The paternalistic emphasis insured that a real effort would be made to meet needs. You were automatically a respected member of the family but relationships would remain formal. I was "Professor Schein" even after five years and many informal meetings. I should point out that in the case of both companies there were strong links to the host culture—New England for DEC and Basel, Switzerland for Ciba-Geigy.

Assumptions such as those just described will, of course, reflect the even more basic assumptions about the nature of human nature. For example, if we assume that humans are inherently aggressive, we will develop a society built around controls of such aggression, with relationship assumptions such as "One must take care of oneself" or "One must compete, but compete fairly." If we assume that humans are inherently cooperative, the assumptions about relationships may well emphasize how to cooperate to accomplish external goals.

Individualism and Groupism

If one looks at cultures around the world and their assumptions about how people relate to each other and what the basic relational units are, obvious differences appear. Some cultures are what Kluckhohn and Strodtbeck (1961) call *individualistic* and Havrylyshyn (1980) calls *individual competitive* (the United States, for example). Other cultures are said to be *collateral, group cooperative*, or *communitarian* in emphasizing that the group is more important than the individual (Japan, for example). Hofstede's (2001) comparative study reinforces this point in identifying individualism as one of the core dimensions along which countries differ. For example, countries such as the United States, Canada, Australia, and the United Kingdom come out highest on this dimension, while Pakistan, Indonesia, Colombia, Venezuela, and Ecuador come out lowest.

One of the deepest elements of culture will be based on this dimension, in the sense that it reflects whether ultimately a society sees as its basic building block the individual or the group. If group interests and individual interests differ, which will be sacrificed and which will be protected? In the U.S. our Constitution and Bill of Rights ultimately protect the individual, whereas in more communitarian cultures the individual is expected to sacrifice himself or herself for the greater good of the group. At the extreme this assumption has led to the glorification by their people of Japanese kamikaze pilots in World War II and of terrorist suicide bombers in the Palestinian/Israeli conflict.

In practice every society and organization must honor both the group and the individual in the sense that neither makes sense without the other. Cultures differ dramatically, however, in the degree to which tacit norms reflect the deeper assumption. On the surface both the United States and Australia appear to be individualistic cultures, yet it is in Australia (and New Zealand) that one hears many references to the "tall poppy syndrome" (i.e., it is the tall poppy that gets cut off); illustrating this, a teenager reported that after a brilliant ride on his surfboard he had to say to his buddies, "Gee, that was a *lucky* one." In contrast, though the United States espouses teamwork, it is evident in sports that it is the superstar who is admired and that building teams is seen as pragmatically necessary, not intrinsically desirable.

Power Distance

Hofstede also identified the dimension of *power distance* and notes that countries vary in the degree to which people in a hierarchical situation perceive a greater or lesser ability to control each other's behavior. People in high-power-distance countries, such as the Philippines, Mexico, and Venezuela, perceive more inequality between superiors and subordinates than do people in low-power-distance countries, such as Denmark, Israel, and Austria. If one looks at the same index by occupation, one finds higher power distance among unskilled and semiskilled workers than among professional and managerial workers, as would be expected.

These dimensions also reflect even deeper cultural assumptions about the nature of the self. For example, Redding and Martyn-Johns (1979) point out that Western and Asian societies have strikingly different core concepts of the self. Asians are less focused on differentiating the individual from the group and therefore put less emphasis on self-actualization as a core personality process, whereas Westerners have developed strong concepts of the individual and the self as something potentially quite distinct from the group and something to be developed in its own right. In some cultures the self is compartmentalized, so that work, family, and leisure involve different aspects of the self; in other cultures the self is more of a whole, and even the idea of separating work from family does not make any sense. The core question of identity and role is thus answered in very different ways in different cultures.

At the organizational level, assumptions about relationships will, of course, reflect the assumptions of the wider culture, but they become elaborated and differentiated. The founder/leader may believe that the only way to run an organization is to assign individual tasks, hold individuals accountable for performance, and minimize group and cooperative work because that would only lead to lowest-common-denominator group solutions or, worse, diffusion of responsibility. Another leader might emphasize cooperation and communication among subordinates as the best means of solving problems and implementing solutions because that would lead to the level of teamwork that task accomplishment requires. These two leaders would develop quite different working styles, which would be reflected ultimately in the organization's processes, reward systems, and control systems.

DEC reduced the power distance between superiors and subordinates as much as possible, building on the assumption that good ideas can come from anyone at any time. Senior managers were always available and willing to talk to anyone about any issue, constrained only by the practicalities of time and space. (To overcome time and space barriers, DEC built a worldwide electronic mail network that was frequently used.) A senior manager in R&D left DEC for a bigger and better job, only to return three months later with the following comment: "In the new company I had an idea for a new product and was told that I would have to talk first to my boss, then to the director of R&D, and then to the senior vice president. At Digital, if I have an idea, I go straight to Ken Olsen [the founder and CEO] and we kick it around. This is the kind of place in which I want to work."

In contrast, Ciba-Geigy valued hierarchy, formality, and protocol. One did not approach people informally. Meetings and conferences had to be well defined, have a clear purpose accepted by all, and be planned with rank and appropriate deference in mind. During my consulting visits, I saw only people who had specifically requested some of my time concerning some specific problems that they were concerned about. It would not have been appropriate for me to drop in on people or to strike up conversations beyond the minimal cordialities in the executive dining room.

Basic Characteristics of Role Relationships

Human relationships can also be usefully analyzed with the aid of Parsons's (1951) original "pattern variables." It is these fundamental characteristics of all role relationships that led to the Kluckhohn and Strodtbeck model and the currently popular model of Hampden-Turner and Trompenaars (2000), which was referred to in Chapter Eight.

In any relationship between people, one can ask these questions:

How much emotionality is appropriate? Should the relationship be (1) very *aloof* and "professional," as in a doctor-patient relationship, or (2) very *emotionally charged*, as in friendship?

Should the relationship be (1) very *specific*, dealing only with the exact reason for the relationship, as in a sales-customer relationship, or (2) *diffuse*, as in most friendships?

Do the participants view each other in (1) very general *universalistic* terms based on stereotypes, as in most sales relationships, or (2) a very *particularistic* way as whole persons?

Are social rewards, such as status and rank, assigned on the basis of (1) what the person is by birth or family membership—what is *ascribed* to him or her—or (2) what the person has actually accomplished—his or her *achievements*?

Using these variables, we would say that relationships at DEC were emotionally charged, diffuse, particularistic, and highly achievement oriented; at Ciba-Geigy they were emotionally aloof, specific, somewhat (though not totally) universalistic, and somewhat mixed on ascription versus achievement. Achievement clearly counted at Ciba-Geigy, but ascriptive criteria such as the right family background and the right level of education also were considered to be very important. One of the high-potential division managers who was a widower was strongly encouraged to remarry as a prerequisite to being promoted to the internal board of the company. People at Ciba-Geigy were assumed to be ambitious, but the good of the company was taken into account more than it was at DEC, where the assumption seemed to be that if everyone did the correct thing—that is, made her or his best individual effort—that would turn out to be best for the company as a whole.

These dimensions identify the specific areas where consensus is needed if the organization is to function smoothly. Consensus in these areas then becomes a deep layer of the culture and surfaces only when someone challenges or violates one of the assumptions. For example, an American manager brought up with strong beliefs in achievement as the basis for status could not cope with the fact that Steinbergs, a Canadian family firm into which he had moved as a general manager, was completely dominated by assumptions of ascription, particularism, and emotional diffuseness. Tasks were assigned on the basis of who was who, decisions were made on the basis of who liked whom, and promotions were clearly reserved for family members. After a year or more of turmoil and conflict he left the organization.

Activity Orientation and Role Definition

One element of activity orientation that is increasingly important today relates to underlying assumptions about the nature of work and the relationships among work, family, and personal concerns. One assumption would be that work is primary; another, that the family is primary; another, that self-interest is primary; and still another, that some form of integrated lifestyle is possible and desirable for both men and women (Bailyn, 1978, 1982, 1993; Schein, 1978, 1990). If members of a given organization have different assumptions about the nature of work activity and its relative importance to other activities, those differences will manifest themselves in frustration and communication breakdowns.

How activity orientation is linked to sex roles also must be examined. Hofstede (2001) found in his survey a basic dimension labeled *masculinity*, reflecting the degree to which, in a given country, male and female roles are clearly distinguished. Countries that come out highest on his combined index are Japan, Austria, and Venezuela; countries at the lowest end are Denmark, Norway, Sweden, and the Netherlands. The United States is near the middle of the distribution on this measure.

As was noted in the discussion of assumptions about human nature, the validity of this dimension is marginal in that it is based on fundamentally Western assumptions about the separation of self from other aspects of society and nature. In particular, the way we categorize sex roles and differentiate work from family and self is clearly not the way some other cultures conceive of human nature, and it is difficult for Westerners even to imagine how human nature and human activity are conceptualized in non-Western cultures.

In the United States we are also discovering, through a painful process of consciousness-raising, how gender- and race-related assumptions come to be so taken for granted that they function to create de facto kinds of discrimination through stereotyping and the creation of various kinds of barriers such as "glass ceilings." In these areas many culture researchers have found the best evidence of culture conflict and genuine ambiguities about roles, influencing even the kinds of problems that researchers have identified and studied (Martin, 1991, 2002).

Rules of Interaction—The Joint Effect of Time, Space, and Relationship Assumptions

In the section on space we saw how intimacy is defined by distance and position. If we combine such assumptions with assumptions about timing and about the appropriate way for people to relate to each other, we have, in effect, the assumption set that specifies what in most cultures are thought of as the basic rules of interaction (Goffman, 1967; Van Maanen, 1979b). What we think of as tact, poise, good manners, and etiquette can be deconstructed into a set of rules that preserve the social order—what Goffman and others have called "face work." In other words, in every human group, the members sooner or later learn that in order to survive as a group, they must develop rules and norms that make the environment safe for all. Members must learn to preserve each other's face and self-esteem, lest the social environment become dangerous. If I humiliate you, I license you to humiliate me.

The content of these basic rules of interaction will differ from group to group, but the existence of some set of such rules can be safely predicted for any group that has had some stability and joint history. For example, both DEC and Hewlett-Packard (HP) strongly espoused teamwork as a necessary condition for successful performance, and in both companies it was considered bad not to be a team player. But when one examines the actual rules of interaction in operation, one discovers almost diametrically opposed assumptions. At DEC, to be a team player meant to be open and truthful and trustworthy. If you agreed to do something, you did it. If you did not agree, you did not promise to do something that you did not intend to do.

At HP, on the other hand, the assumption grew up that groups should reach consensus, that being nice to each other and being cooperative were important in reaching consensus, and that arguing too much or sticking to your own point of view too much was equivalent to not being a team player. Consequently, decisions were reached much more quickly, but they did not stick. People agreed in public to uphold the norms but then in private failed to follow through, forcing the decision process to start all over again.

At DEC it was considered timely to speak up right away if you didn't agree; at HP it was considered timely to agree right away even if you didn't intend to follow up on your own words or if you had reservations about the decision. DEC put more ultimate weight on truth, whereas HP put more ultimate weight on the creation of a certain kind of work climate. The important point is that the new member of either of these organizations had to acquire knowledge of how to manage their relationships in terms of all the dimensions we have reviewed. Superficially, many people saw DEC and HP as basically similar organizations. In terms of the parts of their cultures that dealt with relationship management and decision making, they were quite different.

Summary and Conclusions

This chapter has reviewed the deeper cultural dimensions that deal with human nature, human activity, and human relationships. The set of issues and dimensions reviewed constitutes a kind of grid against which to map a given organizational culture, but one should always remember that not all dimensions are equally salient or important in a given culture. Furthermore, the dimensions interact to form a kind of pattern or paradigm, as was shown in Chapter Two for DEC and Ciba-Geigy.

We reviewed the basic assumptions about human nature as being calculative, social, self-actualizing, or complex; as being positive and malleable (Theory Y) or negative and fixed (Theory X). We noted that some cultures emphasize "doing" and conquering, other cultures emphasize "being" and accepting one's fate and niche, and still others emphasize "being in becoming" in focusing on self-development as the fundamentally "right" way to be. These dimensions characterize how organizations view their relationship to the environment in which they operate.

We then reviewed basic dimensions that have been used to characterize human relationships. The most fundamental of these is whether the group is primarily individualistic and competitive or communitarian and cooperative. All groups have some form of hierarchy, but a relevant cultural dimension is the degree of distance that is felt between higher-ups and lower-downs in the hierarchy.

In the formation of any group, all members must solve for themselves the problem of identity: who to be in that group, how much influence or control they will have, whether their needs and goals will be met, and how intimate the group will become. In that process, groups will learn how to structure a given relationship in terms of the dimensions of how emotionally charged or neutral it should be, how diffuse or specific it is to be, how universalistic or particularistic it is to be, and how much the value placed on the other person is to be based on achievement.

We noted that at a deeper level cultures differ in the degree to which the self is seen as differentiated from work and family roles and that gender roles vary in the degree to which masculinity and femininity are seen as different. We also noted that all groups form rules of interaction around proper behavior in relation to these role dimensions and that adherence to those rules is fundamental to any kind of social order.

We should note that culture is deep, wide, and complex and we should avoid the temptation to stereotype organizational phenomena in terms of one or two salient dimensions. Many such typologies have been suggested, as will be examined in the next chapter.

10

CULTURAL TYPOLOGIES

In the previous several chapters I reviewed a great many dimensions that have been used to characterize cultures. I chose to focus on those that are useful for describing organizational cultures in particular. Other dimensions have been proposed and these are often presented as universal typologies that are presumed to help us understand all organizations. Before reviewing some of those typologies we need to understand what role typologies play in trying to understand an abstract concept like organizational culture.

Why Typologies?

When we observe the "natural" world, what we see, hear, taste, smell, and feel is potentially overwhelming. By itself "raw experience" does not make sense, but our own cultural upbringing has taught us how to make sense of it through conceptual categories that are embedded in our language. What we experience as an infant is a "blooming, buzzing confusion" that is slowly put into order as we learn to discriminate objects such as chairs and tables, mother and father, light and dark and to associate words with those experienced objects and events.

By the time we are young adults we have a complete vocabulary and set of conceptual categories that allow us to discriminate and label most of what we experience. We must not forget, however, that these categories and the language that goes with them are *learned* within a given culture and such learning continues as we move into new subcultures such as occupations and organizations.

The engineer learns new categories and words, as do the doctor, the lawyer, and the manager. The employee going into DEC and the employee going into Ciba-Geigy learn different things.

The scientist trying to study a given area such as human behavior in organizations, leadership, and organizational culture must develop categories that are useful for helping to make sense of the variations that he or she observes. Such categories can derive from cultural categories that already exist or can be invented and labeled with new words, such as monochronic and polychronic as dimensions of the concept of time.

Such new concepts become useful if they (1) help make sense and provide some order out of the observed phenomena, and (2) help to define what may be the underlying structure in the phenomena by building a theory of how things work, which, in turn, (3) enables us to predict to some degree how other phenomena that may not yet have been observed are going to look.

In the process of building new categories—which can be thought of as defining the dimensions to be studied—we inevitably must become more abstract. And as we develop abstractions it becomes possible to develop hypothetical relationships among such abstractions, which we then can think of as typologies or theories of how things work. The advantage of such typologies and the theories they permit us to postulate is that they attempt to order a great variety of different phenomena. The disadvantage and danger is that they are so abstract that they do not reflect adequately the reality of a given set of phenomena being observed. In this sense, typologies can be useful if we are trying to compare many organizations but can be quite useless if we are trying to understand one particular organization.

For example, extroversion and introversion as a personality typology is enormously useful in broadly categorizing observed social behavior, but may be too general to enable us to understand a particular person. Noting that cultures around the world are individualistic or communitarian can be very useful in making sense out of the huge variation we observe, but can be quite useless in trying to understand a particular organization, as was noted in describing Ciba-Geigy as a complex mix of both. The dilemma in building dimensions for study and organizing them into typologies is, therefore, ultimately a pragmatic one of what one is trying to observe and describe and how general or specific one wants one's categories to be.

Typologies That Focus on Assumptions about Participation and Involvement

Organizations are ultimately the result of people doing things together for a common purpose. The basic relationship between the individual and the organization can, therefore, be thought of as the most fundamental dimension around which to build a typology. One of the most general theories here is Etzioni's (1975), which distinguishes among three types of organization:

1. *Coercive* organizations, in which the individual is essentially captive for physical or economic reasons and must, therefore, obey whatever rules are imposed by the authorities

2. *Utilitarian* organizations, in which the individual provides "a fair day's work for a fair day's pay" and therefore abides by whatever rules are essential; however, the group often develops countercultural norms and rules to protect itself

3. *Normative* organizations, in which the individual contributes his or her commitment because the goals of the organization are basically the same as the individual's goals

In the coercive system, members are assumed to be alienated and will exit if possible; in the utilitarian system, they are assumed to be rationally economic calculative; and in the normative consensus system, they are assumed to be morally involved and to identify with the organization.

Assumptions about peer relationships can be derived from this typology. In the coercive system, peer relationships develop as a defense against authority, leading to unions and other forms of self-protective groups. In the utilitarian system, peer relations evolve around the work group and typically reflect the kind of incentive system that management uses. In the normative system, they evolve naturally around tasks and in support of the organization. Some typologies add a dimension of professional or collegial relationships in an organization in which individuals have broad vested rights and a "moral" orientation toward organizational goals, such as in professional partnerships in law or medicine (Jones, 1983; Shrivastava, 1983).

The value of this typology is that it enables us to differentiate business organizations that tend to be utilitarian from coercive total institutions such as prisons and mental hospitals, and from normative organizations such as schools, hospitals, and nonprofits (Goffman, 1961). The difficulty is that within any given organizational type one may see variations of all three dimensions operating, which requires us to invent still other dimensions to capture the uniqueness of a given organization.

A number of typologies focus specifically on how authority is used and what level of participation is expected in the organization: (1) autocratic, (2) paternalistic, (3) consultative or democratic, (4) participative and power sharing, (5) delegative, and (6) abdicative (which implies delegating not only tasks and responsibilities but power and controls as well) (Bass, 1981, 1985; Harbison and Myers, 1959; Likert, 1967; Vroom and Yetton, 1973).

These organizational typologies deal much more with aggression, power, and control than with love, intimacy, and peer relationships. In that regard they are always built on underlying assumptions about human nature and activity. The arguments that managers get into about the "correct" level of participation and use of authority usually reflect the different assumptions they are making about the nature of the subordinates they are dealing with. Looking at participation and involvement as a matter of cultural assumptions makes clear that the debate about whether leaders should be more autocratic or participative is ultimately highly colored by the assumptions of a particular group in a particular context. The search for the universally correct leadership style is doomed to failure because of cultural variation by country, by industry, by occupation, and by the particular history of a given organization.

Typologies of Corporate Character and Culture

The concept of corporate *character* was first introduced into the culture literature by Wilkins (1989), who saw it as a component of culture consisting of "shared vision," "motivational faith" that things would be fair and that abilities would be used, and "distinctive skills," both overt and tacit. In his view, "building character" was possible by emphasizing programs dealing with each of the components, but he did not build a typology around the dimensions.

Goffee and Jones (1998), on the other hand, saw character as equivalent to culture and created a typology based on two key dimensions: "solidarity"—the tendency to be like-minded, and "sociability"—the tendency to be friendly to each other. These dimensions are measured with a twenty-three-item self-description questionnaire. They closely resemble and are derivative from the classical group dynamics distinction between task variables and building and maintenance variables. These same two dimensions were also used extensively by Blake and Mouton (1964, 1969, 1989) in their organization development grid, which was built on the two dimensions of task and group building, each to be measured on a scale of 1 to 9. A highly sociable, person-oriented organization that cared little for task accomplishment would be rated as 1,9, whereas a highly task-oriented, driven, and insensitive organization would be rated 9,1. Various other combinations were possible, ranging from 1,1 (which is virtually a state of anomie) to 5,5 (a compromise solution) to 9,9, the hero of the model, in which task and personal factors are given equal weight.

Goffee and Jones use these dimensions to identify four types of cultures:

1. Fragmented—low on both dimensions
2. Mercenary—high on solidarity, low on sociability
3. Communal—high on sociability, low on solidarity
4 Networked—high on both.

Each type has certain virtues and liabilities that are described, but the typology misses a crucial dimension that has been identified by Ancona (1988) and others: the relationship between the group (organization) and its external environments, the boundary management function that must be added to the task and maintenance functions. Without a model of what happens at the boundary it is not possible to determine which of the types of culture is effective under given conditions.

The Goffee and Jones dimensions are useful for diagnosing some elements of a culture, and the authors provide self-diagnostic questionnaires, but it is somewhat presumptuous to assert that a questionnaire designed just to measure the dimensions that the authors have started with should be adequate to capturing something as complex as an organizational culture. They provide no validation of any sort that the dimensions and how they are measured are related to other organizational indicators or even measure what they are supposed to measure.

Aspects of physical space, time, communication, and identity are made derivative from the two core dimensions, which means that the diagnostician sees everything through those lenses. More problematic is that there is no way of knowing how important these dimensions are in the total *pattern* of dimensions that make up any given culture. One may decide in a given company that we are a communal culture, and this judgment may be valid, but it may be culturally irrelevant in that the important tacit assumptions driving the behavior of that organization may have very little to do with either sociability or solidarity. Recall that in the case of Digital and

Ciba-Geigy, it was the *interaction* of many dimensions that explained the organization's behavior, not any one or two dimensions.

Cameron and Quinn (1999) also developed a four-category typology based on two dimensions, but in their case the dimensions are more structural—how stable or flexible the organization is and how externally or internally focused it is. These dimensions are seen as perpetually competing values. An internally focused flexible organization is thought of as a *clan*, whereas an internally focused stable organization is thought of as a *hierarchy*. An externally focused flexible organization is labeled an *adhocracy*, and an externally focused stable organization is thought of as a *market*.

Whereas the Goffee and Jones typology was built on basic dimensions that derived from group dynamics (task versus maintenance), the Cameron and Quinn typology was built on factor analyzing large numbers of indicators of organizational performance and finding that these reduce to two clusters that correlate closely with what cognitive researchers have found to be "archetypical" dimensions as well. Markets, hierarchies, and clans as organizational types were also identified earlier by Ouchi (1978, 1981) and markets versus hierarchies were analyzed in detail by economists such as Williamson (1975).

Cameron and Quinn argue that, based on six self-description questions, one can build organizational profiles that show the relative tendency toward each of the four types of organization; and that this permits one to decide what kind of change is needed for increased organizational effectiveness in a given external environment. Again, using a few self-description questions as a basis for identifying location on a cultural dimension is questionable and even if valid as a measure, how would one know the relative importance of these dimensions in a given organization's cultural paradigm? Furthermore, how would a researcher know which of these typologies is the more valid or useful without having to know much more about the culture to which they are being applied?

Can the two typologies be reconciled? The mercenary culture seems to map clearly on the market culture. But can we say that a clan is a high-sociability, high-solidarity networked culture? No, because a clan is inwardly focused, whereas a networked culture is, by implication, externally focused. And the communal and fragmented cultures clearly do not map onto hierarchy or adhocracy. So we are left with a dilemma that, in my view, derives from trying to build simple typologies in the first place. In order to determine which typology works better, we would have to assess a given organization with a much more open-ended, multidimensional approach of the sort I will describe in the next chapter.

Intraorganizational Typologies

The most obvious of intraorganizational typologies is the traditional distinction between management and labor or salaried and hourly. In every organization one can distinguish some version of this typology—those who run the place and those who do the daily work. There is no doubt that where these groups are more or less stable and develop a history of their own, they will become cultural units. The best example is the use of the concept of "command and control" as a *type* of organization.

Historically, an important element of such culture formation has been opposition—the deep assumption in both cultures that the conflict between them is intrinsic and inevitable. In a labor union a strong tradition may arise and get passed on from generation to generation that "management will always exploit you and screw you if it can," and within management the assumption may be passed on that "labor will always do as little as possible"—what McGregor identified as Theory X. This tendency leads to characterizing whole organizations as Theory X or Theory Y.

However, if one observes organizations more closely, one will find evidence for another kind of typology based on a combination of the task to be done and the occupational reference groups involved (Schein, 1996a). One can think of these as generic subcultures that every group or organization needs in order to survive. The problem is that in many organizations these subcultures conflict with each other, causing the organization to be less effective than it could be (Schein, 1996a).

Every organization has a task to be performed, and the set of people who get the work done—the line organization—can be thought of as the operator group that will typically form an *operator culture*. At the same time, every organization has a set of people whose job it is to design the work products and processes, who are more concerned about innovation, improvement, and redesign; this group can be thought of as the engineers whose *engineering culture* will be based externally in their occupational reference group. If the organization is a high-tech company, the engineers will evolve their assumptions from their engineering education and the current profession. If the organization is a hospital, the primary care physicians and nurses can be thought of as the operators and the research physicians as the engineers, who are more concerned about their innovations in their specialty than daily patient care.

Every organization must somehow survive economically in order to continue to fulfill its functions, its primary task. The ultimate survival task falls to what we can think of as the executive group, whose fundamental task is not only to ensure that the organization survives and continues to be effective, but who must integrate or at least align the other two cultures to maximize long-run effectiveness. In most organizations the executive function is tied in to the financial community in some way. Therefore, the *executive culture* that evolves is inevitably built around financial matters. Exhibit 10.1 shows the assumptions that are typically found in members of these three cultures and highlights the potential conflict between them. As with all typologies, these are abstractions that will not fit every case, but in every organization one can find some version of each of these cultures and one can then attempt to assess the degree to which they are in conflict or are constructively aligned.

The point of treating these as separate "occupational" cultures is to highlight the fact that each of these sets of assumptions is valid and necessary for organizations to remain effective. People are truly needed to deal with unforeseen contingencies and surprises; engineers and

Exhibit 10.1. The Assumptions of the Three Organizational Subcultures.

1. The Operator Culture (organization based)

   - The action of any organization is ultimately the action of people (operators)

   - The success of the enterprise therefore depends on people's knowledge, skill, and commitment

   - The knowledge and skill required are local and based on the organization's "core technology"

   - No matter how carefully engineered the production process is or how carefully rules and routines are specified, operators will have to deal with unpredictable contingencies

   - Therefore, operators have to have the capacity to learn and to deal with surprises

   - Because most operations involve interdependencies between separate elements of the process, operators must be able to operate as a collaborative team in which openness and mutual trust are highly valued

2. The Engineering Culture (global community)

   - Nature can and should be mastered: "That which is possible should be done"

   - Operations should be based on science and available technology

   - The most fun is solving puzzles and overcoming problems

   - Products and outcomes should be useful and be improvements

   - Solutions should be oriented toward elegance, simplicity, and precision: "Keep it neat and simple"

   - The ideal world is one of elegant machines and processes working in perfect precision and harmony without human intervention

   - People are the problem—they make mistakes and hence should be designed out of the system wherever possible

3. The Executive Culture (global community)

   - Without financial survival and growth there are no returns to shareholders or to society

   - The economic environment is perpetually competitive and potentially hostile: "In a war one cannot trust anyone"

   - Therefore, the CEO must be the "lone hero," isolated and alone, yet appearing to be omniscient and in total control, and feeling indispensable: "I'm OK; after all, I'm here; they are not OK; they have not made it to the top"

Exhibit 10.1. The Assumptions of
the Three Organizational Subcultures, Cont'd.

- One cannot get reliable data from below because subordinates will tell one what they think one wants to hear; therefore, as CEO one must trust one's own judgment more and more (i.e., lack of accurate feedback increases the sense of one's own rightness and omniscience)

- Organization and management are intrinsically hierarchical; the hierarchy is the measure of status and success and the primary means of maintaining control

- Because the organization is very large it becomes depersonalized and abstract, and, therefore, has to be run by rules, routines (systems), and rituals ("machine bureaucracy")

- Though people are necessary, they are a necessary evil, not an intrinsic value; people are a resource like other resources, to be acquired and managed, not ends in themselves

- The well-oiled machine organization does not need whole people, only the activities that are contracted for

---

designers are truly needed in order to invent new and better products and processes, even though some of those processes make some people superfluous or obsolete; and executives are truly needed to worry about the financial viability of the whole organization even though that sometimes requires curbing expensive innovations or laying people off. In terms of a competing values model described above, the issue is how to align the goals of the three subcultures: focusing on doing the job, remaining innovative to deal with changes in the environment, and staying economically healthy. When one of these subcultures becomes too dominant, the organization cannot survive—as was the case with DEC, where the engineering innovation mentality overrode both the operations and executive cultures.

Summary and Conclusions

The value of typologies is that they simplify thinking and provide useful categories for sorting out the complexities we must deal with when we confront organizational realities. They provide categories for thinking and classifying, which is useful. The weakness of culture typologies is that they oversimplify these complexities and may provide us categories that are incorrect in terms of their relevance to what we are trying to understand. They limit our perspective by prematurely focusing us on just a few dimensions, they limit our ability to find complex patterns among a number of dimensions, and they do not reveal what a given group feels intensely about.

Typologies also introduce a bias toward what Martin (2002) calls the "integration perspective" in culture studies—an approach that emphasizes those dimensions on which there is a high degree of consensus. She notes that many organizations are "differentiated" or even "fragmented" to the extent that there is little consensus on any cultural dimensions. An integrated culture is one in which the whole organization shares a single set of assumptions; a differentiated culture is an organization in which powerful subcultures disagree on certain crucial issues, such as labor and management; and a fragmented culture is an organization such as a financial conglomerate that has a great many subcultures and no single overarching set of assumptions that are shared. Clearly the effort to classify a given organization into a single typological category, such as "clan" or "networked," presumes not only integration around two dimensions but also the assumption that those dimensions can be measured well enough to determine the degree of consensus.

Martin's categories are a powerful way to describe organizations that have different kinds of cultural landscapes within them, but they do not require any redefinition of the basic concept of culture as a *shared* set of assumptions that is taken for granted. It is then an empirical matter whether in a given organization we find various levels of integration, differentiation, and/or fragmentation.

Typologies reflect organizational theory and can enhance theory. For example, the distinction between the operator, engineering, and executive cultures *within* organizations is derived from basic theory about labor and management but elaborates that theory by sharpening the cultural distinctions between these three groups and identifying the engineering/design/innovation group as a cultural unit that is often overlooked.

Having provided some conceptual categories and cultural typologies, we must turn next to the problem of empirically deciphering what is actually going on in a given organization. In the next chapter we address this issue of how to assess cultural dimensions.

11

DECIPHERING CULTURE

Organizational culture can be studied in a variety of ways. The method one chooses should be determined by one's purpose. Just assessing a culture is as vague as just assessing personality or character in an individual. We usually think of such an assessment when there is some problem to be illuminated or some specific purpose for which we need information. And, as we will see, how we go about the assessment and what tools we use are very much dependent on our purpose in making it.

Why Might One Want to Decipher or Assess Culture?

The purpose of deciphering or assessing culture can range from pure research, in which the researcher is trying to present a picture of a culture to fellow researchers and other interested parties, to helping an organization come to terms with its own culture because the leaders of the organization are engaged in some change project. The researcher may be an outsider gathering data from insiders for research purposes or to provide information to insiders on some issue that they are exploring. The researcher may be an insider gathering data in relation to some change agenda or some questions raised by management. In *all* of these cases, the researcher must realize that gathering valid data from a complex human system is intrinsically difficult, involves a variety of choices and options, and *is always an intervention into the life of the organization if the research involves any contact with the organization.*

The most obvious difficulty in gathering valid cultural data is a well-known phenomenon: when human subjects are involved in research, there is a tendency for them either to resist and hide data that they feel defensive about or to exaggerate in order to impress the researcher or to get cathartic relief—"Finally someone is interested enough in us to listen to our story." The need for such cathartic relief derives from the fact that even the best of organizations generates "toxins"—frustrations with the boss, tensions over missed targets, destructive competition with peers, scarce resources, exhaustion from overwork, and so on (Frost, 2003). In the process of trying to understand how the organization really works, the researcher may find him- or herself listening to tales of woe from anxious or frustrated employees who have no other outlet. If the researcher is to get any kind of accurate picture of what is going on in the organization, a method must be found that encourages the insiders to "tell it like it is" rather than trying to impress the researcher, hide data, or blow off steam.

If the researcher makes any kind of contact with the organization, even if it is only the getting of permission to observe silently, the human system has been perturbed in unknown ways. The employees being observed may view the observer as a spy or as an opportunity for catharsis, as noted above. Motives may be attributed to management. The observer may be seen as a nuisance, a disturbance, or an audience to whom to play. The key point is that the observer has no way of knowing which of the many possible intervention outcomes are happening and whether or not they are desirable either from a data gathering or ethical point of view. For this reason, one should examine carefully the broad range of interventions available and choose carefully which method to use.

Alternative Data-Gathering Methods

There are many ways of gathering data (as shown in Table 11.1) that differ along two dimensions—how involved the researcher becomes with the organization being studied and how involved the members

Table 11.1 Categories of Research on Organizations.

Level of "Subject" Involvement	Level of Researcher Involvement	
	Low to Medium; Quantitative	High; Qualitative
Minimal	Demographics: measurement of "distal variables"	Ethnography: participant observation; content analysis of stories, myths, rituals, symbols, other artifacts
Partial	Experimentation: questionnaires, ratings, objective tests, scales	Projective tests; assessment centers; interviews
Maximal	Total quality tools such as statistical quality control; action research	Clinical research; organization development

Copyright © E. H. Schein.

of the organization become in the data gathering process. Some cultural artifacts can be gathered by purely demographic methods or by observation at a distance, such as photographing buildings, observing action in the organization without getting involved, entering the organization incognito, and so on. As was pointed out in Chapter Two, the problem with this method is that the data may be clear but undecipherable. I could see all the fighting at DEC from a distance, but I had no idea what it meant.

If we want to understand more of what is going on, we must get more involved through becoming a participant observer/ethnographer, but we do not, in this role, want the subjects to become too directly involved lest we unwittingly change the very phenomena we are trying to study. To minimize the inevitable biases that result from our own involvement, we may use informants to help us clarify what we observe or to decipher the data we are gathering, but we limit the organization's involvement as much as possible.

The middle row of Table 11.1, depicting partial subject involvement, illustrates data gathering methods that involve the members of the organization to a greater degree. If we want to minimize our outsider involvement, we try to rely on objective measurements such as experiments or questionnaires. Experiments are usually not possible, for ethical reasons, but surveys and questionnaires are often used, with limitations that will be discussed in detail below. If we recognize that the interpretation of cultural data may require interaction with the subjects, we settle for semistructured interviews and projective tests that still require the researcher's interpretations but add the data from the interaction itself to aid in that interpretation.

Questionnaires and individual interview surveys can be the best way to compare and contrast sets of organizations efficiently, but if culture is the researcher's target, the limitations of these methods for gathering cultural data must be taken seriously. In using a questionnaire or survey instrument, one runs the risk that

- One will select dimensions to measure that are not relevant or important in terms of the cultural dynamics of a particular organization
- One will measure only superficial characteristics of the culture because survey instruments cannot get at the deeper shared tacit assumptions that define the essence of cultures
- The survey instrument will be neither reliable nor valid, because to validate formal measures of something as deep and complex as cultural assumptions is intrinsically very difficult
- The *patterning* of cultural assumptions into a paradigm cannot be revealed by a questionnaire
- Individual respondents will not be able to answer survey questions reliably because cultural assumptions are tacit
- The questionnaire or survey process, as a very powerful intervention, will have unpredictable consequences for the organization's normal processes (too many researchers gather their data and disappear into their ivory tower without ever consid-

ering whether the way in which they gathered the data influenced and possibly upset the organization in which the data were gathered)

Individual interviews present many of the same problems but at least they do not limit the dimensions to be explored. In an interview one can ask broad questions like "What was it like to come to work in this organization?" "What did you notice most as being important to getting along?" and so on. The main problem with this approach is that it is very time consuming and it may be hard to put data from different individuals together into a coherent picture because each person may see things slightly differently.

The critique of typologies in the last chapter was based in part on these issues—too few dimensions are measured; the measurement tools are short, unvalidated self-report questionnaires; and the taking of the self-report questionnaires biases organization members' perception and thought to an unknown degree.

In Table 11.1, the bottom left cell indicates a methodology for studying the organization by making a direct intervention in how the members work and observing the results; for example, by management's hiring a researcher on a contract to measure the impact of a new process that is being introduced. In this case the intervention was made primarily by the management of the organization itself; the researcher's only job is to measure the effects, although the measurement still will have additional unpredictable effects. In the right cell of that row is the methodology that I believe is most appropriate to cultural deciphering: what I call the *clinical research* model.

The Clinical Research Model

Most of the information I have provided so far about cultural assumptions in different kinds of organizations was gathered by clinical research (Schein, 1987a, 2001). The critical distinguishing feature of the clinical research model is that the data come *voluntarily* from the members of the organization because either *they initiated* the process and have something to gain by revealing themselves to the clinician, consultant, or researcher (hereafter called the *researcher/consultant*) or, if the consultant initiated the project, they feel *they have something to gain from cooperating with him or her.*

Often, the researcher/consultant is invited into the organization to help with some problem that has been presented, but then, in the process of working on the problem, he or she *discovers* culturally relevant information—particularly if the process consultation model is used, with its emphasis on inquiry and helping the organization to help itself (Schein, 1999a). If the initiative comes from an outsider who has obtained permission to "study" some segment of the organization, the clinical approach argues that the cultural data will not be valid until the members of the organization feel they have something to gain and that in some way they will be helped. In other words, to gather valid cultural data the "subjects" must come to view themselves in some sense as "clients" who will be helped in some way by the research process. Only when the outsider in effect becomes a researcher/consultant, will he or she be able to gather valid cultural data.

What makes this data gathering method more powerful than the other methods reviewed is that if the researcher/consultant is *helping* the organization, he or she is thereby licensed to ask all kinds of questions that can lead directly into cultural analysis and thereby allow the development of a research focus as well. Both the consultant and the client become fully involved in the problem solving process; therefore the search for relevant data becomes a joint responsibility. This process does not avoid the potential biases of hiding, exaggerating, and blowing off steam, but in the clinical model the researcher/consultant has the license to go beyond this, to ask further questions and even to ask the respondent to help figure out what is going on.

The researcher/consultant is not, of course, limited to the data that surface in specific diagnostic activities such as individual or group interviews. In most consulting situations there are extensive opportunities to hang around and observe what is going on, allowing the observer to combine some of the best elements of the clinical and the participant observer ethnographic models. The researcher/consultant can, as well, gather demographic information and measure various things unobtrusively, but if the subjects are to be involved at all, they must be involved on their own terms around problems they have identified.

How is one to judge the validity of the data gathered by this clinical model? The validity issue has two components: (1) factual accuracy based on whatever contemporary or historical data we can gather, and (2) interpretative accuracy in terms of representing cultural phenomena in a way that communicates what members of the culture really mean. To fully understand cultural phenomena thus requires at least a combination of history and clinical research, as some anthropologists have argued persuasively (Sahlins, 1985).

Factual accuracy can be checked by the usual methods of triangulation, multiple sources, and replication. Interpretative accuracy is more difficult with subjective interpretations, but two criteria can be applied. First, if the cultural analysis is valid, an independent observer going into the same organization should be able to see the same phenomena. Second, if the analysis is valid, one should be able to predict the presence of other phenomena and anticipate how the organization would handle future issues. In other words, predictability becomes a key validity criterion.

How is a researcher who has not been invited in as a consultant to gather cultural data? How does the ethnographer gain entry and access to informants? The solution to this problem of entry is, in my view, for the ethnographer/researcher to analyze carefully what he or she may genuinely have to offer the organization and work toward a psychological contract in which the organization benefits in some way or, as I put it above, becomes a client. This way of thinking requires the researcher to recognize from the outset that his or her presence will be an intervention in the organization and that the goal should be how to make that intervention useful to the organization. Whether they like it or not, once researchers are in the organization they become de facto researcher/consultants or even part-time employees.

Ethnographers tell stories of how they were not "accepted" until they became helpful to the members of the organization in some way, by either doing a job that needed to be done or contributing in some other way (Van Maanen, 1979a; Barley, 1988; Kunda, 1992). The contribution can be entirely symbolic or unrelated to the work of the group being studied. For example, Kunda tells of his work in a DEC engineering group that he was invited into by the senior manager. The group tolerated his presence but was quite aloof, which made it hard to inquire about what certain rituals and events in the group meant. However, Kunda was a very good soccer player and was asked to join the lunchtime games. He made a goal for his team one day; from that day forward, he reports, his relationship to the group changed completely. He was suddenly "in" and "of" the group, and that made it possible to discuss many issues that had previously been off-limits.

Barley, in his study of the introduction of computerized tomography into a hospital radiology department, offered himself as a working member of the team and was accepted to the extent that he actually contributed in various ways to getting the work done. Researchers who want to gain entry into organizations can explore not only taking a job but also other roles, such as being an intern. The important point is to approach the organization with the intention of *helping*, not just gathering data.

The clinical model makes explicit two fundamental assumptions: (1) it is not possible to study a human system without intervening in it, and (2) one can only fully understand a human system by trying to change it. In this regard, the clinical and the ethnographic models appear to differ sharply in that the stated aim of the ethnographer is generally to leave the system as intact as possible. Not only do I believe that this view of ethnography is invalid—in that the very presence of the ethnographer or participant observer is an intervention of unknown consequence—but ethnographers admit that they get better data when they begin to intervene more actively. The important point is that the intervention goal must be shared by outsider and insider. If the outsider researcher tries to change the organization in terms of his or her own goals, the risk of defensiveness and withholding of data rises dramatically. If the researcher/consultant is helping the organization to make some changes that it wants, the probability rises that organization members will reveal what is really going on.

Ethical Problems in Studying Organizational Cultures

The deciphering of culture has some inherent risks that both the insider and the outsider should assess before proceeding. The risks differ, depending on the purpose of the analysis, and they are often subtle and unknown. Therefore, the desire to go ahead and the organization's permission to do so may not be enough to warrant proceeding. The outside professional, whether consultant or ethnographer, must make a separate assessment and sometimes limit his or her own interventions to protect the organization.

Risks of an Analysis for Research Purposes

Regardless of the way in which the basic cultural data are gathered, the organization can be made vulnerable through having its culture revealed to outsiders. The obvious solution is always to disguise the organization in published accounts, but if the intent is to communicate accurately to outsiders, the data are much more meaningful if the organization and the people are identified. Naming the organizations, as I have done in most of the examples used in this book, makes it possible to gain a deeper understanding of cultural phenomena and also makes it possible for others to check for accuracy and replicate the findings.

On the other hand, if a correct analysis of an organization's culture becomes known to outsiders because it either is published or is simply discussed among interested parties, the organization or some of its members may be put at a disadvantage because data that would ordinarily remain private now may become public. For various reasons the members of the organization may not want their culture laid bare for others' viewing. If the information is inaccurate, potential employees, customers, suppliers, and any other categories of outsiders who deal with the organization may be adversely influenced.

Here again we can draw on the analogy that culture is to the organization as character is to the individual, in that we clearly would not publish an accurate personality profile of a living individual unless that person, for reasons of his or her own, wanted such a publication. If it is important to the scientific community to have such material published or if psychiatrists or clinical psychologists want to inform their colleagues about the cases they have treated, the cases must be sufficiently disguised to ensure the absolute anonymity of the individuals involved. Paradoxically, cases used in business schools are rarely disguised, even though they often include revealing details about an organization's culture. If the organization fully understands what it is revealing and if the information is accurate, no harm is done. But if the case reveals material that the organization is not aware of, such publication can produce undesirable insight or tension on the part of members and can create undesirable impressions on the part of outsiders. If the information is not accurate, then both insiders and outsiders may get wrong impressions and may base decisions on incorrect information.

For example, when I was teaching at the Centre d'Etudes Industrielle in Geneva in the early 1980s they were using a case about DEC that was outdated and gave an entirely incorrect impression of what was going on at DEC, yet students were influenced by this case in terms of whether or not they would apply for jobs at DEC. Furthermore, most cases are only a slice through the organization at a particular time and do not consider historical evolution. The case material about DEC may have been accurate at only one point in time but may be presented as a general picture.

Researchers often attempt to avoid this danger by providing their analysis to the members of the organization before it is published. This step has the advantage of also testing, to some degree, the validity of the information. However, it does not overcome the risk that the members of the organization who clear the data for publication may not be aware of how the analysis might make others in the organization more vulnerable. Nor does it overcome the risk that the members of the organization who review the material may want to play it safe and forbid the publication of anything that names the organization. For the most part, therefore, the ultimate ethical responsibility falls to the researcher. Whenever a researcher publishes information about an individual or organization, he or she must think carefully about the potential consequences. Where I have named organizations in this book, I have either gotten permission or have decided that the material can no longer harm organizations or individuals.

The dilemmas one may encounter are well illustrated in the following example. A doctoral student interviewed a large number of managers and observed the behavior of a subgroup in a company for nine months in order to decipher and describe its culture. The study was carefully done and the final write-up of the organization was fairly well disguised. The write-up was intended to report objectively without evaluating. When it was presented to the organization for clearance and final approval, members of the group pronounced the description to be accurate but asked, "Couldn't you say it in a way that would not make us look so bad?" (It should be noted that only *some* insiders had this reaction.)

One of the managers who did not like the report discovered that a company policy formulated within the preceding year prohibited the publication of case studies about the company—probably for reasons of avoiding inaccurate impressions. Several insiders who felt that they had an obligation to the student fought to have the description released, but several other insiders were sufficiently nervous about the description—even though it was completely disguised—that it took several months and many rewrites before they felt relatively comfortable about the paper.

When the insiders initially approved this project, they did not know what the cultural description would actually look like; they had no way of assessing whether they should approve the project. Since they did not have a particular need to gain insight into their own culture at this point in their history, the actual confrontation with the data was uncomfortable for some members of the company. Truths were spelled out that they felt would have been better left implicit or buried, and the fact that outsiders probably would not recognize the company was small comfort because everyone knew that other insiders would immediately recognize it. The availability of the description in written form became a further intervention in this company's functioning because it articulated many thoughts, values, and assumptions in ways that had never been articulated before. The company had not contracted for anything other than giving a student permission to interview and observe, yet it found itself in some degree of turmoil over material that had not yet even been published.

Risks of an Internal Analysis

If an organization is to understand its own strengths and weaknesses and to make informed strategic choices based on realistic assessments of external and internal factors, it must at some point study and understand its own culture. However, this process is not without its problems, risks, and potential costs. Basically, two kinds of risks must be assessed: (1) the analysis of the culture could be incorrect and (2) the organization might not be ready to receive feedback about its culture.

If the analysis of what the culture's basic assumptions are and how they fit into a pattern or paradigm is wrong it may give the decision maker incorrect data on which to base decisions. If decisions are made on the basis of incorrect assumptions about the culture, serious harm could be done to the organization. Such errors are most likely to occur if culture is defined at too superficial a level—if espoused values or data based on questionnaires are taken to be an accurate representation of the underlying assumptions without conducting group and individual interviews that specifically dig for deeper assumptions and patterns. As I have indicated before, this is the major risk in the use of typologies.

On the other hand, the analysis may be correct, but insiders other than those who made the analysis may not be prepared to digest what has been learned about them. If culture is like character—functioning in part as a set of defense mechanisms to help avoid anxiety and to provide positive direction, self-esteem, and pride—then various conditions might make an organization reluctant to accept the cultural truth about itself. Psychotherapists and counselors constantly must deal with resistance or denial on the part of patients and clients. Similarly, unless an organization's personnel recognize a real need to change, unless they feel psychologically safe enough to examine data about the organization, they will not be able to hear the cultural truths that inquiry may have revealed, or, worse, they may lose self-esteem because some of their myths or ideals about themselves may be destroyed by the analysis.

A potentially even more dangerous risk is that some members will achieve instant insight and automatically and thoughtlessly attempt to produce changes in the culture that (1) some other members of the organization may not want, (2) some other members may not be prepared for and therefore may not be able to implement, and (3) may not solve the problem.

One reason people avoid therapy is that they are not ready for the insights that therapy inevitably brings. Insight sometimes produces change "automatically" because certain illusions and defenses can no longer be used. If culture is to the organization what character is to the individual, then insight into that culture may remove defenses that had been operating and on which the organization had been relying. To study a culture and reveal that culture to the insiders, then, can be likened to an invasion of privacy, which under many conditions is not welcome. Therefore, the student of culture should make the client system fully aware that there are consequences to having elements of one's culture laid bare, so to speak.

A clear example of my misunderstanding of assumptions occurred at a 1970s meeting of the senior management of General Foods, a company that prided itself on taking into account the feelings and preferences of its personnel and their families when they made job assignments. The group was discussing succession in several key jobs, including the job of president. At one point in the discussion, a person was nominated to become head of the international division—a job that was considered a key stepping stone up the corporate ladder and that could eventually lead to the position of executive vice president and ultimately president.

The personnel vice president and one other group member had talked to this individual and reported that he did not want to move to the overseas headquarters because of the critical age of his children. At this point the president entered the discussion and said, "Let me talk to him. Maybe I can explain the situation to him more clearly." My own reaction at this moment was one of dismay because this apparent attempt at persuasion seemed to me a clear violation of the company's principle that personal feelings should weigh heavily in such decisions. Others in the group felt the same way and challenged the wisdom of the president's intervening on the grounds that it would put too much pressure on the individual. We were all assuming that the president was operating from the assumption that this candidate was "corporate property" and that it would be legitimate to persuade him to do his "duty" for the corporation. This assumption would clearly be in violation of the espoused assumption that family issues were taken seriously in the company.

The president then explained his logic, and a deeper assumption emerged. The president said: "I understand that we should not pressure him to take the job if he does not want it and if he understands fully what he is giving up. I want to explain to him that we consider the international VP job a crucial stepping-stone, that we consider him the logical candidate to move up the ladder, and that we will be forced to move him off the ladder if he does not take this job. We don't have time to develop him in an alternate fashion, and he may not realize the consequences of rejecting the offer. But if he understands what he would be giving up and still feels that he should reject it, we will respect that decision and look for another candidate."

The deeper assumption, then, was that "a key executive must be given full organizational information and allowed to make his own choice." If the person knew that he was in line for the presidency, he might want to reassess the family priorities and consider other options—he could move, he could commute, he could leave his family behind, he could leave the children in their school but have them live with someone else, and so on. The implied assumption was that the individual is the only one who could ultimately make the choice. Had the group simply moved this person off the ladder based on their prior conversations with him, it would have been making the choice for him. Once we dug into the issue in this way, it became clear to everyone that the deeper assumption was the one they really lived by and it would have been a mistake to jump to the conclusion that "explanation" would automatically be inappropriate "pressure." Everyone acknowledged that it would certainly put pressure on the individual, but that was less damaging to the total culture than to not give people a choice. The group then approved the decision to have the president talk to the individual and lay out the options.

Another example is what happened when I was asked in 1979 to present my analysis of the Ciba-Geigy culture to its top management. I had been asked to observe and interview people to get a sense of the key assumptions forming the paradigm that was presented in Chapter Three. From my point of view I had clear data and I attempted to be objective and neutral in my analysis. At one point during my presentation, I likened certain aspects of Ciba-Geigy's culture to a military model. Several members of the executive committee who were themselves former military men and who loved the Swiss Army took offense at what they viewed as a derogatory depiction of the army (though I believed I had been neutral in my statements). Their perception that I misunderstood and had challenged one of their values led to an unproductive argument about the validity of the cultural description and to some degree discredited me as a consultant in their eyes.

There are several possible lessons here. The most obvious one is that the outsider should never lecture insiders on their own culture because one cannot know where the sensitivities will lie and one cannot overcome one's own subtle biases. Perhaps if I had stated each of my points carefully as hypotheses or questions for them to react to, I might have avoided this trap.

Second, I learned that my analysis plunged the group members into an internal debate that they were not prepared for and that had multiple unanticipated consequences. The people who objected to my analogy revealed some of their own biases at the meeting in ways they might not have intended, and comments made later suggested that some people were shocked because so-and-so had revealed himself to be a such-and-such kind of person.

The analogy itself, likening aspects of the organization's functioning to the military, unleashed feelings that had more to do with the larger Swiss-German culture in which Ciba-Geigy operated and it introduced a whole set of irrelevant feelings and issues. Many people in the group were made very uncomfortable by the insight that they were indeed operating like the military because they had either forgotten this aspect or had illusions about it. My comments stripped away those illusions.

Third—and this is perhaps the most important lesson—giving feedback to an individual is different from giving feedback to a group, because the group very likely is not homogeneous in its reactions. My "lecture" on the culture was well received by some members of the group, who went out of their way to assure me that my depiction was totally accurate. Obviously, this segment of the group was not threatened by what I had to say. But with others I lost credibility, and with still others I created enough of a threat to unleash defensiveness, plunging the group into an uncomfortable new agenda that then had to be managed.

The point is that I had been doing what *they* requested me to do, yet it had unanticipated consequences that I, as a culture researcher, should have anticipated and controlled for. At the minimum, I should have forewarned my clients that if I gave this lecture it might unleash a variety of group feelings—and were we prepared for this?

Professional Obligations of the Culture Analyst

If the foregoing risks are real, then who should worry about them? Is it enough to say to an organization that we will study your culture and let you know what we find and that nothing will be published without your permission? If we are dealing with surface manifestations, artifacts, and publicly espoused values, then the guideline of letting members clear the material seems sufficient. However, if we are dealing with the deeper levels of the culture, the assumptions and the patterns among them, then the insiders clearly may not know what they are getting into and the obligation shifts to the outsider as a professional, in the same way that it would be the psychiatrist's or counselor's job to make the client genuinely aware of the consequences of proceeding in an investigation of personality or character. The principle of informed consent does not sufficiently protect the client or research subject if he or she cannot initially appreciate what will be revealed.

The analyst of a culture undertakes a professional obligation to understand fully the potential consequences of an investigation. Such consequences should be carefully spelled out before the relationship reaches a level at which there is an implied psychological contract that the outsider will give feedback to the insiders on what has been discovered about the culture, either for inside purposes of gaining insight or for clearing what may eventually be published.

The Inquiry/Assessment Process

As the discussion of Table 11.1 revealed, there is no simple formula for gathering cultural data. Artifacts can be directly observed; espoused values are revealed through the questions the researcher/consultant asks of whoever is available; and shared tacit assumptions have to be inferred from a variety of observations and further inquiry around inconsistencies and puzzlements. Since culture is a shared group phenomenon, the best way to gather systematic data is to bring representative groups of ten to fifteen people together and ask them to discuss artifacts and the values and assumptions that lie behind them. A detailed way to do this when the process is used to help the organization to solve problems is described in Chapter Seventeen.

If the researcher is simply trying to gather information for his or her own purposes and if problems of reliability and validity can afford to be ignored, then the various culture content categories described in the previous chapters are perfectly adequate guidelines for what to ask about. The actual questions around each of the content areas should be constructed by the researcher in terms of the goals of the research, bearing in mind that culture is broad and deep. To capture a whole culture is probably impossible, so the researcher must have some more specific goal in mind before a set of questions for the groups can be designed. And even if the goal is "pure research," data gathering will work best and is most likely to be valid if group interviews are used, of the sort described in Chapter Seventeen.

Summary and Conclusions

There are many methods for assessing cultural dimensions, which can be categorized in terms of the degree to which the researcher is directly involved with the organization and the degree to which organization members become directly involved in the research process. For purposes of academic research or theory building, it is essential that the *outsider*—the person inquiring about the culture—learn what is really going on, and this requires real entry into and involvement with the organization beyond what questionnaires, surveys, or even individual interviews can provide. The researcher must create a relationship with the organization that permits him or her to become a researcher/consultant to insure that reliable and valid data will be forthcoming.

If the consultant is helping leaders manage cultural issues in their own organizations, he or she may design a culture assessment process and may learn some things about the culture, but it is only essential that the *insiders* learn what is really going on. I have been in many situations where insiders achieved clarity about essential elements of their culture while I went away from the project not really understanding their culture at all. In any case the deeper cultural data will reveal themselves only if the consultant establishes a helping relationship with the organization, such that the organization members feel they have something to gain by revealing what they really think and feel. Such a "clinical inquiry" relationship is the minimum requirement for getting valid cultural data.

The process of deciphering a culture for purposes of an insider or for purposes of describing that culture to outsiders each has a set of associated risks and potential costs. These risks are internal in the sense that the members of the organization may not want to know or may not be able to handle the insights into their own culture, and they are external in that the members of the organization may not be aware of the manner in which they become vulnerable once information about their culture is made available to others. In either case, there is the danger that the interpretation is incorrect or so superficial that the deeper layers remain unknown.

In our effort to define a culture, we may discover that no single set of assumptions has formed as a deep-down paradigm for operating, or that the subgroups of an organization have different paradigms that may or may not conflict with each other. Furthermore, culture is perpetually evolving; the cultural researcher must be willing to do perpetual searching and revising. To present "data" about that organization to either an insider or an outsider is inherently risky.

Even if we begin to have an intuitive understanding of an organization's culture, we may find it extraordinarily difficult to write down that understanding in such a way that the essence of the culture can be communicated to someone else. We have so few examples in our literature that it is hard even to point to models of how it should be done (Van Maanen, 1988). But when we see the essence of a culture—the paradigm by which people operate—we are struck by how powerful our insight into that organization now is, and we can see instantly why certain things work the way they do, why certain proposals are never bought, why change is so difficult, why certain people leave, and so on. Few concepts are so powerful in the degree to which they help us decipher what may be a very opaque area. It is the search for and the occasional finding of this central insight that make it all worthwhile. Suddenly we understand an organization; suddenly we see what makes it tick. This level of insight is worth working for, even if in the end we can share it only with colleagues.

The implication for leaders is "Be careful." Cultural analysis can be very helpful if the leader knows what she or he is doing and why. By this I mean that there must be some valid purpose to a cultural analysis. If it is done for its own sake, the risks of either wasting time or doing harm increase. However, the potential for insight and constructive action is tremendous if the leader works with a responsible outsider to analyze and decipher culture in the service of legitimate organizational ends. A specific process for working with culture for purposes of organizational development is described in Chapter Seventeen.

Part Three

THE LEADERSHIP ROLE IN CULTURE BUILDING, EMBEDDING, AND EVOLVING

Part Two focused on the content of culture and the process of deciphering cultural assumptions. The primary focus was on culture. We now shift the focus to leadership, especially the role that leadership plays in creating and embedding culture in a group. As I have argued throughout, the unique function of leadership that distinguishes it from management and administration is this concern for culture. Leaders begin the culture creation process and, as we will see, must also manage and sometimes change culture.

To fully understand the relationship of leadership to culture, we also have to take a developmental view of organizational growth. The role of leadership in beginning the formation of an organizational culture will be covered in Chapter Twelve. Chapter Thirteen examines how leaders of a young and successful organization can systematically embed their own assumptions in the daily workings of the organization, thereby creating a stable culture. In Chapter Fourteen the growth and evolution of the organization into subunits is described and the growth of subcultures is noted.

As organizations grow and evolve, so do their cultures. In Chapter Fifteen I describe ten different mechanisms or processes that cause cultures to change, and I point out the role that leaders can and should play in using these processes to skew cultural evolution to their purposes. All of these are natural processes that should be distinguished from what I call *managed change*, the process by which leaders set out to solve specific organizational problems that may or may not involve cultural elements. In Chapter Sixteen I provide a general model of managed change that needs to be understood by leaders as change agents. Then in Chapter Seventeen I lay out a focused process of culture assessment that should be used in the context of change programs. Finally, in Chapter Eighteen I describe in detail how Ciba-Geigy made a major change involving culture assessment and in Chapter Nineteen I conclude with implications for leadership of this kind of cultural perspective.

12

HOW LEADERS
BEGIN CULTURE CREATION

One of the most mysterious aspects of organizational culture is how it comes to be that two companies with similar external environments, working in similar technologies on similar tasks and with founders of similar origins, come to have entirely different ways of operating over the years. In Chapter Four I tried to illustrate and analyze this process in terms of the spontaneous events that occur in an unstructured group. In this chapter we further analyze this process, considering what happens when a leader builds a group and launches an organization.

As we think about this formation process, we must not confuse the individual assumptions of the leader with the shared assumptions that define the concept of culture. Culture only arises when those individual assumptions lead to shared experiences that solve the group's problems of external survival and internal integration. Culture is created by shared experience, but it is the leader who initiates this process by imposing his or her beliefs, values, and assumptions at the outset.

Culture Beginnings and
the Impact of Founders as Leaders

Cultures basically spring from three sources: (1) the beliefs, values, and assumptions of founders of organizations; (2) the learning experiences of group members as their organization evolves; and (3) new beliefs, values, and assumptions brought in by new members and leaders.

Though each of these mechanisms plays a crucial role, by far the most important for cultural beginnings is the impact of founders. Founders not only choose the basic mission and the environmental context in which the new group will operate, but they choose the group members and bias the original responses that the group makes in its efforts to succeed in its environment and to integrate itself.

Organizations do not form accidentally or spontaneously; rather, they are goal oriented, have a specific purpose, and are created because one or more individuals perceive that the coordinated and concerted action of a number of people can accomplish something that individual action cannot. Social movements or new religions begin with prophets, messiahs, or other kinds of charismatic leaders. Political groups are initiated by leaders who sell new visions and new solutions to problems. Firms are created by entrepreneurs who have a vision of how the concerted effort of the right group of people can create a new good or service in the marketplace.

The process of culture formation is, in each case, first a process of creating a small group. In the typical business organization, this process will usually involve some version of the following steps:

1. One or more people (founders) have an idea for a new enterprise.

2. The founder brings in one or more other people and creates a core group that shares a common goal and vision with the founder; that is, they all believe that the idea is a good one, workable, worth running some risks for, and worth the investment of time, money, and energy required.

3. The founding group begins to act in concert to create an organization by raising funds, obtaining patents, incorporating, locating work space, and so on.

4. Others are brought into the organization, and a common history begins to be built. If the group remains fairly stable and has significant shared learning experiences, it will gradually develop assumptions about itself, its environment, and how to do things to survive and grow.

Founders usually have a major impact on how the group initially defines and solves its external adaptation and internal integration problems. Because they had the original idea, they will typically have their own notion, based on their own cultural history and personality, of how to fulfill the idea. Founders not only have a high level of self-confidence and determination, but they typically have strong assumptions about the nature of the world, the role that organizations play in that world, the nature of human nature and relationships, how truth is arrived at, and how to manage time and space (Schein, 1978, 1983). They will, therefore, be quite comfortable in imposing those views on their partners and employees as the fledgling organization copes, and they will cling to them until such time as they become unworkable or the group fails and breaks up (Donaldson and Lorsch, 1983).

Steinbergs

Sam Steinberg was an immigrant whose parents had started a corner grocery store in Montreal. His parents, particularly his mother, taught him some basic attitudes toward customers and helped him form the vision that he could succeed in building a successful enterprise. He assumed from the beginning that if he did things right, he would succeed and could build a major organization that would bring him and his family a fortune. Ultimately, he built a large chain of supermarkets, department stores, and related businesses that became for many decades the dominant force in its market area.

Sam Steinberg was the major ideological force in his company throughout its history and continued to impose his assumptions on the company until his death in his late seventies. He assumed that his primary mission was to supply a high-quality, reliable product to customers in clean, attractive surroundings and that his customers' needs were the primary consideration in all major decisions. There are many stories about how Sam Steinberg, as a young man operating the corner grocery store with his wife, gave customers credit and thus displayed trust in them. He always took products back if there was the slightest complaint, and he kept his store absolutely spotless to inspire customer confidence in his products. Each of these attitudes later became a major policy in his chain of stores and was taught and reinforced by close personal supervision.

Sam Steinberg believed that only personal examples and close supervision would ensure adequate performance by subordinates. He would show up at his stores unexpectedly, inspect even minor details, and then—by personal example, by stories of how other stores were solving the problems identified, by articulating rules, and by exhortation—would "teach" the staff what they should be doing. He often lost his temper and berated subordinates who did not follow the rules or principles he had laid down.

Sam Steinberg expected his store managers to be highly visible, to be very much on top of their own jobs, and to supervise closely in the same way he did, reflecting deep assumptions about the nature of good management. These assumptions became a major theme in later years in his concept of "visible management"—the assumption that a good manager always has to be around to set a good example and to teach subordinates the right way to do things.

Most of the founding group in this company consisted of Sam Steinberg's three brothers, but one "lieutenant" who was not a family member was recruited early and became, in addition to the founder, the main leader and culture carrier. He shared the founder's basic assumptions about how to run a business and he set up formal systems to ensure that those assumptions became the basis for operating realities. After Sam Steinberg's death this man became the CEO; he continued to articulate the theory of visible management and tried to set a personal example of how to perpetuate this by continuing the same close supervision policies that Sam Steinberg had used.

Sam Steinberg assumed that one could win in the marketplace only by being highly innovative and technically in the forefront. He always encouraged his managers to try new approaches; brought in a variety of consultants who advocated new approaches to human resource management; started selection and development programs through assessment centers long before other companies tried this approach; and traveled to conventions and other businesses where new technological innovations were displayed. This passion for innovation resulted in Steinbergs being one of the first companies in the supermarket industry to introduce the bar code technology and one of the first to use assessment centers in selecting store managers. Steinberg was always willing to experiment in order to improve the business. His view of truth and reality was that one had to find them wherever one could; therefore, one must be open to one's environment and never take it for granted that one has all the answers.

If things worked, Sam Steinberg encouraged their adoption; if they did not, he ordered them to be dropped. Measuring results and solving problems were, for him, intensely personal matters, deriving from his theory of visible management. In addition to using a variety of traditional business measures, he always made it a point to visit all his stores personally. If he saw things not to his liking, he corrected them immediately and decisively even if that meant going around his own authority chain. He trusted only those managers who operated by assumptions similar to his own and he clearly had favorites to whom he delegated more authority.

Power and authority in this organization remained very centralized, in that everyone knew that Sam Steinberg or his chief lieutenant could and would override decisions made by division or other unit managers without consultation and often in a very peremptory fashion. The ultimate source of power, the voting shares of stock, were owned entirely by Sam Steinberg and his wife, so that after his death his wife was in total control of the company.

Sam Steinberg was interested in developing good managers throughout the organization, but he never assumed that sharing ownership through granting stock options would contribute to that process. He paid his key managers very well, but his assumption was that ownership was strictly a family matter, to the point that he was not willing to share stock even with his chief lieutenant, close friend, and virtual cobuilder of the company.

Sam Steinberg introduced several members of his own family into the firm and gave them key managerial positions and favored treatment in the form of good developmental jobs that would test them early for ultimate management potential. As the firm diversified, family members were made heads of divisions, often with relatively little management experience. If a family member performed poorly, he would be bolstered by having a good manager introduced under him. If the operation then improved, the family member would likely be given the credit. If things continued badly, the family member would be moved out, but with various face-saving excuses.

Peer relationships among nonfamily members inevitably became highly politicized. They were officially defined as competitive, and Sam Steinberg believed firmly in the value of interpersonal competition. Winners would be rewarded and losers discarded. However, since family members were in positions of power, one had to know how to stay on the good side of those family members without losing the trust of one's peers, on whom one was dependent.

Sam Steinberg wanted open communication and a high level of trust among all members of the organization, but his own assumptions about the role of the family and the correct way to manage were, to a large degree, in conflict with each other. Therefore, many members of the organization banded together in a kind of mutual protection society that developed a culture of its own. They were more loyal to each other than to the company and had a high rate of interaction with each other, which bred assumptions and norms that became to some degree countercultural to the founder's.

Several points should be noted about the description given thus far. By definition, something can become part of the culture only if it works in the sense of making the organization successful and reducing the anxiety of the members, including Sam Steinberg. His assumptions about how things should be done were congruent with the kind of environment in which he operated, so he and the founding group received strong reinforcement for those assumptions. As the company grew and prospered, Sam Steinberg felt more and more confirmation of his assumptions and thus more and more confidence that they were correct. Throughout his lifetime he steadfastly adhered to those assumptions and did everything in his power to get others to accept them. However, as already noted, some of those assumptions made nonfamily managers anxious and led to the formation of a counterculture.

Sam Steinberg also learned that he had to share some concepts and assumptions with a great many other people. As a result, as his company grew and learned from its own experience, he gradually had to modify his assumptions in some areas or withdraw from those areas as an active manager. For example, in its diversification efforts, the company bought several production units that would enable it to integrate vertically in certain food and clothing areas where that was economically advantageous. But because Sam Steinberg realized that he knew relatively little about manufacturing, he brought in strong managers and gave them a great deal of autonomy in those areas. Some of those production divisions never acquired the culture of the main organization, and the heads of those divisions never enjoyed the status and security that insiders had.

Sam Steinberg eventually also had to learn, somewhat painfully, that the signals he sent were not as clear and consistent as he thought they were. He did not perceive his own conflicts and inconsistencies and hence could not understand why some of his best young managers failed to respond to his competitive incentives and even left the company. He thought he was adequately motivating them and could not see that for some of them the political climate, the absence of stock options, and the arbitrary rewarding of family members made their own career progress too uncertain. Sam Steinberg was perplexed and angry about much of this, blaming the young managers while holding onto his own assumptions and conflicts.

Following Sam Steinberg's death, the company experienced a long period of cultural turmoil because of the vacuum created by both his absence and the retirement of several other key culture carriers, but the basic philosophy of how to run stores was thoroughly embedded and remained. Various family members continued to run the company, though none of them had Sam Steinberg's business skills. With the retirement of Sam Steinberg's chief lieutenant, a period of instability set in; marked by the discovery that some of the managers who had been developed under Sam Steinberg were not as strong and capable as had been assumed. Because none of Sam Steinberg's children or their spouses were able to take over the business decisively, an outside person was brought in to run the company. This person predictably failed because he could not adapt to the culture and to the family.

After two more failures with CEOs drawn from other companies, the family turned to a manager who had originally been with the company and had subsequently made a fortune outside the company in various real estate enterprises. This manager stabilized the business because he had more credibility by virtue of his prior history and his knowledge of how to handle family members. Under his leadership some of the original assumptions began to evolve in new directions. Eventually, the family decided to sell the company, and this manager and one of Sam Steinberg's cousins started a company of their own, which ended up competing with Steinbergs.

One clear lesson from this example is that a culture does not survive if the main culture carriers depart and if the bulk of the members of the organization are experiencing some degree of conflict because of a mixed message that emanates from the leaders during the growth period. Steinbergs had a strong culture, but Sam Steinberg's own conflicts became embedded in that culture, creating conflict and ultimately lack of stability.

Smithfield Enterprises

Smithfield built a chain of financial service organizations, using sophisticated financial analysis techniques in an area of the country where insurance companies, mutual funds, and banks were only beginning to use such techniques. He was the conceptualizer and salesman, but once he had the idea for a new kind of service organization, he got others to invest in, build, and manage it.

Smithfield believed that he should put only a very small amount of his own money into each enterprise because if he could not convince others to put up money, maybe there was something wrong with the idea. He made the initial assumption that he did not know enough about the market to gamble with his own money, and he reinforced this assumption publicly by telling a story about the one enterprise in which he had failed. He had opened a retail store in a Midwestern city to sell ocean fish because he loved it; he assumed others felt as he did, trusted his own judgment about what the marketplace would want, and failed. Had he tried to get many others to invest in the enterprise, he would have learned that his own tastes were not necessarily a good predictor of what others would want.

Because Smithfield saw himself as a creative conceptualizer but not as a manager, he not only kept his financial investment minimal but also did not get very personally involved with his enterprises. Once he put together the package, he found people whom he could trust to manage the new organization. These were usually people like himself who were fairly open in their approach to business and not too concerned with imposing their own assumptions about how things should be done.

One can infer that Smithfield's assumptions about concrete goals, the best means to achieve them, how to measure results, and how to repair things when they were going wrong were essentially pragmatic. Whereas Sam Steinberg had a strong need to be involved in everything, Smithfield seemed to lose interest once the new organization was on its feet and functioning. His theory seemed to be to have a clear concept of the basic mission, test it by selling it to the investors, bring in good people who understand what the mission is, and then leave them alone to implement and run the organization, using only financial criteria as ultimate performance measures.

If Smithfield had assumptions about how an organization should be run internally, he kept them to himself. The cultures that each of his enterprises developed therefore had more to do with the assumptions of the people he brought in to manage them. As it turned out, those assumptions varied a good deal. And if one analyzed Smithfield Enterprises as a total organization, one would find little evidence of a *corporate* culture because there was no group that had a shared history and shared learning experiences. But each of the separate enterprises would have a culture that derived from the beliefs, values, and assumptions of their Smithfield-appointed managers.

This brief case illustrates that there is nothing automatic about founder leaders imposing themselves on their organizations. It depends on their personal needs to externalize their various assumptions. For Smithfield, the ultimate personal validation lay in having each of his enterprises become financially successful and in his ability to continue to form creative new ones. His creative needs were such that after a decade or so of founding financial service organizations, he turned his attention to real estate ventures, then became a lobbyist on behalf of an environmental organization, tried his hand at politics for a while, then went back into business, first with an oil company and later with a diamond mining company. Eventually, he became interested in teaching and ended up at a Midwestern business school developing a curriculum on entrepreneurship.

DEC

The culture of DEC has been described in detail in Chapter Three. In this section I want to focus more specifically on how DEC's founder, Ken Olsen, created a management system that led eventually to the culture I described in Chapter Three. Olsen developed his beliefs, attitudes, and values in a strong Protestant family and at MIT, where he worked on Whirlwind, the first interactive computer. He and a colleague founded DEC in the mid-1950s because they believed they could build interactive computers for which there would eventually be a very large market. They were able to convince investors because of their own credibility and the clarity of their basic vision of the company's core mission. After some years the two founders discovered that they did not share a vision of how to build an organization, so Olsen became the CEO.

Olsen's assumptions about the nature of the world and how one discovers truth and solves problems were very strong at this stage of DEC's growth and were reflected in his management style. He believed that good ideas could come from anyone regardless of rank or background, but that neither he nor any other individual was smart enough to determine whether a given idea was correct. Olsen felt that open discussion and debate in a group was the only way to test ideas and that one should not take action until the idea had survived the crucible of an active debate. One might have intuitions, but one should not act on them until they have been tested in the intellectual marketplace. Hence, Olsen set up a number of committees and groups and insisted that all ideas be discussed and debated before they were acted on.

Olsen bolstered his assumptions with a story that he told frequently to justify his thrusting issues onto groups. He said that he would often *not make a decision* because "I'm not that smart; if I really knew what to do I would say so. But when I get into a group of smart people and listen to them discuss the idea, I get smart very fast." For Ken Olsen, groups were a kind of extension of his own intelligence and he often used them to think out loud and get his own ideas straight in his head.

Olsen also believed that one cannot get good implementation of ideas if people do not fully support them and that the best way to get support is to let people debate the issues and convince themselves. Therefore, on any important decision, Olsen insisted on a wide debate, with many group meetings to test the idea and sell it down the organization and laterally. Only when it appeared that everyone wanted to do it and fully understood it would he ratify it. He even delayed important decisions if others were not on board, though he was personally already convinced of the course of action to take. He said that he did not want to be out there leading all by himself and run the risk that the troops were not committed and might disown the decision if it did not work out. Past experiences of this kind had taught him to ensure commitment before going ahead on anything, even if the consensus-building procedure was time consuming and frustrating.

Although Olsen's assumptions about decision making and implementation led to a very group-oriented organization, his theory

about how to organize and manage work led to a strong individua-
tion process, which reinforced his assumption that individuals are
ultimately the source of creativity. His theory was that one must
give clear and simple individual responsibility and then measure the
person strictly on that area of responsibility. Groups could help to
make decisions and obtain commitment, but they could not under
any circumstances be responsible or accountable.

Olsen believed completely in a proactive model of human
nature and in people's capacity to master nature, a set of assumptions that appear to correlate closely with his own engineering
background. He believed that if one gave people responsibility they
would exercise it responsibly. He always expected people to be on
top of their jobs and was very critical of them, both in public and in
private, if he felt that they were not completely in control.

Recognizing that circumstances might change the outcome of
even the best-laid plans, Olsen expected his managers to renegotiate those plans as soon as they observed a deviation. Thus, for example, if an annual budget had been set at a certain level and the
responsible manager noticed after six months that he would over-
run it, he was expected to get the situation under control according
to the original assumptions or to come back to senior management
to renegotiate. It was absolutely unacceptable either to not know
what was happening or to let it happen without informing senior
management and renegotiating.

Olsen believed completely in open communications and the
ability of people to reach reasonable decisions and make appropriate compromises if they openly confronted the problems and issues,
figured out what they wanted to do, and were willing to argue for
their solution and honor any commitments they made. He assumed
that people have "constructive intent," a rational loyalty to organizational goals and shared commitments. Withholding information,
playing power games, competitively trying to win out over another
member of the organization on a personal level, blaming others for
one's failures, undermining or sabotaging decisions one has agreed

to, and going off on one's own without getting others' agreement were all defined as sins and brought public censure.

As previously noted, the architecture and office layout of DEC reflected Olsen's assumptions about creativity and decision making. He insisted on an open-office layout, preferred cubicles instead of offices with doors for engineers, encouraged individualism in dress and behavior, and minimized the use of status symbols such as private offices, special dining rooms for executives, and personal parking spaces. Instead, there were many conference rooms and attached kitchens to encourage people to interact comfortably.

This model of how to run an organization to maximize individual creativity and decision quality worked very successfully in that the company experienced dramatic growth for over thirty years and had exceptionally high morale. However, as the company grew larger, people found that they had less time to negotiate with each other and did not know each other as well personally, making these processes more frustrating. Some of the paradoxes and inconsistencies among the various assumptions came to the surface. For example, to encourage individuals to think for themselves and do what they believed to be the best course for DEC, even if it meant insubordination, clearly ran counter to the dictum that one must honor one's commitments and support decisions that have been made. In practice, the rule of honoring commitments was superseded by the rule of doing only what one believes is right, which meant that sometimes decisions would not stick.

DEC had increasing difficulty in imposing any kind of discipline on its organizational processes. If a given manager decided that for organizational reasons a more disciplined autocratic approach was necessary, he ran the risk of Olsen's displeasure because freedom was being taken away from subordinates and that would undermine their entrepreneurial spirit. Olsen felt he was giving his immediate subordinates great freedom, so why would they take it away from the levels below them? At the same time, Olsen recognized that at certain levels of the organization, discipline was essential to getting anything done; the difficulty was in deciding just which areas required discipline and which areas required freedom.

When the company was small and everyone knew everyone else, when "functional familiarity" was high, there was always time to renegotiate, and basic consensus and trust were high enough to ensure that if time pressure forced people to make their own decisions and to be insubordinate, others would, after the fact, mostly agree with the decisions that had been made locally. In other words, if initial decisions made at higher levels did not stick, this did not bother anyone—until the organization became larger and more complex. Then what was initially a highly adaptive system began to be regarded by more and more members of the organization as disorganization and chaos.

Ken Olsen believed that those processes that could be simplified should be routinized and that high discipline should be imposed in enforcing them, but as the company became more complex it became more difficult to agree on which processes could and should be simplified and subjected to arbitrary discipline. Olsen believed in the necessity of organization and hierarchy, but he did not trust the authority of position nearly as much as the authority of reason. Hence, managers were granted de facto authority only to the extent that they could sell their decisions, and as indicated above, insubordination was not only tolerated but positively rewarded if it made sense and led to better outcomes. Managers often complained that they could not control any of the things for which they were responsible, yet at the same time they believed in the system and shared Olsen's assumptions because of the kinds of people they were, the degree to which they had been socialized into the system, and the obvious success of this way of managing in building a company.

Olsen also believed that the intellectual testing of ideas, which he encouraged among individuals in group settings, could be profitably extended to organizational units if it was not clear which products or markets should be pursued. He was willing to create overlapping product and market units and to let them compete with each other—not realizing, however, that such internal competition undermined openness of communication and made it more difficult for groups to negotiate decisions. Yet this way of doing things had enough success in the marketplace that DEC managers came to believe in it as a way of operating in a rapidly shifting market environment.

The company thrived on intelligent, assertive, individualistic people who were willing and able to argue for and sell their ideas. The hiring practices of the company reflected this bias clearly in that each new applicant had to undergo many interviews and be convincing in each one of them to be viewed as a positive candidate. So over the course of its first decade the organization tended to hire and keep only those kinds of people who fitted the assumptions and were willing to live in the system even though it might at times be frustrating. The people who were comfortable in this environment and enjoyed the excitement of building a successful organization found themselves increasingly feeling like members of a family and they were emotionally treated as such. Strong bonds of mutual support grew up at an interpersonal level, and Ken Olsen functioned symbolically as a brilliant, demanding, but supportive and charismatic father figure. These familial feelings were implicit but important because they provided subordinates with a feeling of security that made it possible for them to challenge each other's ideas. When a proposed course of action did not make sense, the proposer might be severely challenged and even accused of having dumb ideas, but he could not lose his membership in the family. However, frustration and insecurity grew as the size of the company made it more difficult to maintain the level of personal acquaintance that would make familial feelings possible.

Ken Olsen is an example of an entrepreneur with a clear set of assumptions about how things should be, in terms of both how to relate externally to the environment and how to arrange things internally in the organization. His willingness to be open about his theory and his rewarding and punishing behavior in support of it led both to the selection of others who shared the theory and to strong socialization practices that reinforced and perpetuated it. Consequently, the founder's assumptions were reflected in how the organization operated well into the 1990s. DEC's economic collapse and eventual sale to Compaq in the late 1990s also illustrate how a set of assumptions that works under one set of circumstances may become dysfunctional under other sets of circumstances.

Apple, IBM, and Hewlett-Packard (HP)

I know less about the details of the founding of these companies, but taking a cultural perspective and analyzing cultures from the point of view of what we do know about the founders produces some immediate insights into their cultures. Apple was founded by Steve Jobs and Steve Wozniak, both engineers, with the intention of creating products for children in the education market and products that would be fun and easy to use for "yuppies." Their base was clearly technical, as in the case of DEC, and this showed up in the aggressively individualistic "do your own thing" mentality that I will describe in detail in Chapter Seventeen. When Apple attempted to become more market oriented by bringing in John Scully from PepsiCo, the company grew but many insiders felt that the technical community within Apple never accepted the marketing-oriented executive. It is perhaps significant that Apple eventually returned to its roots in bringing back Steve Jobs. If one observes the direction of Apple today (in 2004) one can see a return to its roots of creating products that are easy to use and fun, such as the I-Pod for music and the I-Chat camera for video conferencing. The attractive design of products and the use of stores to display them suggests that Apple now has very much a marketing orientation but that this orientation had to be combined with their technical skills, something that perhaps only Steve Jobs could do.

Many people point out that IBM did much better, in its efforts to revitalize its business in the 1990s, by bringing in an outside marketing executive, Lou Gerstner. The insight that cultural analysis provides is that IBM was not founded by a technical entrepreneur and never built an engineering-based organization in the first place. Tom Watson was a sales/marketing manager who left National Cash Register Company to found IBM (Watson and Petre, 1990). He thought like a salesman marketer throughout his career and his son Tom Watson, Jr. had the same kind of marketing mentality. Building a clear image with the public became an IBM hallmark, symbolized by its insistence on blue suits and white shirts for all its salespeople. The Watsons clearly had the wisdom to become strong technically, but the deeper cultural assumptions were always derived more from sales and marketing. Is it any surprise, then, that an outstanding marketing executive would be accepted as an outsider to help the company regain its competitive edge?

What of HP? Dave Packard and Bill Hewlett both came out of Stanford with the intention of building a technical business, initially in measurement and instrumentation technology (Packard, 1995). Computers were only brought in later as adjuncts to this core technology and, as was pointed out previously, this led to the discovery that the kinds of people working in these technologies were different from each other and to some degree incompatible, leading ultimately to the splitting off of Agilent to pursue the original technology while HP evolved computers, printers, and various other related products.

HP's growth and success reflected an effective division of labor between Hewlett, who was primarily a technical leader, and Packard, who was more of a business leader. Their ability to collaborate well with each other was undoubtedly one basis for "teamwork" becoming such a central value in the "HP Way." What we know of Packard's managerial style contrasts strongly with Ken Olsen's, in that HP formed divisions early on in its history, put much more emphasis on teamwork and consensus, and became much more dogmatic about standardizing processes throughout the company. HP was much more formal and deliberate than DEC, which made the computer types at HP uncomfortable. Whereas teamwork in HP was defined as coming to agreement and not fighting too hard for your own point of view if the consensus was headed in a different direction, in DEC teamwork was defined as fighting for your own point of view until you either convinced others or truly changed your own mind.

Subsequent to the splitting off of Agilent, the most significant event in the HP story is the introduction of an outsider, Carly Fiorina, as CEO. It appears that her strategy for making HP a successful global player in a variety of computer-related markets is to evolve the HP culture by the mega merger with Compaq, acquiring in that process a large segment of DEC employees who had remained at Compaq.

Summary and Conclusions

The several cases presented in this chapter illustrate how organizations begin to create cultures through the actions of founders who operate as strong leaders. It is important to recognize that even in mature companies one can trace many of their assumptions to the beliefs and values of founders and early leaders. The special role that these leaders play is to propose the initial answers to the young group's questions about how to operate internally and externally. The group cannot test potential solutions if nothing is proposed. Once a leader has activated the group, it can determine whether its actions solve the problems of working effectively in its environment and create a stable internal system. Other solutions can then be proposed by strong group members, and the cultural learning process becomes broadened. Nevertheless, we cannot overlook the tremendous importance of leadership at the very beginning of any group process.

I am not suggesting that leaders consciously set out to teach their new group certain ways of perceiving, thinking, and feeling. Rather, it is in the nature of entrepreneurial thinking to have strong ideas about what to do and how to do it. Founders of groups tend to have well-articulated theories of their own about how groups should work, and they tend to select as colleagues and subordinates others who they sense will think like them. Both founders and the new group members will be anxious in the process of group formation and will look for solutions. The leader's proposal, therefore, will always receive special attention in this phase of group formation.

Early group life also will tend toward intolerance of ambiguity and dissent. In the early life of any new organization one can see many examples of how partners or cofounders who do not think alike end up in conflicts that result in some people leaving, thus creating a more homogeneous climate for those who remain. If the original founders do not have proposals to solve the problems that make the group anxious, other strong members will step in and leaders other than the founders will emerge. I did not observe this in the cases reviewed in this chapter, but I have seen it happen in many other organizations. The important point to recognize is that the anxiety of group formation is typically so high and covers so many areas of group functioning that leadership is highly sought by group members. If the founder does not succeed in reducing the group's anxiety, other leaders will be empowered by the group.

Because founder leaders tend to have strong theories of how to do things, their theories get tested early. If their assumptions are wrong, the group fails early in its history. If their assumptions are correct, they create a powerful organization whose culture comes to reflect their original assumptions. If the environment changes and those assumptions come to be incorrect, the organization must find a way to change its culture—a process that is exceptionally difficult if the founder is still in control of the organization. Such change is difficult particularly because over time the founder leaders have multiple opportunities to embed their assumptions in the various routines of the organization. How this process occurs is detailed in Chapter Thirteen.

13

HOW LEADERS EMBED
AND TRANSMIT CULTURE

In Chapter Twelve we saw how leaders, in their role as founders of organizations, start the culture formation process by imposing their own assumptions on a new group. In this chapter we will explore this process further by examining the many mechanisms that leaders have available to them to reinforce the adoption of their own beliefs, values, and assumptions as the group gradually evolves into an organization. As the organization stabilizes because of success in accomplishing its primary task, the leader's assumptions become shared and the embedding of those assumptions can then be thought of more as a process of socializing new members or acculturating them to the group. From the point of view of a new member, it is a process of the leader and old-timers in the group teaching the new member how to get along in the group and become accepted as a member.

The simplest explanation of how leaders get their message across is that they do it through *charisma*—that mysterious ability to capture the subordinates' attention and to communicate major assumptions and values in a vivid and clear manner (Bennis and Nanus, 1985; Conger, 1989; Leavitt, 1986). The problem with charisma as an embedding mechanism is that leaders who have it are rare and their impact is hard to predict. Historians can look back and say that certain people had charisma or had a great vision. It is not always clear at the time, however, how they transmitted the vision. On the other hand, leaders without charisma have many ways of getting their message across and it is these other ways that will be the focus of this chapter.

Primary Embedding Mechanisms

Taken together, the six primary embedding mechanisms shown in Exhibit 13.1 are the major tools that leaders have available to them to teach their organizations how to perceive, think, feel, and behave based on their own conscious and unconscious convictions. They are discussed in sequence but they operate simultaneously. They are visible artifacts of the emerging culture and they directly create what would typically be called the "climate" of the organization (Schneider, 1990; Ashkanasy, Wilderom, and Peterson, 2000).

What Leaders Pay Attention to, Measure, and Control

One of the most powerful mechanisms that founders, leaders, managers, or even colleagues have available for communicating what they believe in or care about is what they systematically pay atten-

Exhibit 13.1. How Leaders Embed Their Beliefs, Values, and Assumptions.

Primary Embedding Mechanisms

- What leaders pay attention to, measure, and control on a regular basis
- How leaders react to critical incidents and organizational crises
- How leaders allocate resources
- Deliberate role modeling, teaching, and coaching
- How leaders allocate rewards and status
- How leaders recruit, select, promote, and excommunicate

Secondary Articulation and Reinforcement Mechanisms

- Organizational design and structure
- Organizational systems and procedures
- Rites and rituals of the organization
- Design of physical space, facades, and buildings
- Stories about important events and people
- Formal statements of organizational philosophy, creeds, and charters

tion to. This can mean anything from what they notice and comment on to what they measure, control, reward, and in other ways *deal with systematically*. Even casual remarks and questions that are consistently geared to a certain area can be as potent as formal control mechanisms and measurements.

If leaders are aware of this process, then being systematic in paying attention to certain things becomes a powerful way of communicating a message, especially if leaders are totally consistent in their own behavior. On the other hand, if leaders are not aware of the power of this process or they are inconsistent in what they pay attention to, subordinates and colleagues will spend inordinate time and energy trying to decipher what a leader's behavior really reflects and will even project motives onto the leader where none may exist. This mechanism is well captured by the phrase "you get what you settle for."

As a consultant, I have learned that my own consistency in what I ask questions about sends clear signals to my audience about my priorities, values, and beliefs. It is the consistency that is important, not the intensity of the attention. To illustrate, at a recent conference on safety in industrial organizations, the speaker from Alcoa pointed out that one of their former CEOs, Paul O'Neill, wanted to get across to workers how important safety was, and did this by insisting that the first item on *every* meeting agenda was to be a discussion of safety issues.

Douglas McGregor (1960) tells of a company that wanted him to help install a management development program. The president hoped that McGregor would propose exactly what to do and how to do it. Instead, McGregor asked the president whether he really cared about identifying and developing managers. On being assured that he did, McGregor proposed that he should build his concern into the reward system and set up a consistent way of monitoring progress; in other words, he should start to pay attention to it.

The president agreed and announced that henceforth 50 percent of each senior manager's annual bonus would be contingent on what he had done to develop his own immediate subordinates during the past year. He added that he himself had no specific program in mind, but that in each quarter he would ask each senior manager what had been done. One might think that the bonus was the primary incentive for the senior managers to launch programs, but far more important was the fact that they had to report regularly on what they were doing. The senior managers launched a whole series of different activities, many of them pulled together from work that was already going on piecemeal in the organization. A coherent program was forged over a two-year period and has continued to serve this company well. The president continued his quarterly questions and once a year evaluated how much each manager had done for development. He never imposed any program, but by paying consistent attention to management development and by rewarding progress, he clearly signaled to the organization that he considered management development to be important.

At the other extreme, some DEC managers illustrated how inconsistent and shifting attention causes subordinates to pay less and less attention to what senior management wants, thereby empowering the employee level by default. For example, a brilliant manager in one technical group would launch an important initiative and demand total support, but two weeks later he would launch a new initiative without indicating whether or not people were supposed to drop the old one. As subordinates two and three levels down observed this seemingly erratic behavior, they began to rely more and more on their own judgment of what they should actually be doing.

Some of the most important signals of what founders and leaders care about are sent during meetings and in other activities devoted to planning and budgeting, which is one reason why planning and budgeting are such important managerial processes. In questioning subordinates systematically on certain issues, leaders can transmit their own view of how to look at problems. The ultimate content of the plan may not be as important as the learning that goes on during the planning process.

For example, in his manner of planning, Smithfield (see Chapter Twelve, "Smithfield Enterprises") made it clear to all his subordinates that he wanted them to be autonomous, completely responsible for their own operation, but financially accountable. He got this message across by focusing only on financial results. In contrast, both Sam Steinberg and Ken Olsen asked detailed questions about virtually everything during a planning process. Steinberg's obsession with store cleanliness was clearly signaled by the fact that he always commented on it, always noticed deviations from his standards, and always asked what was being done to ensure it in the future. Olsen's assumption that a good manager is always in control of his own situation was clearly evident in his questions about future plans and his anger when plans did not reveal detailed knowledge of product or market issues.

Emotional Outbursts.   Founders and leaders also let members know what they care about with an even more powerful signal: their emotional reactions, especially their emotional outbursts when they feel that one of their important values or assumptions is being violated. Such outbursts are not necessarily very overt, because many managers believe that one should not allow one's emotions to become too involved in the decision-making process. But subordinates generally know when their bosses are upset. On the other hand, some leaders do allow themselves to get overtly angry and upset and use those feelings as messages.

Subordinates find their bosses' emotional outbursts painful and try to avoid them. In the process, they gradually come to condition their behavior to what they perceive the leader to want, and if, over time, that behavior produces desired results they adopt the leader's assumptions as well. For example, Olsen's concern that line managers stay on top of their jobs was originally signaled most clearly in an incident at an executive committee meeting when the company was still very young. A newly hired chief financial officer (CFO) was asked to make his report on the state of the business. He had analyzed the three major product lines and brought his analysis to the meeting. He distributed the information and then pointed out that one product line in particular was in financial difficulty because of falling sales, excessive inventories, and rapidly rising manufacturing costs. It became evident in the meeting that the vice president (VP) in charge of the product line had not seen the CFO's figures and was somewhat embarrassed by what was being revealed.

As the report progressed, the tension in the room rose because everyone sensed that a real confrontation was about to develop between the CFO and the VP. The CFO finished and all eyes turned toward the VP. The VP said that he had not seen the figures and wished he had had a chance to look at them; since he had not seen them, however, he had no immediate answers to give. At this point Olsen blew up, but to the surprise of the whole group he blew up not at the CFO but at the VP. Several members of the group later revealed that they had expected Olsen to blow up at the CFO for his obvious grandstanding in bringing in figures that were new to everyone. However, no one had expected Olsen to turn his wrath on the product line VP for not being prepared to deal with the CFO's arguments and information. Protests that the VP had not seen the data fell on deaf ears. He was told that if he were running his business properly he would have known everything the treasurer knew, and he certainly should have had answers about what should now be done.

Suddenly everyone realized that there was a powerful message in Olsen's behavior. He clearly expected and assumed that a product-line VP would always be totally on top of his own business and would never put himself in the position of being embarrassed by financial data. The fact that the VP did not have his own numbers was a worse sin than being in trouble. The fact that he could not respond to the troublesome figures was also a worse sin than being in trouble. Olsen's blowup at the line manager was a far clearer message than any amount of rhetoric about delegation, accountability, and the like would have been.

If a manager continued to display ignorance or lack of control of his own situation, Olsen would continue to get angry at him and accuse him of incompetence. If the manager attempted to defend himself by noting that his situation either was the result of actions on the part of others over whom he had no control or resulted from prior agreements made by Olsen himself, Olsen would emotionally tell him that he should have brought the issue up right away to force a rethinking of the situation and a renegotiation of the prior decision. In other words, Olsen made it very clear, by the kinds of things to which he reacted emotionally, that poor ultimate performance could be excused but that not being on top of one's own situation and not informing others of what was going on could never be excused.

Olsen's deep assumption about the importance of always telling the truth was signaled most clearly on the occasion of another executive committee meeting, when it was discovered that the company had excess inventory because each product line, in the process of protecting itself, had exaggerated its orders to manufacturing by a small percentage. The accumulation of these small percentages across all the product lines produced a massive excess inventory, which the manufacturing department disclaimed because it had only produced what the product lines had ordered.

At the meeting in which this situation was reviewed, Olsen indicated that he had rarely been as angry as he was then because the product-line managers had *lied*. He stated flatly that if he ever caught a manager exaggerating orders again, it would be grounds for instant dismissal no matter what the reasons. The suggestion that manufacturing could compensate for the sales exaggerations was dismissed out of hand because that would compound the problem. The prospect of one function lying while the other function tried to figure out how to compensate for it totally violated Olsen's assumptions about how an effective business should be run.

Both Steinberg and Olsen shared the assumption that meeting the customer's needs was one of the most important ways of ensuring business success, and their most emotional reactions consistently occurred whenever they learned that a customer had not been well treated. In this area the official messages, as embodied in company creeds and the formal reward system, were completely consistent with the implicit messages that could be inferred from founder reactions. In Steinberg's case, the needs of the customer were even put ahead of the needs of the family, and one way that a family member could get in trouble was by mistreating a customer.

Inferences from What Leaders Do Not Pay Attention To. Other powerful signals that subordinates interpret for evidence of the leader's assumptions are what leaders *do not react to*. For example, at DEC, managers were frequently in actual trouble with cost over-runs, delayed schedules, and imperfect products, but such trouble rarely caused comment if the manager had evidenced that he or she was in control of the situation. Trouble could be expected and was assumed to be a normal condition of doing business; only failure to cope and regain control was unacceptable. In DEC's product design departments, one frequently found excess personnel, very high budgets, and lax management with regard to cost controls, none of which occasioned much comment. Subordinates correctly interpreted this to mean that it was far more important to come up with a good product than to control costs.

Inconsistency and Conflict. The combinations of what founder leaders do and do not pay attention to can be challenging to decipher because they reveal the areas where unconscious conflicts may exist. For example, at DEC the clear concern for customers was signaled by outbursts after customers complained. But this attitude coexisted with an implicit arrogance toward certain classes of customers because the engineers often assumed that they knew what the customer would like in the way of product design and Olsen implicitly reinforced this attitude by not reacting in a corrective way when engineers displayed such attitudes. Olsen's own attitudes toward more or less technically sophisticated customers were not clear, but his silent condoning of his engineers' behavior made it possible for others to assume that Olsen also believed, deep down, that he knew better what the less sophisticated customer really wanted.

Some of the mechanisms that leaders use to communicate their beliefs, values, and assumptions are conscious, deliberate actions; others are unconscious and may even be unintended (Kunda, 1992). The leader may be conflicted and may be sending mutually contradictory messages (Kets de Vries and Miller, 1987). Among the leaders described in Chapter Twelve, Sam Steinberg officially stated a philosophy of delegation and decentralization but retained tight centralized control, intervened frequently on very detailed issues, and felt free to go around the hierarchy. Ken Olsen sent inconsistent signals concerning simplicity and complexity. He always advocated simple structures in which accountability was clearly visible, yet his decision-making style forced high degrees of complexity as various managers worked their proposed solutions through various committees. Managers who grew up in the company understood that one could simultaneously advocate both, but newcomers often had difficulty with what seemed to be obvious inconsistencies. On the one hand, Olsen wanted simplicity, clarity, and high levels of cooperation, but on the other, he often supported and even encouraged overlaps, ambiguity, and competitiveness.

Subordinates will tolerate and accommodate contradictory messages because, in a sense, founders, owners, and others at higher levels are always granted the right to be inconsistent or, in any case, are too powerful to be confronted. The emerging culture will then reflect not only the leader's assumptions but also the complex internal accommodations created by subordinates to run the organization in spite of or around the leader. The group, sometimes acting on the assumption that the leader is a creative genius who has idiosyncrasies, may develop compensatory mechanisms, such as buffering layers of managers, to protect the organization from the dysfunctional aspects of the leader's behavior. In those cases the culture may become a defense mechanism against the anxieties unleashed by inconsistent leader behavior. In other cases the organization's style of operating will reflect the very biases and unconscious conflicts that the founder experiences, thus causing some scholars to call such organizations neurotic (Kets de Vries and Miller, 1984, 1987). At the extreme, subordinates or the board of directors may have to find ways to move the founder out altogether, as has happened in a number of first-generation companies.

In summary, what leaders consistently pay attention to, reward, control, and react to emotionally communicates most clearly what their own priorities, goals, and assumptions are. If they pay attention to too many things or if their pattern of attention is inconsistent, subordinates will use other signals or their own experience to decide what is really important, leading to a much more diverse set of assumptions and many more subcultures.

Leader Reactions to Critical Incidents and Organizational Crises

When an organization faces a crisis, the manner in which leaders and others deal with it creates new norms, values, and working procedures and reveals important underlying assumptions. Crises are especially significant in culture creation and transmission because the heightened emotional involvement during such periods increases the intensity of learning. Crises heighten anxiety, and the need to reduce anxiety is a powerful motivator of new learning. If people share intense emotional experiences and collectively learn how to reduce anxiety, they are more likely to remember what they have learned and to ritually repeat that behavior in order to avoid anxiety.

For example, a company almost went bankrupt because they overengineered their products and made them too expensive. They survived by hitting the market with a lower-quality, less expensive product. Some years later the market required a more expensive, higher-quality product but this company was not able to produce such a product because they could not overcome their anxiety based on their memories of almost going under with the more expensive high-quality product.

What is defined as a crisis is, of course, partly a matter of perception. There may or may not be actual dangers in the external environment, and what is considered to be dangerous is itself often a reflection of the culture. For purposes of this analysis, a crisis is what is perceived to be a crisis and what is defined as a crisis by founders and leaders. Crises that arise around the major external survival issues are the most potent in revealing the deep assumptions of the leaders and therefore the most likely to be the occasions when those assumptions become the basis of shared learning and thus become embedded.

According to a story told about Tom Watson, Jr., in the context of IBM's concern for people and for management development, a young executive had made some bad decisions that cost the company several million dollars. He was summoned to Watson's office, fully expecting to be dismissed. As he entered the office, the young executive said, "I suppose after that set of mistakes you will be wanting to fire me." Watson replied, "Not at all, young man; we have just spent a couple of million dollars educating you."

Innumerable organizations have faced the crisis of shrinking sales, excess inventories, technological obsolescence, and the subsequent necessity of laying off employees in order to cut costs. How leaders deal with such a crisis reveals some of their assumptions about the importance of people and their view of human nature. Ouchi (1981) cites several dramatic examples in which U.S. companies faced with layoffs decided instead to go to short workweeks or to have all employees and managers take cuts in pay to manage the cost reduction without people reduction.

The DEC assumption that "we are a family who will take care of each other" came out most clearly during periods of crisis. When the company was doing well, Olsen often had emotional outbursts reflecting his concern that people were getting complacent. When the company was in difficulty, however, Olsen never punished anyone or displayed anger; instead, he became the strong and supportive father figure, pointing out to both the external world and the employees that things were not as bad as they seemed, that the company had great strengths that would ensure future success, and that people should not worry about layoffs because things would be controlled by slowing down hiring.

On the other hand, Steinberg displayed his lack of concern for his own young managers by being punitive under crisis conditions, sometimes impulsively firing people only to have to try to rehire them later because he realized how important they were to the operation of the company. This gradually created an organization built on distrust and low commitment, leading good people to leave when a better opportunity came along.

Crises around issues of internal integration can also reveal and embed leader assumptions. I have found that a good time to observe an organization very closely is when acts of insubordination take place. So much of an organization's culture is tied up with hierarchy, authority, power, and influence that the mechanisms of conflict resolution have to be constantly worked out and consensually validated. No better opportunity exists for leaders to send signals about their own assumptions about human nature and relationships than when they themselves are challenged.

For example, Olsen clearly and repeatedly revealed his assumption that he did not feel that he knew best through his tolerant and even encouraging behavior when subordinates argued with him or disobeyed him. He signaled that he was truly depending on his subordinates to know what was best and that they should be insubordinate if they felt they were right. In contrast, a bank president with whom I have worked, publicly insisted that he wanted his subordinates to think for themselves, but his behavior belied his overt claim. During an important meeting of the whole staff, one of these subordinates, in attempting to assert himself, made some silly errors in a presentation. The president laughed at him and ridiculed him. Though the president later apologized and said he did not mean it, the damage had been done. All the other subordinates who witnessed the incident interpreted the outburst to mean that the president was not really serious about delegating to them and having them be more assertive. He was still sitting in judgment on them, still operating on the assumption that he knew best.

How Leaders Allocate Resources

The creation of budgets in an organization is another process that reveals leader assumptions and beliefs. For example, a leader who is personally averse to being in debt will bias the budget-planning process by rejecting plans that lean too heavily on borrowing and favoring the retention of as much cash as possible, thus undermining potentially good investments. As Donaldson and Lorsch (1983) show in their study of top-management decision making, leader beliefs about the distinctive competence of their organization, acceptable levels of financial crisis, and the degree to which the organization must be financially self-sufficient strongly influence their choices of goals, the means to accomplish them, and the management processes to be used. Such beliefs not only function as criteria by which decisions are made but are constraints on decision making in that they limit the perception of alternatives.

Olsen's budgeting and resource allocation processes clearly revealed his belief in the entrepreneurial bottom-up system. He consistently resisted letting senior management set targets, formulate strategies, and set goals, preferring instead to stimulate the engineers and managers below him to come up with business plans and budgets that he and other senior executives would approve if they made sense. He was convinced that people would give their best efforts and maximum commitment only to projects and programs that they themselves had invented, sold, and were accountable for.

This system created problems as the DEC organization grew and found itself increasingly operating in a competitive environment in which costs had to be controlled. In its early days the company could afford to invest in all kinds of projects whether they made sense or not. In the late 1980s environment, one of the biggest issues was how to choose among projects that sounded equally good when there were insufficient resources to fund them all. The effort to fund everything resulted in several key projects being delayed, and this became one of the factors in DEC's ultimate failure as a business (Schein, 2003).

Deliberate Role Modeling, Teaching, and Coaching

Founders and new leaders of organizations generally seem to know that their own visible behavior has great value for communicating assumptions and values to other members, especially newcomers. At DEC, Olsen and some other senior executives made videotapes that outlined their explicit philosophy, and these tapes were shown to new members of the organization as part of their initial training. However, there is a difference between the messages delivered by videos or from staged settings, such as when a leader gives a welcoming speech to newcomers, and the messages received when that leader is observed informally. The informal messages are the more powerful teaching and coaching mechanism.

Steinberg, for example, demonstrated his need to be involved in everything at a detailed level by his frequent visits to stores and the minute inspections he made once he got there. When he went on vacation, he called the office every day at a set time and asked detailed questions about all aspects of the business. This behavior persisted into his semiretirement, when he would call every day from his retirement home thousands of miles away. Through his questions, his lectures, and his demonstration of personal concern for details, he hoped to show other managers what it meant to be highly visible and on top of one's job. Through his unwavering loyalty to family members, Steinberg also trained people in how to think about family members and the rights of owners.

Olsen made an explicit attempt to downplay status and hierarchy at DEC because of his assumption that good ideas can come from anyone at any level. He communicated this assumption in many formal and informal ways. For example, he drove a small car, had an unpretentious office, dressed informally, and spent many hours wandering among the employees at all levels, getting to know them personally.

An example of more explicit coaching occurred at Steinbergs when the Steinberg family brought back a former manager as the CEO after several other CEOs had failed. One of the first things this CEO did was to display at a large meeting his own particular method of analyzing the performance of the company and planning its future. He said explicitly to the group: "Now that's an example of the kind of good planning and management I want in this organization." He then ordered his key executives to prepare a long-range planning process in the format in which he had just lectured and gave them a target time to be ready to present their own plans in the new format. At the presentation meeting he coached their presentations, commented on each one, corrected the approach where he felt it had missed the point, and gave them new deadlines for accomplishing their goals as spelled out in the plans. Privately, he told an observer of this meeting that the organization had done virtually no planning for decades and that he hoped to institute formal strategic planning as a way of reducing the massive deficits that the organization had been experiencing. From his point of view, he had to change the entire mentality of his subordinates, which he felt required him to instruct, model, correct, and coach.

How Leaders Allocate Rewards and Status

Members of any organization learn from their own experience with promotions, from performance appraisals, and from discussions with the boss what the organization values and what the organization punishes. Both the nature of the behavior rewarded and punished and the nature of the rewards and punishments themselves carry the messages. Leaders can quickly get across their own priorities, values, and assumptions by consistently linking rewards and punishments to the behavior they are concerned with.

What I am referring to here are actual practices—what really happens—not what is espoused, published, or preached. For example, product managers at General Foods were each expected to develop a successful marketing program for their specific product and then were rewarded by being moved to a better product after about eighteen months. Since the results of a marketing program could not possibly be known in eighteen months, what was really rewarded was the performance of the product manager in creating a "good" marketing program—as measured by the ability to sell it to the senior managers who approved it, not by the ultimate performance of the product in the marketplace.

The implicit assumption was that only senior managers could be trusted to evaluate a marketing program accurately; therefore, even if a product manager was technically accountable for his product, it was, in fact, senior management that took the real responsibility for launching expensive marketing programs. What junior managers learned from this was how to develop programs that had the right characteristics and style from senior management's point of view. If junior-level managers developed the illusion that they really had independence in making marketing decisions, they had only to look at the relative insignificance of the actual rewards given to successful managers: they received a better product to manage, they might get a slightly better office, and they received a good raise—but they still had to present their marketing programs to senior management for review, and the preparations for and dry runs of such presentations took four to five months of every year even for very senior product managers. An organization that seemingly delegated a great deal of power to its product managers was, in fact, limiting their autonomy very sharply and systematically training them to think like senior managers.

To reiterate the basic point, if the founders or leaders are trying to ensure that their values and assumptions will be learned, they must create a reward, promotion, and status system that is consistent with those assumptions. Although the message initially gets across in the daily behavior of the leader, it is judged in the long run by whether the important rewards are allocated consistently with that daily behavior. If these levels of message transmission are inconsistent, one will find a highly conflicted organization without a clear culture or any culture at all at a total organizational level.

How Leaders Recruit, Select, Promote, and Excommunicate

One of the most subtle yet most potent ways in which leader assumptions get embedded and perpetuated is the process of selecting new members. For example, Olsen assumed that the best way to build an organization was to hire very smart, articulate, tough, independent people and then give them lots of responsibility and autonomy. Ciba-Geigy, on the other hand, hired very well educated, smart people who would fit into the more structured culture that had evolved over a century.

This cultural embedding mechanism is subtle because in most organizations it operates unconsciously. Founders and leaders tend to find attractive those candidates who resemble present members in style, assumptions, values, and beliefs. They are perceived to be the best people to hire and are assigned characteristics that will justify their being hired. Unless someone outside the organization is explicitly involved in the hiring, there is no way of knowing how much the current implicit assumptions are dominating recruiters' perceptions of the candidates.

If organizations use search firms in hiring, an interesting question arises as to how much the search firm will understand some of the implicit criteria that may be operating. Because they operate outside the cultural context of the employing organization, do they implicitly become culture reproducers or changers, and are they aware of their power in this regard? Do organizations that employ outside search firms do so in part to get away from their own biases in hiring? In any case, it is clear that initial selection decisions for new members, followed by the criteria applied in the promotion system, are powerful mechanisms for embedding and perpetuating the culture, especially when combined with socialization tactics designed to teach cultural assumptions.

Basic assumptions are further reinforced through criteria of who does or does not get promoted, who is retired early, and who is, in effect, excommunicated by being actually fired or given a job that is clearly perceived to be less important, even if at a higher level (being "kicked upstairs"). At DEC any employee who was not bright or articulate enough to play the idea-debating game and to stand up for his own ideas soon became walled off and eventually was forced out through a process of benign but consistent neglect. At Ciba-Geigy a similar kind of isolation occurred if an employee was not concerned about the company, the products, or senior management. Neither company fired people except for dishonesty or immoral behavior, but at both companies such isolation became the equivalent of excommunication.

Primary Embedding Mechanisms: Some Concluding Observations

These embedding mechanisms all interact and tend to reinforce each other if the leader's own beliefs, values, and assumptions are consistent. By breaking out these categories I am trying to show the many different ways in which leaders can and do communicate their assumptions. Most newcomers to an organization have a wealth of data available to them to decipher the leader's real assumptions. Much of the socialization process is, therefore, embedded in the organization's normal working routines. It is not necessary for newcomers to attend special training or indoctrination sessions to learn important cultural assumptions. These become quite evident through the daily behavior of the leaders.

Secondary Articulation and Reinforcement Mechanisms

In a young organization, design, structure, architecture, rituals, stories, and formal statements are cultural reinforcers, not culture creators. Once an organization has matured and stabilized, these same mechanisms come to be primary culture-creating mechanisms that will constrain future leaders. But in a growing organization these mechanisms are secondary because they work only if they are consistent with the primary mechanisms discussed above. When they are consistent, they begin to build organizational ideologies and thus to formalize much of what is informally learned at the outset. If they are inconsistent, they will either be ignored or be a source of internal conflict.

All these secondary mechanisms can be thought of at this stage as cultural artifacts that are highly visible but may be difficult to interpret without insider knowledge obtained from observing leaders' actual behaviors. When an organization is in its developmental phase, the driving and controlling assumptions will always be manifested first and most clearly in what the leaders demonstrate through their own behavior, not in what is written down or inferred from visible designs, procedures, rituals, stories, and published philosophies. However, as we will see later, these secondary mechanisms can become very strong in perpetuating the assumptions even when new leaders in a mature organization would prefer to change them.

Organizational Design and Structure

As I have observed executive groups in action, particularly first-generation groups led by their founder, I have noticed that the design of the organization—how product lines, market areas, functional responsibilities, and so on are divided up—elicits high degrees of passion but not too much clear logic. The requirements of the primary task—how to organize in order to survive in the external environment—seem to get mixed up with powerful assumptions about internal relationships and with theories of how to get things done that derive more from the founder's background than from current analysis. If it is a family business, the structure must make room for key family members or trusted colleagues, cofounders, and friends. Even in publicly held companies, the organization's design is often built around the talents of the individual managers rather than the external task requirements.

Founders often have strong theories about how to organize for maximum effectiveness. Some assume that only they can ultimately determine what is correct; therefore they build a tight hierarchy and highly centralized controls. Others assume that the strength of their organization is in their people; therefore they build a highly decentralized organization that pushes authority down as low as possible. Still others, like Olsen, believe that their strength is in negotiated solutions; therefore they hire strong people but then create a structure that forces such people to negotiate their solutions with each other—creating, in the process, a matrix organization. Some leaders believe in minimizing interdependence in order to free each unit of the organization; others believe in creating checks and balances so that no one unit can ever function autonomously.

Beliefs also vary about how stable a given structure should be, with some leaders seeking a solution and sticking with it, while others, like Olsen, perpetually redesign their organization in a search for solutions that better fit the perceived problems of the ever-changing external conditions. The initial design of the organization and the periodic reorganizations that companies go through thus provide ample opportunities for the founders and leaders to embed their deeply held assumptions about the task, the means to accomplish it, the nature of people, and the right kinds of relationships to foster among people. Some leaders are able to articulate why they have designed their organization the way they have; others appear to be rationalizing and are not really consciously aware of the assumptions they are making, even though such assumptions can sometimes be inferred from the results. In any case, the organization's structure and design can be used to reinforce leader assumptions but rarely does it provide an accurate initial basis for embedding them because structure can usually be interpreted by the employees in a number of different ways.

Organizational Systems and Procedures

The most visible parts of life in any organization are the daily, weekly, monthly, quarterly, and annual cycles of routines, procedures, reports, forms, and other recurrent tasks that have to be performed. The origins of such routines are often not known to participants—or, in some cases, even to senior management—but their existence lends structure and predictability to an otherwise vague and ambiguous organizational world. The systems and procedures thus serve a function quite similar to the formal structure in that they make life predictable and thereby reduce ambiguity and anxiety. Though employees often complain of stifling bureaucracy, they need some recurrent processes to avoid the anxiety of an uncertain and unpredictable world.

Given that group members seek this kind of stability and anxiety reduction, founders and leaders have the opportunity to reinforce their assumptions by building systems and routines around them. For example, Olsen reinforced his belief that truth is reached through debate by creating many different kinds of committees and attending their meetings. Steinberg reinforced his belief in absolute authority by creating review processes in which he would listen briefly and then issue peremptory orders. Ciba-Geigy reinforced its assumptions about truth deriving from science by creating formal research studies before making important decisions.

Systems and procedures can formalize the process of "paying attention" and thus reinforce the message that the leader really cares about certain things. This is why the president who wanted management development programs helped his cause immensely by formalizing his quarterly reviews of what each subordinate had done. Formal budgeting or planning routines are often adhered to less for producing plans and budgets and more to provide a vehicle for reminding subordinates of what the leader considers to be important matters to pay attention to.

If founders or leaders do not design systems and procedures as reinforcement mechanisms, they open the door to historically evolved inconsistencies in the culture or weaken their own message from the outset. Thus, a strong CEO who believes, as Olsen did, that line managers should be in full control of their own operation must ensure that the organization's financial control procedures are consistent with that belief. If he allows a strong centralized corporate financial organization to evolve and if he pays attention to the data generated by this organization, he is sending a signal inconsistent with the assumption that managers should control their own finances. Then one subculture may evolve in the line organization and a different subculture in the corporate finance organization. If those groups end up fighting each other, it will be the direct result of the initial inconsistency in design logic, not the result of the personalities or the competitive drives of the managers of those functions.

Rites and Rituals of the Organization

Some students of culture would view the special organizational processes of rites and rituals as central to the deciphering as well as to the communicating of cultural assumptions (Deal and Kennedy, 1982, 1999; Trice and Beyer, 1984, 1985). I suspect that the centrality of rites in traditional anthropology has something to do with the difficulty of observing firsthand the primary embedding mechanisms described earlier in this chapter. When the only salient data we have are the rites and rituals that have survived over a period of time, we must, of course, use them as best we can. As with structure and processes, however, if we have only these data, it is difficult to decipher just what assumptions leaders have held that have led to the creation of particular rites and rituals. On the other hand, from the point of view of the leader, if one can ritualize certain behaviors that one considers important, that becomes a powerful reinforcer.

At DEC, for example, the monthly "Woods meetings" devoted to important long-range strategic issues were always held off-site in highly informal surroundings that strongly encouraged informality, status equality, and dialogue. The meetings usually lasted two or more days and involved some joint physical activity such as a hike or a mountain climb. Olsen strongly believed that people would learn to trust and be more open with each other if they did enjoyable things together in an informal setting. As the company grew, various functional groups adopted this style of meeting as well, to the point where periodic off-site meetings became corporate rituals with their own various names, locales, and informal procedures.

In Ciba-Geigy, the annual meeting always involved the surprise athletic event that no one was good at and that would therefore equalize status. The participants would let their hair down, try their best, fail, and be laughed at in a good-humored fashion. It was as if the group were trying to say to itself, "We are serious scientists and business people, but we also know how to play." During the play, informal messages that would not be allowed in the formal work world could be conveyed, thus compensating somewhat for the strict hierarchy.

One can find examples of ritualized activities and formalized ritual events in most organizations, but they typically reveal only very small portions of the range of assumptions that make up the culture of an organization. Therein lies the danger of putting too much emphasis on the study of rituals. One can perhaps decipher one piece of the culture correctly, but one may have no basis for determining what else is going on and how important the ritualized activities are in the larger scheme of things.

Design of Physical Space, Facades, and Buildings

Physical design encompasses all the visible features of the organization that clients, customers, vendors, new employees, and visitors would encounter. The messages that can be inferred from the physical environment, as in the case of structure and procedures, potentially reinforce the leader's messages, but only if they are managed to accomplish this (Steele, 1973). If they are not explicitly managed, they may reflect the assumptions of architects, the organization's planning and facilities managers, local norms in the community, or other subcultural assumptions.

Leaders who have a clear philosophy and style often choose to embody that style in the visible manifestations of their organization. For example, DEC, with its assumptions about truth through conflict and the importance of open communications, chose the open-office layout described earlier. This layout clearly articulated the emphasis on equality, ease of communication, and importance of relationships. The office location in the old woolen mill also communicated Olsen's strong emphasis on frugality and simplicity. What the visitor experienced visually in this organization was an accurate reflection of deeply held assumptions, and one indicator of this depth was that the effects were reproduced in the offices of this organization all over the world.

Ciba-Geigy strongly valued individual expertise and autonomy. But because of its assumption that the holder of a given job becomes the ultimate expert on the area covered by that job, it physically symbolized turf by giving people privacy. Managers at Ciba-Geigy spent much more time thinking things out alone, having individual conferences with others who were centrally involved, and protecting the privacy of individuals so that they could get their work done. At Ciba-Geigy, as at DEC, these were not incidental or accidental physical artifacts. They reflected the basic assumptions of how work gets done, how relationships should be managed, and how one arrives at truth.

Stories About Important Events and People

As a group develops and accumulates a history, some of this history becomes embodied in stories about events and leadership behavior (Allan et al., 2002; Martin and Powers, 1983; Neuhauser, 1993; Wilkins, 1983). Thus, the story—whether in the form of a parable, legend, or even myth—reinforces assumptions and teaches assumptions to newcomers. However, since the message to be found in the story is often highly distilled or even ambiguous, this form of communication is somewhat unreliable. Leaders cannot always control what will be said about them in stories, though they can certainly reinforce stories that they feel good about and perhaps can even launch stories that carry desired messages. Leaders can make themselves highly visible, to increase the likelihood that stories will be told about them, but sometimes attempts to manage the message in this manner backfire because the story may reveal inconsistencies and conflicts in the leader.

Efforts to decipher culture from collecting stories encounter the same problem as the deciphering of rituals: unless one knows other facts about the leaders, one cannot always correctly infer the point of the story. If one understands the culture, then stories can be used to enhance that understanding and make it concrete, but it is dangerous to try to achieve that understanding in the first place from stories alone.

For example, there's a story told about Ken Olsen that when he first saw the IBM PC he said, "Who would ever want a computer in their home?" and "I would fire the engineer who designed that piece of junk." This story sends strong messages about Olsen's prejudices, but it turns out that only one of the messages is correctly interpreted. Olsen did think the PC was less elegant than what he would have wanted to produce, but his remark about computers in the home was in the context of computers *controlling* everything in the home. This remark was made at a time when fears of computers taking over all functions in our lives was very real, as viewers of the film *2001: A Space Odyssey* will recall. Olsen welcomed computers in his home as work and play stations but not as mechanisms for organizing and controlling daily activities.

Formal Statements of Organizational Philosophy, Creeds, and Charters

The final mechanism of articulation and reinforcement to be mentioned is the formal statement—the attempt by the founders or leaders to state explicitly what their values or assumptions are. These statements typically highlight only a small portion of the assumption set that operates in the group and, most likely, will highlight only those aspects of the leader's philosophy or ideology that lend themselves to public articulation. Such public statements have a value for the leader as a way of emphasizing special things to be attended to in the organization, as values around which to rally the troops, and as reminders of fundamental assumptions not to be forgotten. However, formal statements cannot be viewed as a way of defining the organization's culture. At best they cover a small, publicly relevant segment of the culture: those aspects that leaders find useful to publish as an ideology or focus for the organization.

Summary and Conclusions

This chapter examined how leaders embed the assumptions that they hold and thereby create the conditions for culture formation. Six of the mechanisms discussed are powerful primary means by which founders or leaders are able to embed their own assumptions in the ongoing daily life of their organizations. Through what they pay attention to and reward, through the ways in which they allocate resources, through their role modeling, through the manner in which they deal with critical incidents, and through the criteria they use for recruitment, selection, promotion, and excommunication, leaders communicate both explicitly and implicitly the assumptions they actually hold. If they are conflicted, the conflicts and inconsistencies are also communicated and become a part of the culture or become the basis for subcultures and countercultures.

Less powerful, more ambiguous, and more difficult to control are the messages embedded in the organization's structure, its procedures and routines, its rituals, its physical layout, its stories and legends, and its formal statements about itself. Yet these six secondary mechanisms can provide powerful reinforcement of the primary messages if the leader is able to control them. The important point to grasp is that all these mechanisms do communicate culture content to newcomers. Leaders do not have a choice about whether or not to communicate, only about how much to manage what they communicate.

At the organization's early growth stage, the secondary mechanisms of structure, procedures, rituals, and formally espoused values are only supportive, but as the organization matures and stabilizes they become primary maintenance mechanisms—what we ultimately call institutionalization or bureaucratization. The more effective they are in making the organization successful, the more they become the filter or criteria for the selection of new leaders. As a result, the likelihood of new leaders becoming cultural change agents declines as the organization matures. The socialization process then begins to reflect what has worked in the past, not what may be the primary agenda of the current leadership. The dynamics of the "midlife" organization are, therefore, quite different from those of the young and emerging organization, as will be shown in the following chapters.

Though the leadership examples in this chapter come primarily from founders, any manager can begin to focus on these mechanisms when attempting to teach subordinates some new ways of perceiving, thinking, and feeling. What the manager must recognize is that all of the primary mechanisms must be used, and all of them must be consistent with each other. Many change programs fail because the leader who wants the change fails to use the entire set of mechanisms described. To put it positively, when a manager decides to change the assumptions of a work group by using all of these mechanisms, that manager is becoming a leader.

14

THE CHANGING ROLE OF LEADERSHIP IN ORGANIZATIONAL "MIDLIFE"

If an organization is successful in fulfilling its mission it will mature and probably grow. Founders will age or die and be replaced by leaders who have been promoted within the organization. Ownership by founders or founding families will evolve into public ownership and governance by boards of directors. The decision whether to retain private ownership or go public may appear to be a financial decision, but it has enormous cultural consequences. With private ownership the leaders can continue to enforce their own values and assumptions through all of the mechanisms cited in the last chapter. Once governance has shifted to a CEO and a board of directors, the leadership role becomes more diffuse and transient because CEOs and board members usually have limited terms of office and are more accountable to stock holders.

On the one hand, this means that treasured values will be eroded if new CEOs don't adhere to them; on other hand, it makes it possible for the organization to make necessary changes in its goals and means, and, if necessary, to change elements of the culture. Founders may be blind to these issues and may, therefore, have to be made aware of them by their own managements or outside board members if such are in the picture.

With growth will come differentiation into various subgroups, which will, over time, evolve their own cultures. The environmental context within which the organization and these various subgroups operate will evolve, requiring new responses from the organization. Leadership, especially at the level of the executive culture (see Chapter Ten), can influence the nature of this differentiation in important ways. Here again, the criteria that executives use to evolve their organization are usually related to finances, marketing, technology, and products. What is overlooked are the cultural implications of various ways of differentiating the organization.

The culture of the organization that has been built on past success may become, to varying degrees, dysfunctional, requiring what the leader may come to perceive as a need for "culture change," and the way in which growth is managed can facilitate such change. All of these organizational midlife phenomena produce new culture dynamics that require a very different kind of leadership behavior if the organization is to continue to survive.

Differentiation into Subgroups and the Growth of Subcultures

All organizations undergo a process of differentiation as they age and grow. This is variously called division of labor, functionalization, divisionalization, or diversification. The common element, however, is that as the number of people, customers, goods, and services increases, it becomes less and less efficient for the founder to coordinate everything. If the organization is successful, it inevitably creates smaller units that begin the process of culture formation on their own with their own leaders. The major bases on which such differentiation occurs are as follows:

1. Functional/occupational differentiation
2. Geographical decentralization
3. Differentiation by product, market, or technology
4. Divisionalization
5. Differentiation by hierarchical level

Functional/Occupational Differentiation

The forces creating functional subcultures derive from the technology and occupational culture of the function. The production department hires people trained in manufacturing and engineering, the finance department hires economics and finance types, the sales department hires sales types, research and development hires technical specialists, and so on. Even though these newcomers to the organization will be strongly socialized into the basic culture, as described in Chapters Twelve and Thirteen, they will bring with them other cultural assumptions derived from their education and from association with their occupational community (Van Maanen and Barley, 1984). Such differences arise initially from personality differences that cause people to choose different occupations and from the subsequent education and socialization into an occupation (Holland, 1985; Schein, 1971, 1978, 1987b; Van Maanen and Schein, 1979).

The cultures of different occupations, in the sense of the shared assumptions that members of that occupation hold, will differ because of the core technology that is involved in each occupation. Thus engineers, doctor, lawyers, accountants, and so on will differ from each other in their basic beliefs, values, and tacit assumptions because they are doing fundamentally different things, have been trained differently, and have acquired a certain identity in practicing their occupation. One therefore will find in each functional area a blend of the founder assumptions and the assumptions associated with that functional/occupational group.

Recall Dougherty's (1990) study (see Chapter Seven, "What Is 'Information'?") of successful and unsuccessful new product introductions, in which she found that all product development teams agreed that one needed to know as much as possible about one's potential customers, but subcultural assumptions about the customers biased the kind of information each functional group possessed.

A powerful subculture based on technology and occupation is *information technology* (IT), built around a number of assumptions that conflict with other subcultural assumptions. The IT culture is a prime example of what I labeled in Chapter Ten an *engineering culture*, dedicated primarily to improvement and innovation. For example, IT makes the following assumptions:

- Information can be packaged into bits and transmitted electronically

- More information is always better than less
- The more quantifiable information is, the better
- Information can be captured and frozen in time on the computer screen, and so on; hence a paperless office is possible and desirable
- Technology leads and people should adapt
- People can and should learn the language and methods of IT
- Management will give up hierarchy if IT provides better coordination mechanisms
- The more fully connected an organization is, the better it will perform
- People will use information responsibly and appropriately
- Paper can be replaced by electronically stored information

By way of contrast, both the operator culture and the executive culture might hold contrary assumptions. For example, operators and/or executives often make the following assumptions:

- Information relevant to operations must include face-to-face human contact in order to be accurately understood
- Information must be extracted from raw data and will be meaningful only in a particular context that is itself perpetually changing
- Meaning derives only from complex patterns
- The costs associated with speed may not be worth it
- Too much connectivity produces information overload
- The more information you have, the more you need
- Certain kinds of information, such as personal feedback in performance appraisal, should *not* be quantitative and should not be computerized
- The ability to see and manipulate paper is intrinsic to many kinds of tasks

- Technology should adapt to people and be user friendly
- Hierarchy is intrinsic to human systems and a necessary coordination mechanism, no matter how efficient networked communications are
- Control of information is a necessary management tool and the only way of maintaining power and status

If a CEO understands the different assumptions of these sub-cultures, he or she must realize that they can influence the course of the organization's evolution through the kinds of incentives and controls they create. They can grant more power to the IT function to further its assumptions, or they can tell their operational units that they do not have to follow a common solution proposed by the IT function.

With organizational growth and continued success, functional subcultures become stable and well articulated. Organizations acknowledge this most clearly when they develop rotational programs for the training and development of future leaders. When a young manager is rotated through sales, marketing, finance, and production, she or he is learning not only the technical skills in each of these functions but also the point of view, perspective, and underlying assumptions of that function; that is, its subculture. Such deeper understanding is thought to be necessary to doing a good job as a general manager later in the career. Organizations in which general management have always come from just one function often complain that their leaders make less effective integrative decisions because they do not really understand the requirements of the other functions.

In some cases the communication barriers between functional subcultures become so powerful and chronic that organizations have had to invent new boundary-spanning functions or processes. The clearest example is production engineering, a function whose major purpose is to smooth the transition of a product from engineering into production. If one asks why this function is necessary, one finds that without it engineering often designs things that cannot be built or are too expensive to build and that the "normal" communication process between production and engineering is not sufficient to cure the problem. Engineering is likely to perceive production as lazy and unimaginative, while production perceives engineering to be unrealistic, lacking in cost consciousness, and too concerned with product elegance instead of the practicalities of how to build the product. Executive leaders must recognize these as *cultural* issues that need to be managed.

The subcultures of sales/marketing and R&D are often so out of line with each other that organizations have learned to create task forces or project teams that bring all the functions together in the initial product development process. But as Dougherty's (1990) research showed, even that is not, by itself, enough to guarantee understanding across the subcultural boundaries.

In summary, functional subcultures bring in the diversity that is associated with the occupational communities and technologies that underlie the functions. This diversity creates the basic problem of integration and coordination that is often the most difficult part of general management, in that the leader now has to bring into alignment organizational members who have genuinely different points of view based on their education and experience in the organization. If these problems are anticipated, the leader can either avoid organizing by function, or bring the different functions together in dialogues that stimulate mutual understanding of each other's taken-for-granted assumptions. To facilitate such communication across subcultural boundaries requires cultural humility from the leader and the ability not only to perceive subcultural differences but also to respect them.

Geographical Differentiation

A second and equally powerful basis for the creation of subcultures is established when the organization grows to the point that the leadership decides to break it into several geographical units because of any of the following imperatives:

- The need to get closer to different customer bases and the discovery that geographically dispersed customers often require genuinely different goods and services
- The need to take advantage of local labor costs in some geographical areas
- The cost advantages of getting closer to where raw materials, sources of energy, or suppliers are located
- The requirement by local customers that if products are to be sold in a local market, they must be produced in that market area as well, to protect local labor and to gain knowledge of relevant manufacturing technology

The cultural consequences, however, are often unanticipated because the geographical units inevitably adopt some of the asumptions of the host culture in which they operate. Subsidiaries or sales units that operate in different countries are inevitably influenced by the cultures of those countries, even if they are staffed primarily by employees and managers from the home country. If local nationals are hired, this influence of course becomes even greater. The process of local influence becomes most salient where business ethics are involved, as when giving money to suppliers or local government officials in one country is defined as a bribe or kickback and deemed illegal and unethical, while in another country the same act is not only legal but considered an essential and normal part of doing business.

The selection of people to run geographically dispersed units is itself a culturally related decision. If the organization's leadership feels strongly about perpetuating and extending its core assumptions, it tends to send senior managers from the home country into the regions, or if it selects local managers, it tends to put them through an intensive socialization process. For example, I remember meeting in Singapore an Australian who had just been named head of Hewlett-Packard's local plant there. Though he had been hired in Australia and was to spend most of his career in Singapore, he was a dedicated HPer. When I asked him how come, he explained that shortly after being hired he had been flown to California, where he had immediately been met by Mr. Packard himself and then spent six hours with all the top managers. In the following two weeks he was given a thorough indoctrination in the HP Way and was encouraged to visit headquarters often. What impressed him most was how important his appointment was to senior management. Their willingness to spend time with him motivated him to really get to know and perpetuate the central values embodied in the HP Way.

At DEC the senior managers responsible for large regions and countries were based in those countries, but they spent two to three days of every month in meetings with Olsen and other senior managers at headquarters, so the basic assumptions under which DEC operated were constantly reinforced, even though most of the employees were locals.

I was once invited to address a group of Ciba-Geigy managers at the U.S. subsidiary to tell them about the Ciba-Geigy culture as I had experienced it in the Basel headquarters. I had had no contact with the U.S. subsidiary group up to that time. After I described the cultural paradigm to them as I saw it (as outlined in Chapter Three), there was a real sense of shock in the audience, articulated by one manager who said, "My God, you're describing us!" He was particularly shocked because he had believed that the Ciba-Geigy's U.S. group, by virtue of the fact that most of the members were American, would be very different. Clearly, however, the company culture had asserted itself across national boundaries.

On the other hand, the local culture inevitably shapes the geographic subculture as well. One finds a different blend of assumptions in each geographical area, reflecting the local national culture but also the business conditions, customer requirements, and the like. For example, I am familiar with several European pharmaceutical companies that operate in the United States. In each case the U.S. subsidiary mirrors many of the basic assumptions of the European parent (even if it has an American president), but its day-to-day practices in research and in clinical testing reflect the requirements of the U.S. Food and Drug Administration and the U.S. medical establishment. The U.S. pharmaceutical researcher will say that the European is much less thorough in his testing of compounds, not because his research is inferior but because many European countries do not require the same amount of testing before a drug is approved. Over time, these testing methods become habits and become embedded, leading to real conflict between the research organizations in Europe and the United States.

As organizations mature, the geographical units may take over more and more of the functions. Instead of being just local sales or production units, they may evolve into integrated divisions, including even engineering and R&D. Then one sees in those divisions the additional subcultural difficulty of integrating across functional boundaries where the home functional culture is geographically distant. For example, DEC's various European divisions, typically organized by country, found that the customers in different countries wanted different versions of the basic products, leading to the question: Where should the engineering for the local needs be done? On the one hand, it was very important to maintain common engineering standards worldwide, but on the other hand, those common standards made the product less attractive in a given geographical region. Engineering units that were placed in various countries then found themselves in conflict with local marketing and sales units about maintaining standards and in conflict with their home engineering department over the need to deviate from standards.

If a common culture and good understanding exist across the subcultural boundaries, this kind of problem can be resolved rationally in terms of the costs and benefits of different solutions. However, if there is misunderstanding because of a lack of common language and concepts in terms of how to communicate and state the problem, it is likely that the organization will generate conflict and ineffective solutions. At Ciba-Geigy, I encountered one situation in which the U.S. research and development group in one division totally mistrusted the research conducted in the headquarters labs and felt that it had to repeat everything, at enormous cost, to determine whether the results were usable in the U.S. market.

One of the reasons that the marketing and sales departments of an organization often develop communication problems with each other is that the salespeople develop part of their culture from their constant interaction with the customer, whereas the marketing group is generally more immersed in the headquarters culture and its technical subculture. The salespeople deal in daily face-to-face contacts, whereas the marketing people deal with data, long-range strategy, broad concepts, and sales tools such as advertising and promotional programs. Often, marketing sees itself as creating the strategies and tactics that sales must then implement, leading to potential status conflicts. At General Foods this led to conflict because salespeople knew how the stores stocked their shelves and thereby made some products more visible and attractive—something that market research could not possibly reveal. Yet marketing saw itself as the decision maker on product promotions and did not provide salespeople any opportunities to give their input.

The important point to recognize is that the difficulty often encountered between these functions can be seen to result from genuine subcultural differences that are predictable and can be analyzed. To get marketing and sales to work together effectively requires more than a proper reward and incentive system. It requires the development of a common language and common shared experiences.

In summary, as geographical units mature and become divisions and integrated subsidiaries, one will find in them a number of cultural and subcultural phenomena: (1) a blend of the total organization's culture and the geographic host culture, (2) a local version of the functional subcultural issues that exist in the total organization, and (3) more complicated communication problems based on the fact that the functional subcultures will also take on a local character as they hire locals to perform tasks and thereby introduce host country assumptions. Leaders must recognize these cultural issues as inevitable consequences of the kind of organization they have fostered, have the humility to accept them as real issues to be dealt with, and stimulate the necessary dialogue to foster cross cultural understanding.

Differentiation by Product, Market, or Technology

As organizations mature, they typically differentiate themselves in terms of the basic technologies they employ, the product sets this leads to, and the types of customers they ultimately deal with. Founders and promoted leaders in older companies must recognize and decide at what point it is desirable to differentiate products, markets, or technologies, knowing that this will create a whole new set of cultural integration problems down the line. For example, the Ciba-Geigy Company started out as a dyestuffs company, but its research on chemical compounds led it into pharmaceuticals, agricultural chemicals, and industrial chemicals. Though the core culture was based on chemistry, as described previously, one could clearly observe subcultural differences that reflected the different product sets.

The forces that created such subcultural differences were of two kinds. First, different kinds of people with different educational and occupational origins were attracted into the different businesses; second, the interaction with the customer required a different mindset and led to different kinds of shared experiences. I remember at one point suggesting a marketing program that would cut across the divisions and was asked, "Professor Schein, what do you really think an educated salesman who deals all day with doctors and hospital administrators has in common with an ex-farm boy slogging around in manure talking farmers into buying the newest pesticide?"

One of the most innovative and culturally evolutionary steps Ciba-Geigy took in its efforts to become more of a marketing-based organization was to promote a manager who had grown up in the agricultural division to head of the U.S. pharmaceutical division. It happened that this man was such a good manager and such a good marketer that he overcame the stereotypes based on where he had grown up in the business. Although he was ultimately successful, when he first took over he had a tough time winning the respect of the pharmaceutical managers.

Contact with customers is a very powerful force in creating local subcultures that can appropriately interact with the customer's culture. A vivid example is provided by Northrop, a large aerospace company that prided itself on its egalitarianism, high trust, and participative approach to its employees. An analysis of the company's artifacts revealed that the headquarters organization based in Los Angeles was very hierarchical; even the architecture and office layout of the headquarters building strongly reflected hierarchy and status. The managers themselves felt this to be anomalous, but upon reflection they realized that they had built such a headquarters organization to make their primary customers, representatives of the U.S. Defense Department, feel comfortable. They pointed out that the Pentagon is highly structured in terms of hierarchy and that customer teams on their visits to this company were only comfortable if they felt they were talking to managers of a status equivalent to or higher than their own. To make this visible, the company introduced all kinds of status symbols, such as graded office sizes, office amenities, office locations in the building, private dining rooms, and reserved parking spaces.

A trivial but amusing example of the same phenomenon occurred at DEC, when a young employee who ordinarily drove vans to deliver mail or parts internally was assigned to drive board members and other outsiders with high status to special meetings. On one such occasion, he was allowed to drive the one fancy company car, and he dressed for the event by putting on a black pinstriped suit! Only if the passenger interrogated the driver would he or she discover that this was a special assignment, not a routine job.

Divisionalization

As organizations grow and develop different markets, they often divisionalize in the sense of decentralizing most of the functions into the product, market, or geographical units. This process has the advantage of bringing all the functions closer together around a given technology, product set, or customer set, allowing for more integration across the functional subculture boundaries. The forces driving subculture formation then begin to play out more at the divisional level.

Typically, to run an integrated division requires a strong general manager, and that manager is likely to want a fair amount of autonomy in the running of his or her division. As that division develops its own history, it will begin to develop a divisional subculture that reflects its particular technology and market environment, even if it is geographically close to the parent company.

Strong divisional subcultures will not be a problem to the parent organization unless the parent wants to implement certain common practices and management processes. Two examples from my own experience highlight this issue. In the first case, I was asked to work with the senior management of the Swedish government-owned conglomerate of organizations to help headquarters decide whether or not it should work toward developing a common culture. This conglomerate included ship building, mining, and, at the other extreme, consumer products like Ramlosa bottled water. We spent two days examining all of the pros and cons and finally decided that the only two activities that required a common perspective were financial controls and human resource development. In the financial area the headquarters staff had relatively little difficulty establishing common practices, but in the human resource area they ran into real difficulty.

From the point of view of headquarters it was essential to develop a cadre of future general managers, requiring that divisions allow their high-potential young managers to be rotated across different divisions and headquarters functional units. But the division subcultures differed markedly in their assumptions about how to develop managers. One division considered it essential that all of its people be promoted from within because of their knowledge of the business, so its members rejected out of hand the idea of cross-divisional rotation of any sort. In another division, cost pressures were so severe that the idea of giving up a high-potential manager to a development program was unthinkable. A third division's norm was that one rose by staying in functional stovepipes, and managers were rarely evaluated for their generalist potential. When the development program called for that division to accept a manager from another division in a rotational developmental move, it rejected the candidate outright as not knowing enough about the division's business to be acceptable at any level. The divisional subcultures won out and the development program was largely abandoned, to the possible detriment of the parent organization.

In the other case, a similar phenomenon occurred in relation to the introduction of information technology. Interviews with many CEOs in different kinds of industries revealed that one of the biggest problems of those who headed large multidivisional organizations was trying to introduce an electronic mail system across all the divisions. Typically, each division had developed its own system and become highly committed to it. When the corporate information systems department proposed a common system, it encountered strong resistance, and when it imposed a common system, it encountered subversion and refusal to use the system. Several CEOs even commented that information technology was the single hardest thing to get implemented across autonomous divisions.

One of the significant facts about DEC's evolution is that it did create product lines, but never divisions, and that allowed functions such as sales and engineering to remain very dominant. In contrast, HP divisionalized very early in its history. Many managers within DEC speculated that the failure to divisionalize was one of the major reasons for DEC's ultimate economic difficulties.

Differentiation by Hierarchical Level

As the number of people in the organization increases, it becomes increasingly difficult to coordinate their activities. One of the simplest and most universal mechanisms that all groups, organizations, and societies use to deal with this problem is to create additional layers in the hierarchy so that the span of control of any given manager remains reasonable. Of course, what is defined as reasonable will itself vary from five to fifty; nevertheless, it is clear that every organization, if it is successful and grows, will sooner or later differentiate itself into more and more levels.

The interaction and shared experience among the members of a given level provide an opportunity for the formation of common assumptions—a subculture based on rank or status. The strength of such shared assumptions will be a function of the relative amount of interaction and the intensity of the shared experience that the members of that level have with each other as contrasted with members of other levels. Thus a top-management team that functions in isolation at corporate headquarters is quite likely to form a subculture. Similarly, a group of supervisors in a large geographically isolated plant or a group of workers in a union will interact primarily with each other and therefore eventually form a subculture.

In Chapter Ten I described operator, engineering, and executive cultures within organizations. These subcultures are generally correlated with rank as well as with occupation and organizational tasks. For example, Donaldson and Lorsch (1983), in their study of how senior executives make decisions, found that they were guided and constrained by a "dominant belief system" about the necessity of balancing the requirements of their major constituencies—the capital markets from which they must borrow, the labor markets from which they must obtain their employees, the suppliers, and most important, the customers. Scarce resources must be allocated in such a way that the needs of each group are met to an optimal degree.

Senior managers had complex mental equations by which they made their decisions. Constraining such broad strategic decisions was a set of interrelated beliefs about (1) the distinctive competence of their organization, (2) the degree of financial risk that was appropriate for their organization, and (3) the degree to which they felt their organization should be financially self-sufficient. The specifics of such beliefs differed from industry to industry and company to company, but at each company studied, senior management had strong beliefs in these three areas, and those beliefs guided specific decisions about goals, means, and management practices.

What we can say about the nature of hierarchical cultures, then, is that they are similar in *structure*; the basic assumptions are concerned with the same kinds of issues that all top managers face. How they resolve those issues, however, depends on other factors, such as the technology, the maturity of the products and markets, and the unique historical experience of each company.

One could extrapolate further and hypothesize that the subculture at each level of the organization will, over time, structurally reflect the major issues and tasks that must be confronted at that level and that the resolution of those tasks will provide different kinds of cultural content in different industries and companies. Thus all first-line supervisors will develop assumptions about human nature and how to manage employees, but whether they develop idealistic assumptions or cynical assumptions will depend more on the industry and actual company experience. Similarly, all sales managers will develop assumptions about human motivation on the basis of their experience in managing salespeople, but whether they come to believe in salary plus commission, pure commission, bonus systems, or individual or team reward systems will again depend upon the industry and the company.

In other words, the structure of any given hierarchical level's culture will be primarily defined by the tasks that must be achieved at that level. One can also anticipate that the group will have only weak assumptions or no assumptions at all in other areas because its members have not faced tasks or had shared experiences in those areas. To again use the first-line supervisor as an example, he or she may have very strong assumptions about human nature and either weak assumptions or no assumptions about how much debt a company should carry. On the other hand, top management will have very strong assumptions about debt level and only weak ones about how to manage technology or specific customer sets.

Summary and Conclusions

Organizational success usually produces the need to grow, and with growth and aging organizations need to differentiate themselves into functional, geographic, product, market, or hierarchical units. One of the critical functions of leadership in this process is to recognize the *cultural* consequences of various ways of differentiating. New subgroups will eventually share enough experience to create subcultures based on occupational, national, and uniquely historic experiences. Once such differentiation has taken place, the leader's task is to find ways of coordinating, aligning, or integrating the different subcultures.

Leaders should not be surprised when they find that different functions seem to be talking completely different languages, or that geographically isolated managers do not interpret headquarters memos accurately, or that the concerns of senior management about costs and productivity are not shared by employees. Building an effective organization is ultimately a matter of meshing the different subcultures by encouraging the evolution of common goals, common language, and common procedures for solving problems.

It is essential that leaders recognize that such cultural alignment requires not only cultural humility on the leader's part, but skills in bringing different subcultures together into the kind of dialogue that will maintain mutual respect and create coordinated action. Some ideas for how to do this will be covered in the Chapters Seventeen, Eighteen, and Nineteen on leaders as change agents.

15

WHAT LEADERS NEED TO KNOW
ABOUT HOW CULTURE CHANGES

The role of the leader in "managing" culture differs at the different stages of organizational evolution. We have already discussed in Chapter Twelve how founders of organizations initially impose their assumptions on a new group and how that group evolves its culture as a result of success. We have also shown, in Chapter Thirteen, how leaders embed their assumptions as groups evolve. Chapter Fourteen examined how organizations evolve as they become larger and more differentiated. We now need to analyze the processes by which culture evolves and changes as organizations grow and age, and we need to examine how leaders can influence these processes. In this chapter we will examine culture evolution and change mechanisms that tend to occur naturally at different stages of organizational evolution. In Chapters Sixteen and Seventeen we will examine "planned managed culture change"—which is undertaken if and when a leader decides that the evolutionary processes are too slow or inappropriate.

Mechanisms and Forces
That Initiate Culture Change

The way in which culture can and does change depends on the stage at which the organization finds itself. For example, when a culture is in the growth stage, the ways for manipulating the mechanisms of embedding discussed in Chapter Thirteen are also the ways to initiate change in the culture; that is, leaders can change what they pay attention to, control, and reward; their role modeling and coaching; how they allocate resources; how they select, promote, and "deselect" people; and the organizational structures and processes they create. However, once the culture has stabilized because of a long history of success, leaders find that such manipulations are often limited or superficial in their effects. They discover that to change deeply embedded assumptions requires far more effort and time.

Nevertheless, at different stages in the evolution of a given organization different possibilities for culture change arise, because of the particular function that culture plays at each developmental stage. Table 15.1 shows these stages and identifies the particular change mechanisms that are most relevant at each stage. These mechanisms are cumulative in the sense that at a later stage, all the prior change mechanisms are still operating but additional ones become relevant.

Founding and Early Growth

In the first stage—the founding and early growth of a new organization—the main cultural thrust comes from the founders and their assumptions. The cultural paradigm that becomes embedded, if the

Table 15.1. Culture Change Mechanisms.

Organizational Stage	Change Mechanism
Founding and early growth	1. Incremental change through general and specific evolution 2. Insight 3. Promotion of hybrids within the culture
Midlife	4. Systematic promotion from selected subcultures 5. Technological seduction 6. Infusion of outsiders
Maturity and decline	7. Scandal and explosion of myths 8. Turnarounds 9. Mergers and acquisitions 10. Destruction and rebirth

Copyright © E. H. Schein.

organization succeeds in fulfilling its primary task and survives, can then be viewed as that organization's distinctive competence, the basis for member identity, and the psychosocial "glue" that holds the organization together. The emphasis in this early stage is on differentiating the organization from the environment and from other organizations, as the organization makes its culture explicit, integrates it as much as possible, and teaches it firmly to newcomers (and/or selects them for initial compatibility).

The distinctive competences in young companies are usually biased toward certain business functions reflecting the occupational biases of the founders. At DEC the bias was clearly in favor of engineering and manufacturing. Not only was it difficult for the other functions to acquire status and prestige, but professionals in those functions, such as professional marketers, were often told by managers who had been with the company from its origin that "marketers never know what they are talking about." At Ciba-Geigy a similar bias persisted for science and research, even though the company was much older. Because R&D was historically the basis of Ciba-Geigy's success, science was defined as the distinctive competence, even though more and more managers were admitting overtly that the future hinged more on marketing, tight financial controls, and efficient operations.

The implications for change at this stage are clear. The culture in young and successfully growing companies is likely to be strongly adhered to because (1) the primary culture creators are still present, (2) the culture helps the organization define itself and make its way into a potentially hostile environment, and (3) many elements of the culture have been learned as defenses against anxiety as the organization struggles to build and maintain itself.

It is therefore likely that proposals to *deliberately change* the culture from either inside or outside will be totally ignored or strongly resisted. Instead, dominant members or coalitions will attempt to preserve and enhance the culture. The only force that might unfreeze such a situation is an external crisis of survival in the form of a sharp drop in growth rate, loss of sales or profit, a major product failure, or some other event that cannot be ignored. If such a crisis occurs, the founder may be discredited and a new senior manager may be brought into the picture. If the founding organization itself stays intact, so will the culture.

How then does culture change in the growth phase of an organization? Several change mechanisms can be identified.

Incremental Change Through General and Specific Evolution

If the organization is not under too much external stress and if the founder or founding family is around for a long time, the culture evolves in small increments by continuing to assimilate what works best over the years. Such evolution involves two basic processes: general evolution and specific evolution (Sahlins and Service, 1960).

General Evolution. General evolution toward the next stage of development involves diversification, growing complexity, higher levels of differentiation and integration, and creative syntheses into new and higher-level forms. The various impacts of growth and success, which were described in Chapter Fourteen, provide the basis for a more detailed analysis of how this occurs. Implicit in this evolutionary model is the assumption that social systems do have an evolutionary dynamic. Just as groups go through logical stages, so organizations go through logical stages, especially with respect to changing their ownership structure from private to public. However, if a crisis brings in new leadership, there is evidence to suggest that the new direction in which the culture will move is quite unpredictable (Gersick, 1991; Tushman and Anderson, 1986).

The elements of the culture that operate as defenses are likely to be retained and strengthened over the years, but they may be refined and developed into an integrated and more complex structure. Basic assumptions may be retained, but the form in which they appear may change, creating new behavior patterns that ultimately feed back into the basic assumptions. For example, at DEC the assumptions that one must find "truth through debate" and always "do the right thing" evolved from being individual-level principles to being embedded in intergroup dynamics. Whereas in the early DEC culture individuals were able to stay logical in their debate, as DEC became a large conglomerate of powerful groups those same individuals argued from their positions as representatives and defenders of their projects and groups. Doing the right thing for DEC became doing what that particular *group* wanted to do.

Specific Evolution. Specific evolution involves the adaptation of specific parts of the organization to their particular environments and the impact of the subsequent cultural diversity on the core culture. This is the mechanism that causes organizations in different industries to develop different industry cultures and causes subgroups to develop different subcultures. Thus, a high-technology company will develop highly refined R&D skills, whereas a consumer products company in foods or cosmetics will develop highly refined marketing skills. In each case such differences will come to reflect important underlying assumptions about the nature of the world and the actual growth experience of the organization. In addition, because the different parts of the organization exist in different environments, each of those parts will evolve to adapt to its particular environment, as discussed in Chapter Fourteen.

As subgroups differentiate and subcultures develop, the opportunity for more major culture change will arise later, but in this early stage those differences will only be tolerated and efforts will be made to minimize them. For example, it was clear that the service organization at DEC was run more autocratically, but this was tolerated because everyone recognized that a service organization required more discipline if the customers were to get timely and efficient service. The higher-order principle of "do the right thing" justified all kinds of managerial variations in the various functions.

Self-Guided Evolution Through Insight

If one thinks of culture as, in part, a learned defense mechanism to avoid uncertainty and anxiety, then one should be able to help the organization assess for itself the strengths and weaknesses of its culture and to help it modify cultural assumptions if that becomes necessary for survival and effective functioning. Members of the organization can collectively achieve insight if they collectively examine their culture and redefine some of the cognitive elements. Such redefinition involves either changing some of the priorities within the core set of assumptions or abandoning one assumption that is a barrier by subordinating it to a higher-order assumption. The internal deciphering process that will be described in Chapter Seventeen typically produces a level of cultural insight that allows a group to decide the direction of its future evolution. The key role of the leader in this process is to recognize the need for such an intervention and to manage the internal deciphering.

Many of the interventions that have occurred over the years at DEC can be viewed as producing insight. For example, at an annual meeting where the company's poor performance was being discussed, a depressive mood overtook senior management and was articulated as "We could do better if only our president or one of his key lieutenants would decide on a direction and tell us which way to go." A number of us familiar with the culture heard this as a wish for a magic solution, not as a realistic request. I was scheduled to give a short presentation on the company's culture at this meeting and used the opportunity to raise the following question: "Given the history of this company and the kinds of managers and people that you are, if Ken Olsen marched in here right now and told everyone in what direction he wanted you to go in, do you think you would follow?" There was a long silence, followed gradually by a few knowing smiles and ultimately by a more realistic discussion. In effect, the group reaffirmed and strengthened its assumptions about individual responsibility and autonomy but also recognized that its wish for marching orders was really a wish for more discipline in the organization and that this discipline could be achieved among the senior managers by more negotiation and tighter coordination at their own level.

Defenses do not always have to be given up. Sometimes it is enough to recognize how they operate so that their consequences can be realistically assessed. If they are considered too costly, one can engage in compensatory behavior. For example, DEC's commitment to checking all decisions laterally (getting buy-in) before moving ahead was a defense against the anxiety of not knowing whether a given decision was correct. As the company grew, the costs of such a defense mounted because it not only took longer and longer to make a decision but also the process of checking with others who had not grown up in the company, with whom one was not functionally familiar, often could not resolve issues.

The options then were to (1) give up the mechanism, which was difficult to do unless some way was found to contain the anxiety that would be unleashed in the short run (for example, finding a strong leader who would absorb the anxiety), (2) design compensatory mechanisms (for example, having less frequent but longer meetings, classifying decisions and seeking consensus only on certain ones, or finding ways to speed up meetings), or (3) break the company down into smaller units in which the consensual process could work because people could be functionally familiar with each other and build efficient consensual processes. In DEC's evolution all of these mechanisms were discussed and tried from time to time, but breaking up into smaller units was not ever implemented sufficiently to avoid the dysfunctional intergroup negotiations that arose.

Managed Evolution Through Hybrids

The above two mechanisms serve to preserve and enhance the culture as it exists, but changes in the environment often create disequilibria that force more transformational change—change that challenges some of the basic assumptions of the cultural paradigm itself. How can a young organization highly committed to its identity make such changes? One mechanism of gradual and incremental change is the systematic promotion of insiders whose own assumptions are better adapted to the new external realities. Because they are insiders, they accept much of the cultural core and have credibility. But, because of their personalities, their life experiences, or the subculture in which their career developed, they hold assumptions that are to varying degrees different from the basic paradigm and thus can move the organization gradually into new ways of thinking and acting. When such managers are put in key positions, they often elicit the feeling from others: "We don't like what he is doing in the way of changing the place, but at least he is one of us."

For this mechanism to work, some of the most senior leaders of the company must have insight into what is missing, which implies that they first must get somewhat outside their own culture and obtain insight from their own cultural assessment activities, through the questions of board members and consultants, or through educational programs at which they meet other leaders. If the leaders then recognize the need for change, they can begin to select "hybrids" for key jobs—that is, those members of the old culture who best represent the new assumptions that they want to enhance.

For example, at one stage in its history, DEC found itself increasingly losing the ability to coordinate the efforts of large numbers of units. Olsen and other senior managers knew that a proposal to bring an outsider into a key position would be rejected, so they gradually filled several of the key management positions with managers who had grown up in manufacturing and in field service, where more discipline and centralization had been the norm. These managers operated within the culture but gradually imposed more centralization and discipline. In DEC's case the cultural paradigm was strong enough that it overrode their efforts, but it was clearly the correct strategy at that time in DEC's history.

Similarly, when Ciba-Geigy recognized the need to become more marketing oriented, it began to appoint to more senior positions managers who had grown up in the pharmaceutical division, in which the importance of marketing had been recognized earlier.

In that case the process worked to make Ciba-Geigy both more marketing oriented and more strategically focused on pharmaceuticals, ultimately resulting in the merger with Sandoz to create Novartis. Filling key positions with people who have the beliefs, values, and assumptions that are viewed by senior leaders as the necessary ones for the future growth and survival of the organization is, in fact, the commonest culture change mechanism observed.

Transition to Midlife: Problems of Succession

The succession from founders and owning families to midlife under general managers often involves many substages and processes. There are so many ways in which companies actually move from being under the domination of a founder or a founding family to a state of being managed by second-, third-, and fourth-generation general managers that one can only identify a few prototypical processes and events.

The first and often most critical of these processes is the shift from founder to a second-generation chief executive officer. Even if that person is the founder's son or daughter or another trusted family member, it is in the nature of founders and entrepreneurs to have difficulty giving up what they have created (Dyer, 1986, 1989; Schein, 1978; Watson and Petre, 1990). During the transition phase, conflicts over which elements of the culture employees like or do not like become surrogates for what they do or do not like about the founder, since most of the culture is likely to be a reflection of the founder's personality. Battles develop between "conservatives" who like the founding culture and "liberals" or "radicals" who want to change the culture, partly because they want to enhance their own power position. The danger in this situation is that feelings about the founder are projected onto the culture, and, in the effort to displace the founder, much of the culture comes under challenge. If members of the organization forget that the culture is a set of learned solutions that have produced success, comfort, and identity, they may try to change the very things they value and need.

Often missing in this stage is an understanding of what the organizational culture is and what it is doing for the organization, regardless of how it came to be. Succession processes must therefore be designed to enhance those parts of the culture that provide identity, distinctive competence, and protection from anxiety. Such a process can probably be managed only from within, because an outsider could not possibly understand the subtleties of the cultural issues and the emotional relationships between founders and employees.

The preparation for succession is usually psychologically difficult both for the founder and for potential successors, because entrepreneurs typically like to maintain high levels of control. They may officially be grooming successors, but unconsciously they may be preventing powerful and competent people from functioning in those roles. Or they may designate successors but prevent them from having enough responsibility to learn how to do the job—what we might call the "Prince Albert" syndrome, remembering that Queen Victoria did not permit her son many opportunities to practice being king. This pattern is particularly likely to operate with a father-to-son transition as was the case at IBM (Watson and Petre, 1990).

When senior management or the founder confronts the criteria for a successor, some cultural issues are forced into the open. It is now clear that much of the culture has become an attribute and property of the organization, even though it may have started out as the property of the founder. It is said that at Kodak "the ghost of George Eastman still walks the halls." If the founder or the founder's family remains dominant in the organization, one may expect little culture change but a great deal of effort to clarify, integrate, maintain, and evolve the culture, primarily because it is identified with the founder. For example, David Packard turned over the management of HP to a promoted general manager, but when Packard saw decisions being made that violated some of his own values, he stepped back into the picture and brought in a different CEO who would reinforce those values.

Formal management succession, when the founder or founding family finally relinquishes control, provides an opportunity to change the direction of the cultural evolution if the successor is the right kind of hybrid: representing what is needed for the organization to survive, yet seen as acceptable "because he is one of us" and therefore also a conserver of the valued parts of the old culture. At Steinbergs, after several outsiders had failed as CEOs, someone was found who had been with the company earlier and was therefore perceived by the family to "understand the company" even though he brought in many new assumptions about how to run the business. After hiring several outside CEOs, Apple brought back Steve Jobs, who had run another company and presumably learned some valuable things to bring back to the organization he had founded.

Whereas during the growth period culture is an essential glue, at midlife the most important elements of the culture have become embedded in the structure and major processes of the organization. Hence, consciousness of the culture and the deliberate attempt to build, integrate, or conserve the culture have become less important. The culture that the organization has acquired during its early years now comes to be taken for granted. The only elements that are likely to be conscious are the credos, dominant espoused values, company slogans, written charters, and other public pronouncements of what the company wants to be and claims to stand for— its philosophy and ideology.

At this stage it is more difficult to decipher the culture and make people aware of it because it is so embedded in routines. It may even be counterproductive to make people aware of the culture, unless there is some crisis or problem to be solved. Managers view culture discussions as boring and irrelevant, especially if the company is large and well established. On the other hand, geographical expansions, mergers and acquisitions, and introductions of new technologies require a careful self-assessment to determine whether the new cultural elements to be integrated or merged are, in fact, compatible.

At this stage there may also be strong forces toward cultural diffusion, toward loss of integration, because powerful subcultures will have developed and because a highly integrated culture is difficult to maintain in a large, differentiated, geographically dispersed organization. Furthermore, it is not clear whether or not all the cultural units of an organization should be uniform and integrated. Several conglomerates I have worked with have spent a good deal of time wrestling with the question of whether to attempt to preserve or, in some cases, build a common culture, as the Swedish government example showed (see Chapter Fourteen, "Divisionalization"). Are the costs associated with such an effort worth it? Might there even be a danger that one will impose assumptions on a subunit that might not fit its situation at all? On the other hand, if subunits are all allowed to develop their own cultures, what is the competitive advantage of being a single organization? At this stage it is less clear which functions are served by the total culture, so the problem of managing cultural change is more complex and diverse.

Forces that cause organizations to launch change programs at this stage can come, as in the first stage, either from the outside or from the inside; that is, (1) the entire organization or parts of it may experience economic difficulty or in some other way fail to achieve key goals because the environment has changed in a significant manner, or (2) the organization may develop destructive internal power struggles among subcultures. For example, at Ciba-Geigy prior to its launching of its redirection project (described in Chapter Eighteen), some of the divisions, such as Chemicals, were consistently declining, to the point where the total economic health of Ciba-Geigy was called into question. At the same time, the functional groups in the country companies were increasingly fighting the headquarters organization and were complaining that profits were undermined by the heavy overhead burdens imposed on them by the "fat" Basel headquarters.

A number of change mechanisms can be identified that can occur spontaneously or be systematically managed by and manipulated by leaders. In mid-life organizations these mechanisms will operate *in addition* to the ones previously mentioned.

Change Through Systematic Promotion from Selected Subcultures

The strength of the midlife organization is in the diversity of its sub-cultures. Whether leaders are conscious of it or not, they evolve midlife organizations culturally by assessing the strengths and weak-nesses of different subcultures and then biasing the total culture toward one of those subcultures by systematically promoting people from that subculture into power positions in the total culture. This is an extension of the previously mentioned use of hybrids, but has a more potent effect in midlife because preservation of the total cul-ture is not as big an issue as it was in the young and growing orga-nization. Also, the midlife organization is led by general managers who are not as emotionally embedded in the original culture and are therefore better able to assess needed future directions.

Whereas the diversity of subcultures is a threat to the young organization, in midlife it can be seen as an advantage. The only dis-advantage to this change mechanism is that it is very slow. If the pace of culture change is to be increased, systematic planned change projects, of the kind that will be described in Chapters Sixteen and Seventeen, must be launched. It is also the case, as DEC illustrated, that the basic culture can survive and outlive what a hybrid group of managers tries to impose. When the head of Service was given the Sales organization as well, he began to promote a lot of his own peo-ple into key sales positions, leading many to complain that Sales was becoming too much like a service organization. However, after DEC was sold to Compaq and eventually was merged with HP, it became clear that it was the service culture that was attractive to Compaq and it is still alive and well within HP. In any case, one of the quick-est ways of diagnosing the direction in which an organization's cul-ture is heading is to track the occupational and subcultural origins of the people being promoted into senior positions.

Culture Change Through Technological Seduction

One of the less obvious ways in which the leaders of midlife organizations change cultural assumptions is through the subtle, cumulative, and sometimes unintended impacts of new technology that they introduce deliberately. At one extreme, one can observe the gradual evolutionary diffusion of technological innovation; for example, a new technology—the automobile—displacing not only the horse and buggy but also, eventually, many of the assumptions and rituals that accompanied the old technology. At the other extreme, technological seduction involves the deliberate, managed introduction of specific technologies for the sake of seducing organization members into new behavior, which will, in turn, require them to reexamine their present assumptions and possibly adopt new values, beliefs, and assumptions.

My focus here will be on situations in which a leader consciously decides to introduce a new technology in order to initiate cultural change. Sometimes the goal is to reduce what the leader perceives to be too much cultural diversity by deliberately introducing a seemingly neutral or progressive technology that has the effect of getting people to think and behave in common terms. Sometimes the goal is to force assumptions out into the open in a neutral and ostensibly nonthreatening way. Sometimes the technology is physical, such as the introduction of robots into an assembly line or the automation of a chemical or nuclear plant, and sometimes it is a sociotechnical process, such as the introduction of a formal total quality program.

Many companies have used educational interventions to introduce a new social technology as part of an organization development program, with the avowed purpose of creating some common concepts and language in a situation where they perceive a lack of shared assumptions; for example, Blake's Managerial Grid (Blake and Mouton, 1969; Blake, Mouton, and McCanse, 1989). The most recent and increasingly popular versions of this type of intervention are Systems Dynamics, as presented in Senge's *The Fifth Discipline* (1990) and Total Quality Management, as presented in a variety of books and programs (e.g., Ciampa, 1992). The assumption underlying this strategy is that a new common language and concepts in a given cultural area, such as "how one relates to subordinates" or "how one defines reality in terms of one's mental models," will gradually force organization members to adopt a common frame of reference that will eventually lead to common assumptions. As the organization builds up experience and resolves crises successfully, new shared assumptions gradually come into being.

The current practice of introducing personal computers to several layers of management as a vehicle for networking the organization, the mandatory attendance at training courses, the introduction of expert systems to facilitate decision making, and the use of various kinds of "groupware" to facilitate meetings across time and space barriers all clearly constitute another version of technological seduction, though perhaps unintended by the original architects (Gerstein, 1987; Grenier and Metes, 1992; Johansen, 1991; Savage, 1990; Schein, 1992).

Sometimes leaders perceive that there is too much diversity in the assumptions governing management decisions and they bring this issue into the open by introducing a technology that forces decision-making premises and styles into consciousness. Some leaders also see in the technology the opportunity to impose the assumptions that underlie the new technology itself, such as the importance of precision, measurement, quantification, and model building. In some cases the effects are unintended—as when information technology is brought in to enable everyone to communicate more effectively with each other and to reduce the impact of formal hierarchy, but the CEO uses the information for control purposes and unwittingly increases the impact of hierarchy.

An unusual example of technological seduction was provided by a manager who took over a British transportation company that had grown up with a royal charter one hundred years earlier and had developed strong traditions around its blue trucks with the royal coat of arms painted on their sides (Lewis, 1988). The company was losing money because it was not aggressively seeking new concepts of how to sell transportation. After observing the company for a few months, the new chief executive officer abruptly and without giving reasons ordered that the entire fleet of trucks be painted solid white. Needless to say, there was consternation. Delegations urging the president to reconsider, protestations about loss of identity, predictions of total economic disaster, and other forms of resistance arose. All of these were patiently listened to, but the president simply reiterated that he wanted it done, and soon. He eroded the resistance by making the request nonnegotiable.

After the trucks were painted white, the drivers suddenly noticed that customers were curious about what they had done and inquired what they would now put on the trucks in the way of new logos. This got the employees at all levels thinking about what business they were in and it initiated the market-oriented focus that the president had been trying to establish in the first place. Rightly or wrongly, he assumed that he could not get this focus just by requesting it. He had to seduce the employees into a situation in which they had no choice but to rethink their identity.

Managed Culture Change Through Infusion of Outsiders

Shared assumptions can be changed by changing the composition of the dominant groups or coalitions in an organization—what Kleiner in his research has identified as "the group who really matters" (Kleiner, 2003). The most potent version of this change mechanism occurs when a board of directors brings in a new CEO, or when a new CEO is brought in as a result of an acquisition, merger, or leveraged buyout. The new CEO usually brings in some of his or her own people and gets rid of people who are perceived to represent the old and increasingly ineffective way of doing things. In effect, this destroys the group or hierarchical subculture that was the originator of the total culture and starts a process of new culture formation. If there are strong functional, geographic, or divisional subcultures, the new leaders usually have to replace the leaders of those units as well.

Dyer (1986) has examined this change mechanism in several organizations and found that it follows certain patterns:

1. The organization develops a sense of crisis, because of declining performance or some kind of failure in the marketplace, and concludes it needs new leadership

2. Simultaneously, there is a weakening of "pattern maintenance" in the sense that procedures, beliefs, and symbols that support the old culture break down

3. A new leader with new assumptions is brought in from the outside to deal with the crisis

4. Conflict develops between the proponents of the old assumptions and the new leadership

5. If the crisis is eased and the new leader is given the credit, he or she wins out in the conflict and the new assumptions begin to be embedded and reinforced by a new set of pattern maintenance activities

People may feel "We don't like the new approach, but we can't argue with the fact that it made us profitable once again, so maybe we have to try the new ways." Members who continue to cling to the old ways are either forced out or leave voluntarily because they no longer feel comfortable with where the organization is headed and how it does things. However, if improvement does not occur, or the new leader is not given credit for the improvement that does occur, or the new assumptions threaten too much of the core of the culture, the new leader will be discredited and forced out. This situation occurs frequently when this mechanism is attempted in young companies in which the founders or owning families are still powerful. In those situations the probability is high that the new leader will violate the owners' assumptions and be forced out by them.

To understand fully the dynamics of the process described by Dyer, one would, of course, need to know more about why and how the pattern maintenance mechanisms have become weakened. One common cause of such weakening is a change in ownership. For example, when founders or founding families give up ownership of the company or ownership changes as a result of a merger, acquisition, or leveraged buyout, this structural change substantially reduces the supports to the present cultural assumptions and opens the door to power struggles among diverse elements, which further weakens whatever cultural assumptions were in place. If strong subcultures have formed and if one or more of those subcultures is strongly tied to outside constituencies that hold different assumptions, the existing culture is further weakened. For example, when employees vote in a union and that union is part of a strong international union, management loses some degrees of freedom and new assumptions are likely to be introduced in the internal integration area. A similar effect can occur when senior management is increasingly selected from one function, such as finance, and that function becomes more responsive to the stockholders, whose interests may not be the same as those of the marketing, manufacturing, or technical people inside the organization.

Culture change is sometimes stimulated by systematically bringing outsiders into jobs below the top management level and allowing them gradually to educate and reshape top management's thinking. This is most likely to happen when those outsiders take over subgroups, reshape the cultures of those subgroups, become highly successful, and thereby create a new model of how the organization can work (Kuwada, 1991). Probably the most common version of this process is that of bringing in a strong outsider or an innovative insider to manage one of the more autonomous divisions of a multidivisional organization. If that division becomes successful, it not only generates a new model for others to identify with but it also creates a cadre of managers who can be promoted into more senior positions and thereby influence the main part of the organization.

For example, the Saturn division of General Motors and the NUMMI plant—a joint venture of GM and Toyota—were deliberately given freedom to develop new assumptions about how to involve employees in the design and productions of cars and thus learned what amount to some new cultural assumptions about human relationships in a manufacturing plant context. Similarly, GM also acquired EDS (Electronic Data Systems) as a technological stimulus to organizational change. But in each of these cases we also see that having an innovative subculture within the larger culture does not guarantee that the larger culture will reexamine or change its culture. The innovative subculture helps in disconfirming some of the core assumptions, but again, unless there is sufficient anxiety or sense of crisis, the top management culture may remain impervious to the very innovations they have created.

The infusion of outsiders inevitably brings various cultural assumptions into conflict with each other, raising discomfort and anxiety levels. Leaders who use this change strategy therefore also have to figure out how to manage the high levels of anxiety and conflict that they have wittingly or unwittingly unleashed.

Culture Change Through Scandal and Explosion of Myths

As an organization matures, it develops a positive ideology and a set of myths about how it operates—what Argyris and Schön (1974, 1978) have labeled *espoused theories* and what I have called the level of *espoused values* in the culture model. At the same time, the organization continues to operate by the shared tacit assumptions that have worked in practice, which Argyris and Schon label *theories-in-use* and which more accurately reflect what actually goes on. And it is not unlikely that the espoused theories, the announced values of the organization come to be, to varying degrees, out of line with the actual assumptions that govern daily practice.

For example, an organization's espoused theory may be that it takes individual needs into consideration in making geographical moves; yet its theory-in-use may be that anyone who refuses an assignment is taken off the promotional list. An organization's espoused theory may be that when it introduces new products it uses rational decision-making techniques based on market research; yet its theory-in-use may be that it indulges the biases and pet projects of a certain key manager. An organization may espouse the value of teamwork, but all of its practices may be strongly individualistic and competitive. An organization may espouse concern for the safety of its employees, but its practices may be driven by assumptions that one must keep costs down to remain competitive, leading to the encouragement of unsafe practices. If, in the history of the organization, nothing happens to expose these incongruities, myths may grow up that support the espoused theories and values, thus even building up reputations that are out of line with reality. The most common example in the 1990s was the myth in many companies that they would never lay anybody off.

It is where such incongruities exist between espoused values and shared tacit assumptions that scandal and myth explosion become relevant as mechanisms of culture change. Nothing changes until the consequences of the actual operating assumptions create a public and visible scandal that cannot be hidden, avoided, or denied. One of the most powerful triggers to change of this sort occurs when a company experiences a disastrous accident, such as the near-meltdown at Three Mile Island, the losses of the *Challenger* and *Columbia* space shuttles, or the Bhopal chemical explosion or the Alpha Power Company that was ordered by the court to improve environmental management because of its explosion that blew asbestos into the neighborhood. In these cases the norms and practices surrounding environmental and safety concerns in relation to productivity and cost concerns have to be re-examined and new norms are then proposed and implemented. If those new norms work better a new cultural element is gradually created.

Another kind of example involves career movement practices. A company that prided itself on a career system that gave managers real choices in overseas assignments had to face the reality that one of their key overseas executives committed suicide and stated in his suicide note that he had been pressured into this assignment in spite of his personal and family objections. At the espoused values level they had idealized their system. The scandal exposed the shared tacit assumption by which they operated: that people were expected to go where senior executives wanted them to go. The recognition of this discrepancy then led to a whole program of revamping the career assignment system to bring espoused values and assumptions into line with each other.

In another example, a product development group operated by the espoused theory that its decisions were based on research and careful market analysis, but in fact one manager dominated all decisions and he operated from pure intuition. Eventually, one of the products he had insisted on failed in such a dramatic way that a reconstruction of why it had been introduced had to be made public. The manager's role in the process was revealed by unhappy subordinates and was labeled as scandalous. He was moved out of his job, and a more formal process of product introduction was immediately mandated.

What public scandals produce is a situation that forces senior executives to examine norms and practices and assumptions that were taken for granted and operated out of awareness. Disasters and scandals do not automatically cause culture *change*, but they are a powerful disconfirming force that cannot be denied and that starts, therefore, some kind of change program. At a national level this kind of public reexamination is starting in the culture of finance through the public scandals involving Enron and various other organizations that have evolved questionable financial practices. The new practices that may be launched do not automatically create new cultures but create the conditions for new practices and values to come into play that may eventually become new cultural elements.

Insiders sometimes create or "engineer" scandals in order to induce some of the changes they want by leaking information to the right place at the right time. Such leaks are sometimes defined as *whistle-blowing,* in the sense of exposing internal inconsistencies. Since whistle-blowing has the potential for precipitating a crisis that may force some cultural assumptions to be reexamined, one can see why people are cautious about it and why the organization often punishes it. On the other hand, the revelation by organization members that something is wrong and needs to be fixed is one of the only mechanisms whereby leaders can find out when espoused values and tacit assumptions are out of line with each other. From a cultural analysis perspective, it is predictable that the whistle-blower's message would tend to be ignored, because most likely it challenges some of the myths by which the organization is working. One of the most difficult aspects of leadership, therefore, is to stay open to this kind of critical information and even to encourage it.

Organizational Maturity and Potential Decline

Continued success creates strongly held shared assumptions and thus a strong culture. If the internal and external environments remain stable, this is an advantage. However, if there is a change in the environment, some of those shared assumptions can become a liability, precisely because of their strength. This stage is sometimes reached when the organization is no longer able to grow, because it has saturated its markets or become obsolete in its products. It is not necessarily correlated with age, size, or number of managerial generations, but rather reflects the interaction between the organization's outputs and the environmental opportunities and constraints.

Age does matter, however, if culture change is required. If an organization has had a long history of success based on certain assumptions about itself and the environment, it is unlikely to want to challenge or reexamine those assumptions. Even if the assumptions are brought to consciousness, the members of the organization are likely to want to hold on to them because they justify the past and are the source of their pride and self-esteem. Such assumptions now operate as filters that make it difficult for key managers to understand alternative strategies for survival and renewal (Donaldson and Lorsch, 1983; Lorsch, 1985).

Outside consultants can be brought in and clear alternatives can be identified. But no matter how clear and persuasive the consultant tries to be, some alternatives will not even be understood if they do not fit the old culture, and some alternatives will be resisted even if understood because they create too much anxiety or guilt. Even if top management has insight, some new assumptions cannot be implemented down the line in the organization because people simply would not comprehend or accept the changes that might be required (Davis, 1984).

For example, DEC understood very well that the computer market had shifted toward commodities that could be built cheaply and efficiently by using components from other organizations, but to take this path would have required both a whole different approach to manufacturing and the abandonment of the company's commitment to the fun and excitement of technical innovation.

Similarly, several parts of Ciba-Geigy had to confront the unpleasant realities that patents on some of their better products had run out; that younger, more flexible, and more aggressive competitors were threatening them; that there was overcapacity in several of their major chemical markets because of the overestimation by the whole industry of the market potential; and that it was not clear whether there was enough "left to be invented" to warrant the continued emphasis on research. The company needed to become more innovative in marketing and had to shift its creative energy from R&D to manufacturing process innovation in order to bring its costs down. But the culture was built around research, so the creative marketers and the innovative production engineers had a hard time getting attention from senior management. The research department itself needed to become more responsive to the marketplace, but it still believed that it knew best. Even senior managers who could see the dilemma were caught in their own shared assumptions. They could not challenge and overrule some of the powerful research people and the culture dictated that they stay off of each other's turf.

In such a situation, the basic choices are between more rapid transformation of parts of the culture to permit the organization to become adaptive once again through some kind of "turnaround," or destruction of the organization and its culture through a process of total reorganization via a merger, acquisition, or bankruptcy proceedings. In either case, strong new change managers or "transformational leaders" are likely to be needed to unfreeze the organization and launch the change programs (Kotter and Heskett, 1992; Tichy and Devanna, 1986).

Culture Change Through Turnarounds

Turnaround, as a mechanism of cultural change, is actually a combination of many of the above mechanisms, fashioned into a single program by a strong leader or team of change agents. In turnaround situations I have observed or heard about, what strikes me is that all the mechanisms previously described may be used in the total change process, especially the replacement of key people with internal hybrids and outsiders who bring in different assumptions. In addition, the turnaround leader will launch planned change programs of the type that will be described in the next two chapters.

Turnarounds usually require the involvement of all organization members, so that the dysfunctional elements of the old culture become clearly visible to everyone. The process of developing new assumptions then is a process of cognitive redefinition through teaching, coaching, changing the structure and processes where necessary, consistently paying attention to and rewarding evidence of learning the new ways, creating new slogans, stories, myths, and rituals, and in other ways coercing people into at least adopting new behaviors. All the other mechanisms described earlier come into play, but it is the willingness to coerce that is the key to turnarounds.

Two fundamentally different leadership models have been promulgated for managing turnarounds—or, as they have come to be more popularly known, "transformations." In the *strong vision model*, the leader has a clear vision of where the organization should end up, specifies the means by which to get there, and consistently rewards efforts to move in that direction (Tichy and Devanna, 1986; Bennis and Nanus, 1985; Leavitt, 1986). This model works well if the future is reasonably predictable and if a visionary leader is available. If neither of these conditions can be met, organizations can use the *fuzzy vision model*, whereby the new leader states forcefully that the present is intolerable and that performance must improve within a certain time frame, but then relies on the organization to develop visions of how to actually get there (Pava, 1983). The "We need to change" message is presented forcefully, repeatedly, and to all levels of the organization, but it is supplemented by the message "and we need your help." As various proposals for solutions are generated throughout the organization, the leader selects and reinforces the ones that seem to make the most sense. This model is obviously more applicable in situations in which the turnaround manager comes from the outside and therefore does not initially know what the organization is capable of. It is also more applicable when the future continues to appear turbulent, in that this model begins to train the organization to become conscious of how to change its own assumptions as part of a continuous adaptive process. Turnarounds usually have to be supplemented with longer-range organization development programs to aid in new learning and to help embed new assumptions. To embed new assumptions in a mature organization is much more difficult than in a young and growing organization because all of the organization structures and processes have to be rethought and, perhaps, rebuilt.

Culture Change Through Mergers and Acquisitions

When one organization acquires another organization or when two organizations are merged, there is inevitable culture clash, because it is unlikely that two organizations will have the same cultures. The leadership role is then to figure out how best to manage this clash. The two cultures can be left alone to continue to evolve in their own way. A more likely scenario is that one culture will dominate and gradually either convert or excommunicate the members of the other culture. A third alternative is to blend the two cultures by selecting elements of both cultures for the new organization, either by letting new learning processes occur or by deliberately selecting elements of each culture for each of the major organizational processes.

For example, in the merger of HP with Compaq, though many felt that it was really an acquisition that would lead to domination by HP, in fact the merger implementation teams examined each business process in both organizations, chose the one that looked better, and imposed it immediately on everyone. Elements of both cultures were imported by this means and this accomplished the goal of eliminating those elements that the HP leadership felt had become dysfunctional in the HP culture.

Culture Change Through Reorganization and Rebirth

Little is known or understood about this process, so little will be said about it here. Suffice it to say that if one physically destroys the organization that is the carrier of a given culture, by definition that culture is destroyed and whatever new organization begins to function begins to build its own new culture. This process is traumatic and therefore not typically used as a deliberate strategy, but it may be relevant if economic survival is at stake.

Organizational changes that are true transformations—not merely incremental adaptations—probably reflect culture changes at this level. In the evolution of companies, such transformations occur periodically and at those times the direction of the change is not always predictable (Tushman and Anderson, 1986; Gersick, 1991). Change at this level sometimes results from mergers, acquisitions, or leveraged buyouts if the new owners decide to completely restructure the organization and are willing to get rid of most of the key managers of the old culture in the process.

Summary and Conclusions

I have described various mechanisms and processes by which culture changes. As was noted, different functions are served by culture at different organizational stages, and the change issues are therefore different at those stages. In the formative stage of an organization, the culture tends to be a positive growth force, which needs to be elaborated, developed, and articulated. In organizational midlife the culture becomes diverse, in that many subcultures will have formed. Deciding which elements need to be changed or preserved then becomes one of the tougher strategic issues that leaders face, but at this time leaders also have more options to change assumptions by differentially rewarding different subcultures. In the maturity and decline stage, the culture often becomes partly dysfunctional and can only be changed through more drastic processes such as scandals and turnarounds.

Culture change also occurs from the entry into the organization of people with new assumptions and from the different experiences of different parts of the organization. For purposes of this analysis, those changes are captured in the observation that organizations differentiate themselves over time into many subcultures. But the important point to focus on is that it is within the power of leaders to enhance diversity and encourage subculture formation, or they can, through selection and promotion, reduce diversity and thus manipulate the direction in which a given organization evolves culturally.

Cultural change in organizational midlife is primarily a matter of deliberately taking advantage of the diversity that the growth of subcultures makes possible. Unless the organization is in real difficulty, there will be enough time to use systematic promotion, organization development, and technological change as the main mechanisms in addition to normal evolution and organizational therapy. What can leaders do to speed up and systematically manage such culture change? In the next three chapters we will examine both the theory and practice of planned culture change.

16

A CONCEPTUAL MODEL
FOR MANAGED CULTURE CHANGE

In Chapter Fifteen I reviewed all the ways in which culture can and does change, noting how leaders can influence these processes. However, many of the mechanisms described are either too slow or inaccessible. Subcultural diversity may not be sufficient, outsiders with the right new assumptions may be unavailable, and creating scandals or introducing new technology may not be practical. How then does a leader systematically set out to change how an organization operates, recognizing that such change may involve varying degrees of culture change? In this chapter I will describe a model of planned, managed change and discuss the various principles that have to be taken into account if the changes involve culture. In Chapter Seventeen I will show how this process leads to cultural assessment and describe the role of such assessment in the overall change process It is my presumption that culture change per se is not usually a valid goal. Instead, the organization typically has some problems that need fixing or some new goals that need to be achieved. In the context of such organizational changes culture becomes involved, but it is essential to understand first the general processes of organizational change before managed culture change as such becomes relevant.

The Psychosocial Dynamics of
Transformative Organizational Change

The fundamental assumptions underlying *any* change in a human system are derived originally from Kurt Lewin (1947); I have elaborated and refined his basic model in my studies of coercive persuasion, professional education, group dynamics training, and management development (Schein, 1961a, 1961b, 1964, 1972; Schein and Bennis, 1965). All human systems attempt to maintain equilibrium and to maximize their autonomy vis-à-vis their environment. Coping, growth, and survival all involve maintaining the integrity of the system in the face of a changing environment that is constantly causing varying degrees of disequilibrium. The function of cognitive structures such as concepts, beliefs, attitudes, values, and assumptions is to organize the mass of environmental stimuli, to make sense of them, and to thereby provide a sense of predictability and meaning to the individual. The set of shared assumptions that develop over time in groups and organizations serves this stabilizing and meaning-providing function. The evolution of culture is therefore one of the ways in which a group or organization preserves its integrity and autonomy, differentiates itself from the environment and other groups, and provides itself an identity.

Unfreezing/Disconfirmation

If any part of the core cognitive structure is to change in more than minor incremental ways, the system must first experience enough disequilibrium to force a coping process that goes beyond just reinforcing the assumptions that are already in place. Lewin called the creation of such disequilibrium *unfreezing*, or creating a motivation to change. Unfreezing as I have subsequently analyzed it is composed of three very different processes, each of which must be present to a certain degree for the system to develop any motivation to change: (1) enough *disconfirming data* to cause serious discomfort and disequilibrium; (2) the connection of the disconfirming data to important goals and ideals, causing *anxiety and/or guilt*; and (3) enough *psychological safety*, in the sense of being able to see a possibility of solving the problem and learning something new without loss of identity or integrity (Schein, 1980, 1999b).

Transformative change implies that the person or group that is the target of change must *unlearn* something as well as learn something new. Transformative change will therefore almost always involve culture change to some degree. Most of the difficulties of such change have to do with the *unlearning*, because what we have learned has become embedded in various routines and may have become part of our personal and group identity. The key to understanding resistance to change is to recognize that some behavior that has become dysfunctional for us may nevertheless be difficult to give up because this might make us lose group membership or may violate some aspect of our identity.

For example, in the case of Amoco, first described in Chapter One, the new reward and control system required engineers to change their self-image from being members of an organization to being self-employed consultants who must sell their services. In the case of the Alpha Power Company, the electrical workers had to change their self-image from being employees who heroically kept power and heat on to being responsible stewards of the environment, preventing and cleaning up spills produced by their trucks or transformers. The new rules required them to report incidents that might be embarrassing to their group, and even to report on each other if they observed environmentally irresponsible behavior in fellow workers. Finally, transformative change at DEC would have required engineers to give up their passion for innovation and learn how to design and manufacture computers that were cheaper and less elegant, a degree of identity change that they would probably not have tolerated.

Disconfirming data are any items of information that show the organization that some of its goals are not being met or some of its processes are not accomplishing what they are supposed to: sales are off, customer complaints are up, products with quality problems are returned more frequently, managers and employees are quitting in greater numbers than usual, employees are sick or absent more and more, and so on. Disconfirming information can be economic, political, social, or personal—as when a charismatic leader chides a group for not living up to its own ideals and thereby induces guilt. However, the information is usually only symptomatic. It does not automatically tell the organization what the underlying problem might be, but it creates disequilibrium in pointing up that something is wrong somewhere. It makes members of the organization uncomfortable and anxious—a state that we can think of as *survival anxiety*, in that it implies that *unless we change, something bad will happen to the individual, the group, and/or the organization.*

Disconfirmation and its attendant survival anxiety does not, by itself, automatically produce a motivation to change, because members of the organization can rationalize or deny by perceiving the information as being basically irrelevant to important goals or ideals they may hold. For example, if employee turnover suddenly increases, it is still possible for organization members to say, "It is only the bad people who are leaving, the ones we don't want anyway." Or if sales are down, it is possible to say, "This is only a reflection of a minor recession." Members of the organization will only feel anxious or guilty if the disconfirming information relates to important goals or ideals and if it is cognitively impossible to deny such connections. But anxiety and guilt can be denied and repressed as well, so even if the disconfirming information registers, so to speak, that is still not enough to motivate change if the change implies some threat to the more basic sense of identity or integrity that the person or group feels.

What often makes this level of denial and repression likely is the fact that the prospect of learning new ways of perceiving, thinking, feeling, and behaving itself creates anxiety—what we can think of as *learning anxiety*, a feeling that "I cannot learn this without losing a feeling of self-esteem or group membership." It is the reduction of this anxiety that is meant by the third component of unfreezing—the creation of *psychological safety*. The learner must come to feel that the new way of being is possible and achievable, and that the learning process itself will not be too anxiety provoking or demeaning.

The Amoco engineers simply could not imagine how they could function as freelance consultants. They had no skills along those lines. Alpha Power electrical workers were in a panic because they did not know how to diagnose environmentally dangerous conditions—how to determine, for example, whether a spill requires a simple mop-up or is full of dangerous chemicals such as PCBs, or whether a basement is merely dusty or is filled with asbestos dust, and so on. At DEC, engineers knew how to do things differently, but it was a formidable task for them to change manufacturing processes from building everything to just putting together components purchased from others. At Ciba-Geigy, when patents ran out and more cost-effective manufacturing processes had to be invented and implemented, massive amounts of learning anxiety were unleashed.

In some cases, disconfirming data have existed for a long time but because of a lack of psychological safety the organization has avoided anxiety or guilt by repressing it or by denying the data's relevance or validity—or even its existence. Data that make it clear that something is wrong can easily be ignored or denied as invalid if to take them seriously would unleash learning anxiety. Once a new leader makes the organization feel safe in learning something new, the change can occur rapidly because the motivation was there all the time. The essence of psychological safety, then, is that we can imagine a needed change without feeling a loss of integrity or identity. If the change I have to make threatens my whole self, I will deny the data and the need for change. Only if I can feel that I will retain my identity, my integrity, and my membership in groups that I care about as I learn something new or make a change, will I be able to even contemplate doing so.

The importance of visionary leadership can be understood in this context, in that the vision sometimes serves the function of providing the psychological safety that permits the organization to move forward. For example, a visionary leader could have created a new positive image of the freelance consultant for Amoco engineers and provided role models of engineers who had successfully made the transition. However, without a period of prior disconfirmation it is not clear that a visionary leader would be given much attention. New visions are most important when people are ready to pay attention, and they are only ready to pay attention when they are consciously or unconsciously hurting because of an accumulation of disconfirming information. One might speculate that the reason why we have had so many books on transformational visionary leadership in the last decade is because the United States, as a society, is hurting and the need for some psychological safety through new visions is particularly acute.

Does disconfirmation always have to be present to start the change process? Is there not a *natural instinct* to learn and improve? Isn't natural curiosity enough of a motive to try new things and overcome old habits of thought? New learning that does not require unlearning probably occurs, though even then one could argue that curiosity is driven to some degree by dissatisfaction with one's present state of perception and thought. The organizational question is this: can a *successful* organization make transformational changes or must there be some threat or sense of failure or crisis before people will be motivated to make such changes? Does there have to be a "wake-up call" or "burning platform" before the need for real change is accepted? In other words, must the process of organizational transformation *always* start with some form of survival anxiety? My own experience convinces me that some sense of threat, crisis, or dissatisfaction must be present before enough motivation is present to start the process of unlearning and relearning.

The disconfirming data are only symptoms, which should trigger some diagnostic work, focusing on the underlying problem or issue that needs to be addressed. Before one even starts to think about culture, one needs to (1) have a clear definition of the operational problem or issue that started the change process and (2) formulate *specific* new behavioral goals. It is in this analysis that one may first encounter the need for some culture assessment in order to determine to what degree cultural elements are involved in the problem situation. It is at this point that an assessment of the kind I will describe in the next chapter first becomes relevant. This should not be undertaken, however, until some effort has been made to identify which changes are going to be made and which "new way of working" will fix the problem, and some assessment has been made of how difficult and anxiety-provoking the learning of the new way will be (Schein, 1999b).

Changes in self-image or group norms that will be required to fix the problem do not automatically make clear how other elements of the culture will be impacted. More important, if we are to make changes we must look to other elements of the culture that will *help* us in making them—as the highly organized, autocratically administered training program was able to do at Alpha Power, to give employees a sense of comfort in dealing with new environmental hazards.

Cognitive Restructuring

Once an organization has been unfrozen, the change process proceeds along a number of different lines that reflect either new learning, through trial and error based on *scanning* the environment broadly, or imitation of role models, based on psychological *identification* with the role model. In either case, the essence of the new learning is usually some cognitive redefinition of some of the core concepts in the assumption set. For example, when companies that assume they are lifetime employers who never lay anyone off are faced with the economic necessity to reduce payroll costs, they cognitively redefine layoffs as "transitions" or "early retirements," make the transition packages very generous, provide long periods of time during which the employees can seek alternative employment, offer extensive counseling, provide outplacement services, and so on, all to preserve the assumption that "we treat our people fairly and well." This process is more than rationalization. It is a genuine cognitive redefinition on the part of the senior management of the organization and is viewed ultimately as "restructuring."

Most change processes emphasize the need for behavior change. Such change is important in laying the groundwork for cognitive redefinition but is not sufficient unless such redefinition takes place. Behavior change can be coerced, but it will not last once the coercive force is lifted unless cognitive redefinition has preceded or accompanied it. Some change theories (for example, Festinger, 1957) argue that if behavior change is coerced for a long enough period of time, cognitive structures will adapt to rationalize the behavior change that is occurring. The evidence for this is not clear, however, as recent developments in former Communist countries reveals. People living under communism did not automatically become Communists even though they might be coerced for fifty years or more.

Lorsch (1985), in his study of top management, shows how they attempted to make changes, with small incremental adjustments, to individual beliefs but that the kinds of changes that were necessary to improve adaptation to a rapidly changing environment really required more substantial restructuring of concepts, such as appropriate levels of risk and acceptable level of debt that a company could carry. At both DEC and Ciba-Geigy the concept of what "marketing" was underwent substantial cognitive redefinition as those companies attempted to cope with their changing environments.

Learning New Concepts and New Meanings for Old Concepts. If one has been trained to think in a certain way and has been a member of a group that has also thought that way, how can one imagine changing to a new way of thinking? As pointed out above, if you were an engineer in Amoco, you would have been a member of a division working as an expert technical resource with a clear career line and a single boss. In the new structure of a centralized engineering group "selling its services for set fees," you were now asked to think of yourself as a member of a consulting organization selling its services to customers who could purchase those services elsewhere if they did not like your deal. For you to make such a transformation would require you first of all to develop several *new* concepts—"freelance consultant," "selling services for a fee," and "competing with outsiders who could underbid you." In addition, you would have to learn a new meaning for the concept of what it means to be an engineer, and what it means to be an employee of that organization. You would have to learn a new reward system: being paid and promoted based on your ability to bring in work. You would have to learn to see yourself as much as a salesman as an engineer. You would have to define your career in different terms and learn to work for lots of different bosses.

Along with new concepts would come new standards of evaluation. Whereas in the former structure you were evaluated largely on the quality of your work, now you would have to estimate more accurately just how many days a given job would take, what quality level could be achieved in that time, and what it would cost if you tried for the higher-quality standard you were used to.

If standards do not shift, problems do not get solved. The computer designers at DEC who tried to develop products competitive with the IBM PC never changed their standards for evaluating what a customer expected. They overdesigned the products, building in far too many bells and whistles, and made them too expensive, thus failing to capture enough of the market to make them financially viable.

Imitation and Identification Versus Scanning and Trial-and-Error Learning. There are basically two mechanisms by which we learn new concepts, new meanings for old concepts, and new standards of evaluation: either we learn through imitating a role model and psychologically identifying with that person, or we keep inventing our own solutions until something works. The leader as change manager has a choice as to which mechanism to encourage. For example, the leader can "walk the talk" in the sense of making him or herself a role model of the new behavior that is expected. As part of a training program, the leader can provide role models through case materials, films, role-plays, or simulations. One can bring in learners who have acquired the new concepts and encourage others to get to know how they did it. This mechanism works best when (1) it is clear what the new way of working is to be and (2) the concepts to be taught are themselves clear. However, we sometimes can learn things through imitation that do not really fit into our personality or our ongoing relationships. Once we are on our own and the role models are no longer available, we often revert to our old behavior.

If we want to learn things that really fit into our personality, then we must learn to scan our environment and develop our own solutions. For example, Amoco could have developed a training program for how to be a consultant, built around engineers who had made the shift successfully. However, senior management felt that such a shift was so personal that they decided merely to create the structure and the incentives but to let the individual engineers figure out for themselves how they wanted to manage the new kinds of relationships. In some cases this meant people leaving the organization. But those engineers who learned from their own experience how to be consultants genuinely evolved to a new kind of career that they integrated into their total lives.

The general principle here is that the leader as change manager must be clear about the ultimate goals—the new way of working that is to be achieved—but that does not necessarily imply that everyone will get to that goal in the same way. Involvement of the learner does not imply that the learner has a choice about the ultimate *goals*, but does imply that he or she has a choice of the *means* to get there.

Refreezing

The final step in any given change process is *refreezing*. This refers to the necessity for the new behavior and set of cognitions to be reinforced, to produce once-again confirming data. If such new conformation is not forthcoming, the search and coping process continues. As soon as confirming data from important environmental sources, external stakeholders, or internal sources are produced, the new beliefs and values gradually stabilize, become internalized, and, if they continue to work, become taken-for-granted assumptions until new disconfirmations start the change process all over again.

Identification and imitation will produce quicker learning that will be reinforced by the group and the leader who models the behavior, but this may only be as stable as the relationship with that group or leader. If we want real internalization of the new cognitive constructs and standards of evaluation, we need to encourage scanning and trial-and-error learning from the outset. As we will see below, that outcome is best achieved when the learner is actively involved in the design of the learning process.

Survival Anxiety Versus Learning Anxiety

If the disconfirming data "get through" the learners' denial and defensiveness, they will feel either survival anxiety or guilt. They will recognize the need to change, to give up some old habits and ways of thinking, and to learn some new habits and ways of thinking. But the minute the learners accept the need to change they will also begin to experience learning anxiety. It is the interaction of these two anxieties that creates the complex dynamics of change.

The easiest way to illustrate this dynamic is in terms of learning a new stroke in tennis or golf. The process starts with disconfirmation—you are not beating some of the people you are used to beating, or your aspirations for a better score or a better-looking game are not met, so you feel the need to improve your game. But as you contemplate the actual process of unlearning your old stroke and developing a new stroke, you realize that you may not be able to do it or you may be temporarily incompetent during the learning process. These feelings are learning anxiety. Similar feelings arise in the cultural area when the new learning involves becoming computer competent, changing one's supervisory style, transforming competitive relationships into teamwork and collaboration, changing from high-quality, high-cost strategy to becoming the low-cost producer, moving from engineering domination and product orientation to a marketing and customer orientation, learning to work in nonhierarchical diffuse networks, and so on.

Sociopsychological Bases of Learning Anxiety. Learning anxiety is a combination of several specific fears, all of which may be active at any given time as one contemplates having to unlearn something and learn something new.

Fear of Temporary Incompetence. During the transition process one will be unable to feel competent because one has given up the old way and has not yet mastered the new way. The best examples probably come from the efforts to learn to use computers.

Fear of Punishment for Incompetence. If it takes one a long time to learn the new way of thinking and doing things, one will fear that one will be punished for lack of productivity. In the computer arena there are some striking cases in which employees never learned the new system sufficiently to take advantage of its potential, because they felt they had to remain productive and thus spent insufficient time on the new learning.

Fear of Loss of Personal Identity. If one's current way of thinking identifies one to oneself and to others, one may not wish to be the kind of person that the new way of working would require one to be. For example, in the early days of the breakup of the Bell System many old-time employees left because they could not accept the identity of being a member of a hard-driving, cost-conscious organization that would take phones away from consumers who could not afford them.

Fear of Loss of Group Membership. The shared assumptions that make up a culture also identify who is in and who is out of the group. If by developing new ways of thinking one will become a deviant in one's group, one may be rejected or even ostracized. To avoid loss of group membership one will often resist learning the new ways of thinking and behaving. This fourth force is perhaps the most difficult to overcome because it requires the whole group to change its ways of thinking and its norms of inclusion and exclusion.

Defensive Responses to Learning Anxiety. As long as learning anxiety remains high, one will be motivated to resist the validity of the disconfirming data or will invent various excuses why one cannot really engage in a transformative learning process right now. These responses come in the following stages (Coghlan, 1996):

1. *Denial.* You will convince yourself that the disconfirming data are not valid, are temporary, don't really count, reflect someone just crying "wolf," and so on.

2. *Scapegoating, passing the buck, dodging.* You will convince yourself that the cause is in some other department, that the data do not apply to you, and that others need to change first before you do.

3. *Maneuvering, bargaining.* You will want special compensation for the effort to make the change; you will want to be convinced that it is in your own interest and will be of long-range benefit to you.

Given all of these bases of resistance to change, how then does the change leader create the conditions for transformative change? Two principles come into play:

PRINCIPLE 1: *Survival anxiety or guilt must be greater than learning anxiety.*

PRINCIPLE 2: *Learning anxiety must be reduced rather than increasing survival anxiety.*

From the change leader's point of view, it might seem obvious that the way to motivate learning would be simply to increase the survival anxiety or guilt. The problem with that approach is that greater threat or guilt may simply increase defensiveness to avoid the threat or pain of the learning process. And that logic leads to the key insight about transformative change embodied in Principle 2: the change leader must reduce learning anxiety by increasing the learner's sense of psychological safety—the third component of unfreezing.

How to Create Psychological Safety

Creating psychological safety for organizational members who are undergoing transformational learning involves eight steps that must be taken almost simultaneously. They are listed chronologically but the change leader must be prepared to implement all of them.

1. *A compelling positive vision.* The targets of change must believe that the organization will be better off if they learn the new way of thinking and working. Such a vision must be articulated and widely held by senior management.

2. *Formal training.* If the new way of working requires new knowledge and skill, members must be provided with the necessary formal and informal training. For example, if the new way of working requires teamwork, then formal training on team building and maintenance must be provided.

3. *Involvement of the learner.* If the formal training is to take hold, the learners must have a sense that they can manage their own informal training process, practice, and method of learning. Each learner will learn in a slightly different way, so it is essential to involve learners in designing their own optimal learning process.

4. *Informal training of relevant "family" groups and teams.* Because cultural assumptions are embedded in groups, informal training and practice must be provided to whole groups so that new norms and new assumptions can be jointly built. Learners should not feel like deviants if they decide to engage in the new learning.

5. *Practice fields, coaches, and feedback.* Learners cannot learn something fundamentally new if they don't have the time, the resources, the coaching, and valid feedback on how they are doing. Practice fields are particularly important so that learners can make mistakes without disrupting the organization.

6. *Positive role models*. The new way of thinking and behaving may be so different from what learners are used to that they may need to be able to see what it looks like before they can imagine themselves doing it. They must be able to see the new behavior and attitudes in others with whom they can identify.

7. *Support groups in which learning problems can be aired and discussed*. Learners need to be able to talk about their frustrations and difficulties in learning with others who are experiencing similar difficulties so that they can support each other and jointly learn new ways of dealing with the difficulties.

8. *A reward and discipline system and organizational structures that are consistent with the new way of thinking and working*. For example, if the goal of the change program is to learn how to be more of a team player, the reward system must be group oriented, the discipline system must punish individually aggressive selfish behavior, and the organizational structures must make it possible to work as a team.

Most transformational change programs fail because they do not create the eight conditions outlined above. And when one considers the difficulty of achieving all eight conditions and the energy and resources that have to be expended to achieve them, it is small wonder that changes are often short-lived or never get going at all. On the other hand, when an organization sets out to really transform itself, real and significant cultural changes can be achieved.

Organizing a Change Program That May Involve Culture Change

When an organization encounters disconfirming information and launches a change program, it is not clear at the outset whether culture change will be involved and how the culture will aid or hinder the change program. To clarify these issues, a culture assessment process of the kind described in the next chapter becomes appropriate. However, it is generally better to be very clear about the change goals before launching the culture assessment. Several more principles apply at this point.

PRINCIPLE 3: *The change goal must be defined concretely in terms of the specific problem you are trying to fix, not as "culture change."*

For example, in the Alpha Power Company case, the court said that the company had to become more environmentally responsible and more open in its reporting. The change goal was to get employees to (1) be more aware of environmental hazards, (2) report them immediately to the appropriate agencies, (3) learn how to clean up the hazardous conditions, and (4) learn how to prevent spills and other hazards from occurring in the first place. Whether or not the culture needed to be changed was not known when the change program was launched. Only as specific goals were identified could one determine whether cultural elements would aid or hinder the change; as it turned out, large portions of the culture were used positively to change some specific elements in the culture that did have to be changed. For example, workers had to learn that containing oil spills from their vehicles was just as important as fixing the hospital generator, which was, for many of them, a major shift in their sense of identity.

One of the biggest mistakes that leaders make when they undertake change initiatives is to be vague about their change goals and to *assume* that culture change will be needed. When someone asks me to help him or her with a culture change program, my most important initial question is "What do you mean? Can you explain your goals without using the word *culture*?"

PRINCIPLE 4: *Old cultural elements can be destroyed by eliminating the people who "carry" those elements, but new cultural elements can only be learned if the new behavior leads to success and satisfaction.*

Once a culture exists, once an organization has had some period of success and stability, *the culture cannot be changed directly, unless one dismantles the group itself*. A leader can impose new ways of doing things, can articulate new goals and means, can change reward and control systems, but none of those changes will produce *culture* change unless the new way of doing things actually works better and provides the members a new set of shared experiences.

PRINCIPLE 5: *Culture change is always transformative change that requires a period of unlearning that is psychologically painful.*

Many kinds of changes that leaders impose on their organizations require only new learning and therefore will not be resisted. These are usually new behaviors that make it easier to do what we want to do anyway, such as learning a new software program to make our work on the computer more efficient. However, once we are adults and once our organizations have developed routines and processes that we have become used to, we may find that new proposed ways of doing things look like they will be hard to learn or will make us feel inadequate in various ways. We may feel comfortable with our present software and may feel that to learn a new system is not worth the effort. The change leader therefore needs a model of change that includes "unlearning" as a legitimate stage and that can deal with transformations, not just enhancements. This is why a model of *transformative* change, such as was described in this chapter, must underlie any culture change initiative.

Once the change goals are clearly understood in concrete behavioral terms, it becomes appropriate to do a culture assessment to determine how the culture may aid or hinder the change program. The mechanics of this process are described in Chapter Seventeen.

Summary and Conclusions

Culture change inevitably involves unlearning as well as relearning and is therefore, by definition, transformative. This chapter describes a general change model that acknowledges from the outset the difficulty of launching any transformative change because of the anxiety associated with new learning. The change process starts with disconfirmation, which produces survival anxiety or guilt—the feeling that one must change—but the learning anxiety associated with having to change one's competencies, one's role or power position, one's identity elements, and possibly one's group membership causes denial and resistance to change. The only way to overcome such resistance is to reduce the learning anxiety by making the learner feel psychologically safe. The conditions for creating psychological safety were described. If new learning occurs, it usually reflects cognitive redefinition, which consists of learning new concepts and new meanings for old concepts and adopting new standards of evaluation.

The change goals should initially be focused on the concrete problems to be fixed; only when those goals are clear is it appropriate to do a culture assessment to determine how the culture may aid or hinder the change process.

17

ASSESSING CULTURAL DIMENSIONS: A TEN-STEP INTERVENTION

This chapter describes a process for enabling members of the organization to identify important cultural assumptions and to evaluate the degree to which those assumptions aid or hinder some changes that the organization is trying to make. Because this process is only useful in the context of a change program, the leader or consultant/facilitator should not get involved in a culture assessment unless the organizational "clients" know precisely what they are trying to achieve.

If you are the leader and know what your change goals are, you can proceed on your own or work with a consultant who has familiarity with culture inquiry. If you are the consultant/facilitator and the client says they just want "to assess the culture" or "change the culture," that is not specific enough for you to proceed. You should probe what the organizational client means by *culture* and why he or she thinks a culture assessment would be useful. The answers will typically reveal some change agenda that the client has, and it is important to specify clearly what that change agenda is, as was pointed out in the last chapter. Once the client has identified in concrete terms what the desired "new way of working" is, the culture assessment can then be done in order to identify what elements of the culture will aid the change program and what elements will hinder it (Schein, 1999b).

For example, at Alpha Power the court-appointed monitor defined the problem as "Alpha's culture"; this launched a "culture change" program and led to my being hired as a consultant to help design it. A culture assessment was not relevant, however, until it was determined that a "new way of working" was required that involved: (1) more sense of responsibility on the part of the hourly employees for identifying, reporting, and remediation of environmental spills and other environmental, health, and safety (EH&S) problems; (2) more openness in reporting EH&S problems rather than continuing the tendency to cover up to protect the work group from embarrassment or disciplinary action; and (3) more teamwork in dealing with EH&S problems.

The culture *change* portion of this larger agenda then concerned primarily (1) the change in the self-image of the hourly workers, (2) a change in the role of their immediate supervisors toward delegating more responsibility, and (3) changes in the supporting structures, such as the discipline system and reward system. But the bulk of the Alpha Power culture—which was built on traditions of technical excellence, performance reliability, a strong but highly paternalistic hierarchy, and a commitment to extensive and detailed training and development of the work force—not only did not change but should not have changed. The bulk of the culture was used to make significant changes in one portion of the culture, and was, in fact, essential to achieving the changes that were made in the way work was done at the front line and the way supervisors restructured their role.

Once the purpose of the assessment has been made clear, the essence of the assessment process is to bring together one or more representative groups in the organization, provide them a model of how to think about organizational culture and subcultures, and then ask them to identify the main artifacts, the espoused values, and the shared tacit assumptions, with an outsider playing the role of facilitator, documenter and, when necessary, gadfly and question asker. A member of the organization in a leader role can be the facilitator, so long as it is not his or her own department and as long as they have an understanding of how culture works.

A number of important assumptions lie behind this approach:

- Culture is a set of *shared* assumptions; hence, obtaining the initial data in a *group* setting is more appropriate and valid than conducting individual interviews.

- The contextual meaning of cultural assumptions can only be fully understood by members of the culture; hence, creating a vehicle for *their understanding* is more important than for the researcher or consultant to obtain that understanding.

- Not all parts of a culture are relevant to any given issue the organization may be facing; hence, attempting to study an entire culture in all of its facets is not only impractical but also usually inappropriate.

- Insiders are capable of understanding and making explicit the shared tacit assumptions that make up the culture, but they need outsider help in this process. The helper/consultant should therefore operate primarily from a process-consulting model and should avoid, as much as possible, operating as an expert on the content of any given group's culture (Schein, 1999a).

- Some cultural assumptions will be perceived as helping the organization to achieve its strategic goals or resolving its current issues, while others will be perceived as constraints or barriers; hence it is important for the group members to have a process that allows them to sort cultural assumptions into both of these categories.

- Changes in organizational practices to solve the problems that initiated the culture analysis can usually be achieved by building on existing assumptions; that is, the culture-deciphering process often reveals that new practices not only can be derived from the existing culture, but *should* be—as the Alpha Power example shows.

- If changes in the culture are discovered to be necessary, those changes will rarely involve the entire culture; it will almost always be a matter of changing one or two assumptions. Only rarely does the basic paradigm have to change, but if it does, the organization faces a multi-year major change process of the sort described in Chapter Sixteen.

The Ten-Step Culture Assessment Process

The implementation of a culture-deciphering process based on these assumptions can now be described in terms of the following ten steps.

Step One: Obtaining Leadership Commitment

Deciphering cultural assumptions and evaluating their relevance to some organizational purpose must be viewed as a major intervention in the organization's life and therefore must only be undertaken with the full understanding and consent of the leaders of the organization. In practical terms this means that if someone from an organization calls or writes me to ask if I will help her or him figure out their organization's culture, my first question is always some form of "Why do you want to do this?" or "What problem are you having that makes you think a cultural analysis is relevant?" The only times I have tried to help a group analyze its own culture without a problem or issue to motivate the process, the analysis has essentially failed for lack of interest on the part of the group.

Step Two: Selecting Groups for Interviews

The next step is for the consultant/researcher to work with the leaders/executives to determine how best to select some groups representative of the culture. The criteria for selection will usually depend on the concrete nature of the problem to be solved. Groups can either be homogeneous with respect to a given department or rank level or made deliberately heterogeneous by selecting diagonal slices from the organization. The group can be as small as three and as large as thirty. If important subcultures are believed to be operating, one can repeat the process in different groups or deliberately bring in samples of members from different groups in order to test, in the meetings, whether the assumed differences exist.

The composition of the group is further determined by the client's perception of the level of trust and openness in the group, especially in regard to deciding whether senior people who might inhibit the discussion should be present. On the one hand, it is desirable to have a fairly open discussion, which might mean keeping higher levels out. On the other hand, it is critical to determine the extent to which the assumptions that eventually come out in the group meetings are shared by the leaders, which argues for their presence. Because the level of trust and openness across various boundaries is itself likely to be a cultural issue, it is best to start with a heterogeneous group and let the group experience the extent to which certain areas of communication are or are not inhibited by the presence of others.

Once groups have been chosen, it should be the leader/executives who inform the groups of the purpose of the meetings. Just being summoned to a meeting to do a culture assessment is too vague. The participants must know either what change problems are being worked on or what research problems the outsider has brought in and gotten commitment to pursue.

Step Three: Selecting an Appropriate Setting for the Group Interviews

An appropriate locale and setting for doing the exercise is usually a large, comfortable room with lots of wall space for hanging flip-chart pages, with a set of breakout rooms available in which sub-groups can meet.

Step Four: Explaining the Purpose of the Group Meeting

The large group meeting should start with a restatement, by someone from the organization who is perceived to be in a leadership or authority role, of the purpose of the meeting, so that openness of response is encouraged. The process consultant is then introduced as the outsider who will help the group conduct an analysis of how the organization's culture is an aid or a constraint in solving the problem or resolving the issue. The process consultant can be an outsider, a member of the organization who is part of a staff group devoted to providing internal consulting services, or a leader from another department if he or she is familiar with how culture works.

Step Five: A Short Lecture on How to Think About Culture

It is essential for the group to understand that culture manifests itself at the level of artifacts and espoused values, but that the goal is to try to decipher the shared tacit assumptions that lie at a lower level. The consultant should, therefore, present the model shown in Chapter Two and ensure that everyone understands the distinction among the three levels and that culture is a learned set of assumptions based on a group's shared history. It is important for the group to understand that what they are about to assess is a product of their own history and that the culture's stability rests on the organization's past success.

Step Six: Eliciting Descriptions of the Artifacts

The consultant then tells the group that they are going to start by describing the culture through its artifacts. A useful way to begin is to find out who has joined the group most recently and ask that person what it felt like to enter the organization and what he or she noticed most upon entering it. Everything mentioned is written down on a flip chart, and as the pages are filled, they are torn off and hung on the wall so that everything remains visible.

If group members are active in supplying information, the consultant can stay relatively quiet, but if the group needs priming, the consultant should suggest categories such as dress codes, desired modes of behavior in addressing the boss, the physical layout of the workplace, how time and space are used, what kinds of emotions one would notice, how people get rewarded and punished, how one gets ahead in the organization, and so forth. The consultant can use the categories reviewed in Chapters Four and Five to ensure that many different categories of artifacts are covered, but it is important not to give out such a list before a spontaneous group discussion has occurred because it may bias the group's perception of what is important. The consultant does not know initially what areas of the culture are especially salient and relevant and so should not bias the process of deciphering.

This process should continue for about one hour or until the group clearly runs dry, and it should produce a long list of artifacts covering all sorts of areas of the group's life. Being visually surrounded by the description of their own artifacts is a necessary condition for the group to begin to stimulate its own deeper layers of thinking about what assumptions its members share.

Step Seven: Identifying Espoused Values

The question that elicits artifacts is "*What* is going on here?" By contrast, the question that elicits espoused values is "*Why* are you doing what you are doing?" Typically, I pick an artifactual area that is clearly of interest to the group and ask people to articulate the reasons why they do what they do. For example, if they have said that the place is very informal and that there are few status symbols, I ask why. This usually elicits value statements such as "We value problem solving more than formal authority" or "We think that a lot of communication is a good thing" or even "We don't believe that bosses should have more rights than subordinates."

As values or beliefs are stated, I check for consensus; if there appears to be consensus, I write down the values or beliefs on a new chart pad. If members disagree, I explore why by asking whether this is a matter of different subgroups having different values or there is genuine lack of consensus, in which case the item goes on the list with a question mark to remind us to revisit it. I encourage the group to look at all the artifacts they have identified and to figure out as best they can what values seem to be implied. If I see some obvious ones that they have not named, I will suggest them as possibilities— but in a spirit of joint inquiry, *not* as an expert conducting a content analysis of their data. Once we have a list of values to look at, which usually occurs within another hour or so, we are ready to push on to shared tacit assumptions.

Step Eight: Identifying Shared Tacit Assumptions

The key to getting at the underlying assumptions is to check whether the espoused values that have been identified really explain all of the artifacts or whether things that have been described as going on have clearly *not* been explained or are in actual conflict with some of the values articulated. For example, the members of a group from Apple Computer conducted some cultural assessments in 1991 and noted that they spend a great deal of time in planning activities but that the plans usually got overridden by the needs of a here-and-now crisis. They put planning on their list of espoused values and felt genuinely puzzled and ashamed that they followed through so little on the plans they had made. This raised the whole issue of how time was perceived; after some discussion, the group members agreed that they operated from a deeper shared assumption that could best be stated as "Only the present counts." Once they stated the assumption in this form, they immediately saw on their own artifact list other items that confirmed this and thought of several new artifacts that further reinforced their orientation toward the immediate present (see pages 351–55).

The same group identified many different informal activities that members engaged in, including parties at the end of workdays, celebrations when products were launched, birthday parties for employees, joint travel to recreational areas such as ski resorts, and so on. The *value* they espoused was that they liked being with each other. But as we pondered the data, it became clear that a deeper *assumption* was involved, namely, "Business can and should be more than making money; it can and should be *fun* as well." Once this assumption was articulated, it immediately led the group to realize that a further assumption was operating: "Business not only should be more than just making money; it can and should be *socially significant*."

The latter assumption reminded the group members of a whole series of artifacts concerning the value they put on their products, why they liked some products better than others, why they valued some of their engineers more than others, how their founders had articulated their original values, and so on. A whole new issue was raised about the pros and cons of selling to the government and to the defense industries versus continuing to focus on the education sector.

Assumptions that are important and salient trigger a whole new set of insights and begin to make sense of a whole range of things that previously had not made sense. Often these salient assumptions reconcile what the group may have perceived as value conflicts. For example, in doing this exercise a group of human resource professionals at an insurance company identified as an important value "becoming more innovative and taking more risks as the environment changes," but the members could not reconcile this goal with the fact that very little actual innovation was taking place. In pushing deeper, to the assumption level, they realized that throughout its history the company had operated on two very central assumptions about human behavior: (1) people work best when they are given clear rules to cover all situations (among the artifacts the group had listed was a "mile-long shelf of procedure manuals"), and (2) people like immediate feedback and will not obey rules unless rule violation is immediately punished. Once the group stated these tacit assumptions, they realized that these assumptions were driving their behavior far more than the espoused value of innovation and risk taking. Not only was there no real positive incentive for innovating, but in fact it was risky because any false steps would immediately be punished.

Another example was the previously cited case of the engineering group at HP that discovered that the espoused values of "teamwork" and "being nice to each other" were overruled by the tacit assumptions that individualistic competitive behavior was the way to get things done and get ahead.

This phase of the exercise is finished when the group and the process consultant feel that they have identified most of the critical assumption areas and participants are now clear on what an assumption is. In terms of time estimates, these steps should have taken three to four hours. At this point I have also found that if the group is larger than ten or so people, it is necessary to do the next step in smaller breakout groups.

Step Nine: Identifying Cultural Aids and Hindrances

The task for subgroups depends in part on what the presenting problems were, whether or not subcultures were identified in the large group exercise, and how much time is available. For example, if there was evidence in the large group meeting that there are functional, geographical, occupational, or hierarchical subcultures, the consultant may wish to send off subgroups that reflect those presumed differences and have each subgroup further explore its own assumption set. Or, if the consultant finds that there is reasonable consensus in the large group on the assumptions identified, he or she can compose the subgroups randomly, by business unit, or by any other criterion that makes sense given the larger problem or issue that is being addressed.

In any case, the task for the subgroups consists of two parts: (1) spending some time (an hour or so) refining assumptions and identifying other assumptions that may have been missed in the large group meeting, and (2) categorizing the assumptions according to whether they will aid or hinder the solution of the problem that is being addressed. The groups need to review what the "new way of working" is and how the assumptions identified will help or hinder in getting there. I ask the subgroups to report back to the total group the two or three main assumptions that will aid and the two or three that will hinder the desired changes.

It is very important to require the participants to look at assumptions from this dual point of view because of a tendency to see culture only as a constraint and thus put too much emphasis on the assumptions that will hinder. In fact, successful organizational change probably arises more from identifying assumptions that will aid than from changing assumptions that will hinder, but groups initially have a harder time seeing how the culture can be a source of positive help.

Step Ten: Reporting Assumptions and Joint Analysis

The purpose of this step is to reach some kind of consensus on what the important shared assumptions are and their implications for what the organization wants to do. The process starts when the subgroups report their own separate analyses to the full group. If there is a high degree of consensus, the process consultant can go straight into a discussion of implications. More likely there will be some variations, and possibly disagreements, which will require some further inquiry by the total group with the help of the process consultant.

For example, the group may agree that there are strong subculture differences that must be taken into account. Or some of the assumptions may have to be reexamined to determine whether they reflect an even deeper level that would resolve disagreements. Or the group may come to recognize that for various reasons it does not have many shared assumptions. In each case, the role of the process consultant is to raise questions, force clarification, test perceptions, and in other ways help the group achieve as clear a picture as possible of the assumption set that is driving the group's day-to-day perceptions, feelings, thoughts, and ultimately, behavior.

Once there is some consensus on what the shared assumptions are, the discussion proceeds to the role of those assumptions in aiding or hindering what the group wants to do. As previously stated, one of the biggest insights for the group comes from seeing how some of the assumptions will aid them, creating the possibility that their energy should go into strengthening those positive assumptions instead of worrying about overcoming the constraining ones.

If, however, real constraints are identified, the group discussion then has to shift to an analysis of how culture can be managed and what it would take to overcome the identified constraints. At this point a brief further lecture on the material described in Chapters

Fourteen, Fifteen, and Sixteen may be needed to review some of the culture change mechanisms that are implied, and a new set of subgroups may be formed to develop a change strategy. Typically, this would require, at a minimum, an additional half day. Thus, if culture *change* is now to be undertaken, additional time beyond the original one-day meeting is required. Notice, however, that this group process produces a large amount of cultural data in a single day. It is not necessary to think of culture assessment as a slow, time-consuming process. The cases that follow will illustrate various aspects of this ten-step assessment process, especially the importance of getting at deeper assumptions.

Case Example One: MA-COM

The lesson of this case example is that culture assessment done for one purpose can reveal cultural elements that were not anticipated yet explain much of the observed behavior of the organization and its leaders. In this case, once the deeper and unanticipated elements of the culture were identified, the change agenda was revised toward a better solution.

The recently appointed CEO of MA-COM, a high-tech company that consisted of ten or more divisions, asked me to help him figure out how the organization could develop a "common culture." He felt that its history of decentralized autonomous divisions was now dysfunctional and that the company should work toward a common set of values and assumptions. The CEO, the director of human resources, and I were the planning group to decide how to approach the problem. We reached the conclusion that all of the division directors, all of the heads of corporate staff units, and various other individuals who were considered to be relevant to the discussion would be invited to an all-day meeting whose purpose was to identify the elements of a common culture for the future. Thirty people attended the meeting.

We began with the CEO stating his goals and why he had asked the group to come together. He introduced me as the person who would stage-manage the day, but made it clear that we were working on his agenda. I then gave a thirty-minute lecture on how to think about culture and launched into the process described above by asking some of the less-senior people in the group to share what it was like to enter this company. As people brought out various artifacts and norms, I wrote them down on flip charts and hung up the filled pages around the room. This was symbolically important to immerse the group in its own culture. It appeared clear that there were powerful divisional subcultures, but it was also clear that there were many common artifacts across the group. My role, in addition to writing things down, was to ask for clarification or elaboration as seemed appropriate to me.

As we worked into our second and third hours, some central value conflicts began to emerge. The various divisional units really favored the traditional assumption that high degrees of decentralization and divisional autonomy were the right way to run the overall business, but at the same time they longed for strong centralized leadership and a set of core values that they could rally around as a total company. My role at this point was to help the group confront the conflict and to try to understand both its roots and its consequences. We broke at lunchtime and instructed randomly selected subgroups of seven to eight members to continue the analysis of values and assumptions for a couple of hours after lunch and then met at around three o'clock for a final two-hour analysis and wrap-up session.

To start off the final session, each group gave a brief report of the assumptions that it felt aided and those it felt hindered achievement of a common corporate culture. In these presentations the same divisional-versus-corporate conflict kept emerging, so when the reports were done, I encouraged the group to dig into this a little more. Because some mention had been made of strong founders, I asked the group to talk further about how the divisions had been acquired. This discussion led to a major insight. It turned out that almost every division had been acquired with its founder still in place and that the early corporate headquarters policy of granting autonomy had encouraged those founders to remain as CEOs even though they had given up ownership.

Most of the managers in the room had grown up under those strong leaders and had enjoyed that period of their history very much. Now, however, all the founders had either retired, left, or died, and the divisions were led by general managers who did not have the same charisma the founders had. What the group longed for was the *sense of unity and security they each had had in their respective divisions under their founders*. They did not, in fact, want a strong *corporate* culture and leadership, because the businesses of the divisions were really quite different. What they wanted was stronger leadership at the *divisional* level but the same degree of divisional autonomy that they had always had. They realized that their desire for a stronger corporate culture was misplaced.

These insights, based on historical reconstruction, led to a very different set of proposals for the future. The group, with the blessing of corporate leadership, agreed that they only needed a few common corporate policies in areas such as public relations, human resources, and research and development. They did not need common values or assumptions, though if such developed naturally over time that would be fine. On the other hand, they wanted stronger leadership at the divisional level and a development program that would maximize their chances to obtain such leadership. Finally, they wanted to strongly reaffirm the value of divisional autonomy to enable them to do the best possible job in each of their various businesses.

MA-COM *Lessons Learned.* This case illustrates the following important points about deciphering culture and managing cultural assumptions:

1. A senior management group with the help of an outside facilitator is able to decipher key assumptions that pertain to a particular business problem—in this case, whether or not to push for a more centralized common set of values and assumptions.

2. The cultural analysis revealed several assumptions that were centrally related to the business problem, as judged by the participants. However, other elements of the culture that were clearly revealed in the artifacts were not judged to be relevant. Inasmuch as every culture includes assumptions about virtually everything, it is important to have a deciphering technique that permits one to set priorities and to discover what aspects of a culture are relevant.

3. The resolution of the business problem did not require any culture change. In fact, the group reaffirmed one of its most central cultural assumptions. In this context the group did, however, define some new priorities for future action—to develop common policies and practices in certain business areas. Often what is needed is a change in business practices within the context of the given culture, not necessarily a change in the culture.

Case Example Two: Apple Computer

This example illustrates how cultural assessment can aid in the process of long-range planning.

Apple Computer decided in 1991 to conduct a cultural analysis as part of a long-range planning exercise focused on human resource issues. How big would the company be in five years, what kind of people would it need, and where should it locate itself geographically under different size scenarios? A ten-person working group, consisting of several line managers and several members of the human resource function, was assigned the task of figuring out how Apple's culture would influence growth and what impact it might have on the kinds of people who would be attracted to it in the future. The vice president for human resources knew of my work on culture and asked me to be a consultant to this working group. He functioned as its chairman.

The original plan was to sort out various planning tasks and delegate these to other committees for more detailed work, because the presentation to the company meeting was six months off. One of these other groups was charged with analyzing the impact of Apple's culture on future growth. My role was to help organize the study, teach the group how best to study culture, and consult with the culture subcommittee down the line.

The first meeting of the group was scheduled for a full day and involved the planning of several different kinds of activities, of which the culture study was just one. When it came to deciding how to study the Apple culture, I had twenty minutes in which to describe the model of artifacts, espoused values, and basic underlying assumptions. I also described in general terms how I had used the model with other organizations to help them decipher their culture. The group was intrigued enough to accept my next suggestion, which was to try the process out in this group if we were willing to commit a couple of hours to it. The group agreed, so after the twenty-minute lecture, we launched directly into uncovering artifacts and values.

Because this group was used to thinking in these terms, it was easy for them to mix the analysis of assumptions, values, and artifacts, so we ended up rather quickly with a provisional set of tacit assumptions backed by various kinds of data that the group generated. These were written down in draft form on flip charts; that evening I organized them into a more ordered set of what we ended up calling Apple's "governing assumptions":

1. *We are not in the business for the business alone but for some higher purpose—to change society and the world, create something lasting, solve important problems, have fun.*

One of Apple's major products was designed to help children learn. Another major product was designed to make computing easier and more fun. Apple engaged in many rituals designed to be fun—for example, after-hours parties, playfulness at work, and magic shows at executive-training events. The group felt that only what is fun and what is unique gets the big rewards.

It was alleged that many people at Apple would object if the company went after the broad business market and if it sold products to selected groups who would misuse the product (for example, the Department of Defense).

2. *Task accomplishment is more important than the process used or the relationships formed.*

The group listed several versions of this assumption:

- When you fail at Apple, you are alone and abandoned; you become a "boat person."
- Seniority, loyalty, past experience don't count relative to present task achievements.
- When you trip, no one picks you up.
- Out of sight, out of mind; you are only as good as your latest hit; relationships formed at work do not last.
- People are so intent on their mission that they don't have time for you or to form relationships.
- Bonding occurs only around tasks and is temporary.
- Groups are security blankets.
- Apple views itself as a club or a community, not a family.

3. *The individual has the right and obligation to be a total person.*

This showed up as the following assumptions:

- Individuals are powerful, can be self-sufficient, and can create their own destiny.
- A group of individuals motivated by a shared dream can do great things.
- People have an inherent desire to be their best and will go for it.
- Apple neither expects company loyalty from individuals nor expects to guarantee employment security to individuals.

- Individuals have the right to be fully themselves at work, to express their own personality and uniqueness, to be different.
- There is no dress code and no restriction on how personal space is decorated.
- Children or pets can be brought to work.
- Individuals have the right to have fun, to play, to be whimsical.
- Individuals have the right to be materialistic, to make lots of money, to drive fancy cars no matter what their formal status.

4. *Only the present counts.*

This assumption was discussed earlier in this chapter, but it had some other ramifications, expressed as norms and artifacts:

- Apple has no sense of history or concern for the future.
- Seize the moment; the early bird gets the worm.
- Apple does not see itself as a lifetime employer.
- Longer-range plans and tasks get discussed but not done.
- People do not build long-range cross-functional relationships.
- Nomadic existence inside Apple is normal; people don't have offices, only "campsites" and "tents."
- The physical environment is constantly rearranged.
- It is easier to fix things than to plan for perfection; flexibility is our greatest skill.
- People are forgotten quickly if they leave a project or the company.
- "We learn by doing."

These governing assumptions and the supporting data were passed on to the subcommittee dealing with the Apple culture, where they were tested and refined with further interviews. Interestingly enough, after several more months of work no substantial changes had been made to the list, suggesting that a group can get at the essentials of its culture very rapidly.

Apple Lessons Learned. This case illustrates the following important points:

1. If a motivated insider group is provided with a process for deciphering its culture, members can rather quickly come up with some of their most central driving assumptions. I revisited Apple several years after this event and was shown a recent report on the company's culture. The same set of assumptions was written down in this report as still being the essence of the culture, though the various assumptions were stated in somewhat different order and with some additional comments about areas that needed to change.

2. Stating these governing assumptions allowed the company managers to assess where their strategy might run into cultural constraints. In particular, they realized that if they were to grow rapidly and enter the broad business market, they would have to deal with members of their organization who grew up under the assumption that business should involve more than just making money. They also realized that they lived too much in the present and would have to develop longer-range planning and implementation skills.

3. Apple reaffirmed its assumptions about task primacy and individual responsibility by starting to articulate explicitly a philosophy of no mutual obligation between the company and its employees. When layoffs became necessary, the company simply announced them without apology and carried them out. Apple was one of the first companies to articulate that *employment* security would gradually have to give way to *employability* security, by which they meant that one would learn enough during some years at Apple to be attractive to another employer if laid off. There should be no loyalty in either direction, in that employees should feel free to leave if a better opportunity came along.

Case Example Three: U.S. Army Corps of Engineers

This case example illustrates the culture-deciphering process in a different type of organization. As part of a long-range strategy-planning process, I was asked in 1986 to conduct an analysis of the culture of the U.S. Army Corps of Engineers because of concerns that their mission was changing and they were uncertain what future sources of funding would be. In attendance were the twenty-five or so senior managers, both military and civilian, with the specific purpose of analyzing their culture in order to (1) remain adaptive in a rapidly changing environment, (2) conserve those elements of the culture that are a source of strength and pride, and (3) manage the evolution of the organization realistically. The managers knew that the Corps' fundamental mission had changed over the last several decades and that the survival of the organization hinged on getting an accurate self-assessment of its strengths and weaknesses.

The usual assessment procedure was followed, and the discussion developed the following themes, stated as either key values or assumptions, depending on how the group itself experienced that element.

- Our mission is to solve problems of river control, dams, bridges, and so forth pragmatically, not aesthetically, but our responsiveness to our environment leads to aesthetic concerns within the context of any given project.

- We always respond to crisis and are organized to do so.

- We are conservative and protect our turf, but value some adventurism.

- We are decentralized and expect decisions to be made in the field, but control the field tightly through the role of the district engineer.

- We are numbers driven and always operate in terms of cost/benefit analyses, partly because quality is hard to measure.

- We minimize risk because we must not fail; hence things are overdesigned, and we use only safe, well-established technologies.

- We exercise professional integrity and say no when we should.

- We try to minimize public criticism.

- We are responsive to externalities but attempt to maintain our independence and professional integrity.

- We are often an instrument of foreign policy through our non-U.S. projects.

The group identified as its major problem that the traditional mission of flood control was largely accomplished, and, with changing patterns in Congress, it was not easy to tell what kinds of projects would continue to justify the budget. Financial pressures were seen to cause more projects to be cost-shared with local authorities, requiring degrees of collaboration that the Corps was not sure it could handle. The culture discussion provided useful perspectives on what was ahead, but did not provide clues as to the specific strategy to pursue in the future.

Corps of Engineers Lessons Learned. This case, like the others, illustrates that one can get a group to decipher major elements of its culture and that this can be a useful exercise in clarifying what is strategically possible.

Case Example Four: The Delta Pharmaceuticals Sales Organization

This example illustrates the use of a cultural assessment to determine whether a management succession should emphasize culture preservation by hiring an insider or begin a process of cultural evolution by hiring an outsider (Schein, 1999b).

Delta is the U.S. subsidiary of a large European pharmaceutical company. The vice president of sales had been in his job for thirty years and was widely credited with having built up a very successful sales organization. The culture issue came up around the question of whether to replace him with an inside candidate, thereby reinforcing the culture that had been built, or bring in an outsider, thereby setting in motion cultural changes toward another type of sales organization.

In this case the goal of the assessment was not only to understand the present culture of the sales organization but also to evaluate whether they were indeed open to either alternative. What they wanted was an effective sales organization; they would measure this by determining first, how they felt about the culture that we would uncover and second, how the members of the sales organization felt about their own culture.

The basic assessment plan was to work my way down through the organization, doing either individual or group interviews as seemed appropriate. In planning this process an important issue came up. The current VP of sales expected me to do extensive *individual* interviews to decipher the culture. I had to convince him that it was not only more valid but far more efficient to work with *groups,* unless there was reason to believe that group members would be inhibited in talking about the culture in front of others. Based on his understanding of his own organization, we jointly decided that at the top level of this organization, where inhibition might operate, I would interview individuals, but as I got to the regional and district organizations I would run group meetings along the lines described above, unless I encountered evidence of inhibition there. After completing the group meetings I was to write up an analysis of the culture that would enable senior management to decide on the succession process.

Exhibit 17.1 presents some of the excerpts from my report, which led eventually to the appointment of the inside candidate and reflected the decision to preserve and reinforce the existing culture. Notice that in this case the artifacts and values are more salient and the tacit assumptions are implied but not made explicit.

Delta Pharmaceutical Lessons Learned. This report illustrates how a culture assessment can be used to deal with a very specific question—in this case, a senior management succession decision. If there had been more conflict or discord in the culture, the decision would have been more complex; as it turned out, throughout the organization there was unanimity that the present culture was well adapted to the business situation and should therefore be preserved and enhanced.

The assessment process was adapted to the particular problem the organization faced, and the key members of the client system

Exhibit 17.1. Excerpts from the Delta Sales Culture Report.

- There is a very strong sales culture that was largely created over the last several decades by the present VP, who is about to retire.

- This sales culture is credited with being the reason why the company has been as successful as it has been.

- The present sales culture is perceived to be the company's best hope for the future. The sales organization feels strongly that it should not be tampered with.

- The key elements of the sales culture, its strengths, are

  The high morale, dedication, and loyalty of the sales reps

  The high degree of flexibility of the reps in responding to changing management demands in the marketing of the existing products

  The high degree of openness of communication that permits rapid problem solving, collaboration, and shifting of strategy when needed

  Good communication and collaboration between district managers and reps

  A strong family feeling—informal relationships up and down the hierarchy; everyone is known to management on a first-name basis and employees trust management

  A strong development program that permits sales reps multiple career options according to their talents and needs

  High ethical and professional standards in selling; focus on educating doctors, not just pushing individual products

  High degree of discipline in following company directives in how to position products; feeling of "management showed us how to do it, and it worked"

- There was a strong feeling that only an insider would "understand" the culture they had built. Bringing in an outsider would be very risky because he or she might undermine or destroy the very things they felt made them effective.

- Though the culture is authoritarian and hierarchic, it works very well because top management gets across the message that it is the reps and the districts that make the system go, and that what higher management is doing is in support of the front lines. It is a very people-oriented culture, which allows for both flexibility and discipline. For example, every district will follow the sales/marketing plan, but every district manager will allow his reps to use their own skills and biases to their own best advantage and will not impose arbitrary methods to be used in every case. Reps feel they have some autonomy but also feel obligated and committed to company plans.

(Continued)

Exhibit 17.1. Excerpts from the Delta Sales Culture Report, Cont'd.

- The individual and group incentive and bonus systems are working well in keeping an optimum balance between individual competition and teamwork. The management system is very sensitive to the need to balance these forces and does so at the higher level as well between the sales and marketing organizations.
- The wider company culture is very people oriented and makes multiple career paths available. The personal growth and development emphasis, supplemented by thorough training, emanates from the top of the company and is perceived as the reason why people are so motivated.

Copyright © E. H. Schein.

were instrumental in designing a process that would best reveal the essential elements of their culture.

Case Example Five: The Naval Research Labs

This case illustrates how the decision to assess the culture of an organization because of some concern about lack of communication between presumed geographic subcultures led to a completely unexpected set of insights about other subcultural dynamics that were operating. The initial goal was to determine how the geographical and structural differences between the research unit in New England and its administrative/political unit in Washington, D.C., might have created differences in their subcultures. The two units were populated by different kinds of people and had different tasks, so it was anticipated that there would be important subcultural differences that would create communication and coordination problems.

I was contacted by an MIT alumnus who worked in the Labs and knew about my work on culture. He introduced me to the senior management of the Labs and we decided to create a one-day assessment workshop in which we would explore the geographic subculture differences, using my methodology. The group doing the assessment was a senior management slice representing both the research and administrative units. As we proceeded, it was revealed that an important set of structural differences not previously noticed had to be taken into account. The Labs worked in terms of projects that were local, and each had a different financial sponsor in Washington. Therefore, *each project* had its own administrative staff working in Washington to develop budgets, keep sponsors informed, and generally manage all of the external political issues that might come up.

What had originally been perceived as two units, one in Washington and one in New England, turned out to be nine units, *each of which* had both a New England and a Washington subunit. Because it was so critical for each project to work smoothly, the geographic factor was quickly overcome in each of the nine projects through multiple meetings and constant communication. Each *project* thus developed a subculture based on the nature of its work and its people, and there were indeed subculture differences among the projects, but the original notion that there was a geographic problem had to be dropped completely.

The important learning from this culture exercise was that the focus on culture revealed some important structures in the organization that had not really been noticed before. And where the geographic separation mattered, each project had already done a great deal to ameliorate the potential negative consequences. As in the previous case, the assessment revealed that the subcultures needed to be preserved rather than changed.

Summary and Conclusions

The assessment process described and illustrated reflects a number of conclusions:

1. Culture *can* be assessed by means of various individual and group interview processes, with group interviews being by far the better method in terms of both validity and efficiency. Such assessments can be usefully made in as little as a half day.

2. Culture *cannot* be assessed by means of surveys or questionnaires, because one does not know what to ask and cannot judge

the reliability and validity of the responses. Survey responses can be viewed as cultural artifacts and as reflections of the organization's climate, but they do not tell you anything about the deeper values or shared assumptions that are operating.

3. A culture assessment is of little value unless it is tied to some organizational problem or issue. In other words, diagnosing a culture for its own sake is not only too vast an undertaking but also can be viewed as boring and useless. On the other hand, when the organization has a purpose, a new strategy, a problem to be solved, a change agenda, then to determine how the culture impacts the issue is not only useful but in most cases necessary. The issue should be related to the organization's effectiveness and should be stated in as concrete a way as possible. One cannot say that the culture itself is an issue or problem. The culture impacts how the organization performs and the initial focus should always be on where the performance needs to be improved.

4. The assessment process should first identify cultural assumptions, then assess them in terms of whether they are a strength or a constraint on what the organization is trying to do. In most organizational change efforts, it is much easier to draw on the strengths of the culture than to overcome the constraints by changing the culture.

5. In any cultural assessment process one should be sensitive to the presence of subcultures and be prepared to do separate assessments of them in order to determine their relevance to what the organization is trying to do.

6. Culture can be described and assessed at the artifact, espoused values, or shared tacit assumptions level; the importance of getting to the assumptions level derives from the insight that unless you understand the shared tacit assumptions, you cannot explain the discrepancies that almost always surface between the espoused values and the observed behavioral artifacts.

It should be noted that the ten-step group process described here is extremely fast. Within a few hours one can get a good approximation of what some of the major assumptions are. If it is important for the outsider/researcher to be able to describe the culture in more detailed terms, then additional observations, participant observation, and more group assessments can be made until a complete picture emerges. In terms of implications for leadership, I would argue that in most situations in which leaders need to manage some element of their culture, this internal deciphering process is sufficient and the approach is likely to be useful.

18

A CASE OF ORGANIZATIONAL (CULTURAL?) CHANGE

The purpose of this chapter is to further illustrate the complexity of culture and culture change when one applies it to a particular organization faced with particular problems over a period of time. In practice, the drive for culture change derives from the need to solve organizational problems. It is only when cultural assumptions get in the way that the culture change issue arises. In this chapter I will examine a case of a major multiyear turnaround that was designed to fix a great many problems that Ciba-Geigy had generated in the 1970s and that was viewed at the time as a real example of culture change. The story illustrates many of the mechanisms discussed in the preceding chapters but also raises some fundamental questions about whether or not real culture change took place at Ciba-Geigy.

In the earlier description of the Ciba-Geigy paradigm, I tried to show how certain deep shared assumptions related to each other, and how that pattern of assumptions explained a great deal of the day-to-day behavior of the organization. In this chapter I also want to show how a change process revealed some of the elements of the Ciba-Geigy culture and how that culture did and did not change, even as the organization changed. In laying out the case it will also become clearer what I mean by a clinical approach to studying culture. I will present data from Ciba-Geigy along with contrasting observations from other cases to illustrate, through concrete events, how the change process unfolds and how the consultant gets involved with it.

The cultures of DEC and Ciba-Geigy did not reveal themselves easily or automatically; rather, I had to reconstruct, with the help of members of the organization, why certain events that struck me as incongruent made sense if viewed from a cultural point of view. I will therefore interweave into the account below how I made some of the cultural inferences that have been reported in this book.

The information I will present here is, of course, not complete, either historically or ethnographically. It is limited by the clinical perspective I am taking and is therefore biased by the client's purpose in involving me. But culture is pervasive, so the deeper assumptions of a cultural paradigm will show through in any of the settings that can be observed. What is less clear is the structure and content of the various subcultures that may have existed, though the impact of some of those subcultures became quite visible during the change process.

Initial Contact and First Annual Meeting

My involvement with Ciba-Geigy began in 1979 with a major "educational intervention" for the top management group at its annual worldwide meeting. Dr. Leupold, the manager of Ciba-Geigy's management development function, had heard me speak at a 1978 open seminar on career development and career anchors (Schein, 1978, 1993b). He suggested to his boss, Sam Koechlin, the chairman of the executive committee (the group accountable for the company's performance), that my material on career dynamics might be worth sharing with Ciba-Geigy's senior management.

Koechlin's goal for the annual meeting was to combine work on company problems with some stimulating input for the group, broadly in the area of leadership and creativity. He saw that the company was moving into a more turbulent economic, political, and technological environment that would require new kinds of responses. Koechlin was a descendant of one of the Swiss founding families of the company but had spent ten years of his career in the U.S. subsidiary and had come to appreciate that the more dynamic U.S. environment stimulated a level of creativity that he saw as lacking in the home country. His own educational background was not in science but in law. He was a good example of the kind of marginal leader who could simultaneously be in his culture, yet perceive it somewhat objectively. His bringing of various outside speakers into the annual meeting was a deliberate attempt to broaden the perception of his top management. My two days of lecturing were to be focused on leadership and creativity in the context of individual career development.

Both the topic of creativity and the approach of lecturing to the group were completely congruent with Ciba-Geigy's assumptions that (1) creativity is important in science, (2) knowledge is acquired through a scientific process, and (3) knowledge is communicated through experts in a didactic way. By way of contrast, in the pragmatic environment at DEC it would have been inconceivable to devote two whole days of senior management time to a seminar involving primarily outside lecturers, and the topic of creativity would not have interested the senior managers—it would have been viewed as much too abstract. In fact, if I did attempt to lecture the group, even for fifteen minutes, I was interrupted and forced to either make my comments immediately relevant or let the group get back to work.

Whereas at DEC much took place without preplanning, at Ciba-Geigy everything was planned to the level of the smallest detail. After Koechlin and Leupold had agreed between themselves on the general topic, it was necessary for me to meet Koechlin to see whether my general approach and personal style was compatible with what he was looking for. I was invited to spend a day and night at his house outside of Basel, where I also met his wife. Koechlin and I got along well, so it was agreed that we would go ahead with my sessions at the 1979 annual meeting in Merlingen, Switzerland.

Some weeks later, a Mr. Kunz visited me at MIT to discuss the details. Kunz was the seminar administrator responsible for the detailed agenda of the three days, and, as it turned out, also had to indoctrinate me on how to deal with this group. He had been a line manager who had moved into executive training, but, by virtue of his prior experience, was familiar with the expectations of senior line management. Kunz met with me at MIT for many hours some months prior to the seminar to plan for the materials to be used, the exercise to be designed to involve the participants, the schedule, and so on.

In this process I observed firsthand how carefully Ciba-Geigy managers planned for every detail of an activity for which they were responsible. I had to provide a plan that showed virtually minute by minute what would happen during the two days, and the company was clearly willing to commit all the time and energy it might take to design as nearly perfect a meeting as possible. Not only was Ciba-Geigy's high degree of commitment to structure revealed in this process, but, in retrospect, it also revealed how basic the assumption was about managerial turf. Kunz had clear responsibility for the conduct of the meeting, though he was two levels below the participants in the hierarchy. He had formed a review committee, including Koechlin and some members of the executive committee, to review the seminar plan and to obtain their involvement, but this group gave considerable freedom to Kunz to make final decisions on seminar format. Thus, both at DEC and at Ciba-Geigy, the culture was displaying itself in the manner in which I encountered the organization, but I did not know this at the time.

The participants at the Ciba-Geigy annual meeting were the chairman of the board, Koechlin's boss, several board members who showed up as visitors, the nine-person executive committee, all the senior functional and divisional managers, and the most important country managers; a total of forty-five. This group met annually for five days or less, depending on the specific agenda to be covered.

Though I did not know it at the time, the meeting served a major integrative and communication function in that it legitimized during the meeting what culturally did not happen in day-to-day operations—a high level of *open* and *lateral* communication. It also reflected the hierarchical emphasis, however, in that this sharing across units took place in public under the scrutiny of the executive committee and board members. Moreover, there was still a strong tendency to be deferential toward others and to share ideas only when information was specifically asked for. The meeting also provided an opportunity for senior management to get a major message across quickly to the entire organization and, as we will see, to involve the entire organization in crisis management when that was needed.

The meeting took place at a pleasant Swiss mountain resort and, as described earlier, always included a special recreational event that helped the group loosen up with each other. My talks were delivered on the second and third day, and I included in the day's activities a set of mutual interviews on career histories to help participants to determine their "career anchors." I put creativity into the context of innovation—especially role innovation—to highlight that scientific creativity was by no means the only kind, and that managers in any role could become more innovative in their approach. Determining the career anchor requires pairs of people who had to interview each other about their educational and career history. I asked people to pair themselves up in any way that seemed comfortable to them to avoid having to make up formal pairs that might bring people together who would not be comfortable sharing with each other. The chairman of the board enthusiastically participated, and thereby set a good tone for the meeting.

I learned on the third day about the meeting tradition that highlighted the ability of the group to shed its hierarchy and have fun together. Kunz was empowered to locate some fun activity somewhere in the neighborhood that would allow all of us to try our hand at something none of us was good at. It was deliberately planned to be a surprise to everyone except Kunz and Koechlin, and each year anticipation ran high as to what Kunz would come up with. Early in the afternoon we all boarded buses and were taken twenty-five miles to a site where crossbow shooting was being done recreationally, and each of us had to take our turn trying to learn to hit a target with this rather novel and different weapon. The activity reduced everyone to the same level of incompetence and thereby provided an opportunity for much teasing across hierarchical boundaries.

Following the crossbow shooting we were all bussed to a nearby castle where a large, informal dinner, accompanied by much wine and beer, topped off the day. At this dinner the chairman spoke very informally and made reference to his career anchor, thereby legitimating the previous day's input, and again illustrating how ready the group was to listen to authority and utilize academic inputs.

Impact of First Annual Meeting

The three major effects of this meeting, were as follows:

1. The group obtained new insights and information about creativity and innovation, especially the insight that innovation occurs within a variety of careers and organizational settings and should not be confused with the pure creative process that scientists are engaged in. The assumption had crept in that only scientists are creative, so those managers who had left their technical identities behind long ago were reassured by my message that managerial role innovations in all the functions of the business were much needed in a healthy organization. This legitimized as "creative" a great many activities that had previously not been perceived as such and liberated some problem-solving energy by linking innovation to day-to-day problem solving. This insight would not have been all that important but for the fact that the group was so embedded in assumptions about science and the creative process within science. I learned later that it was Koechlin's intention all along to broaden the group's perspective and to lay the groundwork for changes that he had in mind.

2. The group obtained new insights from the discussion of career anchors, which emphasized the variety of careers and the different things people are looking for in their careers. The effect was to unfreeze some of the monolithic notions about careers and the role of scientific backgrounds in careers. The chairman's humorous talk legitimized the notion of individual differences in careers, particularly since the chairman was a lawyer, not a scientist.

3. The group got to know me and my style as a responsive process consultant through several spontaneous interventions that I made during the three days. In particular, I was allowed to attend Kunz's planning committee meetings to review each day's activities and found in that context a number of occasions on which my ideas for process and design facilitated the group's planning. Koechlin and other members of the executive committee were able to observe that a process consultant could be very helpful at a meeting.

During the informal times at meals and in the evening, my spontaneous responses were geared to getting out of the expert role. For example, if I was asked what companies were doing today in the field of participative management, I would give examples and highlight the diversity of what I observed rather than generalizing as I was expected to do. I had the sense that in this process I was disappointing some of the managers with whom I was speaking, because I did not fit the stereotype of the scientist who is willing to summarize the state of knowledge in a field. On the other hand, my willingness to delve into the problems of Ciba-Geigy appealed to some managers, and they accepted my self-definition as a process consultant rather than an expert consultant.

My participation in the meeting ended when my two days were finished, but plans were made to institute career planning and job/role planning in broader segments of the company. Specifically, Koechlin and the executive committee decided to ask all senior managers to do the "job/role planning exercise," which involves rethinking one's own job in the context of how it has changed and will continue to change as one projects ahead five years and analyzes the environment around the job (Schein, 1978, 1995). Koechlin also encouraged more managers to do the "career anchor interview exercise" as an input to the annual management development process and authorized the development of an adaptation of the original interview questionnaire for use specifically in the company. I was asked to work with the headquarters management development group to help implement these two activities by spending roughly ten to fifteen days during the subsequent year as a consultant. My clients were to be Leupold, the management development manager, and Koechlin; the broad mission was to increase the ability of the company to innovate in all areas.

First Year's Work:
Getting Acquainted with the Culture

I visited the company several times during the year, each time for two to three days. During these visits I learned more about the management development system, met some of the members of the executive committee, and gradually got involved in what I considered to be my most important activity: the planning of the next annual meeting. From my point of view, if innovation was to take hold, the most important thing to take advantage of was the relatively more open climate of the annual meeting. My goal was to be accepted as a process consultant to the entire meeting, not as an educator coming in with wisdom for one or two days.

But the notion that I could help "on line" continued to be quite foreign to most of the managers, though at DEC I had learned the opposite lesson: unless I worked on line with real problems, the group considered me more or less useless. Initially I thought that the reactions of Ciba-Geigy's managers were simply based on misunderstanding. It was only with repeated experiences of not being invited to working meetings at Ciba-Geigy, of always being put into an expert role, and of always having to plan my visits in great detail that I realized I was up against something that could be genuinely defined as cultural. The Ciba-Geigy managers' perception of what consultants do and how they work reflected their more general assumptions about what managers do and how they work.

For example, on several occasions I noticed that managers whom I had met on previous visits looked past me and ignored me when I encountered them in the public lobby or the executive dining room. I later learned that to be seen with a consultant meant that one had problems and needed help—a position that managers in Ciba-Geigy strongly avoided. I could only be accepted in a role that fitted Ciba-Geigy's model, that of educator and expert to management as a whole. The point is important because my request to attend the next annual meeting in a process consultant role was, unbeknownst to me, strongly countercultural. But Koechlin was intrigued, and his own innovativeness swayed other members of the planning committee to accept me in that role.

We compromised on the notion that I would give some lectures on relevant topics based on the events I observed at the meeting, thus legitimizing my attendance. My role as a consultant was further legitimized by my being cast as a scientist who had to be given an opportunity to get to know top management better, so that I could be more helpful in the future. Koechlin and other senior managers had a specific view of what the total group needed, and they were prepared to introduce an outsider in the consultant role to facilitate this process. I came to realize that they wanted to unfreeze the group to get it to be more receptive to the crisis message they were preparing to deliver. An outsider with new ideas was seen as helpful in this process, both as a source of feedback to the group and as an expert on the change process that was about to be launched.

Another outsider, a professor of policy and strategy who also occupied a position on the board of Ciba-Geigy, was invited as well. Our attendance at the meeting was related to a decision made by Koechlin and the executive committee that at the 1980 annual meeting a major review of company performance, division by division, would be undertaken. Such a review, they believed, would bring out the need for change and innovation and, thereby, reverse a slide into unprofitability that had been going on but was not clearly recognized or accepted. They also planned to introduce a program of change called the redirection project.

This business problem had been developing over several years but had not yet been identified as a crisis to be collectively shared with senior management worldwide. The major product divisions of the company were the primary profit centers, but, as I indicated before, were not likely to communicate much with each other, even though their headquarters were all in Basel. These divisions knew what their individual situations were but seemed unaware of the impact on the company as a whole of dropping profit levels in many areas. Only the executive committee had the total picture.

This situation could easily arise because of the low amount of lateral communication, permitting the manager of a division that was losing money to rationalize that his loss was easily compensated for by other divisions and that things would soon improve. The culture encouraged each manager to worry only about his own piece of the organization, not to take a broad corporate view. Although communications that had gone out to the divisions over the year had suggested a total company problem, no one seemed to take it very seriously. Therefore, much of the annual meeting was to be devoted to selling the idea that there was a total company problem and helping managers, in small group meetings, to accept and deal with those problems.

Given these goals, the planning committee saw the point of having me help in the design of the meeting and to plan lectures, as needed, on how to initiate and manage various change projects. In other words, the economic and market environment was creating a financial crisis, top management decided it was time to deal with it, and the consultation process became one piece of management's more general process of launching the redirection project.

Unfreezing at the Second Annual Meeting

The first segment of the meeting was devoted to presenting financial data, division by division, followed by small group meetings to digest and analyze the situation and formulate proposals for reversing the business decline. What made the situation complicated was that some of the divisions—those operating in mature markets—were losing money and needed major restructuring, while other divisions were growing and making good contributions to overall profit levels. The division managers from the problem divisions were embarrassed, apologetic, and overconfident that they could reverse the situation, while others said privately that the losing divisions could not possibly accomplish their goals, were not really committed to change, and would make only cosmetic alterations.

The division managers from the profitable divisions bragged, felt complacent, and wondered when top management would do something about the "losers" who were dragging others down with them. But many people from the losing divisions and from top management said privately that even the profitable divisions, although they might look good relative to others inside the company, were not performing as well as they should compared to outside competitors in their own industrial market segments. Clearly it was up to the hierarchy to fix this problem, as the divisions saw it.

During the divisional reviews and presentations, another important cultural assumption surfaced. As was reported in Chapter Five, the company had been diversifying for a number of years and was attempting to get into consumer goods via a recent acquisition in the United States of Airwick. I learned during the Airwick product review how strongly Ciba-Geigy's self-image revolved around "important" products that cured diseases and prevented starvation. Selling something only because it made money did not fit into some of their cultural assumptions about the nature of their business, and dealing with an organization whose processes were primarily geared to marketing made them uneasy. It was no surprise, therefore, when in 1987 this division was sold off even though it was profitable.

The country managers, representing subsidiary companies in the major countries of the world, acknowledged the cross-divisional issues but were actually more upset by the fact that the headquarters organization—representing such functions as research and development, finance and control, personnel, and manufacturing—had become overgrown. These managers insisted that the headquarters functional staffs should be reduced, because they were an unnecessary overhead and, in many cases, an active interference in running the businesses in the countries. A high degree of centralization of research and development, manufacturing, and financial control had made sense when the company was young and small; but as it expanded and became a worldwide multinational, the small regional sales offices had gradually become large autonomous companies that managed all the functions locally.

Country heads needed their own staffs; but these staffs then came into conflict with the corporate staffs and the division staffs, who felt that they could communicate directly with their division people in each country. Because of the hierarchical nature of the organization, the headquarters groups asked for enormous amounts of information from the regions and frequently visited the regions. They felt that if they had worldwide responsibility for something, they had to be fully informed about everything at all times. Because of the lack of lateral communication, the functional staffs did not realize that their various inquiries and visits often paralyzed local operations because of the amount of time it took to answer questions, entertain visitors, get permission to act, and so on.

As the cost structure of the company came under increasing scrutiny, the country organizations were asked to reduce costs, while the headquarters organizations remained complacent, fat, and happy. The question that most worried the country managers was whether top management considered the profit erosion serious enough to warrant reductions in the headquarters functional staffs. If not, it must mean that this was only a fire drill, not a real crisis.

Inducing Survival Anxiety

By the end of the first day of the meeting, the disconfirming financial data had been presented and groups had met to consider what should be done, but the feedback from the groups indicated neither a complete understanding nor a real acceptance of the problem. There was clearly insufficient anxiety or guilt. The planning committee met to consider what to do and decided that the other consultant could help the group recognize the seriousness of the problem if he interrogated the group members in the style of a Harvard case discussion and led them to the inevitable conclusion that a crisis really existed. He did this very effectively on the second day of the meeting in a two-hour session that proved conclusively to all present that the group could not remain profitable in the long run unless major changes were made. The result was a real sense of survival anxiety and depression. For the first time, the message had really been accepted collectively, setting the stage for the introduction of the redirection project.

Why did this work? I had the sense that, in a culture where senior managers function symbolically as parent figures, it is difficult for the parents to tell the children that the family may fail if they don't shape up. The children find it too easy to blame each other and the parents and to collectively avoid feeling responsible. There was too much of a tradition that senior managers (the parents) would take care of things as they always had. The anxiety of facing up to the "family problem" was too overwhelming, so a great deal of denial had been operating.

The outside consultant could, in this case, take the same information but present it as a problem that the family as a whole owned and had to confront and handle as a total unit. He could be much more direct and confrontational than insiders could be with each other; at the same time, he could remind the total group that everyone was in this together—the executive committee as the symbolic parents along with all the children. This recognition did not reduce the resultant panic; however, it forced it out into the open, since denial was no longer possible. The group had been genuinely disconfirmed and made anxious, but not knowing how to fix problems heightened learning anxiety as well and the group did not yet feel psychologically safe and hence felt paralyzed.

Providing Some Psychological Safety

The next problem, then, was how to reduce the learning anxiety and discouragement now present in the group. How could we provide some psychological safety that would permit the group to redefine the situation, to begin to feel capable of doing something constructive? The other consultant and I took a long walk to think this out and came up with the idea that now would be a good time to give some lectures on the nature of resistance to change and how to overcome it. He had been confrontational, so I should now come on as supportive and facilitative.

I hurriedly pulled together notes, made transparencies, and on the following morning gave lectures on (1) why healthy organizations need to be able to change; (2) why individuals and groups resist change; (3) how to analyze forces that facilitate and forces that constrain change; and (4) how to develop valid change targets for the coming year, in the context of the redirection project, with timetables, measurements of outcomes, and accountabilities. I emphasized a point that is central to change projects: that the period of change has itself to be defined as a stage to be managed, with transition managers specifically assigned (Beckhard and Harris, 1987).

These lectures had the desired effect of giving the group members a way of thinking positively, so that when they were sent back into small groups to develop priority issues for making the redirection project a success, they were able to go off to these meetings with a sense of realism and optimism. The general results of the small group meetings were quite clear. They saw the need for the unprofitable divisions to shrink and restructure themselves, and the need for profitable divisions to become more effective relative to the competition, but they stated clearly that neither of these could happen if the headquarters organization did not confront the excess people in the headquarters and the style of management that was emanating from the functional groups. The ideas were not new, but they were now shared—and with some conviction. The meeting ended with top management making a commitment to confronting all of the issues identified and to the creation of a set of task forces to deal with the problems.

Creating a Structure for the Redirection Project: Project Task Forces as a "Parallel System"

The Ciba-Geigy managers were skillful at working in groups. Koechlin and the executive committee used this skill first by creating a steering committee to organize the redirection project into thirty or so separate, manageable tasks. The steering committee met for several days following the annual meeting to think through the specific tasks to be accomplished in the redirection process and to design the entire parallel system that would implement it.

A separate steering committee was created for each task and one member of the executive committee was made accountable for the performance of that task group. To avoid asking some of the senior managers to shrink and restructure divisions for which they had previously been responsible, responsibilities were reshuffled so that no conflicts of interest would arise and each division would be looked at with fresh eyes.

In addition, each task group was assigned a senior manager to review and challenge the proposed solutions of that task group to ensure that they made sense and had been properly thought through. The steering committee defined the timetables and the broad targets. Each team was also given the services of an internal organizational consultant to help with the organization of the team itself, and several of the teams asked for and obtained my help on how to structure their work.

All of this was communicated clearly by top management in written form, through meetings, and through trips to various parts of the company throughout the following year. Not only the process but also the necessity for it and top management's commitment to it were highlighted in these meetings. Great emphasis was given to the particular project that would reduce the number of people in the Basel headquarters by at least one third—no small task, as this involved in many cases laying off friends and relatives.

These structural changes in job responsibilities were major innovations implemented by the steering committee. The skillful use of groups, both at the annual meeting and in the design of the projects, struck me as paradoxical. How could a company that was so hierarchical and so concerned about individual turf be so effective in inventing groups and in operating within a group context? The answer appeared to be in the fact that the top management of the company was itself a group that had worked together for a long time and felt jointly accountable. The broader Swiss-German culture in which the company functioned also represented this same paradox—strong individualism with, at the same time, a strong sense of community and a commitment to working together in groups to solve problems.

Their respect for groups was confirmed in a meeting in which I was advising two young managers on the design of a one-week middle-management course. I suggested the use of one of the group survival exercises that illustrates clearly how groups can solve some objective problems better than individuals. I was told that they had used this exercise in the past but that participants routinely asked why their time was being wasted, since they were already convinced that groups could do better than individuals in problem solving!

One might also speculate that group work had such importance at Ciba-Geigy because it was virtually the only form of lateral communication available in the company. The sensitivities that might be operating if managers from one division offered help to or asked for help from another division could be overcome, with faces saved, if a task force consisting of members of both divisions adopted a process of taking turns reporting to each other on the progress of effective and ineffective interventions. The listener could then learn and get new ideas without either identifying himself as a problem or having others identify him as a target of their input. Group meetings thus preserved face all the way around.

It was also recognized that groups helped to build commitment to projects even though the implementation system was essentially hierarchical. If groups had discussed the issue, the hierarchy worked more smoothly, as in the Japanese system, where consensus is sought before a decision is announced. In various ways the redirection project was using the cultural strengths of the company and was redefining its formal procedures in order to deal with the business problem without changing the culture overtly.

Second Year: Consolidation of the Redirection Project

During my several visits following the second annual meeting, I worked on three important areas. First, I made myself available to any project group or group members who wished to discuss any aspect of how to proceed, with the appointment to be made at their initiative. If I learned something that would help other projects, I would summarize it and write it up for circulation to others. I was consulted by several managers on how best to think about early retirement, how to ease people out in their home community, how to get managers to think about innovative restructuring, and so on.

As mentioned before, I soon discovered that my memos pulling good ideas together died on the desks of the people to whom I sent them. That was my first encounter with the cultural norm that at Ciba-Geigy information does not circulate laterally. I also spent a good deal of time with the executive committee member who was responsible for the whole project, helping him to keep his role and his leadership behavior in his project group clear and effective. He was the only member of the executive committee who consistently used me as a process consultant. Parenthetically, he was their chief financial officer and also a lawyer. Several project managers wanted help in thinking through their roles as project chairmen and solicited my reactions to proposals prior to running them by the challengers.

Second, I became more familiar with the management development inventory and planning system and began a series of meetings with Leupold, the manager of this function, to see how it could be improved. Bringing in and developing better and more innovative managers was seen as a high-priority longer-range goal of the redirection project. It was also known that Leupold would retire within a year and his successor might need a consultant who had learned something about the company to help him think out his program.

Third, I was asked by Koechlin and the planning group to think about the cultural assumptions operating, to interview managers about the company culture, and to figure out how the culture was aiding or hindering the redirection project. The basic idea was to be prepared to comment on the role of the culture at the third annual meeting.

Third Annual Meeting:
The Culture Lecture Disaster

I had made it clear that one should think of change as a stage to be managed, with targets and assigned change managers (Beckhard and Harris, 1987). From this point of view, the third annual meeting provided a natural opportunity to review progress, check out what problems had been encountered, share successes and good innovations, replan some projects if necessary, and, most important, announce newly defined role relationships among executive committee members, division heads, and country heads.

The headquarters organization was too involved in the day-to-day operation of the local businesses. So as the functions were shrunk and restructured, it also appeared desirable to redefine the corporate headquarters role as more strategic, with the operating units to do more of the day-to-day management. This was possible because country managers were now willing and able to assume more responsibilities and because the executive committee increasingly recognized the importance of its strategic role.

At the opening session I was asked to review the progress of the redirection project, based on interviews with a series of managers about their experiences with the project. This lecture was designed to remind the participants of change theory, to legitimize their individual experiences and frustrations by giving a wide range of examples, to illustrate how restraining forces had been dealt with by innovative managers, and to introduce to the group the concept of corporate culture as a force to be analyzed. Based on my observations and systematic interviews, I was to review some of the major cultural assumptions operating at Ciba-Geigy.

The reaction to the lecture produced an important insight. Many participants said that I had stated things more or less accurately, but they clearly were not pleased that I, as an outsider, had made portions of their culture public. Some of them insisted that I had misunderstood or misinterpreted the culture, and one or two executive committee members subsequently decided that I therefore was not a useful consultant. For me to discuss their cultural assumptions created a polarized situation. Some managers moved closer to me; others moved further away. Internal debates were launched about whether or not certain statements about their culture were correct or not. I concluded that if one did not want that kind of polarization, one should help the group decipher its own culture rather than presenting one's own view of that culture in a didactic manner.

Following the general presentation on culture and change, each of the projects was asked to give a brief review of its status, and small groups met to consider implications and make suggestions. The last part of the meeting—and, from the point of view of the planning group, the most difficult—concerned the problem of how to inform everyone about the new roles of the executive committee, the division heads, and the country heads. The executive committee members were not sure that their planned effort to become more strategic and to have more individual accountabilities would get across just by saying it.

We therefore planned a three-step process: (1) a formal announcement of the new roles; (2) a brief lecture by me on the implications of role realignment, emphasizing the systemic character of role networks and the need for each manager to renegotiate his role downward, upward, and laterally if the new system was to work; and (3) a powerful emotional speech by the chief financial officer on the effect of this new alignment in streamlining the company for the future. The meeting ended on a high note, based on a sense of what had already been accomplished in one year, what accomplishments were in the works, and what improvements could be expected from the new role that the executive committee had taken for itself.

The fact that the headquarters organization had begun to shrink through early retirements and had reduced some of its more bothersome control activities sent the clear message that top management was serious about its role in the redirection project even though the early retirement of headquarters people was an extremely painful process. The fact that people were being retired destroyed the taken-for-granted assumption that people had a guaranteed career in the company, but the highly individualized and financially generous manner in which retirements were handled reinforced another basic assumption: that the company cared very much for its people and would not hurt them if there was any way to avoid it.

Assessment During the Third Year

Most of my regular visits subsequent to the third annual meeting were devoted to working with Joe Wells, the new manager of management development. Leupold had been asked to retire as part of the headquarters restructuring. Though I continued to meet with members of the executive committee on redirection matters, the priority shifted to helping Wells think through his new role and reexamine how the entire process could be improved. Leupold was offered, as part of his retirement package, a consultantship with the company, provided he developed a research project that could be jointly conducted with me.

We proposed a study of the careers of the top two hundred managers in the company, with the purpose of identifying critical success factors or problems in those careers. The project was approved by the executive committee with the condition that I was to act as technical supervisor of the project, reminding me once again that my credibility as a consultant rested heavily on my scientific reputation and that scientific validity was the ultimate decision criterion for the company. The study involved a detailed historical reconstruction of the two hundred careers and revealed surprisingly little geographical, cross-functional, and/or cross-divisional movement as those careers progressed.

A presentation of these and other results was given to the executive committee by Leupold, which led to a major discussion of how future general managers should be developed. A consensus was reached that there should be more early geographic rotation and movement into and out of headquarters, but cross-functional and cross-divisional movement remained a controversial issue. The executive committee members also realized that rotational moves, if they were to be useful, had to occur early in the career. They decided that such early movement would occur only if a very clear message about the importance of career development went out to the entire organization.

This decision led to the design of a half-day segment on management development, which was inserted into the management seminars that were periodically given to the top five hundred managers of the company. A new policy on early rotation was mandated, and the data from the project were used to justify the new policy. Once senior management accepted a conclusion as valid, it was able to move decisively and to impose a proposed solution on the entire company. The message was communicated by having executive committee members at each seminar, but implementation was left to local management.

During this year Koechlin relinquished the job of chairman of the executive committee for reasons of health, which raised a potential succession problem. However, the executive committee had anticipated the problem and had a new chairman and vice-chairman ready. The new chairman was a scientist, but the new vice-chairman was the chief financial officer who had shown great leadership skills during the redirection project. Both of them strongly reaffirmed the scientific and technical assumptions underlying the success of Ciba-Geigy, as if to say "We are making major changes but we are the same kind of culture as before."

By the end of the third year, the financial results were much better, and the restructuring process in the unprofitable divisions was proceeding rapidly. Each unit learned how to manage early retirements, and a measure of interdivisional cooperation was achieved in the process of transferring people who were redundant in one division into other divisions. Initial attitudes were negative, and I heard many complaints from managers that even their best people were not acceptable to other divisions. This attitude was gradually eroded because the assumption that "We don't throw people out without maximum effort to find jobs for them" eventually overrode the provincialism of the divisions. Managers who were too committed to the old strategy of running those divisions were gradually replaced with managers who were deemed to be more innovative in their approach. One of the managers of a division that needed to make major reductions and redesign its whole product line was deemed so successful in this project that he was promoted to the executive committee.

Because it had fulfilled its functions, the redirection project was officially terminated at the end of the third year. Relevant change projects would now be handled by the executive committee, and I was asked to be "on call" to line managers needing help. For example, the new head of one of the previously unprofitable divisions wanted help in restoring the morale of those managers who remained after many of their colleagues were retired or farmed out to other divisions. He sensed a level of fear and apathy that made it difficult to move forward positively. In true Ciba-Geigy fashion, he had tried to solve this problem on his own by bringing in an outside training program, but it had been unsuccessful. He then requested a meeting with me to seek alternative solutions. Given the Ciba-Geigy culture and his own commitment, it was obvious that he should build his program internally and enlist the aid of the corporate training people, who would know how to design a program that would be culturally congruent. He had never considered using the corporate training group to help him, though he knew of it and liked some of the people in it. I found myself being the broker between two parts of the organization that could have been talking to each other directly. He did follow up, and in the subsequent year a successful in-house program was developed.

During the next two years my involvement declined gradually. The head of the redirection project's headquarters reduction team became the chairman of the board and the former head of the division that had needed the most downsizing became the chairman of the executive committee. Both of these managers showed their talent in the way they handled their projects. All of the changes were accomplished without any outsiders being brought into Ciba-Geigy. I continued to work with Wells on management development issues and helped him to implement some of his programs. I also worked with the U.S. subsidiary on projects for which my knowledge of the culture was considered an asset. But the assumption that one uses consultants only when one has serious problems prevailed, so from 1988 on my involvement has been virtually zero.

Summary and Conclusions

Based on what I observed and heard, Ciba-Geigy successfully weathered a major organizational crisis involving many elements of its culture.

1. The financial trend toward nonprofitability was decisively reversed.

2. Two previously unprofitable divisions restructured themselves by drastically cutting products, facilities, and people, and by reorganizing their production and marketing activities to fit the current market and economic realities. One of these divisions was considered a loser, but because of its successful restructuring under a dynamic manager it became the company hero. The manager of this division became the chairman of the executive committee.

3. The functions in the corporate headquarters were reduced by 30 to 40 percent, and more line responsibility was delegated to the countries and divisions.

4. The functions in the divisions were also reassessed, and their role was changed in line with headquarters' becoming more strategic.

5. The profitable divisions thoroughly reassessed themselves and began programs—particularly in the pharmaceutical division—to be more competitive in their particular industries.

6. Executive committee members restructured their own accountabilities so that each division, country, and function had one clear line boss but one whose focus was more strategic. In the previous system, these organizational units had felt accountable to the

entire executive committee and were often micromanaged by head-quarters people from Basel.

7. A major management succession occurred and was negoti-ated successfully, in that the new chairman and vice-chairman of the executive committee were perceived by senior management as good choices and were promoted further in recent years.

8. In this whole three-year change process, many managers who were considered less effective were weeded out through early retirement, permitting the filling of key jobs by managers consid-ered more dynamic and effective.

9. Senior managers acquired insight into the ways in which their culture both constrained and helped them.

10. A major cultural assumption about career stability and "life-time employment," particularly at headquarters, was reassessed and abandoned. In that process another major assumption about dealing with people on an individualized and humane basis was reaffirmed.

11. Managerial career development was redefined in terms of required rotation both geographically and through headquarters.

12. The consumer goods acquisition that did not fit was reeval-uated and a decision made to sell it. At the same time, the corporate acquisition policy was clarified to only look for companies that were based on technologies with which Ciba-Geigy felt comfortable.

Most managers in Ciba-Geigy said that they had undergone some great changes and that many of their assumptions about the world and the company had changed. On the surface it looked like a clear case of major culture change. However, when one looks closely, the cultural paradigm of the company had not really changed at all. There continued to be the same bias toward scientific author-ity; the hierarchy functioned as strongly as ever, but with redefined roles; the assumption that managers do their job best when left alone to learn for themselves was still very strong; and lateral com-munication was still considered mostly irrelevant. For example, there was still no regular meeting of division heads except at the annual meeting, where they met with everyone else, and there were no functional meetings across countries or divisions.

Various projects—for example, to bring in MBAs on a trial basis and to hold worldwide meetings of functional people, such as the management development coordinators from all the divisions and key countries—were pushed, but one senses that they were only tolerated in the culture, not encouraged. On one of my visits, Wells arranged for me to meet five of the MBAs who had been hired into different parts of Ciba-Geigy to see how they were reacting to their different situations. We had a productive and constructive meeting. However, a week later Wells was criticized for organizing the meeting by several of the bosses of the MBAs, because he was stepping onto the turf of these other managers. It turned out that they would not have given permission for such a cross-departmental group to meet.

When the redirection project began, we all talked of culture change. To label a change as culture change enhanced the drama of what was happening, so it may have had some motivational value even if in the end it was inaccurate. At the same time, it focused people on the culture, so that they could identify both the constraints and the enhancing features of the culture. But the important thing to note is that considerable change can take place in an organization's operations without the basic cultural paradigm changing at all. In fact, at Ciba-Geigy some of the assumptions could not have changed but for the even stronger action of deeper assumptions. Thus, some parts of the culture helped many of the changes to happen in other parts of the culture. Specifically, the downsizing of the headquarters organization, which clearly abandoned one cultural assumption, could not have occurred but for the deeper assumption that "we take good care of our people." In their study of major changes in large corporations, Donaldson and Lorsch (1983) report something very similar. The basic deep beliefs of management did not change, but actually were used to fuel the changes that the organizations needed to make to become more adaptive and effective. The constancy of a core set of deep beliefs, values, and assumptions is also one of the keys to the longevity of organizations as shown in the Collins and Porras studies of successful organizations (Collins and Porras, 1994).

This insight leads to a further point. Many assumptions around mission, goals, means, measurement systems, roles, and relationships can be superficial within the total structure of the cultural paradigm yet very important for the organization's functioning on a day-to-day basis. The assumption that the headquarters functional groups had worldwide responsibility for tracking everything was not a very deep assumption within the whole Ciba-Geigy culture, but it had a major impact on business performance and managerial morale in the country companies. Changing some of these superficial assumptions was crucial to Ciba-Geigy's effective adaptation. The deeper assumptions may drive this whole process but may not have to change.

It should also be noted that the deeper assumptions are not necessarily functional. The commitment to science continued to be manifested in commitment to scientists, especially some of the older ones who had helped the company to become successful. In one extreme case such a person was a country manager who was performing poorly in that role. A more skillful general manager had been groomed to take over this country, but the decision to give him authority was held up for two full years in order to let the scientist retire at his normal time. It was felt that to force him into early retirement would not only be destructive to him but would send the wrong signal to the rest of the organization.

What, then, really happened in the redirection project and why? Many in the company asked this question in order to understand the reasons for the success of the change effort. My own observation is that the effort was successful because the executive committee (1) sent a clear message that a change was needed, (2) involved itself fully in the change process, (3) tackled the impossible job of reducing headquarters staff as well as the power of the functional groups, and (4) thereby not only created involvement and ownership down the line in the country groups but made it clear that operational problems would increasingly be delegated down. Even though communication laterally was still minimal, the vertical channels were more opened up. Financial information was shared more than before, suggestions coming up through the project structure were listened to, and proposals that were accepted were effectively implemented through the existing hierarchy as a result of clear top-down signals.

The design of the redirection project—with an externalized steering committee that created project groups with consultants and challenger managers and provided clear goals, timetables, and time off to work on the problem—reflected skills embedded in the Ciba-Geigy culture. They knew very well how to design group projects and work in groups. In this sense Ciba-Geigy used its cultural strength to redirect itself more rapidly than might have been possible in a less structured organization, or one less sensitive to group process issues.

The driving force and the source of many of the key insights behind this change effort was Koechlin, who, as mentioned before, was the kind of leader who could step outside of his own culture and assess it realistically. The willingness of the chief financial officer and various division managers to step outside their own subcultures and learn some new approaches also played a key role. But in the end the culture changed only in peripheral ways by restructuring some minor assumptions. Yet such peripheral culture change is often sufficient to redesign the core business processes and thereby to fix major organizational problems.

As a postscript, Ciba-Geigy eventually merged with Sandoz to become Novartis, a larger multinational now focused more specifically on pharmaceuticals. I had occasion to ask the CEO of Novartis about this later merger and was told that it went very smoothly, even though these two companies had been competitors and "enemies" at the time of my work with them. If this merger went smoothly, it is probably because the two companies had some strong common elements—the Basel culture and the industry culture of pharmaceuticals.

19

THE LEARNING CULTURE
AND THE LEARNING LEADER

In this final chapter I want to shift my focus from analysis to normative inference. There is much speculation nowadays about the direction in which the world is heading and what all of this means for organizations and leadership. My sense of this is that the various predictions about globalism, knowledge-based organizations, the information age, the biotech age, the loosening of organizational boundaries, and so on all have one theme in common—we basically do not know what the world of tomorrow will really be like, except that it will be *different,* more *complex,* more *fast*-paced, and more *culturally diverse* (Hesselbein, Goldsmith, and Somerville, 1999; Global Business Network, 2002; Schwartz, 2003; Michael, 1985, 1991). This means that *organizations and their leaders will have to become perpetual learners.*

When we pose the issue of perpetual learning in the context of cultural analysis, we confront a paradox. Culture is a stabilizer, a conservative force, a way of making things meaningful and predictable. Many management consultants and theorists have asserted that "strong" cultures are desirable as a basis for effective and lasting performance. But strong cultures are by definition stable and hard to change. If the world is becoming more turbulent, requiring more flexibility and learning, does this not imply that strong cultures will increasingly become a liability? Does this not mean, then, that the process of culture creation itself is potentially dysfunctional because it stabilizes things, whereas flexibility might be more appropriate? Or is it possible to imagine a culture that, by its very nature, is learning oriented, adaptive, and flexible? Can one stabilize perpetual learning and change? What would a culture that favored perpetual learning and flexibility look like?

To translate that question into leadership terms, what is the direction in which the leaders of today should be pushing cultural evolution to prepare for the surprises of tomorrow? What sort of characteristics and skills must a leader have to perceive the needs of tomorrow and to implement the changes needed in order to survive?

What Might a Learning Culture Look Like?

The hypotheses spelled out in this chapter have resulted from many conversations with the late Donald Michael (1985, 1991) and with Tom Malone (1987), and Peter Senge (1990) about the organization of the future. They reflect a bringing together of what Michael sees as the learning needs of the future, what Malone sees as the theory and practice of coordination in the information age, what Senge visualizes as the art and practice of the learning organization, and my own thoughts about culture and innovation (Schein, 1990). Combining these ideas leads to a first attempt to describe the characteristics of a learning culture in terms of relevant dimensions and positions on those dimensions.

1. A Proactivity Assumption

A learning culture would have to assume that the appropriate way for humans to behave in relationship to their environment is to be proactive problem solvers and learners. If the culture is built on fatalistic assumptions of passive acceptance, learning will become more and more difficult as the rate of change in the environment increases. It is not clear how this kind of assumption works out in those cultures in which fatalistic acceptance is a central assumption. I would speculate that in those cultures a differentiation will take place between domains such as religion, in which the old assumption will hold, and business, in which new assumptions concerning active problem solving will come to coexist with the old assumptions. A good example of that kind of evolution is seen in Singapore's spectacular economic success, based on combining Asian and Western assumptions (Schein, 1996b).

The learning leader must portray confidence that active problem solving leads to learning, thereby setting an appropriate example for other members of the organization. It will be more important to be committed to the learning *process* than to any particular solution to a problem. In the face of greater complexity, the leader's dependence on others to generate solutions will increase, and we have overwhelming evidence that new solutions are more likely to be adopted if the members of the organization have been involved in the learning process. The *process* of learning must ultimately be made part of the culture, not just the solution to any given problem.

2. Commitment to Learning to Learn

The learning culture must have in its DNA a "learning gene," in the sense that members must hold the shared assumption that learning is a good thing worth investing in and that learning to learn is itself a skill to be mastered. Learning must include not only learning about changes in the external environment but also learning about internal relationships and how well the organization is adapted to the external changes. For example, one way of understanding the failure of DEC is to note that they were committed to continued technological innovation—that is, learning in the technology area—but there was very little reflection or commitment to learning how their own organization was creating destructive intergroup competition. DEC did not learn that achieving truth through debate could only work at the interindividual level. Once the debate became an intergroup debate, truth seeking was undermined by the need to protect turf and people.

The key to learning is to get feedback and to take the time to reflect, analyze, and assimilate the implications of what the feedback has communicated. A further key to learning is the ability to generate new responses; to try new ways of doing things and to obtain feedback on the results of the new behavior. This takes time, energy, and resources. A learning culture must therefore value reflection and experimentation, and must give its members the time and resources to do it.

The learning leader must both believe in the power of learning and personally display an ability to learn, by seeking and accepting feedback and by displaying flexibility of response as conditions change.

3. Positive Assumptions About Human Nature

Learning leaders must have faith in people and must believe that ultimately human nature is basically good and, in any case, malleable. The learning leader must believe that humans can and will learn if they are provided the resources and the necessary psychological safety. Learning implies some desire for survival and improvement. If leaders start with assumptions that people are basically lazy and passive, that people have no concern for organizations or causes above and beyond themselves, they will inevitably create organizations that will become self-fulfilling prophecies. Such leaders will train their employees to be lazy, self-protective, and self-seeking, and they will then cite those characteristics as proof of their original assumption about human nature. The resulting control-oriented organizations may survive and even thrive in certain kinds of stable environments, but they are certain to fail as the environments become more turbulent and as technological and global trends cause problem solving to become increasingly more complex.

Knowledge and skill are becoming more widely distributed, forcing leaders—whether they like it or not—to be more dependent on other people in their organizations. Under such circumstances a cynical attitude toward human nature is bound to create, at best, bureaucratic rigidity and, at the worst extreme, counterorganizational subgroups. In either case, the learning process will be fatally undermined.

Given this hypothesis, one might speculate about why McGregor's (1960) insight into this problem in terms of Theory X (cynical mistrust of people) and Theory Y (idealistic trust of people) still has not taken hold, more than forty years after it was first promulgated. One hypothesis is that he was proposing the more idealistic Theory Y at a time when control-oriented bureaucracies were still working fairly effectively. The real relevance of Theory Y may well be to the learning organization of the future. It is inconceivable to me how a learning-oriented leader could have anything other than Theory Y assumptions about human nature and how an organization in which knowledge and skill are widely distributed can work on any basis other than mutual trust. And this takes us all the way back to Kurt Lewin's classic studies of classrooms under autocratic or democratic leaders (1947). The autocratic classes could match and even outdo the democratic ones in performance when the teacher was present, but if the teacher left, the autocratic ones fell apart, whereas the democratic ones reorganized and continued to perform.

4. The Assumption That the Environment Can Be Dominated

A learning culture must contain in its DNA a gene that reflects the shared assumption that the environment is to some degree manageable. An organization that assumes that it must symbiotically accept its niche will have more difficulty in learning as the environment becomes more turbulent. Adaptation to a slowly changing environment is also a viable learning process, but I am assuming that the way in which the world is changing will make that less and less possible. The more turbulent the environment, the more important it will be for leaders to argue for and show that some level of control over the environment is desirable and possible.

5. Commitment to Truth Through Pragmatism and Inquiry

A learning culture must contain the shared assumption that solutions to problems derive from a deep belief in inquiry and a pragmatic search for truth. The inquiry process itself must be flexible and reflect the nature of the environmental changes encountered. What must be avoided in the learning culture is the automatic assumption that wisdom and truth reside in any one source or method.

As the problems we encounter change, so too will our learning method have to change. For some purposes we will have to rely heavily on normal science; for others, we will have to find truth in experienced practitioners because scientific proof will be impossible to obtain; for still others, we will collectively have to experiment and live with errors until a better solution is found. Knowledge and skill will be found in many forms, and what I am calling a clinical research process—in which helpers and clients work things out together—will become more and more important because no one will be expert enough to provide an answer. One might say that in the learning organization one will have to *learn how to learn*.

The toughest problem for learning leaders is to come to terms with their own lack of expertise and wisdom. Once we are in a leadership position, our own needs and the expectations of others dictate that we know the answer and be in control of the situation. Yet if we provide answers, we are creating a culture that will inevitably take a moralistic position in regard to reality and truth. The only way to build a learning culture that continues to learn is for leaders themselves to realize that there is much that they do not know and must teach others to accept that there is much that they do not know. The learning task then becomes a shared responsibility.

It is also worth noting that in many cultures, notably Western ones, the assumption that one knows and is in control is particularly associated with masculine roles. It is quite possible that women will find it easier, as leaders, to accept a whole range of methods for arriving at solutions and will therefore be more able to function in a learning role. It is also worth noting that required sabbaticals and career development systems that require cross-functional and geographic rotational assignments were probably invented to maximize the learning potential of individual leaders, while the practice of limiting the term of office of leaders was invented to maximize the organization's ability to bring in new points of view and new modes of inquiry.

I am often asked how to make someone more sensitive to culture. My short answer is "*Travel* more." It is through giving ourselves more varied experiences in more different kinds of cultures that we learn about cultural variation and develop cultural humility. The learning leader should make it a point to spend a lot of time outside his or her organization and travel to as many other cultures as is practical.

6. Orientation Toward the Future

The optimal time orientation for learning appears to be somewhere between the far future and the near future. One must think far enough ahead to be able to assess the systemic consequences of different courses of action, but one must also think in terms of the near future to assess whether or not one's solutions are working. If the environment is becoming more turbulent, the assumption that the best orientation is to live in the past or to live in the present clearly seems dysfunctional.

A similar argument can be made about assumptions about optimal units of time—should we think primarily in terms of minutes, hours, days, months, quarters, years, decades? This will, of course, depend on the task and the kind of learning that is going on, but the optimal assumption is that one should pick medium-length time units for assessment: enough time to test whether a proposed solution is working but not so much time that one persists with a proposed solution that is clearly not working.

For any given task, the learning leader will have to make an instant diagnosis of what a medium length of time is, and that will vary from situation to situation. As the world becomes more complex we will be less and less able to rely on standard time units such as quarters or years. Because time has so many symbolic meanings and is so central to our daily conduct, the learning leader must be very conscious of her or his own assumptions about time and make these explicit for others.

7. Commitment to Full and Open Task Relevant Communication

The learning culture must be built on the assumption that communication and information are central to organizational well-being and must therefore create a multichannel communication system that allows everyone to connect to everyone else. This does not mean that all channels will be used or that any given channel will be used for all things. What it does mean is that anyone must be able to communicate with anyone else and that everyone assumes that telling the truth as best one can is positive and desirable.

This principle of openness does not mean that one suspends all the cultural rules pertaining to face and adopts a definition of openness equivalent to the proverbial "letting it all hang out"—there is ample evidence that such interpersonal openness can create severe problems across hierarchical boundaries and in intercultural settings. It means, rather, that one must become sensitive to *task-relevant information* and be as open as possible in sharing that. One of the important roles for the learning leader will be to specify, in terms of any given task, what the minimum communication system must be and what kind of information is critical to effective problem solving and learning. More information is not necessarily a good thing, because the more we know the more questions we develop about what we don't know. However, if a fully connected network ends up overloading everyone with information, certain channels can be voluntarily closed on a temporary basis. But the assumption that it is, in principle, possible and all right for anyone in the system to communicate with anyone else must remain in place.

A fully connected network can only work if high trust or at least high functional familiarity exists among all the participants. High trust is partly a function of leader assumptions that people can be trusted and have constructive intent. High functional familiarity is a function of the leader bringing interdependent people and units together often enough to allow them to become familiar with each other.

Creating an effective communication structure has implications for assumptions about space. The arrangement most likely to support learning is probably a flexible space structure that can be designed and redesigned as communication requirements change (Steele, 1973, 1986).

8. Commitment to Diversity

The more turbulent the environment, the more likely it is that the more diverse organization will have the resources to cope with unpredicted events. Therefore, the learning leader should stimulate diversity and promulgate the assumption that diversity is desirable at the individual and subgroup levels. Such diversity will inevitably create subcultures, and those subcultures will eventually be a necessary resource for learning and innovation.

For diversity to be a resource, however, the subcultures must be connected and must learn to value each other enough to learn something of each other's culture and language. A central task for the learning leader, then, is to ensure good cross-cultural communication and understanding throughout the organization. Creating diversity does not mean letting diverse parts of the system run on their own without coordination. Laissez-faire leadership does not work, because it is in the nature of subgroups and subcultures to protect their own interests. To optimize diversity therefore requires some higher-order coordination mechanisms and mutual cultural understanding.

9. Commitment to Systemic Thinking

As the world becomes more complex and interdependent, the ability to think systemically, to analyze fields of forces and understand their joint causal effects on each other, and to abandon simple linear causal logic in favor of complex mental models will become more critical to learning. There are many variations of systemic thinking, such as "systems thinking" as promulgated by Senge

(1990) and Sterman (2000), systemic thinking in biology, systemic thinking in family therapy, and so on. The learning leader must believe that the world is intrinsically complex, nonlinear, interconnected, and overdetermined in the sense that most things are multiply caused.

10. Commitment to Cultural Analysis for Understanding and Improving the World

The learning culture must understand the concept of culture and the learning leader must be willing and able to work with culture, as will be illustrated in the following case example.

Case Example: Saab Combitech

An excellent example of cultural intervention in the service of organizational learning is the 1997 seminar run by Saab Combitech, the R&D arm of the Saab company and its leader Per Risberg. Combitech consisted of seven separate research units working with different technologies such as developing complex training systems, military hardware, marine electronics, aerospace technology, and space exploration technology. These units had created their own subcultures based on their tasks, technologies and the occupations of their employees. The units were friendly to each other, but did not understand each other well enough to discover how they could all improve if they shared more of their technological and organizational insights.

Risberg recruited me to help him design an intervention that would teach the hundred or so members of these groups about culture and help them to become more familiar with each other's cultures. The groups were required to read portions of my culture book before the seminar and to write me a letter in which they were to compare themselves to DEC and Ciba-Geigy and write out some observations on their own culture.

On the first day I introduced the culture model, gave them more examples, and reviewed their self-analyses. We then had each group volunteer two of its members to become "anthropologists" who would go into one other group to learn what its culture was like. I provided some dimensions of the sort covered in Chapters Five through Nine and gave them several hours to visit, observe, and inquire about the group's artifacts, espoused values, and tacit assumptions. On the second day these observations were reported in a plenary session so that each group heard how it was perceived by its two anthropologists and we all became highly aware of both the communality and diversity of assumptions across the groups.

The third day was devoted to a systematic exploration, in the plenary session, of the ways in which the research units were interdependent and how they could help each other by sharing more of their technology and know-how. That evening Risberg hosted the attendees and their spouses at a final banquet, which began with formal cocktails and a sit-down dinner at long tables. It was very awkward because many of the Combitech people did not know each other very well; the spouses were uncomfortable and we all chafed at the prospect of a long dull evening.

However, after the first course Risberg asked us all to go to our rooms and follow instructions that we would find there. We found a box with some new clothing—tie-dyed shirts, loose pants, slippers, and headbands! We were to put on these clothes and report to the parking lot, where we found a huge audio setup. We were then instructed to line up for dance lessons provided by an instructor— several simple steps that all of us could master. The leader then played some rhythmic music and we practiced our steps until we were able to really do the dance and enjoy it. We could feel ourselves relaxing and getting to know each other at this more primitive level, so that by the time we had danced for twenty minutes and were instructed to go back into dinner, we were all chatting amicably.

Dinner was a big Indian buffet that required much moving around and further loosening up. By the end of the evening there was laughter, backslapping, exchanges of cards, and commitments to get together in the future. Risberg had created a "cultural" event that reinforced beautifully his intention of having his research groups get to know each other and work more with each other. Not only did the group learn about culture as a concept, but the design of the workshop used culture creatively by having the groups play at being "anthropologists."

Having us all change into informal "hippie clothes" and dance together was similar in intent to what Ciba-Geigy did when, during our annual meeting, we would all have to shoot crossbows or engage in some other sport that brought us all down to the same level. Risberg had realized that even though his organization had existed for many years, the members were not well acquainted with each other and needed some event to build commonality.

How Relevant Are Other Dimensions?

Many other dimensions could be analyzed from the point of view of what would aid or hinder learning. With respect to most of those, the conclusions are not clear. For example, with respect to the dimension of individualism and groupism it would appear that both kinds of systems can learn, but perhaps the best prescription for learning is to accept the notion that every system has both elements in it, and the learning culture will be the one that optimizes individual competition and collaborative teamwork, depending on the task to be accomplished. A similar argument can be made around the dimension of task versus relationship orientation. An optimal learning system would balance these as required by the task rather than opting for either extreme.

With respect to degree of hierarchy, autocracy, paternalism, and participation, it is again a matter of what kind of task, what kind of learning is required, and the particular circumstances. In the Alpha Power example we saw that knowledge of environmental hazards and how to deal with them was initially learned in a very autocratic, top-down training program, but as experience in the field accumulated, the learning process has shifted to local innovation, which is then circulated to the rest of the organization. Innovative solutions to environmental, health, and safety issues are captured in videotapes and circulated throughout the organization. Monthly award lunches are held, at which successful teams meet with senior management and each other to share "how they did it" and to communicate solutions to other teams.

In the end we have to recognize that even the concept of *learning* is heavily colored by cultural assumptions and that learning can mean very different things in different cultures and subcultures. The dimensions I listed above reflect only my own cultural understanding and should therefore be taken only as a first approximation of what a learning culture should emphasize.

As we do more research at the national, organizational, and subgroup levels, other dimensions will surface. It does seem obvious, however, that some conceptual clarity about how we get organizations to learn and—to learn faster—is becoming a priority issue, and that we cannot get such clarity without tackling the difficult conceptual problem of how a culture itself can be a perpetual learning system.

To summarize, the learning culture must assume that:

- The world can be managed
- It is appropriate for humans to be proactive problem solvers
- Reality and truth must be pragmatically discovered
- Human nature is basically good and in any case mutable
- The best kind of time horizon is somewhere between far and near future
- The best kinds of units of time are medium-length ones
- Accurate and relevant information must be capable of flowing freely in a fully connected network
- Diverse but connected units are desirable

And finally, the learning culture must assume that the world is intrinsically a complex field of interconnected forces in which multiple causation and overdetermination are more likely than linear or simple causes.

The role of learning-oriented leadership in a turbulent world, then, is to promote these kinds of assumptions. Leaders themselves must first hold such assumptions, become learners themselves, and then be able to recognize and systematically reward behavior based on those assumptions in others.

Programs such as total quality management can be assessed in terms of whether or not they operate on the assumptions outlined above. The overt and espoused values that are stated for such solutions often hide assumptions that are not, in fact, favorable to the kind of learning I have described. If leaders are not aware of the cultural underpinnings of what they are doing or the assumptions of the group on which they are imposing new solutions, they are likely to fail. Learning leaders must be careful to look inside themselves to locate their own mental models and assumptions before they leap into action.

The Role of the Learning Leader in Different Organizational Situations

Having described the generic characteristics of a learning culture and the implications in general for the learning leader, I now turn to some additional factors that affect the different stages of organizational evolution. The learning dilemma will be different at different cultural stages.

Leadership in Culture Creation

In a growing organization, leaders externalize their own assumptions and embed them gradually and consistently in the mission, goals, structures, and working procedures of the group. Whether we call these basic assumptions the guiding beliefs, the theories-in-use, the mental models, the basic principles, or the guiding visions on which founders operate, there is little question that they become major elements of the emerging culture of the organization.

In a rapidly changing world, the learning leader/founder must not only have vision, but also be able both to impose it and to evolve it further as external circumstances change. Inasmuch as the new members of an organization arrive with prior organizational and cultural experiences, a common set of assumptions can be forged only by clear and consistent messages as the group encounters and survives its own crises. The culture creation leader therefore needs persistence and patience, yet as a learner must be flexible and ready to change.

As groups and organizations develop, certain key emotional issues arise, concerning dependence on the leader, peer relationships, and how to work effectively. At each of these stages of group development, leadership is needed to help the group identify the issues and deal with them. During these stages leaders often have to absorb and contain the anxiety that is unleashed when things do not work as they should (Hirschhorn, 1988; Schein, 1983, Frost, 2003). The leader may not have the answer, but he or she must provide temporary stability and emotional reassurance while the answer is being worked out. This anxiety-containing function is especially relevant during periods of learning, when old habits and ways must be given up before new ones are learned. And if the world is becoming more changeable, such anxiety may be perpetual, requiring of the learning leader a perpetual supportive role.

This anxiety-containing function is especially relevant in entrepreneurs and founders of companies. The traumas of growth appear to be so constant and so powerful that unless a strong leader plays the role of anxiety- and risk-absorber, the group cannot get through its early stages of growth and fails. It helps to be in an ownership position, since everyone then realizes that the founder is in fact taking a greater personal financial risk, but ownership does not automatically create the ability to absorb anxiety. As Frost (2003) has shown so cogently, all organizations create toxins as part of their normal functions, so leaders must provide or create the toxin absorption and elimination function if their organizations are to be capable of learning.

The difficult learning agenda for founder leaders is how to be simultaneously clear and strong in articulating their vision and open to change as that very vision becomes maladaptive in a turbulent environment.

Leadership at Organizational Midlife

Once the organization develops a substantial history of its own, its culture becomes more of a cause than an effect. The culture now influences the strategy, the structure, the procedures, and the ways in which the group members will relate to each other. Culture becomes a powerful influence on members' perceiving, thinking, and feeling, and these predispositions, along with situational factors, will influence the members' behavior. Because it serves an important anxiety-reducing function, culture will be clung to even if it becomes dysfunctional in relationship to environmental opportunities and constraints.

Midlife organizations show two basically different patterns, however. Some, under the influence of one or more generations of leaders, develop a highly integrated culture even though they have become large and diversified; others allow growth and diversification in cultural assumptions as well and therefore can be described as culturally diverse with respect to their business, functional, geographical, and even hierarchical subunits. How leaders manage culture at this stage of organizational evolution depends on which pattern they perceive and which pattern they decide is best for the future.

Leaders at this stage need, above all, the insight and skill to help the organization evolve into whatever will make it most effective in the future. In some instances this may mean increasing cultural diversity, allowing some of the uniformity that may have been built up in the growth stage to erode; in other instances it may mean pulling together a culturally diverse set of organizational units and attempting to impose new common assumptions on them. In either case the leader needs to (1) be able to analyze the culture in sufficient detail to know which cultural assumptions can aid and which ones will hinder the fulfillment of the organizational mission and (2) have the intervention skills to make desired changes happen.

Most of the prescriptive analyses of how to bring organizations through this period emphasize that the leader must have certain insights, clear vision, and the skills to articulate, communicate, and implement the vision, but they say nothing about how a given organization can find and install such a leader. In U.S. organizations in particular, the outside board members probably play a critical role in this process, but if the organization has had a strong founding culture, its board may be composed exclusively of people who share the founder's vision. Consequently, real changes in direction may not become possible until the organization gets into serious survival difficulties and begins to search for a person with different assumptions to lead it.

Leadership in Mature and Declining Organizations

In the mature organization, if it has developed a strong unifying culture, that culture now defines even what is to be thought of as leadership, what is heroic or sinful behavior, and how authority and power are to be allocated and managed. Thus, what leadership has created now either blindly perpetuates itself or creates new definitions of leadership, which may not even include the kinds of entrepreneurial assumptions that started the organization in the first place. The first problem of the mature and possibly declining organization, then, is to find a process to empower a potential leader who may have enough insight and power to overcome some of the constraining cultural assumptions.

Leaders capable of such managed culture change can come from inside the organization, if they have acquired objectivity and insight into elements of the culture. However, the formally designated senior managers of a given organization may not be willing or able to provide such culture change leadership. If a leader is imposed from the outside, he or she must have the skill to diagnose accurately what the culture of the organization is, which elements are well adapted and which are problematic for future adaptation, and how to change that which needs changing.

Conceived of in this way, leadership is, first of all, the capacity to surmount one's own organizational culture, to be able to perceive and think about ways of doing things that are different from what the current assumptions imply. To fulfill this role adequately, learning leaders therefore must be somewhat marginal and somewhat embedded in the organization's external environment. At the same time, learning leaders must be well connected to those parts of the organization that are themselves well connected to the environment—the sales organization, purchasing, marketing, public relations, legal, finance, and R&D. Learning leaders must be able to listen to disconfirming information coming from these sources and to assess the implications for the future of the organization. Only when they truly understand what is happening and what will be required in the way of organizational change can they begin to take action in starting a learning process.

Much has been said of the need for vision in leaders, but too little has been said of their need to listen, to absorb, to search the environment for trends, and to build the organization's capacity to learn. It is especially at the strategic level that the ability to see and acknowledge the full complexity of problems becomes critical. The ability to acknowledge complexity may also imply the willingness and emotional strength to admit uncertainty and to embrace experimentation and possible errors as the only way to learn (Michael, 1985). In our obsession with leadership vision, we may have made it difficult for the learning leader to admit that his or her vision is not clear and that the whole organization together will have to learn. And, as I have repeatedly argued, vision only helps when the organization has already been disconfirmed and members feel anxious and in need of a solution. Much of what the learning leader must do occurs before vision even becomes relevant.

Leadership and Culture in Mergers and Acquisitions

When the management of a company decides to merge with or acquire another company, it usually makes careful checks of the financial strength, market position, management strength, and various other concrete aspects pertaining to the health of the other company. Rarely checked, however, are those aspects that might be considered cultural: the philosophy or style of the company, its technological origins, its structure, and its ways of operating—all of which may provide clues as to its basic assumptions about its mission and its future. Yet if culture determines and limits strategy, a cultural mismatch in an acquisition or merger is as great a risk as a financial, product, or market mismatch (Buono and Bowditch, 1989; COS, 1990; McManus and Hergert, 1988).

For example, at one point in its history General Foods (GF) purchased Burger Chef, a successful chain of hamburger restaurants; but despite ten years of concerted effort, GF could not make the acquisition profitable. First of all, GF did not anticipate that many of the best Burger Chef managers would leave because they did not like the GF philosophy. Then, instead of hiring new managers with experience in the fast-food business, GF assigned some of its own managers to run the new business. This was its second mistake, since these managers did not understand the technology of the fast-food business and hence were unable to utilize many of the marketing techniques that had proved effective in the parent company. Third, GF imposed many of the control systems and procedures that had historically proved useful for it; these drove the chain's operating costs up too high. The parent company's managers found that they could never completely understand franchise operations and hence could not get a feel for what it would take to run that kind of business profitably. Eventually GF sold Burger Chef, having lost many millions of dollars over the course of a decade.

Another example highlights the clash of two sets of assumptions about authority. A first-generation company, run by a founder who injected strong beliefs that one succeeds by stimulating initiative and egalitarianism, was bought by another first-generation company, which was run by a strong autocratic entrepreneur who had trained his employees to be highly disciplined and formal. The purchasing company wanted and needed the new managerial talent it acquired, but within one year of the purchase most of the best managers from the acquired company had left because they could not adapt to the formal autocratic style of the parent company. The autocratic entrepreneur could not understand why this had happened and had no sensitivity to the cultural differences between the two companies.

What is striking in both of these cases is the acquiring company's lack of insight into its own organizational culture; its own unconscious assumptions about how a business should be run.

In a third example, we see a case of cultural misdiagnosis. A U.S. company realized that it was about to be acquired by a larger British firm. The company conducted an internal audit of its own culture and concluded that being taken over by the British company would be highly unpalatable. It therefore instituted a set of procedures that made their company unattractive (such as poison pills) and waited for a situation that looked more promising. A French company came onto the scene as a potential buyer; it was perceived to be a much better cultural match, so the company allowed itself to be bought. Six months later the French parent sent over a management team that decimated the U.S. company and imposed all kinds of processes that were much less compatible than anything the U.S. company had imagined. But it was too late.

After mergers, acquisitions, or diversifications have run into trouble, managers frequently say that cultural incompatibilities were at the root of it, but somehow these factors rarely get taken into account during the initial decision-making process. What then is the role of leadership in these situations? Four critical tasks can be identified:

1. Leaders must understand their own culture well enough to be able to detect potential incompatibilities with the culture of the other organization.

2. Leaders must be able to decipher the other culture; to engage in the kinds of activities that will reveal to them and to the other organization what some of its assumptions are.

3. Leaders must be able to articulate the potential synergies or incompatibilities in such a way that others involved in the decision process can understand and deal with the cultural realities.

4. If the leader is not the CEO, he or she must be able to convince the CEO or the executive team to take the cultural issues seriously.

Members of planning groups or acquisition teams often develop the cross-cultural insights necessary to make good decisions about mergers and acquisitions, but lack the skills to convince their own senior managers to take the culture issues seriously. Or, alternatively, they get caught up in political processes that prevent the cultural realities from being attended to until after the key decisions have been made. In any case, cultural diagnosis based on marginality and the ability to surmount one's own culture again surfaces as the critical characteristic of learning leaders.

Leadership and Culture in Partnerships, Joint Ventures, and Strategic Alliances

Joint ventures and strategic alliances require cultural analysis even more than mergers and acquisitions, because in today's rapidly globalizing world, cross-national boundaries are increasingly involved. Deciphering differences between two companies in the same national culture is not as difficult as deciphering both national and company differences when one engages in a partnership or joint venture across national boundaries (Salk, 1997). One of the special difficulties is determining whether the differences that are perceived are attributable to national or organizational cultures, yet it is important to make this determination because one must assume that the likelihood of changing national characteristics is very low.

The role of learning leadership in these situations is much the same as in mergers and acquisitions, except that leaders must even surmount their national identities. For example, Essochem Europe, the European subsidiary of Exxon, could never find local managers to put on their board because they were all "too emotional." They never came to terms with their own stereotype of managers as intrinsically unemotional sorts of people, and never realized or accepted that this was based on their U.S. assumptions. Many organizations make international assignments a requirement for a developing general manager, with the explicit notion that such experiences is essential if potential leaders with broader outlooks are to surface. In other words, the learning leader must become marginal not only with respect to the organizational culture, but even with respect to national and ethnic culture.

Implications for the Selection and Development of Leaders

To summarize at this point, our analysis of organizational culture makes it clear that leadership is intertwined with culture formation, evolution, transformation, and destruction. Culture is created in the first instance by the actions of leaders; culture also is embedded and strengthened by leaders. When culture becomes dysfunctional, leadership is needed to help the group unlearn some of its cultural assumptions and learn new assumptions. Such transformations sometimes require what amounts to conscious and deliberate destruction of cultural elements, which in turn requires the ability to surmount one's own taken-for-granted assumptions, to see what is needed to ensure the health and survival of the group, and to make things happen that enable the group to evolve toward new cultural assumptions. Without leadership in this sense, groups would not be able to adapt to changing environmental conditions. What, then, is really needed to be a leader in this sense?

1. Perception and Insight

First, the leader must be able to perceive the problem, to have insight into the culture and its dysfunctional elements. Such boundary-spanning perception can be difficult because it requires one to see one's own weaknesses, to perceive that one's own defenses not only help in managing anxiety but can also hinder one's efforts to be effective. Successful architects of change must have a high degree of objectivity about themselves and their own organizations; such objectivity results from spending portions of their careers in diverse settings that permit them to compare and contrast different cultures. In the development of future leaders, many organizations are therefore emphasizing international experience.

Individuals often are aided in becoming objective about themselves through counseling and psychotherapy. One might conjecture that leaders could benefit from comparable processes, such as training and development programs that emphasize experiential learning and self-assessment. From this perspective one should also note that one of the most important functions of outside consultants or board members is to provide the kind of counseling that produces cultural insight. It is therefore far more important for the consultant to help the leader figure himself or herself out than to provide recommendations on what the organization should do. The consultant also can serve as a "cultural therapist," helping the leader figure out what the culture is and which parts of it are more or less adaptive.

To become learning oriented, leaders also need to acknowledge their own limitations. As the world becomes more turbulent, it will be more and more difficult to develop clear visions. Instead, leaders will have to admit to not knowing the answer, to admit to not being in control, to embrace trial-and-error learning, and to become supportive of the learning efforts of others.

2. Motivation

Leadership requires not only insight into the dynamics of the culture but also the motivation and skill to intervene in one's own cultural process. To change any elements of the culture, leaders must be willing to unfreeze their own organization. Unfreezing requires disconfirmation, a process that is inevitably painful for many. The leader must find a way to say to his or her own organization that things are not all right and must, if necessary, enlist the aid of outsiders in getting this message across. Such willingness requires a great ability to be concerned for the organization above and beyond the self, to communicate dedication or commitment to the group above and beyond self-interest.

If the boundaries of organizations become looser, a further motivational issue arises in that it is less and less clear where a leader's ultimate loyalty should lie—should it be with the organization, the industry, the country, or some broader professional community whose ultimate responsibility is to the globe and to humanity in some broader sense?

3. Emotional Strength

Unfreezing an organization requires the creation of psychological safety, which means that the leader must have the emotional strength to absorb much of the anxiety that change brings with it as well as the ability to remain supportive to the organization through the transition phase, even if group members become angry and obstructive. The leader is likely to be the target of anger and criticism because, by definition, he or she must challenge some of what the group has taken for granted. This may involve such powerful symbolic acts as closing down a division in the company that was the original source of the company's growth and the basis of many employees' pride and identity. It may involve laying off or retiring loyal, dedicated employees and old friends. Worst of all, it may involve the message that some of the founder's most cherished assumptions are wrong in the contemporary context. It is here that dedication and commitment are especially needed to demonstrate to the organization that the leader genuinely cares about the welfare of the total organization even as parts of it come under challenge. The learning leader must remember that giving up a cultural element requires one to take some risk—the risk that one will be very anxious and, in the end, worse off, yet must have the strength to push into this unknown territory.

4. Ability to Change the Cultural Assumptions

If an assumption is to be given up, it must be replaced or redefined in another form, and it is the burden of learning leadership to make that happen. In other words, leaders must have the ability to induce "cognitive redefinition" by articulating and selling new visions and concepts or creating the conditions for others to find these new concepts. They must be able to bring to the surface, review, and change some of the group's basic assumptions. At Ciba-Geigy this process had only begun in the redirection project described in Chapter Eighteen. Many managers were beginning to doubt that the organization's commitment to science-based technical products could sustain the company in the long run. But so far no strong leader had emerged to convince the organization that consumer goods marketed through strong customer-oriented organizations could be a source of pride for the company.

5. Ability to Create Involvement and Participation

A paradox of learning leadership is that the leader must be able not only to lead but also to listen, to involve the group in achieving its own insights into its cultural dilemmas, and to be genuinely participative in his or her approach to learning and change. The leaders of social, religious, or political movements can rely on personal charisma and let the followers do what they will. But in an organization, the leader has to work with the group that exists at the moment, because he or she is dependent on the people to carry out the organization's mission. The leader must recognize that, in the end, cognitive redefinition must occur inside the heads of many members of the organization, and that will happen only if they are actively involved in the process. The whole organization must achieve some degree of insight and develop motivation to change before any real change will occur—and the leader must create this involvement.

The ability to involve others and to listen to them also protects leaders from attempting to change things that should not be changed. When leaders are brought in from the outside this becomes critical, because some of the assumptions operating in the organization may not fit the leader's own assumptions yet may still be critical to the success of the organization.

Summary and Conclusions

I have tried to articulate in this chapter the characteristics of a *learning culture* and the implications for leadership of the realities of creating such a culture in an increasingly turbulent and unpredictable world. I reviewed the culture change issues at the major stages of organizational development and focused on the leadership role in developing strategy, in mergers and acquisitions, and in joint ventures and strategic alliances.

It seems clear that the leader of the future must be a perpetual learner, which will require (1) new levels of perception and insight into the realities of the world and into him- or herself; (2) extraordinary levels of motivation to go through the inevitable pain of learning and change, especially in a world with looser boundaries in which one's own loyalties become more and more difficult to define; (3) the emotional strength to manage one's own and others' anxiety as learning and change become more and more a way of life; (4) new skills in analyzing and changing cultural assumptions; and (5) the willingness and ability to involve others and elicit their participation.

Learning and change cannot be imposed on people. Their involvement and participation is needed in diagnosing what is going on, in figuring out what to do, and in actually bringing about learning and change. The more turbulent, ambiguous, and out of control the world becomes, the more the learning process must be shared by all the members of the social unit doing the learning.

In the end, we must give organizational culture its due. Can we recognize—as individual members of organizations and occupations, as managers, as teachers and researchers, and sometimes as leaders— how deeply our own perceptions, thoughts, and feelings are culturally determined? Ultimately, we cannot achieve the cultural humility that is required to live in a turbulent culturally diverse world unless we can see cultural assumptions within ourselves. In the end, cultural understanding and cultural learning starts with self-insight.

References

Academy of Management Review, "Special Topic Forum on Time and Organizational Research," 26(4), Oct. 2001.

Adorno, T., & others (1950). *The authoritarian personality.* New York: HarperCollins.

Allan, J., Fairtlough, G., & Heinzen, B. (2002). *The power of the tale.* London: Wiley.

Ancona, D. G. (1988). Groups in organizations. In C. Hendrick (Ed.), *Annual review of personality and social psychology: Group and intergroup processes.* Thousand Oaks, CA: Sage.

Ancona, D. G., & Chong, C. L. (1996). Entrainment: Pace, cycle, and rhythm in organizational behavior. In B. M. Staw & L. L. Cummings (Eds.), *Research in organizational behavior* (Vol. 18, pp. 251–284). Greenwich, CT: JAI Press.

Argyris, C. (1964). *Integrating the individual and the organization.* New York: Wiley.

Argyris, C. (1976). *Increasing leadership effectiveness.* New York: Wiley-Interscience.

Argyris, C., Putnam, R., & Smith, D. M. (1985). *Action science.* San Francisco, CA: Jossey-Bass.

Argyris, C., & Schön, D. A. (1974). *Theory in practice: increasing professional effectiveness.* San Francisco, CA: Jossey-Bass.

Argyris, C., & Schön, D. A. (1978). *Organizational learning.* Reading, MA: Addison-Wesley.

Ashkanasy, N. M., Wilderom, C.P.M., & Peterson, M. F. (Eds.) (2000). *Handbook of organizational culture and climate.* Thousand Oaks, CA: Sage.

Bailyn, L. (1978). Accommodation of work to family. In R. Rapoport & R. N. Rapoport (Eds.), *Working couples.* London: Routledge Kegan Paul.

Bailyn, L. (1982). The apprenticeship model of organizational careers: A response to changes in the relationship between work and family. In P. A. Wallace (Ed.), *Women in the workplace.* Boston: Auburn House.

Bailyn, L. (1985). Autonomy in the industrial R&D lab. *Human Resource Management, 24,* 129–146.

Bailyn, L. (1992). Changing the conditions of work: Implications for career development. In D. H. Montross & C. J. Shinkman (Eds.), *Career development in the 1990s: Theory and practice.* Springfield, IL: Thomas.

Bailyn, L. (1993). *Breaking the mold*. New York: Free Press.

Barley, S. R. (1984a). The professional, the semi-professional, and the machine: The social implications of computer based imaging in radiology. Unpublished doctoral dissertation, Sloan School of Management, MIT.

Barley, S. R. (1984b). *Technology as an occasion for structuration: Observations on CT scanners and the social order of radiology departments*. Cambridge, MA: Sloan School of Management, MIT.

Barley, S. R. (1988). On technology, time, and social order. In F. A. Dubinskas (Ed.), *Making time*. Philadelphia: Temple University Press, 145.

Bartunek, J. (1984). Changing interpretive schemes and organizational restructuring: The example of a religious order. *Administrative Science Quarterly, 29*, 355-372.

Bass, B. M. (1981). *Stogdill's handbook of leadership* (rev. ed.). New York: Free Press.

Bass, B. M. (1985). *Leadership and performance beyond expectations*. New York: Free Press.

Beckhard, R., & Dyer, W. G., Jr. (1983a). Managing continuity in the family-owned business. *Organizational Dynamics*, Summer, 5–12.

Beckhard, R., & Dyer, W. G., Jr. (1983b). Managing change in the family firm: Issues and strategies. *Sloan Management Review, 24*(3), 59–65.

Beckhard, R., & Harris, R. T. (1987). *Organizational transitions: Managing complex change*. Reading, MA: Addison-Wesley.

Bennis, W., & Nanus, B. (1985). *Leaders*. New York: HarperCollins.

Bennis, W. G., & Shepard, H. A. (1956). A theory of group development. *Human Relations, 9*, 415–437.

Berg, P. O., & Kreiner, C. (1990). Corporate architecture: Turning physical settings into symbolic resources. In P. Gagliardi (Ed.), *Symbols and artifacts*. Hawthorne, NY: Walter de Gruyter.

Bion, W. R. (1959). *Experiences in groups*. London: Tavistock.

Blake, R. R., & Mouton, J. S. (1964). *The managerial grid*. Houston: Gulf.

Blake, R. R. & Mouton, J. S. (1969). *Building a dynamic organization through grid organization development*. Reading, MA: Addison-Wesley.

Blake, R. R., Mouton, J. S., & McCanse, A. A. (1989). *Change by design*. Reading, MA: Addison-Wesley.

Bluedorn, A. C. (1997). Primary rhythms, information processing, and planning: Toward a strategic temporal technology. *Technology Studies, 4*, 1–36.

Bluedorn, A. C. (2000). Time and organizational culture. In N. M. Ashkanazy, C.P.M. Wilderom, & M. F. Peterson (Eds.), *Handbook of organizational culture and climate*. Thousand Oaks, CA: Sage.

Bradford, L. P., Gibb, J. R., & Benne, K. D. (Eds.) (1964). *T-group theory and laboratory method*. New York: Wiley.

Buono, A. F., & Bowditch, J. L. (1989). *The human side of mergers and acquisitions*. San Francisco: Jossey-Bass.

Butterfield, F. (1982). *China, alive in the bitter sea*. New York: Times Books.

Cameron, K. S., & Quinn, R. E. (1999). *Diagnosing and changing organizational culture*. Reading, MA: Addison-Wesley.

Castaneda, C. (1968). *The teachings of Don Juan*. New York: Pocket Books.

Castaneda, C. (1972). *Journey to Ixtlan*. New York: Simon & Schuster.

Ciampa, D. (1992). *Total quality: A user's guide for implementation*. Reading, MA: Addison-Wesley.

Coghlan, D. (1996). Mapping the progress of change through organizational levels. *Research in Organizational Change and Development*, 9, 123–150.

Collins, J. C., & Porras, J. I. (1994). *Built to last*. New York: HarperBusiness.

Conger, J. A. (1989). *The charismatic leader*. San Francisco, CA: Jossey-Bass.

Cook, S.D.N., & Yanow, D. (1993). Culture and organizational learning. *Journal of Management Inquiry*, 2(4), 373–390.

COS (Centre for Organizational Studies) (1990). *Mergers and acquisitions: Organizational and cultural issues*. Barcelona, Spain: COS/Foundation Jose M. de Anzizu.

Dandridge, T. C., Mitroff, I. I., & Joyce, W. (1980). Organizational symbolism: A topic to expand organizational analysis. *Academy of Management Review*, 5(1), 77–82.

Davis, S. M. (1984). *Managing corporate culture*. Cambridge, MA: Ballinger.

Davis, S., & Davidson, B. (1991). *2020 vision*. New York: Simon & Schuster.

Deal, T. E., & Kennedy, A. A. (1982). *Corporate cultures*. Reading, MA: Addison-Wesley.

Deal, T. E., & Kennedy, A. A. (1999). *The new corporate cultures*. New York: Perseus.

Denison, D. R. (1990). *Corporate culture and organizational effectiveness*. New York: Wiley.

Donaldson, G., & Lorsch, J. W. (1983). *Decision making at the top*. New York: Basic Books.

Dougherty, D. (1990). Understanding new markets for new products. *Strategic Management Journal*, 11, 59–78.

Douglas, M. (1986). *How institutions think*. Syracuse, NY: Syracuse University Press.

Dubinskas, F. A. (1988). *Making time: Ethnographies of high-technology organizations*. Philadelphia: Temple University Press.

Dyer, W. G., Jr. (1986). *Culture change in family firms*. San Francisco, CA: Jossey-Bass.

Dyer, W. G., Jr. (1989). Integrating professional management into a family-owned business. *Family Business Review*, 2(3), 221–236.

England, G. (1975). *The manager and his values*. Cambridge, MA: Ballinger.

Etzioni, A. (1975). *A comparative analysis of complex organizations*. New York: Free Press.

Festinger, L. A. (1957). *Theory of cognitive dissonance*. New York: HarperCollins.

Forrester, J. (1969). *Urban dynamics*. Cambridge, MA: MIT Press.

Frost, P. J. (2003). *Toxic emotions at work*. Boston: Harvard Business School Press.

Gagliardi, P. (Ed.) (1990). *Symbols and artifacts: Views of the corporate landscape*. New York: Walter de Gruyter.

Geertz, C. (1973). *The interpretation of cultures*. New York: Basic Books.

Gersick, C.J.C. (1991). Revolutionary change theories: A multilevel exploration of the punctuated equilibrium paradigm. *Academy of Management Review, 16*, 10–36.

Gerstein, M. S. (1987). *The technology connection: Strategy and change in the information age*. Reading, MA: Addison-Wesley.

Global Business Network (2002). *What's next? Exploring the new terrain for business*. Cambridge, MA: Perseus Books.

Goffee, R., & Jones, G. (1998). *The character of a corporation*. New York: Harper Business.

Goffman, E. (1959). *The presentation of self in everyday life*. New York: Doubleday.

Goffman, E. (1961). *Asylums*. New York: Doubleday Anchor.

Goffman, E. (1967). *Interaction ritual*. Hawthorne, NY: Aldine.

Grenier, R., & Metes, G. (1992). *Enterprise networking: Working together apart*. Maynard, MA: Digital Press.

Hall, E. T. (1959). *The silent language*. New York: Doubleday.

Hall, E. T. (1966). *The hidden dimension*. New York: Doubleday.

Hall, E. T. (1977). *Beyond culture*. New York: Doubleday.

Hampden-Turner, C., & Trompenaars, A. (1993). *The seven cultures of capitalism*. New York: Doubleday Currency.

Hampden-Turner, C. M., & Trompenaars, F. (2000). *Building cross-cultural competence*. New York: Wiley.

Hanna, D. P. (1988). *Designing organizations for high performance*. Reading, MA.: Addison-Wesley.

Harbison, F., & Myers, C. A. (1959). *Management in the industrial world*. New York: McGraw-Hill.

Hatch, M. J. (1990). The symbolics of office design. In P. Gagliardi (Ed.), *Symbols and artifacts*. New York: Walter de Gruyter.

Havrylyshyn, B. (1980). *Road maps to the future*. Oxford, England: Pergamon Press.

Henderson, R. M., & Clark, K. B. (1990). Architectural innovation: The reconfiguration of existing product technologies and the failure of established firms. *Administrative Science Quarterly, 35*, 9–30.

Herzberg, F. (1968). One more time: How do you motivate employees? *Harvard Business Review*, Jan.–Feb., 53–62.

Hesselbein, F., Goldsmith, M., & Somerville, I. (Eds.). (1999). *Leading beyond the walls*. San Francisco, CA: Jossey-Bass.

Hirschhorn, L. (1988). *The workplace within: Psychodynamics of organizational life*. Cambridge, MA: MIT Press.

Hofstede, G. (1991). *Cultures and organizations*. London: McGraw-Hill.

Hofstede, G. (2001). *Culture's consequences* (2nd ed.). Thousand Oaks, CA: Sage (1st ed. 1980).

Hofstede, G., & Bond, M. H. (1988). The Confucius connection: From cultural roots to economic growth. *Organizational Dynamics, 16*(4), 4–21.

Holland, J. L. (1985). *Making vocational choices* (2nd ed.). Englewood Cliffs, NJ: Prentice Hall.

Homans, G. (1950). *The human group*. New York: Harcourt Brace Jovanovich.

Jaques, E. (1982). *The forms of time*. London: Heinemann.

Jaques, E. (1989). *Requisite organization*. Arlington, VA: Cason Hall.

Johansen, R., & others (1991). *Leading business teams*. Reading, MA: Addison Wesley.

Jones, G. R. (1983). Transaction costs, property rights, and organizational culture: An exchange perspective. *Administrative Science Quarterly, 28*, 454–467.

Jones, M. O., Moore, M. D., & Snyder, R. C. (Eds.). (1988). *Inside organizations*. Thousand Oaks, CA: Sage.

Kets de Vries, M.F.R., & Miller, D. (1984). *The neurotic organization: Diagnosing and changing counterproductive styles of management*. San Francisco, CA: Jossey-Bass.

Kets de Vries, M.F.R., & Miller, D. (1987). *Unstable at the top: Inside the troubled organization*. New York: New American Library.

Kilmann, R. H., & Saxton, M. J. (1983). *The Kilmann-Saxton culture gap survey*. Pittsburgh, PA: Organizational Design Consultants.

Kleiner, A. (2003). *Who really matters*. New York: Doubleday Currency.

Kluckhohn, F. R., & Strodtbeck, F. L. (1961). *Variations in value orientations*. New York: HarperCollins.

Koprowski, E. J. (1983). Cultural myths: Clues to effective management. *Organizational Dynamics*, Autumn, 39–51.

Kotter, J. P., & Heskett, J. L. (1992). *Culture and performance*. New York: Free Press.

Kunda, G. (1992). *Engineering culture*. Philadelphia, PA: Temple University Press.

Kuwada, K. (1991). Strategic learning. Graduate School of Business, Stanford University, Research Paper No. 1121, January.

Lawrence, P. R., & Lorsch, J. W. (1967). *Organization and environment*. Boston: Harvard Graduate School of Business Administration.

Leavitt, H. J. (1986). *Corporate pathfinders*. Homewood, IL: Dow Jones-Irwin.

Lewin, K. (1947). Group decision and social change. In T. N. Newcomb & E. L. Hartley (Eds.), *Readings in social psychology*. New York: Holt, Rinehart and Winston.

Lewis, G. (1988). *Corporate strategy in action: The strategy process in British road services*. London: Routledge.

Likert, R. (1967). *The human organization*. New York: McGraw-Hill.

Lorsch, J. W. (1985). Strategic myopia: Culture as an invisible barrier to change. In R. H. Kilmann, M. J. Saxton, R. Serpa, and associates, *Gaining control of the corporate culture*. San Francisco, CA: Jossey-Bass.

Louis, M. R. (1980). Surprise and sense making. *Administrative Science Quarterly, 25*, 226–251.

Louis, M. R. (1981). A cultural perspective on organizations. *Human Systems Management, 2*, 246–258.

Louis, M. R. (1983). Organizations as culture bearing milieux. In L. R. Pondy & others (Eds.), *Organizational symbolism*. Greenwich, CT: JAI Press.

Malone, T., et al. (1987). Electronic markets and electronic hierarchies. *Communications of the ACM, 30*, 484–497.

Martin, J. (1982). Stories and scripts in organizational settings. In A. Hastorf & A. Isen (Eds.), *Cognitive social psychology*. New York: Elsevier.

Martin, J. (1991). A personal journey: From integration to differentiation to fragmentation to feminism. In P. Frost & others (Eds.), *Reframing organizational culture*. Thousand Oaks, CA: Sage.

Martin, J. (2002). *Organizational culture: Mapping the terrain*. Thousand Oaks, CA: Sage.

Martin, J., & Powers, M. E. (1983). Truth or corporate propaganda: The value of a good war story. In L. R. Pondy & others (Eds.), *Organizational symbolism*. Greenwich, CT: JAI Press.

Maruyama, M. (1974). Paradigmatology and its application to cross-disciplinary, cross-professional, and cross-cultural communication. *Dialectica, 28*, 135–196.

Maslow, A. (1954). *Motivation and personality*. New York: HarperCollins.

McGregor, D. M. (1960). *The human side of enterprise*. New York: McGraw-Hill.

McManus, M. L., & Hergert, M. L. (1988). *Surviving merger and acquisition*. Glenview, IL: Scott Foresman.

Merton, R. K. (1957). *Social theory and social structure* (Rev. ed.). New York: Free Press.

Michael, D. N. (1985). *On learning to plan—and planning to learn*. San Francisco, CA: Jossey-Bass.

Michael, D. N. (1991). Leadership's shadow: The dilemma of denial. *Futures*, Jan./Feb., 69–79.

Miller, D. (1990). *The Icarus paradox*. New York: HarperCollins.

Mitroff, I. I., & Kilmann, R. H. (1975). Stories managers tell: A new tool for organizational problem solving. *Management Review, 64*(7), 18–28.

Mitroff, I. I., & Kilmann, R. H. (1976). On organizational stories: An approach to the design and analysis of organizations through myths and stories. In R. H. Kilmann, L. R. Pondy, & L. Sleven (Eds.), *The management of organization design*. New York: Elsevier.

Neuhauser, P. C. (1993). *Corporate legends and lore*. Austin, TX: Peg. C. Neuhauser.

Onken, M. (1999). Temporal elements of organizational culture and impact on firm performance. *Journal of Managerial Psychology, 14*, 231–243.

Ouchi, W. G. (1981). *Theory Z*. Reading, MA: Addison-Wesley.

Ouchi, W. G., & Johnson, J. (1978). Types of organizational control and their relationship to emotional well-being. *Administrative Science Quarterly, 23*, 293–317.

Packard, D. (1995). *The HP way*. New York: HarperCollins.

Parsons, T. (1951). *The social system*. New York: Free Press.

Pascale, R. T., & Athos, A. G. (1981). *The art of Japanese management*. New York: Simon & Schuster.

Pasmore, W. A., & Sherwood, J. J. (eds.) (1978). *Sociotechnical systems: A sourcebook*. La Jolla, CA: University Associates.

Pava, C.H.P. (1983). *Managing new office technology*. New York: Free Press.

Perin, C. (1991). The moral fabric of the office. In S. Bacharach, S. R. Barley, & P. S. Tolbert (Eds.), *Research in the sociology of organizations* (special volume on the professions). Greenwich, CT: JAI Press.

Peters, T. J. (1987). *Thriving on chaos*. New York: Knopf.

Peters, T. J., & Waterman, R. H., Jr. (1982). *In search of excellence*. New York: HarperCollins.

Pettigrew, A. M. (1979). On studying organizational cultures. *Administrative Science Quarterly, 24*, 570–581.

Pondy, L. R., Frost, P. J., Morgan, G., & Dandridge, T. (Eds.). (1983). *Organizational symbolism*. Greenwich, CT: JAI Press.

Porras, J., & Collins, J. (1994). *Built to last*. New York: HarperBusiness.

Redding, S. G., & Martyn-Johns, T. A. (1979). Paradigm differences and their relation to management, with reference to Southeast Asia. In G. W. England, A. R. Neghandi, & B. Wilpert (Eds.), *Organizational functioning in a cross-cultural perspective*. Kent, Ohio: Comparative Administration Research Unit, Kent State University.

Rice, A. K. (1963). *The enterprise and its environment*. London: Tavistock.

Ritti, R. R., & Funkhouser, G. R. (1987). *The ropes to skip and the ropes to know*. Columbus, OH: Grid (3rd ed.; 1st ed. 1982).

Rockart, J. F., & DeLong, D. W. (1988). *Executive support systems*. Homewood, IL: Dow Jones-Irwin.

Roethlisberger, F. J., & Dickson, W. J. (1939). *Management and the worker*. Cambridge, MA: Harvard University Press.

Sahlins, M. (1985). *Islands of history*. Chicago: University of Chicago Press.

Sahlins, M., & Service, E. R. (Eds.) (1960). *Evolution and culture*. Ann Arbor: University of Michigan Press.

Salk, J. (1997). Partners and other strangers. *International Studies of Management and Organization, 26*(4), 48–72.

Savage, C. M. (1990). *Fifth generation management: Integrating enterprises through human networking*. Maynard, MA: Digital Press.

Schein, E. H. (1961a). *Coercive persuasion*. New York: Norton.

Schein, E. H. (1961b). Management development as a process of influence. *Industrial Management Review (MIT), 2*, 59–77.

Schein, E. H. (1964). Personal change through interpersonal relationships. In W. G. Bennis, E. H. Schein, D. E. Berlew, & F. I. Steele (Eds.), *Interpersonal dynamics*. Homewood, IL: Dorsey, 357–394.

Schein, E. H. (1968). Organizational socialization and the profession of management. *Industrial Management Review, 9*, 1–15.

Schein, E. H. (1969). *Process consultation: Its role in organization development*. Reading, MA: Addison-Wesley.

Schein, E. H. (1971). The individual, the organization, and the career: A conceptual scheme. *Journal of Applied Behavioral Science, 7*, 401–426.

Schein, E. H. (1972). *Professional education: Some new directions*. New York: McGraw-Hill.

Schein, E. H. (1978). *Career dynamics: Matching individual and organizational needs*. Reading, MA: Addison-Wesley.

Schein, E. H. (1980). *Organizational psychology* (3rd ed.). Englewood Cliffs, NJ: Prentice Hall (1st ed. 1965).

Schein, E. H. (1983). The role of the founder in creating organizational culture. *Organizational Dynamics*, Summer, 13–28.

Schein, E. H. (1987a). *The clinical perspective in fieldwork*. Thousand Oaks, CA: Sage.

Schein, E. H. (1987b). Individuals and careers. In J. W. Lorsch (Ed.), *Handbook of organizational behavior*. Englewood Cliffs, NJ: Prentice Hall.

Schein, E. H. (1988). *Process consultation: Vol. 1. Its role in organization development* (2nd ed.). Reading, MA: Addison-Wesley.

Schein, E. H. (1990). Innovative cultures and adaptive organizations. *Sri Lanka Journal of Development Administration*, 7(2), 9–39.

Schein, E. H. (1992). The role of the CEO in the management of change. In T. A. Kochan & M. Useem (Eds.), *Transforming organizations*. New York: Oxford University Press.

Schein, E. H. (1993a). On dialogue, culture, and organizational learning. *Organizational Dynamics*, Autumn, 22, 40–51.

Schein, E. H. (1993b). *Career anchors* (revised). San Diego, CA: Pfeiffer (Jossey-Bass).

Schein, E. H. (1995). *Career survival*. San Francisco, CA: Jossey-Bass.

Schein, E. H. (1996a). Three cultures of management: The key to organizational learning. *Sloan Management Review*, 38, 1, 9–20.

Schein, E. H. (1996b). *Strategic pragmatism: The culture of Singapore's Economic Development Board*. Cambridge, MA: MIT Press.

Schein, E. H. (1999a). *Process consultation revisited*. Englewood Cliffs, NJ: Prentice Hall.

Schein, E. H. (1999b). *The corporate culture survival guide*. San Francisco, CA: Jossey-Bass.

Schein, E. H. (2001). Clinical inquiry/research. In P. Reason & H. Bradbury (Eds.), *Handbook of action research*. San Anselmo, CA: Sage Press, 228–237.

Schein, E. H. (2003). *DEC is dead; long live DEC*. San Francisco, CA: Berrett-Koehler.

Schein, E. H., & Bennis, W. G. (1965). *Personal and organizational change through group methods*. New York: Wiley.

Schneider, B. (Ed.) (1990). *Organizational climate and culture*. San Francisco, CA: Jossey-Bass.

Schultz, M. (1995). *On studying organizational cultures*. New York: Walter de Gruyter.

Schwartz, P. (2003). *Inevitable surprises*. New York: Gotham Books.

Senge, P. M. (1990). *The fifth discipline*. New York: Doubleday Currency.

Senge, P. M., Roberts, C., Ross, R. B., Smith, B. J., & Kleiner, A. (1994). *The fifth discipline field book*. New York: Doubleday Currency.

Shrivastava, P. (1983). A typology of organizational learning systems. *Journal of Management Studies, 20*, 7–28.

Sithi-Amnuai, P. (1968). The Asian mind. *Asia*, Spring, 78–91.

Smircich, L. (1983) Concepts of culture and organizational analysis. *Administrative Science Quarterly, 28*, 339-358.

Sorensen, J. B. (2002). The strength of corporate culture and the reliability of firm performance. *Administrative Science Quarterly, 47*, 70–91.

Steele, F. I. (1973). *Physical settings and organization development*. Reading, MA: Addison-Wesley.

Steele, F. I. (1981). *The sense of place*. Boston: CBI Publishing.

Steele, F. I. (1986). *Making and managing high-quality workplaces*. New York: Teachers College Press.

Sterman, J. D. (2000). *Business dynamics: Systems thinking and modeling for a complex world*. New York: McGraw-Hill/Irwin.

Steward, J. H. (1955). *Theory of culture change*. Urbana: University of Illinois Press.

Tagiuri, R., & Litwin, G. H. (Eds.) (1968). *Organizational climate: Exploration of a concept*. Boston: Division of Research, Harvard Graduate School of Business.

Tichy, N. M., & Devanna, M. A. (1986). *The transformational leader*. New York: Wiley

Trice, H. M., & Beyer, J. M. (1984). Studying organizational cultures through rites and ceremonials. *Academy of Management Review, 9*, 653–669.

Trice, H. M., & Beyer, J. M. (1985). Using six organizational rites to change culture. In R. H. Kilmann, M. J. Saxton, R. Serpa, and associates. *Gaining control of the corporate culture*. San Francisco, CA: Jossey-Bass, 370–399.

Trice, H. M., & Beyer, J. M. (1993). *The cultures of work organizations*. Englewood Cliffs, NJ: Prentice Hall.

Trist, E. L., and others (1963). *Organizational choice*. London: Tavistock.

Turquet, P. M. (1973). Leadership: The individual and the group. In G. S. Gibbard, J. J. Hartman, & R. D. Mann (Eds.), *Analysis of groups: Contributions to theory, research, and practice*. San Francisco, CA: Jossey-Bass.

Tushman, M. L., & Anderson, P. (1986). Technological discontinuities and organizational environments. *Administrative Science Quarterly, 31*, 439–465.

Van Maanen, J. (1976). Breaking in: Socialization at work. In R. Dubin (Ed.), *Handbook of work organization and society*. Skokie, IL.: Rand McNally.

Van Maanen, J. (1977). Experiencing organizations. In J. Van Maanen (Ed.), *Organizational careers: Some new perspectives*. New York: Wiley.

Van Maanen, J. (1979a). The fact of fiction in organizational ethnography. *Administrative Science Quarterly, 24*, 539–550.

Van Maanen, J. (1979b). The self, the situation, and the rules of interpersonal relations. In W. Bennis and others, *Essays in interpersonal dynamics*. Florence, KY: Dorsey Press.

Van Maanen, J. (1988). *Tales of the field: On writing ethnography*. Chicago: University of Chicago Press.

Van Maanen, J., & Barley, S. R. (1984). Occupational communities: Culture and control in organizations. In B. M. Staw & L. L. Cummings (Eds.), *Research in organizational behavior* (Vol. 6). Greenwich, CT: JAI Press.

Van Maanen, J., & Kunda, G. (1989). Real feelings: Emotional expression and organizational culture. In B. Staw (Ed.), *Research in organizational behavior* (Vol. 11). Greenwich, CT: JAI Press.

Van Maanen, J., & Schein, E. H. (1979). Toward a theory of organizational socialization. In B. M. Staw & L. L. Cummings (Eds.), *Research in organizational behavior* (Vol. 1). Greenwich, CT: JAI Press.

Vroom, V. H., & Yetton, P. W. (1973). *Leadership and decision making*. Pittsburgh, PA: University of Pittsburgh Press.

Watson, T. J., Jr., & Petre, P. (1990). *Father, son & co.: My life at IBM and beyond*. New York: Bantam Books.

Weick, K. (1995). *Sensemaking in organizations*. Thousand Oaks, CA: Sage.

Wilkins, A. L. (1983). Organizational stories as symbols which control the organization. In L. R. Pondy and others (Eds.), *Organizational symbolism*. Greenwich, CT: JAI Press.

Wilkins, A. L. (1989). *Developing corporate character*. San Francisco, CA: Jossey-Bass.

Williamson, O. (1975). *Markets and hierarchies, analysis and anti-trust implications: A study in the economics of internal organization*. New York: Free Press.

Index